ASP.NET Site Performance Secrets

Simple and proven techniques to quickly speed up your ASP.NET web site

Matt Perdeck

PUBLISHING

BIRMINGHAM - MUMBAI

ASP.NET Site Performance Secrets

First published: October 2010

Production Reference: 1041010

Published by Packt Publishing Ltd.
32 Lincoln Road
Olton
Birmingham, B27 6PA, UK.

ISBN 978-1-849690-68-3

www.packtpub.com

Cover Image by Asher Wishkerman (a.wishkerman@mpic.de)

Credits

Author
Matt Perdeck

Reviewers
Maarten Balliauw
Ayoosh Joshi
Shivprasad Koirala
Michael Allen Smith

Acquisition Editor
David Barnes

Development Editor
Maitreya Bhakal

Technical Editor
Krutika V. Katelia

Indexer
Rekha Nair

Editorial Team Leader
Aditya Belpathak

Project Team Leader
Lata Basantani

Project Coordinator
Srimoyee Ghoshal

Proofreader
Clyde Jenkins

Graphics
Geetanjali Sawant
Nilesh R. Mohite

Production Coordinator
Arvindkumar Gupta

Cover Work
Arvindkumar Gupta

About the Author

Matt Perdeck has over 20 years of experience in developing high-performance software systems, ranging from the largest ATM network in The Netherlands to embedded software in advanced Wide Area Networks. After graduating as a B.Sc. in Computer Science from the University of Technology Twente, The Netherlands, he designed and developed software in Australia, The Netherlands, Slovakia, and Thailand. Along the way, he also earned an M.B.A. from the University of Western Australia and Copenhagen Business School. He has extensive .NET and SQL Server development experience and has written several .NET articles. As an old school software engineer, he is passionate about making things faster, simpler, and more efficient. His website address is `http://advancedwebsitetechnology.com`.

Every book is a team effort, and this is no exception. I wish to thank David Barnes, who responded to my original book proposal a few hours before I got on a plane to Ethiopia, and helped me have it accepted at Packt. Also, thanks to him, I could maintain a proper structure of the book while writing it. Next, I would like to thank Maitreya Bhakal, who painstakingly reviewed my first drafts, drafted in technical reviewers, and engaged in late night discussions with me about the optimal way to express what I was trying to say in the English language. I am also grateful for the efforts of Krutika Katelia, who checked every detail and made the book ready for publishing. And last but not least, my thanks go out to Srimoyee Ghoshal, who kept the whole project on track, and to Lata Basantani, who looked after the contract.

About the Reviewers

Maarten Balliauw has a Bachelor's degree in Software Engineering, and has eight years of experience in software development. He started his career during his studies, when he founded a company doing web development in PHP and ASP.NET. After graduation, he sold his shares and joined one of the largest ICT companies in Belgium, RealDolmen, where he continued web application development in ASP.NET and application lifecycle management in Visual Studio Team System. He is a Microsoft Certified Technology Specialist ASP.NET and Most Valuable Professional (MVP) ASP. NET, and works with the latest Microsoft technologies, such as LINQ and ASP.NET 3.5. He has published many articles in both PHP and .NET literature, such as MSDN magazine Belgium and PHP Architect. Maarten wrote the book ASP.NET VC 1.0 Quickly with Packt Publishing. Maarten is a frequent speaker at various national and international events.

Blog: http://blog.maartenballiauw.be

E-mail: maarten@maartenballiauw.be

Twitter: http://twitter.com/maartenballiauw

Ayoosh Joshi, MCAD, MCSD.NET, former CTO of CertGuard Inc., has been actively involved with Microsoft technologies since the advent of .NET. He also holds a Masters degree in Computer Applications.

Currently, he is an active partner in the InfoTech firm, Apex Web Solutions, in addition to providing technological consultation and training to various firms including TurkReno Inc.

In his leisure time, he frequents various technology newsgroups, such as StackOverflow.com under the moniker, Cerebrus. He has also been single-handedly moderating the "DotnetDevelopment Google Group" since the past five years.

Since his learning days, he has been obsessed with evaluating and maximizing application performance, and has always kept an eye out for the holy grail of "Optimal Performance".

Shivprasad Koirala, MVP, ASP.NET, MCAD, MCSD.NET, Former CEO of www.questpond.com, has been actively involved in teaching the latest Microsoft technologies for past 14 years.

He is a currently working as the CEO for a leading training company and earns his daily bread by giving training, writing technical books, recording training videos, and providing consultancy to many leading IT firms.

He has authored around 20 books on technology, revolving around interview questions series, which includes the best seller, ".NET Interview Questions".

To get these materialistic benefits (MVP, writing books, and so on), I have often sacrificed my family time. I feel I have been selfish when it comes to kids and family.

I want to say thanks, and sorry too, to Birma, Harisngh, Sanjana, Simran and Vishna.

Michael Allen Smith is a software professional living in Seattle, WA. He has been developing websites since 1995.

Table of Contents

Preface

Do you think that only experts with a deep understanding of the inner workings of ASP.NET, SQL Server, and IIS can improve a website's performance? Think again, because this book tosses that notion out of the window. This book will help you resolve every web developer's nightmare—a slow website with angry managers looking over your shoulder and raging calls from advertisers and clients. You don't have the time or energy to gain a thorough and complete understanding of ASP.NET performance optimization. You just need your site to run faster! This book will show you how.

This hands-on book shows how to dramatically improve the performance of your ASP.NET-based website straight away, without forcing you through a lot of theoretical learning. It teaches you practical, step-by-step techniques that you can use right away to make your site faster with just the right amount of theory; you need to make sense of it all.

Unlike other performance-related books, here you'll first learn how to pinpoint the bottlenecks that hold back your site's performance, so that you can initially focus your time and energy on those areas of your site where you can quickly make the biggest difference. It then shows you how to fix the bottlenecks you found with lots of working code samples and practical advice, and just the right amount of theoretical detail.

What this book covers

Chapter 1, High Level Diagnosis shows how to determine which aspect of loading a web page is taking too long – generating the page on the server, transferring the page to the browser, loading the images, or loading JavaScript and CSS files.

Chapter 2, Reducing Time to First Byte shows how to further pinpoint the bottleneck if you found it takes too long to generate a web page on the server. Examples of possible bottlenecks are lack of memory or CPU resources and slow database access.

Chapter 3, Memory shows how to reduce memory usage.

Chapter 4, CPU shows how to reduce CPU usage.

Chapter 5, Caching shows how to get the most out of the caching features provided by browsers, proxies, ASP.NET, and IIS.

Chapter 6, Thread Usage shows how to use asynchronous programming to prevent your web site from running out of IIS worker threads.

Chapter 7, Reducing Long Wait Times shows how to reduce delays due to off -box session modes, thread locks, disk accesses, and communication with other servers.

Chapter 8, Speeding up Database Access shows how to speed up database accesses on the database server, such as identifying and fixing expensive queries.

Chapter 9, Reducing Time to Last Byte shows how to further pinpoint the bottlenecks if you find that it takes too long to transfer a web page to the browser. It also shows how to reduce ViewState and white space overhead.

Chapter 10, Compression shows how to get the most out of the compression features provided by IIS 6 and IIS 7. This can dramatically reduce the size of web pages and JavasScript and CSS files, as they travel over the Internet.

Chapter 11, Optimizing Forms shows how to reduce the number of form submissions and the delay caused by each submission. This includes implementing client-side form validation and five forms of asynchronous communication with the server.

Chapter 12, Reducing Image Load Times shows how to reduce the number of images on the page and their file sizes, how to better cache images, and how to load more of them concurrently.

Chapter 13, Improving JavaScript Loading shows how to compress JavaScript and CSS files and how to reduce their impact on page rendering.

Chapter 14, Load Testing shows how to do load testing, and how to create a load testing environment using spare computers.

What you need for this book

Software required to run the sample software in the book:

1. Vista Home Premium or higher, or Windows 7 Home Premium or higher

   Note that the Starter and Home Basic versions of these operating systems do not include IIS 7 and so, they can't be used.

2. Visual Studio 2008 Express Web Developer Edition or later, or a paid version of Visual Studio 2008 or later.

   Free download is available at `http://www.microsoft.com/express/Downloads/#2010-Visual-Web-Developer`.

3. SQL Server 2008 Express or later

   Free download is available at `http://www.microsoft.com/express/database/`.

4. .NET Framework 3.5

   Free download is available at `http://www.microsoft.com/downloads/en/details.aspx?FamilyId=333325fd-ae52-4e35-b531-508d977d32a6&displaylang=en`.

   If you have installed a version of Visual Studio 2008, you don't need to install .NET Framework 3.5 because it is included with Visual Studio 2008. If you only have a version of Visual Studio 2010 on your machine, you may need to install .NET Framework 3.5 to be able to run the sample code with Visual Studio 2010.

Who this book is for

This book is written for ASP.NET/SQL Server-based website developers who want to speed up their site using simple, proven tactics without going through a lot of unnecessary theoretical learning. If your website isn't performing well, this is the ideal book for you.

Conventions

In this book, you will find a number of styles of text that distinguish between different kinds of information. Here are some examples of these styles, and an explanation of their meaning.

Code words in text are shown as follows: " This exposes the method `Dispose()`, which disposes the object."

A block of code is set as follows:

```
using (SqlConnection connection = new SqlConnection(connectionString))
{
    // use connection ...
} // connection.Dispose called implicitly
```

Any command-line input or output is written as follows:

```
USE TuneUp
ALTER DATABASE TuneUp SET ENABLE_BROKER WITH ROLLBACK IMMEDIATE
```

New terms and **important words** are shown in bold. Words that you see on the screen, in menus or dialog boxes for example, appear in the text like this: "Check the **Allow** checkbox in the **Modify** row and click on **OK**."

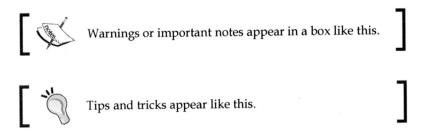

Warnings or important notes appear in a box like this.

Tips and tricks appear like this.

Reader feedback

Feedback from our readers is always welcome. Let us know what you think about this book—what you liked or may have disliked. Reader feedback is important for us to develop titles that you really get the most out of.

To send us general feedback, simply send an e-mail to feedback@packtpub.com, and mention the book title via the subject of your message.

If there is a book that you need and would like to see us publish, please send us a note in the **SUGGEST A TITLE** form on www.packtpub.com or e-mail suggest@packtpub.com.

If there is a topic that you have expertise in and you are interested in either writing or contributing to a book, see our author guide on www.packtpub.com/authors.

Customer support

Now that you are the proud owner of a Packt book, we have a number of things to help you to get the most from your purchase.

Downloading the example code for this book

You can download the example code files for all Packt books you have purchased from your account at http://www.PacktPub.com. If you purchased this book elsewhere, you can visit http://www.PacktPub.com/support and register to have the files e-mailed directly to you.

Errata

Although we have taken every care to ensure the accuracy of our content, mistakes do happen. If you find a mistake in one of our books—maybe a mistake in the text or the code—we would be grateful if you would report this to us. By doing so, you can save other readers from frustration and help us improve subsequent versions of this book. If you find any errata, please report them by visiting http://www.packtpub.com/support, selecting your book, clicking on the **let us know** link, and entering the details of your errata. Once your errata are verified, your submission will be accepted and the errata will be uploaded on our website, or added to any list of existing errata, under the Errata section of that title. Any existing errata can be viewed by selecting your title from http://www.packtpub.com/support.

Piracy

Piracy of copyright material on the Internet is an ongoing problem across all media. At Packt, we take the protection of our copyright and licenses very seriously. If you come across any illegal copies of our works, in any form, on the Internet, please provide us with the location address or website name immediately so that we can pursue a remedy.

Please contact us at copyright@packtpub.com with a link to the suspected pirated material.

We appreciate your help in protecting our authors, and our ability to bring you valuable content.

Questions

You can contact us at questions@packtpub.com if you are having a problem with any aspect of the book, and we will do our best to address it.

1
High Level Diagnosis

Being responsible for a site with slowly loading pages is simply not good. Having twitchy managers look over your shoulder, angry phone calls from advertisers, and other such nastiness is simply no fun. Unfortunately, it can happen to even the best developer—one day your site is cruising along just fine and the next morning, it is really slow. Of course, it may not be completely your fault. Moving the site to that cheap hosting plan may have a bearing on it, or the advertising campaign that marketing just launched without telling you, driving massive traffic to the site. In the end, it doesn't matter—all eyes are on you to make the site faster, and do it quickly. Of course, if you slip in performance improvements in regular releases, there is a better chance you'll avert that sort of crisis.

The problem is that generating even a moderately complex web page involves many lines of code and many different files. Seeing that time is always short, you'll want to zero in on those lines of code and those files that have the biggest impact on performance, leaving everything else for another day. Do this in a structured, top-down way, and you'll get it done more quickly and with a greater chance of success.

In this chapter, you'll learn the following:

- The overall process of assuring good performance, and how performance tuning fits into this.

- How to generate Waterfall charts as a way to identify those aspects of your site that cause web page performance issues.

- A number of scenarios of poor performance and how to recognize each scenario using the Waterfall charts you generated. With each scenario, you'll find a reference to the specific chapter that shows how to further pinpoint the bottleneck, and then eliminate it.

In this chapter, we'll stay at a fairly general level; in the subsequent chapters, we'll dive deeply into the technical aspects of improving your website's performance. This will include performance monitoring (*Chapter 2, Reducing Time to First Byte*), IIS thread usage (*Chapter 6, Thread Usage*), database access (*Chapter 8, Speeding up Database Access*), and on-the-fly JavaScript compression and on-demand loading (*Chapter 13, Improving JavaScript Loding*).

To see how to load test your code without touching your production environment, refer to *Chapter 14, Load Testing*.

Assuring good performance

Before you start diagnosing and fixing performance issues, let's first have a quick look at how this fits in to the overall process of assuring good performance. This process consists of these parts:

- Continuous monitoring
- Setting performance goals
- Iterative improvements

Let's go through each part of the process one-by-one.

Continuous monitoring

The performance of your website is affected by both the things you control, such as code changes, and the things you cannot control such as increases in the number of visitors or server problems. Because of this, it makes sense to monitor the performance of your site continuously. That way, you find out that the site is becoming too slow before your manager does.

At the end of this section, you'll find a list of monitoring services that will keep an eye on your site.

What do you mean by "site is becoming too slow"? Glad you asked.

Setting performance goals

When this books talks about performance, it ultimately talks about page load time—that's what your visitors and potential customers experience.

It pays to have a clear understanding of how fast is fast enough. Spending time and effort on making your site faster is time and effort not spent on other improvements. There is little point in making your site faster if it is already fast enough.

Your manager, client, or marketing department may have ideas about what constitutes "fast enough". Alternatively, visit the page Website Response Times at `http://www.useit.com/alertbox/response-times.html` to gain inspiration for setting performance goals.

Ok, you've been monitoring your site, and found it is getting too slow. What now?

Iterative improvements

Because websites, web servers, and browsers are such complex beasts, it pays to make improvements in a deliberate fashion. Hence, these two golden rules:

- **One change at a time**: Because multiple changes can affect each other in surprising ways, life will be much easier if you implement and evaluate changes one-by-one.

- **Test, test, test**: You don't know whether your change really is an improvement until you have tested it thoroughly. Make sure that performance after the change is better than performance before the change, and be ready to roll back your changes if it isn't; what works for other sites may not work for your site.

This process makes your site run faster. An iterative process is shown as following:

1. Record the current performance.
2. Diagnose the performance problem — identify the single most important bottleneck.
3. Fix that one bottleneck (remember, one change at a time).
4. Test your change. Has performance improved? If it didn't, roll back your change and come up with a better fix. If it did, go back to step 1.

As a result of this, making your site faster is an iterative process:

If you find bottlenecks that currently do not pose a problem, but will come back to bite you in the future, it may be good to fix them, now that they are clear in your head.

We can capture all this in a flowchart:

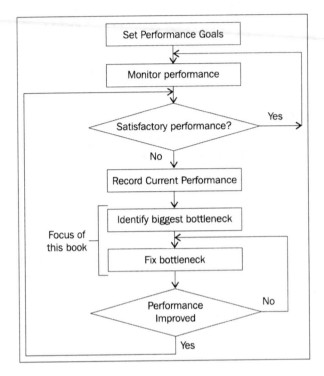

Monitoring services

If you search Google for "site monitoring service", you'll find lots of companies that will monitor your website's performance for you. They also alert you when the response time gets too high, indicating your site is down.

Here are a few of the monitoring services that offer a free plan at the time of this writing. Note that the descriptions below relate to the free plan. If you are prepared to spend a bit of money, check their websites for their offerings:

- **Pingdom**: http://www.pingdom.com/

  Pages you can monitor: 1

  Checking frequency: Once every 1, 5, 15, 30, or 60 minutes

  Checks from: United States, Asia, Europe

  Sends alerts via: E-mail, SMS, Twitter or iPhone

  Reporting: Detailed downloadable stats showing the result of each check

- **Mon.itor.us**: http://mon.itor.us/

  Pages you can monitor: Unlimited (1 per contact e-mail address)

  Checking frequency: Once every 30 minutes

  Checks from: United States, Europe

  Sends alerts via: E-mail, SMS, Twitter, or IM

  Reporting: Weekly reports, real-time graph

- **dotcom-monitor**: http://www.dotcom-monitor.com/

  Free 30-day trial

  Pages you can monitor: Unlimited

  Checking frequency: Once per minute

  Checks from: United States, Europe, Israel

  Sends alerts via: E-mail, Phone, SMS, Pager, SNMP

  Reporting: Daily, weekly, and monthly e-mails, extensive online reports, and graphs

- **247webmonitoring**: http://247webmonitoring.com/

  Pages you can monitor: 5

  Checking frequency: Once every 15, 30, or 60 minutes

  Checks from: United States

  Sends alerts via: E-mail

  Reporting: Real-time graph

Now that we've seen the process of assuring satisfactory performance, let's focus on how to diagnose and fix performance problems. After all, that is what this book is all about.

High-level diagnosis with Waterfall charts

Because our goal is to make a given web page load quicker, let's enumerate the components that make up a web page:

- **The file with the HTML**: In the ASP.NET world, this file normally has the extension .aspx. Because of this, in the remainder of this book, I'll refer to this file as the main .aspx file. Without this file, there is no page. Generating this file most often takes most of the server resources required to generate the overall page.

- **Images and flash files**: These files are often large and numerous.

- **JavaScript and CSS files**: These files can block rendering of the page.

Based on this, we can categorize bottlenecks that slow down the page-loading into these broad categories:

- Main `.aspx` file takes too long to generate
- Main `.aspx` file takes too long to transfer from server to browser
- Images (and flash files) take too long to transfer
- JavaScript and CSS files block page rendering

In order to speed up loading of a page, we need to know in which of these categories the bottleneck falls. This is the focus of the remainder of this chapter. Once you know the broad category, you can further pinpoint the bottleneck and fix it. You'll see how in the subsequent chapters.

How do I figure out in which broad category the bottleneck falls? A simple way to do that is with a **Waterfall chart**.

A Waterfall chart shows the components that make up the page, in which order they get loaded by the browser, and more importantly, how much time they take to load. It looks similar to the following:

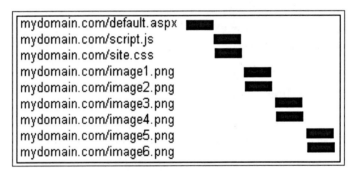

If for example, the main `.aspx` file takes too long to load, the Waterfall chart will show a very long bar for that file.

In a little while, we'll see how to figure out the broad category of the bottleneck in a Waterfall chart. But first, let's see how to produce such a chart.

Creating a Waterfall chart using Firebug

There are many free tools that will generate a Waterfall chart for you. One of those is Firebug, the popular add-on for the Firefox browser. Obviously, this tool works only for Firefox and not Internet Explorer or other browsers; so at the end of this chapter, you'll find other free tools that generate Waterfall charts for those browsers. But given the popularity of Firebug, we'll stick with that for now.

Installing Firebug

To use Firebug, you need to have the Firefox browser installed on your computer. Get it for free at `http://www.mozilla.com/`.

Once you have Firefox running, use it to open the Firebug home page at `http://getfirebug.com/`.

Here you'll find a link that installs Firebug.

Creating the Waterfall chart

Now that you have Firebug installed, create a Waterfall chart:

1. In Firefox, open the **Tools** menu, choose **Firebug**, and then choose **Open Firebug** or press *F12*. The Firebug bar appears at the bottom of the browser window.

2. In the Firebug bar, click on the **Net** drop-down and select **Enable**. Also, make sure that the **All** option is selected below the Firebug bar.

3. Browse to a page in Firefox. You will see the Waterfall chart of the various components on the page appear.

Interpreting the Waterfall chart

That chart is certainly very colorful, but what does it all mean? Actually, Firebug provides a lot of information in the Waterfall chart, including full request and response headers and timeline information. Also, it's easy to save all this information to a file.

Request and response information

Click the little + sign to the left of a filename in the Waterfall chart. You'll see a drop-down with the full request and response headers that were sent when the file was retrieved.

| GET style.css | 200 OK | packtpub.com | 2 KB | 1.06s |

But wait, there is more:

- In the drop-down, click on the **Response** tab to see the contents of the file.
- If the URL of the file had query string parameters, they are shown in a **Params** tab.
- If this was a POST or PUT request, there is a tab with the sent data.
- If it is an HTML file, the HTML tab shows the actual page created by the HTML, which is very handy for iframes.
- If the response came in the form of a JSON file, you'll find a tab with the data in the form of an expandable tree. For more information about JSON, visit `http://www.json.org/`.

Timeline information

Hover the mouse over a colored bar to see detailed timing information:

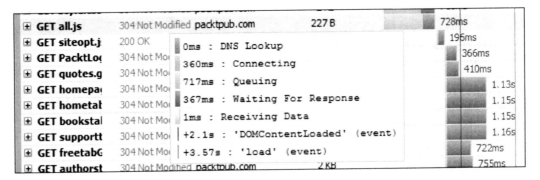

Here is what the numbers mean:

DNS Lookup	Time taken to find the IP address of the server holding the file, based on the file's URL.
Connecting	Time spent creating a TCP connection.
Queuing	Firefox limits the number of outstanding requests. If it finds an image or some other file in the `.aspx` page while Firefox is already at the maximum number of outstanding requests, it queues this new file. Queuing shows the time spent by the file in this queue.
Waiting For Response	Time spent waiting for the first byte of the file from the server.
Receiving Data	Time spent in receiving the file.

'DOMContentLoaded' (event)	Time between the start of the DNS lookup of this request and the entire **DOM (Document Object Model)** being ready. The DOM is the browser's internal representation of the HTML on your page. When the DOM is ready, the visitor can look around the entire page, even while some items are still loading. This number can be negative if the request started after the DOM became ready.
'load' (event)	Time between the start of the DNS lookup of this request and the page having been fully loaded, including the images.

In addition to this timing popup, there are two more. Hover over the file size to see the precise size of the file in bytes. To see the full URL of a file, hover over its name.

Page-level information

At the very bottom of the Waterfall chart, you will find the total number of files making up the page, their total size and the total page-load time:

39 requests		201 KB (189 KB from cache)	4.67s

Saving information

To save the headers to the clipboard, right-click on a file to get a popup with a **save** option. You can then paste the headers to a text file.

To save the entire chart to a file, use the NetExport extension for Firebug available at `http://getfirebug.com/releases/extensions.html`.

Once you have this installed, an **Export** button appears above the Waterfall chart, next to the **All** button. This exports the chart to a `.har` file.

If you open the `.har` file in your favorite text editor, you'll find that the file stores the information in JSON format.

The easiest way to view your `.har` files as a chart is with the online viewer at `http://www.softwareishard.com/har/viewer/`.

This not only shows the Waterfall chart saved in the `.har` file, but also throws in some additional statistics:

- How much of the total wait time was taken by the various components of each request (DNS lookup, receiving the page, and so on)
- The proportion of the total page weight in bytes taken by the `.aspx` file, images, CSS files, and so on
- The proportion of the total page weight that came from the internal browser cache rather than over the Internet
- The size of the request and response headers as compared to the request and response bodies

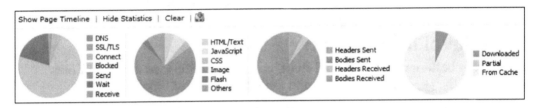

Categorizing bottlenecks using Waterfall charts

Before we saw how to create a Waterfall chart with Firebug, we discussed the four broad categories of bottlenecks that slow down page loading:

- Main `.aspx` file taking too long to generate
- Main `.aspx` file taking too long to load
- Images (and flash files) taking too long to load
- JavaScript and CSS files blocking page rendering

The following sections show how each broad category expresses itself in a Waterfall chart generated by Firebug. Each section also refers you to the chapter where you'll see how to further pinpoint the bottleneck and then fix it.

Scenario 1: Main .aspx file takes long to arrive

In the chart below, the top line is for the main .aspx page. The purple section shows how long the browser waited until it received the first byte. It shows a situation where the browser has to wait a long time for the first byte of the .aspx file. Obviously, this delays loading of all other components, because it is the .aspx file that tells the browser which images, CSS files, and so on to load.

If your web page produces a similar Waterfall chart, you will want to focus on reducing the time it takes the web server to generate the .aspx page. Refer to *Chapter 2, Reducing Time to First Byte*, where you'll see how to pinpoint web server issues, code issues, and so on.

Scenario 2: Main .aspx file takes long to load over the Internet

In the chart below, the top line still refers to the .aspx file. In this scenario, the purple section shows that the browser didn't have to wait long for the first byte of the .aspx file. However, the grey section shows it took a long time to load the entire file over the Internet. This, in turn, delays loading of those images and other files that appear towards the end of the .aspx file.

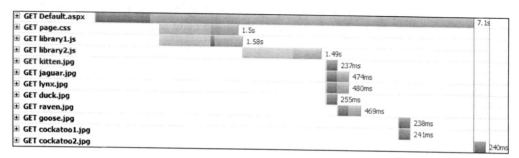

To see how to deal with this scenario, refer to *Chapter 9, Reducing Time to Last Byte*.

Scenario 3: Images take long to load

This chart shows a common scenario, where the `.aspx` file is quick to arrive and load, but the images on the page take a long time to load. Fortunately, browsers will load a number of images in parallel rather than one-by-one, speeding up the process. However, the number of images loaded in parallel is limited by the browser to avoid overloading the connection; the exact limit depends on the browser. As a result, on pages with lots of images, some images will wait for other images to load first, thereby increasing the page load time, as shown in the following screenshot:

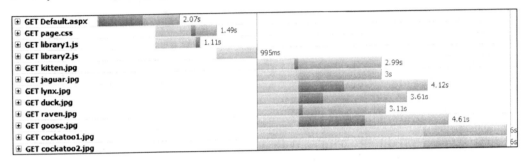

Refer to *Chapter 12, Reducing Image Load Times* to see how to get your images loaded sooner in a variety of ways, including browser caching and removing unused bytes to reduce image file sizes.

Scenario 4: JavaScript file blocks rendering

This chart shows a less common scenario, where a JavaScript file blocks rendering of the rest of the page. This can have a big impact on overall page load time.

When an external JavaScript file starts loading, rendering of the rest of the page is stopped until the file has completed loading and executing. This ensures that the JavaScript coming later in the page can use JavaScript libraries that were loaded and executed earlier on. CSS files also block page rendering in order to ensure that the visitor is not exposed to the "raw", unstyled version of the page.

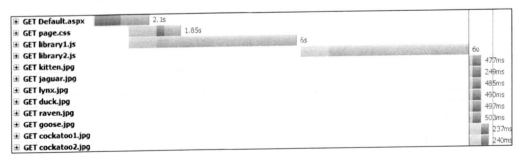

The following chart shows a different scenario where JavaScript code blocks rendering of the rest of the page, not by being slow to load but by taking a long time to execute. This could be caused by both external JavaScript, which is loaded from an external file, and by internal JavaScript which sits in the main .aspx file.

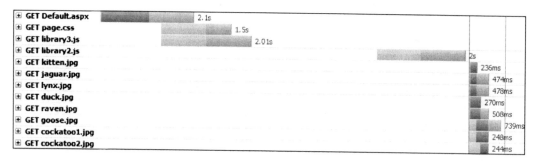

Solutions for this scenario include reducing the download time of JavaScript files, loading them after the page has been rendered, and loading them on demand. *Chapter 13, Improving JavaScript Loading* goes into the details. It also shows how to improve loading of your CSS files, and how to ensure that the advertisements served by external advertisement networks do not block rendering of your page.

Waterfall generators for other browsers

The Waterfall chart generated by Firebug as introduced earlier in this chapter obviously only works with Firefox, because Firebug is a Firefox add-on. This is not convenient if Firefox is not your favorite browser, or if you want to see how other browsers load content. Here are a few free alternatives for other browsers.

Fiddler (browser-independent)

Fiddler is a proxy which logs all HTTP and HTTPS traffic between your browser and the Internet. It also allows you to change the incoming and outgoing data. Because it doesn't integrate with the browser itself as Firebug does, Fiddler works with any browser, including Internet Explorer.

Download at Fiddler from http://www.fiddler2.com/fiddler2/.

To generate a Waterfall chart with Fiddler, follow these steps:

1. Start Fiddler.

2. Make sure that the **Streaming** button is depressed. This ensures that Fiddler doesn't use buffering, which would distort the Waterfall chart.

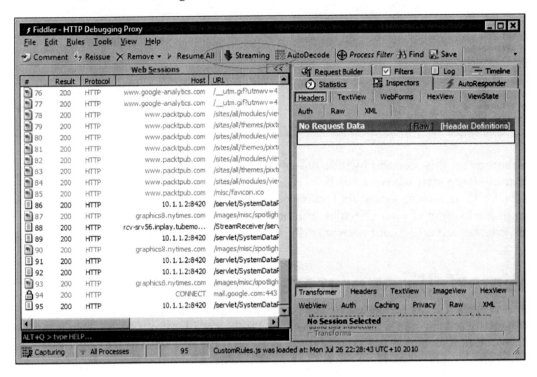

3. Start your favorite browser and load a page. It is the easiest if you have only one page open at a time, because Fiddler will record all traffic to all browser windows.

4. You will see all the files loaded as part of the page in Fiddler, in the left-hand **Web Sessions** window.

5. Press *F12* to stop capturing any more traffic.

6. From the **Edit** menu, choose **Select All**. This way, all files will be shown in the Waterfall chart.

7. Click on the **Timeline** tab on the right-hand side. This will show the Waterfall chart. To see how to interpret the chart, visit http://www. fiddler2.com/fiddler/help/timeline.asp.

If the bars on the timeline look hatched rather than solid, it means that Fiddler has used buffering, which distorted the chart. Click on the **Streaming** button to switch off buffering and start again.

8. If you want to analyze another page, clear out the **Web Sessions** window first by clicking on the **Remove** button. Press *F12* again to start capturing traffic again and visit another page in your browser.

Internet Explorer via WebPagetest

This free, web-based service uses Internet Explorer to produce Waterfall charts. Simply visit their site at http://www.webpagetest.org/test and enter the URL of a page you're interested in. You can run tests from the United States, the UK, and New Zealand.

Because this is a web-based service, there is no software to install. On the other hand, it won't work for you if your site is behind a firewall, which probably applies to your development server.

Also, keep in mind that it runs Internet Explorer to produce its charts, so the charts you see apply to that browser even if you are visiting WebPagetest with Firefox!

Google Chrome

Google's Chrome browser lets you generate a simple Waterfall chart right out of the box. You also get headers and other details about each file.

Download Google Chrome from http://www.google.com/chrome.

To generate a Waterfall chart:

1. Open a web page in Chrome.
2. Right-click anywhere on the page and choose **Inspect element**. The Web Inspector window appears.
3. In the new window, click on the **Resources** button.
4. Choose to enable **Resource Tracking**. Your page reloads and the Waterfall chart appears.

To see request and response headers, parameters, and so on, click on a filename to the left of the Waterfall chart. This replaces the Waterfall chart with detailed information for that file.

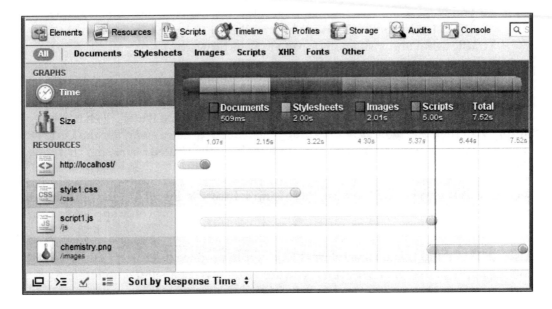

Apple Safari

Apple Safari has the same underlying code base as Google Chrome, including the Web Inspector.

Download Apple Safari from `http://www.apple.com/safari/`.

However, before you can use the Web Inspector on Safari, it needs to be enabled first:

1. Open Safari.
2. Open the Safari settings menu and choose **Preferences**. The **Preferences** popup appears:

3. Check **Show Develop menu in menu bar**.
4. Close the **Preferences** popup.

With the Web Inspector enabled, you can now generate a Waterfall chart in the same way, as with Google Chrome:

1. Open a web page in Safari.

2. Right-click anywhere on the page and choose **Inspect element**. The Web Inspector window appears.

3. In the new window, click on the **Resources** button.

4. Choose to enable **Resource Tracking**. Your page reloads and the Waterfall chart appears.

To see request and response headers, parametes, and so on, click on a filename to the left of the Waterfall chart. This replaces the Waterfall chart with detailed information for that file.

More Waterfall chart generators

- **HttpWatch**: This is paid software. A free evaluation version is also available. It provides more detailed information than Fiddler. Also, it is slightly more advanced than Firebug and works with both Firefox and Internet Explorer.

- **IBM Page Detailer**: This Waterfall chart generator is proxy-based, similar to Fiddler. It provides more details than Fiddler, but is more difficult to use. Visit `http://www.alphaworks.ibm.com/tech/pagedetailer` for more details.

- **Site-Perf.com**: This is a web-based Waterfall chart generator, similar to WebPagetest. It allows you to run tests from both Europe and the United States. Visit `http://site-perf.com/` for more details.

- **Pingdom Page Test**: This is a web-based Waterfall chart generator, with some nice sorting features. Visit `http://tools.pingdom.com/` for more details.

- **Visual Round Trip Analyzer**: This is another proxy-based generator, similar to Fiddler. However, instead of files, this shows TCP packets. It is strictly hardcore only. Visit `http://www.microsoft.com/downloads/details.aspx?FamilyID=119f3477-dced-41e3-a0e7-d8b5cae893a3&displaylang=en` for more details.

Find out more

Here are some more online resources:

- **Response Times: Check the 3 Important Limits**
  `http://www.useit.com/papers/responsetime.html`

- **Performance Research, Part 1: Check what the 80/20 rule tells us about reducing HTTP requests**
  `http://yuiblog.com/blog/2006/11/28/performance-research-part-1/`

- **High Performance Websites: Check the Importance of Front-End Performance**
  `http://developer.yahoo.net/blog/archives/2007/03/high_performanc.html`

Summary

In this chapter, we saw that performance tuning is a part of a continuous effort to assure satisfactory performance for your website. The two golden rules are, as we saw earlier in the chapter, introducing changes one-by-one, and testing every change to see if it really improves the performance of your website.

Then we saw a detailed description of the Waterfall charts generated by Firebug, an add-on for the popular Firefox browser. This was followed by a series of possible scenarios of poor performance, plus references to a specific chapter in this book for each scenario.

A list of tools to generate Waterfall charts for browsers other than Firefox was provided at the end, including tools which are independent of the browser being used.

In the next chapter, we'll see how to reduce the time it takes for the server to generate the page. You'll learn about the Windows performance monitor, and you'll see how to improve the use of system resources.

2
Reducing Time to First Byte

The "time to first byte" is the time it takes your server to generate a page, plus the time taken to move the first byte over the Internet to the browser. Reducing that time is important for visitor retention—you want to give them something to look at, and provide confidence that they'll have the page in their browser soon.

Reducing time to first byte involves making better use of system resources such as memory and CPU. An added benefit of a more efficient code is that there will be less need to buy more hardware when traffic grows.

This chapter consists of two parts, as explained.

The first section *Pinpointing bottlenecks* shows how to pinpoint a number of common bottlenecks, including:

- Memory pressures
- Caching
- CPU usage
- Thread usage
- Long wait times for external resources

You will see how to use system counters to get a better understanding of what is going on inside your code. This will help you prioritize the most promising areas, so that you use your time most effectively.

Once you've determined which bottleneck to address first, you can skip to the chapter that shows how to fix it:

- Memory (chapter 3)
- CPU (chapter 4)

- Caching (chapter 5)
- Thread usage (chapter 6)
- Resolving long wait times (chapter 7)

The second section *Additional measures* shows the additional things you can do, such as reducing unwanted traffic.

Pinpointing bottlenecks

Before diving in and making changes to your website, it makes sense to first identify the most significant bottlenecks. That helps you prioritize areas to fix, so that you make the best use of your time.

Memory

First check whether the server is running out of memory. If it does, that will increase CPU usage and disk I/O (input/output), meaning that solving memory pressures will automatically reduce pressures on the CPU and Disk as well.

Shortage of memory increases CPU usage and disk I/O because when the server runs out of memory, it makes room by swapping pages of less-used data in memory to a swap file on disk, named `pagefile.sys`. Now when that data is needed again, and the server can't find it in memory, it causes a **hard page fault**, meaning that the server has to retrieve the data from the disk. All this takes much more CPU usage and disk I/O than a simple memory access.

The tool to use to see how much page swapping is going on depends on your operating system.

Windows Server 2003

Run `perfmon` from the command prompt. Sadly, this old version of `perfmon` doesn't have the nice display boasted by the Vista and 2008 versions. To see the number of hard page faults in this version, click on the "plus" button in the toolbar, then select **Memory** in the **Performance object** drop-down, and add the **Pages/sec** counter.

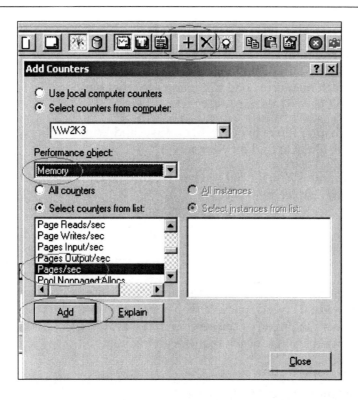

Windows Vista, Windows Server 2008, or Windows 7

On Windows Vista or Windows Server 2008, run the program `perfmon` from the command prompt. This opens the monitor window.

On Windows 7, run `resmon` to start the new Windows 7 resource monitor. For our purpose, `resmon` and `perfmon` are almost identical. Look at **Hard Faults/sec** in the Memory area. If that value is high, the server is running out of memory and spending CPU cycles and disk I/O to swap pages in and out of memory from the disk. *Chapter 3, Memory* shows how to reduce memory usage.

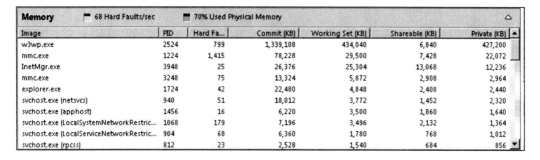

Memory	■ 68 Hard Faults/sec		■ 70% Used Physical Memory			△
Image	PID	Hard Fa...	Commit (KB)	Working Set (KB)	Shareable (KB)	Private (KB)
w3wp.exe	2524	799	1,339,108	434,040	6,840	427,200
mmc.exe	1224	1,415	78,228	29,500	7,428	22,072
InetMgr.exe	3948	25	26,376	25,304	13,068	12,236
mmc.exe	3248	75	13,324	5,872	2,908	2,964
explorer.exe	1724	42	22,480	4,848	2,408	2,440
svchost.exe (netsvcs)	940	51	18,012	3,772	1,452	2,320
svchost.exe (apphost)	1456	16	6,220	3,500	1,860	1,640
svchost.exe (LocalSystemNetworkRestric...	1068	179	7,196	3,496	2,132	1,364
svchost.exe (LocalServiceNetworkRestric...	904	68	6,360	1,780	768	1,012
svchost.exe (rpcss)	812	23	2,528	1,540	684	856

Simulating a memory shortage

To see what this situation looks like in `perfmon`, see the `MemoryBound` folder in the downloaded code bundle. In the folder, a simple website is present inside that consumes too much memory. Load test it and see what happens. To see how to do a load test, refer to *Chapter 14, Load Testing*.

The rest of this chapter refers to `perfmon` on Vista and Windows Server 2008, because that's what you're likely to find on your server.

Keep `perfmon` running. You'll need it when we discuss CPU usage, in the *CPU* section later in the chapter.

Caching

If you already use caching, skip to the next section *CPU*; otherwise, read on.

Caching is one the most effective ways to improve website performance. It allows you to store individual objects, parts of web pages, or entire web pages in memory either in the browser, a proxy, or the server. That way, those objects or pages do not have to be generated again for each request, giving you:

- Reduced response time
- Reduced memory and CPU usage
- Less load on the database
- Fewer round trips to the server, when using browser or proxy caching
- Reduced retrieval times when the content is served from proxy cache, by bringing the contents closer to the browser

Caching is the most useful for objects or pages that are expensive to produce and frequently used. It becomes less useful for objects or pages that take a lot of memory, get outdated very quickly, or are rarely used. Even so, if a page is requested 10 times a second, caching it for just a second will lead to 90 percent of the requests being served from cache.

If you are not using caching already and provided you not are running out of memory, implementing caching can deliver substantial benefits. One line of code at the top of each page may be all it takes. *Chapter 5, Caching* shows you how to implement caching.

CPU

Go back to `perfmon`; if you closed it, run it again from the **Command Prompt**. If you use Windows Server 2003, in `perfmon` choose **Processor** in the **Performance object** drop-down, and then add the **% Processor Time** counter. In later operation systems, you will see the **Resource Overview** again:

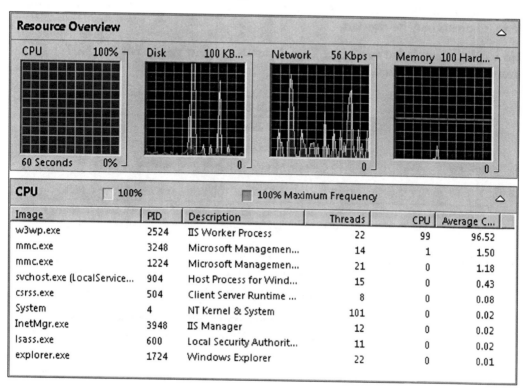

Have a look at the CPU area. The left-most percentage shows the **% Processor Time** counter. If it is over 80 percent, your code is using too many CPU cycles. If that is the case for you, *Chapter 4, CPU* shows how to reduce CPU usage.

What about the **Maximum Frequency** percentage next to the **% Processor Time** counter? This is not directly performance-related. When the CPU is doing little, the operating system throttles it back so it uses less power. That means that if it is 100 percent, the operating system has decided to stop saving power and not necessarily that the CPU is overloaded.

To see what a CPU-stressed situation looks like in `perfmon`, see the `CPUBound` folder in the downloaded code bundle. In the folder, a simple website is present that consumes too much CPU. Load test it and see what happens. To see how to do a load test, refer to chapter 14.

Thread usage

When a request is executed, it runs on a thread within the application pool process on the server. However, the number of threads that can be used to execute requests concurrently gets limited by IIS, because thread switching is expensive. When a request arrives and there are no threads available, it has to wait in a queue for one to become available. That means a longer wait for visitors, and if the queue gets too long, requests may be rejected.

How many threads are available? That depends on your version of the .NET framework and how you use IIS:

Framework Version	Available threads by default
1.1	20 times the number of CPUs* minus 8
2.0	12 times the number of CPUs
3.5, 4.0	IIS 7 Classic Mode: 12 times the number of CPUs
	IIS 7 Integrated Mode: 100 times the number of CPUs

*"Number of CPUs" refers to the number of cores, not the number of packages. So, a computer with a single E8400 Intel Core 2 Duo, which has two cores, is regarded to have two CPUs.

A situation where there are not enough available threads to process incoming requests is called **thread starvation**. To find out whether thread starvation is an issue, check the following system counters on your production server with `perfmon`:

1. On the server, run `perfmon` from the **Command Prompt (Start | All Programs | Accessories | Command Prompt)**. This opens the monitor window.

2. On the left-hand side, expand **Monitoring Tools**. Click on **Performance Monitor**.

3. Click on the green "plus" sign, shown in the following screenshot. The **Add Counters** dialog appears.

4. On the left-hand side of the dialog, expand **ASP.NET**. A series of counters appear:

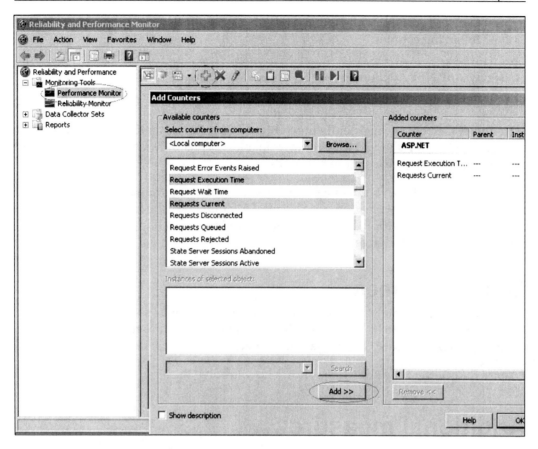

5. Select these counters and add them by clicking on the **Add** button:

Category: ASP.NET	
Request Execution Time	Time in milliseconds it takes for a request to be processed.
Requests Current	Number of requests known to **ASP.NET**. This includes queued requests and requests being executed.

6. Collapse **ASP.NET** and expand **ASP.NET Applications**. Then, add the following counter:

Category: ASP.NET Applications	
Requests Executing	Number of requests that are currently being executed.

If **Requests Current** is consistently much higher than **Requests Executing**, you have requests waiting for a thread to become available. *Chapter 6, Thread Usage* shows how to use the available threads more efficiently.

To see what thread starvation looks like in perfmon, see the ThreadStarvation_ Sleep folder in the downloaded code bundle. A simple website is present inside that holds on to its threads for too long. Load test it and see what happens. To see how to do a load test, refer to chapter 14.

Long wait times

Looking at the performance counters you used in the previous section, if **Request Execution** time tends to be high while the CPU and memory are not stressed, each executing thread probably has to wait for an external resource, such as a database.

Chapter 7, Reducing Long Wait Times shows how to solve this.

Additional measures

Here are a few more ways to reduce the load on your server.

Deployment

The way you deploy your site to production can impact its performance. This section looks at making sure your code runs in the release mode rather than debug mode, and at reducing the number of assemblies making up your site.

Building projects in release mode

If your site is a web-application project rather than a website, or if your website is a part of a solution containing other projects, be sure to build your releases in the release mode. This removes debugging overhead from your code, so it uses less CPU and memory.

For building projects in release mode, follow these steps:

1. In Visual Studio, choose **Build | Configuration Manager**.
2. In the **Active Solution Configuration** drop-down, select **Release** and click on **Close**. The next builds will now be in release mode.
3. If you have a website in your solution, you'll see that it remains in the debug mode. This is because its compile mode is set by the debug flag in web. config, instead of the active solution configuration. You'll see how to deal with this in the *Publishing your website* section.
4. Choose **Build | Rebuild Solution**.

This completely rebuilds the projects in your solution.

Publishing your website

If you use a website rather than a web-application project, follow the steps here to publish your site. This will compile your website in release mode, irrespective of the debug flag in web.config.

It also produces all the files making up your site into a single directory, ready to be copied to the web server.

Note that the Express edition of Visual Studio doesn't support publishing a website.

If you have a solution containing other projects, the assemblies for those projects will go in the bin directory of the website. As shown in the *Building projects in release mode* section, be sure to rebuild your solution in the release mode before publishing your website. Otherwise, you will publish the debug versions of the projects, even though the website itself will be compiled in release mode.

The steps are as follows:

1. In Visual Studio, select your website.
2. Choose **Build | Publish Web Site**.

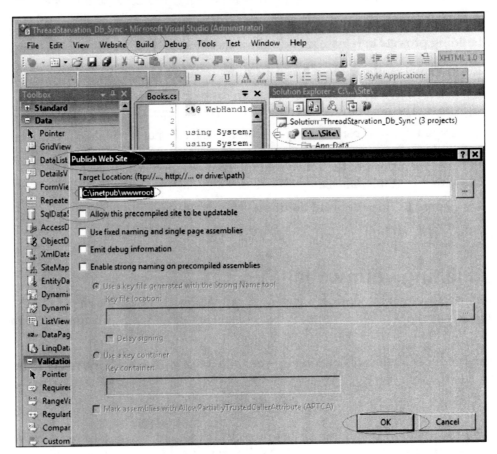

3. In the **Publish Web Site** dialog, enter the target directory in the **Target Location** field where you want to receive the published files. This can also be an FTP site. Uncheck **Allow this precompiled site to be updatable**, unless you want to be able to edit your .aspx files on the production server.

4. Click on **OK**. The publish operation will then compile your website in the release mode. It deletes everything in the target directory and then writes the files making up the website to the directory.

5. If you look in the target directory, you'll find that all the codes behind the files are gone—they have been compiled into DLL files in the bin directory. The .aspx files will be empty, unless you have checked **Allow this precompiled site to be updatable**. If you use a solution with additional projects, the assemblies for the other projects will be in the bin folder as well.

6. Update the web.config in the target folder, so that it uses the connection strings for your production database, and so on. Be sure to set debug to false:

```
<system.web>
  <compilation debug="false">
  ...
  </compilation>
</system.web>
```

 The free **Web Deployment Project** extension by Microsoft allows you to generate the correct connection string and appConfig settings in the web.config automatically based on your build configuration. Visit http://msdn.microsoft.com/en-us/library/aa479568.aspx for more details.

7. Take the server offline and copy the files in the target folder into the root folder of the site on the server. If you have multiple servers, use a script that automatically updates each server one-by-one.

Disabling debug mode

If you keep all your sources on the production server rather than pre-compiling them as shown in the previous section, it is critical that you set the debug flag in web.config to false. Otherwise, the **Just In Time** compiler will compile your sources in debug mode, significantly increasing CPU and memory usage.

Even if you use pre-compilation where your sources are always compiled in the release mode, it makes sense to set debug to false. This is to gain optimizations such as caching and compression of WebResources.axd.

To make sure that no site on the production server uses debug mode, set this in machine.config on the production server:

```
<configuration>
  <system.web>
    <deployment retail="true"/>
  </system.web>
</configuration>
```

This not only overrides the debug flag in web.config, but also disables trace output in a page, and disables showing detailed error messages remotely. This makes it more difficult for hackers to gain information about your website.

A disadvantage of running your code in the release mode is that it provides less debugging information when things go wrong. For example, if you get the yellow screen of death due to an unhandled exception, it won't show line numbers. This means that if performance is not an issue, you might prefer to run your code in debug mode.

Reducing number of assemblies

When you publish a website as described earlier in the *Publish your website* section, it produces an assembly for each directory with compiled source files. In general, you want to reduce the number of assemblies:

- Each assembly carries metadata overhead.
- It is easier for the compiler to optimize code in a single, large assembly.

The disadvantage of having fewer bigger assemblies is that it can make versioning and deployment more difficult. Load test this approach before spending too much time on it (chapter 14 shows how to do load testing).

To compile your site into a single assembly, use the Web Deployment Projects extension to Visual Studio. More information about this free package is available on http://msdn.microsoft.com/en-us/library/aa479568.aspx.

A free download for Visual Studio 2008 is available on http://www.microsoft.com/downloads/details.aspx?FamilyId=0AA30AE8-C73B-4BDD-BB1B-FE697256C459&displaylang=en.

Reducing round trips

Round trips between browser and server can take a long time, increasing wait times for the visitor. Here are some ways to cut down on them.

Using Server.Transfer instead of Response.Redirect

If you need to redirect the visitor to another page on your server, consider using **Server.Transfer** instead of **Response.Redirect**. Response.Redirect sends a message to the browser telling it to load the other page, after which the browser gets back to the server asking for that page.

You can prevent that round trip by using Server.Transfer. This transfers execution to the other page right away. This means the visitor sees the new page, but with the old URL showing in the browser address box.

A disadvantage of this technique is that it confronts the visitor with two different pages having the same URL. That can be confusing, especially if they bookmark the page or share the URL with someone else.

To get around this, transfer only to a page that is clearly associated with the page the visitor came from. For example, when the visitor submits a form, you could transfer to a page that shows the result of the form submission. Don't transfer from your wooden toy page to the gaming page. If you know that a post back from a page will always result in a transfer to another page, consider using **PostBackUrl** to post back to the target page directly.

Always specifying the default file in URLs

IIS will automatically redirect URLs such as `http://mydomain/myfolder` to `http://mydomain/myfolder/`. Also, `http.sys` won't put implied default files in its kernel cache. You can prevent the redirects and allow kernel caching by writing `http://mydomain/myfolder/default.aspx`.

Permanent redirects

If you are redirecting visitors to a new page because the page is outdated, use a permanent 301 redirect. Browsers and proxies will update their caches, and search engines will use them as well. That way, you reduce traffic to the old page.

You can issue a 301 redirect programmatically:

```
Response.StatusCode = 301;
Response.AddHeader("Location", "NewPage.aspx");
Response.End();
```

For .NET 4 or higher:

```
Response.RedirectPermanent("NewPage.aspx");
```

You can also set up the redirect in IIS. If you use IIS 6:

1. In **IIS Manager**, right-click on the file or folder you wish to redirect.
2. Select **A redirection to a URL**.
3. Enter the new page.
4. Check **The exact url entered above** and **A permanent redirection for this resource**.

In IIS 7, HTTP Redirection first needs to be installed. On Windows Server 2008, follow these steps:

1. Click **Start | Administrative Tools | Server Manager**.

2. In the **Server Manager**, expand **Roles**, and then click on **Web Server (IIS)**. The **Web Server (IIS)** dialog opens.

3. Scroll to the **Role Services** section, and then click on **Add Role Services**. The **Add Role Services** wizard opens.

4. Under **Common HTTP Features**, check **HTTP Redirection**, and click on **Next**.

5. Read the messages and click on **Install**.

6. On the last page, click on **Close**.

On Vista or Windows 7, follow these steps to install HTTP Redirection:

1. Click **Start | Control Panel | Programs and Features | Turn Windows Features on or off**.

2. Expand **Internet Information Services**, expand **World Wide Web Services**, expand **Common Http Features**, check **HTTP Redirection**, and click on **OK**.

Now set up your redirects in `web.config`, like this:

```
<configuration>
  <location path="OldPage.aspx">
    <system.webServer>
      httpRedirect enabled="true" destination="NewPage.aspx"
        httpResponseStatus="Permanent" />
    </system.webServer>
  </location>
</configuration>
```

Your site needs to use **Integrated Mode** rather than **Classic Mode** for this to work.

Minimizing CNAME records

When setting up domains and sub-domains, try to use **A** records rather than **CNAME** records. **CNAME** records can take another round trip to resolve.

SSL

When you use SSL for a page, an encrypted session is negotiated between the server and the browser. This mainly affects small static pages, where the overhead of negotiating the session can be significant, relative to the time needed to generate and transfer the page itself. The downside of SSL is less significant if you generate large pages on the server involving database accesses, and so on.

Because encrypted pages use the HTTPS protocol while normal pages use HTTP, use absolute links when referring from encrypted pages to unencrypted pages and vice versa, or just use absolute links throughout the site.

If you have images on encrypted pages, those images need to use HTTPS as well; otherwise, the visitor receives a warning.

Unwanted requests

All requests add to the load on your server, especially if they involve expensive operations such as database accesses. This means that you want to prevent those requests that do not help you achieve the objectives of your site such as selling widgets or disseminating information.

Search engine bots

Having a search engine crawl your site is a good thing. However, you don't want it to request files that are not relevant to the search listing, or that you want to keep private, because that may be a waste of resources. Those files could include:

- Images
- JavaScript, CSS, and other plumbing-related files
- Pages that require authentication

To ask spiders to not access specific areas of your site, put a text file named `robots.txt` in the root folder of your site.

To stop all search engine crawling, use:

```
User-agent: *
Disallow: /
```

To stop search engines from crawling specific folders:

```
User-agent: *
Disallow: /images/
Disallow: /js/
Disallow: /css/
Disallow: /private/
```

Some major search engines allow you to reduce the crawling rate of their spider using the following syntax:

```
User-agent: *
Crawl-delay: 10
```

You'll find more information about `robot.txt` and how the major engines use it, at the following web addresses:

- Robots exclusion standard
  `http://en.wikipedia.org/wiki/Robots_exclusion_standard`

- How to reduce the number of requests the Yahoo! search web crawler makes on your site
  `http://help.yahoo.com/l/us/yahoo/search/indexing/slurp-03.html`

- Crawl delay And the Bing Crawler, MSNBot
  `http://www.bing.com/toolbox/blogs/webmaster/archive/2009/08/10/crawl-delay-and-the-bing-crawler-msnbot.aspx`

- Changing Google's crawl rate
  `http://www.google.com/support/webmasters/bin/answer.py?answer=48620`

Another way of influencing the crawling behavior of search engines is to provide a site map. This is an XML file in your site's root folder containing an entry for each file on your site. You can include an update frequency for your files, so search engines won't read them more often than needed.

The full specification of site maps is present at `http://www.sitemaps.org/`.

Hotlinking

Hotlinking is the practice of linking to someone else's images on your site. If this happens to you and your images, another web master gets to show your images on their site and you get to pay for the additional bandwidth and incur the additional load on your server.

A great little module that prevents hot linking is **LeechGuard Hot-Linking Prevention Module** at `http://www.iis.net/community/default.aspx?tabid=34&i=1288&g=6`.

CAPTCHA

If you have forms on your site that update the database or execute some other expensive action, you will want to make sure that only humans can submit the form, and not robots.

One way to do that is via a CAPTCHA (**Completely Automated Public Turing test to tell Computers and Humans Apart**) image. This is an image showing letters or digits. Because it is an image, it is very hard for robots to read. That means that if the visitor manages to enter the correct letters or digits, they are likely to be human.

There are several CAPTCHA libraries that you can easily plug into your forms, including the following:

- **reCAPTCHA**: http://recaptcha.net/
- **BotDetect CAPTCHA**: http://captcha.biz/

An interesting twist is the **Honeypot CAPTCHA**. Instead of exploiting the inability of robots to read images, it exploits the fact that they don't execute JavaScript.

You simply include a bit of JavaScript on your site that sets a hidden form field to a secret code. If after the post back, you find that the hidden form field isn't there or has the wrong content, you know you're dealing with a robot. More information on this and how to deal with human visitors who don't have JavaScript enabled is available at Lightweight Invisible CAPTCHA Validator Control (http://haacked. com/archive/2006/09/26/Lightweight_Invisible_CAPTCHA_Validator_ Control.aspx).

Scrapers

If you have many pages with useful content, you will be confronted by people using software to read ("scrape") your pages to use it for their own purposes automatically. One example is them creating their own website with your content—the content generates traffic from search engines that the site then monetizes with ads. This is probably one type of traffic you don't want.

As long as the scraper doesn't modify the "from" IP address in its requests and doesn't try to mimic a human visitor by slowing down the frequency of its requests, some simple code can defend against this situation. This would detect whether a given visitor (identified by their IP address) is sending requests at super human speed, and if so, block that IP address, say for 20 minutes.

This doesn't defend against sophisticated **Denial Of Service (DOS)** attacks that bring down a site by bombarding it with requests—the software used in these attacks modifies the "from" IP address of the requests to make detection very difficult.

The code below defends against an unsophisticated scraper by recording how often each visitor sends requests to the site, and blocking those visitors that send too many requests in a given interval (class DOSBotDefence in folder DOSBotDefence in the downloaded code bundle):

```
public class BotDefence
{
```

This code assumes that if a visitor sends over 100 requests in a five-second period, it is a bot attack. This is simply an example. Looking at your logs, you should come up with your own numbers. Make sure that you don't block legitimate visitors or search engine crawlers:

```
private const int intervalSeconds = 5;
private const int maxRequestsInInterval = 100;
```

If a visitor has been deemed to be a bot attack, it will be blocked for 20 seconds:

```
private const int blockedPeriodSeconds = 20;
```

Create a class to hold information about a visitor. You'll see in a moment why these two fields are sufficient.

```
private class VisitorInfo
{
  public int nbrHits;
  public bool blocked;
  public VisitorInfo()
  {
    nbrHits = 1;
    blocked = false;
  }
}
```

Create a method that will tell the page whether a request is a bot attack. It will return `true` if it is, otherwise it will return `false`:

```
public static bool IsBotAttack()
{
```

Find out the IP address of the visitor:

```
string visitorIP =
    HttpContext.Current.Request.UserHostAddress;
```

Retrieve the visitors' information from the cache, using their IP address as the cache key:

```
VisitorInfo visitorInfo =
    (VisitorInfo)HttpContext.Current.Cache[visitorIP];
```

If their information wasn't in cache, create one. Seeing that they just made a single request, set their number of hits to one. Get the cache entry to expire at the end of the request counting interval. That will implicitly reset the counter, so there is no need to explicitly keep track of the interval ourselves, as shown:

```
if (visitorInfo == null)
{
  HttpContext.Current.Cache.Insert(
    visitorIP, new VisitorInfo(), null,
    DateTime.Now.AddSeconds(intervalSeconds),
    System.Web.Caching.Cache.NoSlidingExpiration);
}
else
{
```

If they did have information in cache, check whether they are blocked. If so, return `true` to indicate it is a bot attack:

```
if (visitorInfo.blocked)
{
  return true;
}
```

Increment the number of hits, because `visitorInfo` is simply a reference to the object in cache; there is no need to write the updated value back to cache:

```
visitorInfo.nbrHits++;
```

If the number of hits is too high, block the visitor. Reinsert their info into the cache, but now use the blocked interval as the expiry of the cached item. That way, the cache manager takes care of ending the blocked period by wiping the visitor's slate clean. Return `true` to indicate this is a bot attack:

```
if (visitorInfo.nbrHits > maxRequestsInInterval)
{
  visitorInfo.blocked = true;
  HttpContext.Current.Cache.Insert(
  visitorIP, visitorInfo, null,
  DateTime.Now.AddSeconds(blockedPeriodSeconds),
  System.Web.Caching.Cache.NoSlidingExpiration);
  return true;
}
}
```

If we got this far, the visitor is not deemed to be a bot attack. Return `false`:

```
        return false;
    }
}
```

Finally, pages that execute expensive actions and that are vulnerable to attack include this code:

```
protected void Page_Load(object sender, EventArgs e)
{
  if (BotDefence.IsBotAttack())
  {
    Response.End();
    return;
  }
  ...
}
```

This solution is simply an example. It probably isn't ready to take into production. You will want to build in tracing to keep a track of the IP addresses getting blocked. You will want to white-list IP addresses that are known to be good. Also, try not to block Googlebot or other search engine crawlers.

Finally, keep in mind that IP addresses are not a fool-proof method of identifying visitors:

- An ISP or company may connect users via a proxy or firewall, giving everybody the same IP address
- Some ISPs give dial-up users a dynamic IP address while they are connected, and reuse that IP address for another user when it becomes available

Usability testing

One source of unwanted traffic is visitors looking around your website without finding what they are looking for, or not understanding how to do the things you want them to do, thereby creating more traffic than if your website had been easier to use.

Usability testing is well outside the scope of this book. Search for "usability" and you will find lots of good information.

Find out more

Here are more online resources:

- Anatomy and Performance of SSL Processing
  `http://www.cs.ucr.edu/~bhuyan/papers/ssl.pdfb`
- CAPTCHA: Telling Humans and Computers Apart Automatically
  `http://www.captcha.net/`
- Alternatives to CAPTCHA
  `http://www.w3.org/TR/turingtest/`
- Usability 101: Introduction to Usability
  `http://www.useit.com/alertbox/20030825.html`

Summary

This chapter showed how to pinpoint bottlenecks that slow down the generation of a web page. We discussed memory pressures, caching, CPU usage, thread usage, and long wait times for external resources. For each bottleneck, you were referred to the chapter that shows how to fix it.

We also had a look at some miscellaneous ways to speed up the generation of a web page, including making sure that your code runs in release mode, reducing round trips to the server and reducing unwanted traffic.

In the next chapter, we'll find out how to reduce your application's memory usage.

3
Memory

Along with the CPU, memory is a critical hardware resource that directly affects the performance of any program running on a web server. When it comes to generating web pages using ASP.NET, a shortage of memory reduces performance for two fundamental reasons:

- It forces the server to swap data out of memory to the swap file on disk. This not only increases CPU usage and disk I/O, but also slows down data access because accessing data on disk is much slower than accessing data in memory.

- It prevents you from using caching, a powerful technique that trades off increased memory use for improved performance. Caching is discussed in *Chapter 5, Caching.*

The quickest and cheapest way to overcome memory problems may be to simply add more physical memory to the server, rather than spending the developers' time to fix the issue. On the other hand, if your application is very memory-hungry, you may be better off fixing this to avert running out of memory again in the near future.

This chapter discusses the following:

- The two main classes of objects consuming memory in your site: managed resources and unmanaged resources

- The life cycle of managed resources

- Ways to reduce memory usage by managed and unmanaged resources

- Ways to reduce memory usage by sessions, which can take a lot of memory, if used poorly

Managed resources

Managed resources are the objects you create on the heap in your C# code by calling new. Before going into ways to save memory taken by managed resources, let's have a quick look at their life cycle.

Life cycle

When you call new to create an object, memory is allocated for it on the CLR-managed heap. This always happens from the end of the allocated area, which makes it very quick.

When the CLR tries to allocate memory for an object and finds that enough space is not present at the end of the allocated area, it initiates a garbage collection. This removes all objects that no longer have references, and compresses all the surviving objects. The result is a nice, contiguous space at the end of the allocated area.

Once all references to an object disappear because they have gone out of scope or because they have been set to null, the object becomes eligible for garbage collection. However, it only gets physically removed by the next garbage collection, which may not happen for a while. This means that an object will be using memory for some time after you've stopped using it. Interestingly, the longer you've used the object, the longer it is likely to remain in memory after it loses all references, depending on its generation.

Generations

A garbage collection involves visiting a large number of objects to check whether they can be garbage-collected or not, which is expensive. To cut down on this expense, the CLR uses the fact that objects that have been in use for a long time are less likely to have lost their references than objects that have been recently created. This means that it makes sense to check the younger objects first and then the older ones.

This has been implemented by grouping objects in three generations—Gen 0, Gen 1, and Gen 2. Each object starts life in Gen 0. When it survives a garbage collection, it is promoted to Gen 1. If a Gen 1 object survives a garbage collection, it is further promoted to Gen 2. If a Gen 2 object survives a garbage collection, it simply stays in Gen 2.

Gen 0 objects are collected frequently, so short-lived objects are quickly removed. Gen 1 objects are collected less frequently, and Gen 2 objects even less frequently. So the longer an object lives, the longer it takes for it to be removed from memory once it has lost all references.

When Gen 1 objects are collected, the garbage collector collects Gen 0 objects as well. Also, when Gen 2 objects are collected, those in Gen 1 and Gen 0 too are collected. As a result, higher generation collections are more expensive.

Large Object Heap

In addition to the heap just described, there is a second heap for objects over 85 KB, called the **Large Object Heap** (LOH). If either the Large Object Heap or Gen 2 runs out of space, that triggers both a Large Object Heap collection and a Gen 2 collection. Remember that a Gen 2 collection goes through all objects in all generations, making it expensive.

There is no issue if there aren't many objects in Gen 2 and lower, or if the collection results in a lot of space being cleared. However, if there are lots of allocations on the Large Object Heap triggering lots of collections combined with lots of objects on the normal heap, the resulting Gen 2 collections can have an impact on performance.

A secondary issue is that when a large object is allocated, the CLR first clears the memory to be used for that object. For very large objects, that can take a lot of CPU cycles.

A final twist is that unlike objects on the normal heap, objects on the Large Object Heap are not compacted during a garbage collection. This means that if you allocate large objects of different sizes, you may wind up with a lot of unused space in between objects that cannot be used for memory allocation.

Counters

To keep track of garbage collections, check the following counters in category **.NET CLR Memory** with `perfmon`. To see how to check counters with `perfmon`, refer to *Chapter 2, Reducing Time to First Byte*, the *Pinpointing bottlenecks* section, *Thread usage* subsection, to be precise.

Category: .NET CLR Memory	
Percent Time in GC	The percentage of time spent in the GC since the end of the last collection. A value over 10 percent indicates a high allocation rate, or a high proportion of objects surviving garbage collections.
Gen 0 heap size	Maximum bytes that can be allocated in Gen 0 before the next Gen 0 garbage collection occurs. This is not the current number of bytes allocated for Gen 0 objects.
Gen 1 heap size	The current number of bytes taken by Gen 1 objects. This is not the maximum size of Gen 1.

Category: .NET CLR Memory	
Gen 2 heap size	The current number of bytes taken by Gen 2 objects. This is not the maximum size of Gen 2.
Large Object Heap size	Current size of the Large Object Heap in bytes.
# Bytes in all Heaps	The sum of counters **Gen 0 heap size**, **Gen 1 heap size**, **Gen 2 heap size** and **Large Object Heap size**. It reflects the amount of memory used by managed resources.
# Gen 0 Collections	Number of times Gen 0 objects have been garbage-collected since the start of the application. Do not use the _ Global_ instance of this counter, because it is not accurate.
# Gen 1 Collections	Number of times Gen 1 objects have been garbage-collected since the start of the application. Do not use the _ Global_ instance of this counter, because it is not accurate.
# Gen 2 Collections	Number of times Gen 2 objects have been garbage collected since the start of the application. Do not use the _ Global_ instance of this counter, because it is not accurate.

CLR profiler

CLR Profiler is a free tool by Microsoft that shows how much memory your application uses, broken down by type of object and size of object. Even better, it shows which code is doing most of the allocations. And it comes with an informative 108-page manual.

Download CLR Profiler from:

- CLR Profiler for the .NET Framework 2.0
  `http:// www.microsoft.com/downloads/details.`
  `aspx?familyid=a362781c-3870-43be- 8926-862b40aa0cd0&displaylan`
  `g=en.`

Instead of describing CLR Profiler in detail, I'll take you through the basics, so you can get started with it quickly. Then if you want to go deeper, you can read the manual:

1. Start CLR Profiler.
2. Make sure that **Profiling active**, **Allocations**, and **Calls** are checked.
3. Click on **File | Profile ASP.NET**. This shuts down IIS, inserts instrumentation, and then restarts IIS. The instrumentation seriously slows down the server, making CLR Profiler unsuitable for use in a production environment.

4. Run your ASP.NET website for example, by pressing *F5* in Visual Studio. The remainder of these instructions assume you ran the website in folder `MemoryBound` in the downloaded code bundle. The Page_Load handler of its `default.aspx` page runs a loop that leaves strings of size 2, 4, 8, ..., 16777216 on the heap, making it ideal to test a tool such as CLR Profiler:

```
string s = "x";
for (long i = 0; i < 24; i++)
{
    // double size of s in each iteration
    s += s;
}
```

5. When you have finished with the website, click on **Kill ASP.NET** in CLR Profiler. This removes the instrumentation, and then shows a summary page. This includes the sizes of the Gen 0, Gen 1, Gen 2, and Large Object Heaps. It also has buttons to drill down in the allocation information gathered by CLR Profiler, as shown in the following screenshot:

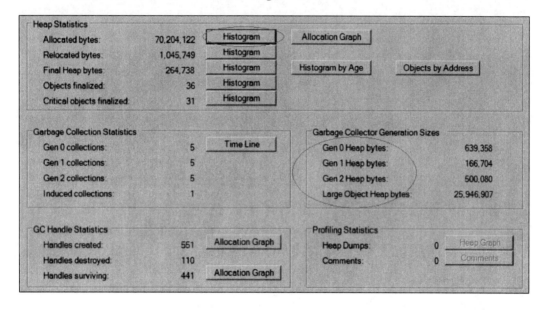

6. For example, click on the **Histogram** button next to **Allocated bytes**. This shows the proportion of the allocated space taken by object size and object type. In this case, the histogram confirms what you already suspected — most of the allocations were for strings, and most of the space went to very large strings:

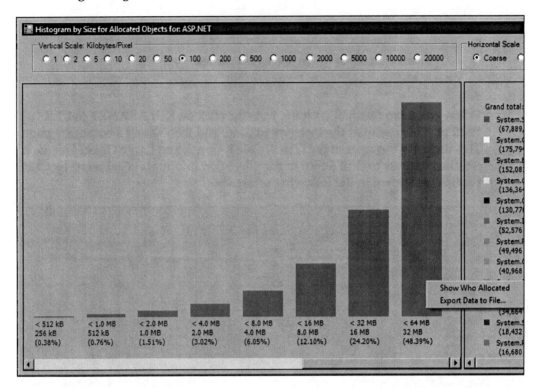

7. While looking at the bar to the right showing massive memory allocations, your first question will be: Where is the code that is allocating all this memory? To find out, right-click on the bar and choose **Show Who Allocated**. This brings up an allocation graph.

8. Scroll to the right in the allocation graph. You should come across the methods responsible for the memory allocations.

See *Chapter 4, CPU* for a number of commercial profiling tools that also give you an insight in your application's memory usage.

Garbage collector versions

The CLR has two versions of the garbage collector:

- The server version, which optimizes throughput, memory use, and processor scalability
- The work station version, which works better for desktop applications

ASP.NET uses the server version, provided your server has more than one CPU. This server version suspends all threads during garbage collection, increasing efficiency at the cost of application responsiveness.

Based on the way the garbage collector works, we can optimize performance in a number of ways:

- Acquire late
- Release early
- Using `StringBuilder` to concatenate strings
- Using `Compare` for case-insensitive compares
- Using `Response.Write` buffer
- Pooling objects over 85 KB

Let's look at each of these points one-by-one.

Acquire late

Create objects as late as you can. That saves memory, and shortens their life span so that they are less likely to be promoted to a higher generation. Specifically:

- Do not create large objects before a long-running call. Instead, do it afterwards if you can.

  Instead of the following:

  ```
  LargeObject largeObject = new LargeObject();
  // Long running database call ...
  largeObject.MyMethod();
  ```

  Use the following:

  ```
  // Long running database call ...
  LargeObject largeObject = new LargeObject();
  largeObject.MyMethod();
  ```

- Do not pre-allocate memory space, except for objects over 85 KB. That practice may be more efficient on some systems that are not based on .NET, such as real-time systems without a garbage collector. However, with the fast allocation in .NET, there is no advantage in doing this. All you do here is to stop the CLR from doling out memory in the most efficient way.

- If you use .NET 4, consider using `Lazy<T>`. This allows you to define an expensive object in a way that postpones its actual creation until it is actually used. You would define the object like the following:

```
Lazy<ExpensiveObject> expensiveObject = new
Lazy<ExpensiveObject>();
```

  As opposed to a normal class instantiation, this doesn't yet create the object. The object only gets created when you reference it for the first time:

```
expensiveObject.Value
```

Release early

If you need an object for only a short time, make sure it doesn't have long-lived references. Otherwise, the garbage collector doesn't know that it can be collected, and may even promote it to a higher generation so it hangs around even longer.

If you need to reference a short-lived object from a long-lived object, set the reference to null once you no longer need the short-lived object, as in the following code:

```
LargeObject largeObject = new LargeObject();

// Create reference from long lived object to new large object
longLivedObject.largeObject = largeObject;

// Reference no longer needed
longLivedObject.largeObject = null;
```

In a class, if a property references a short-lived object and you are about to execute a lengthy operation, set the reference to `null` if you no longer need the short-lived object:

```
private LargeObject largeObject { get; set; }

public void MyMethod()
{
    largeObject = new LargeObject();
    // some processing ...
    largeObject = null;
    // more lengthy processing ...
```

There is no need to do this for local variables, because the compiler figures out when a variable is no longer being used.

Using StringBuilder to concatenate strings

Strings are immutable objects that live on the heap. That means that when you perform an operation on a string, you automatically create a new one. Doing this often enough will quickly fill the heap, causing an expensive garbage collection.

Concatenating strings is a common operation. The StringBuilder class in namespace System.Text allows you to do this without creating large numbers of intermediate strings on the heap. It does this by allocating a buffer and then performing operations on the characters in that buffer.

Using StringBuilder

- Instead of the following:

```
string s = "";
for (int i = 0; i < stringArray.Length; i++)
{
    s += stringArray[i];
}
```

  Use the following:

```
StringBuilder sb = new StringBuilder(capacity);
for (int i = 0; i < stringArray.Length; i++)
{
    sb.Append(stringArray[i]);
}
string s = sb.ToString();
```

- Instead of the following:

```
// Concatenation results in new string object
sb.Append(stringArray[i] + ",");
```

  Use the following:

```
sb.Append(stringArray[i]);
sb.Append(",");
```

- Instead of the following:

```
// Returning a string creates an intermediate string on heap
sb.Append(ReturnString(...));
```

  Use the following:

```
// Method itself adds string to StringBuilder
AddString(sb, ...);
```

When not to use StringBuilder

StringBuilder comes with its own overhead. If you have fewer than about seven concatenations, use simple string concatenation even if you get intermediate strings on the heap.

Secondly, when concatenating strings in one shot, only the final string is created. In that case, do not use StringBuilder:

```
s = s1 + s2 + s3 + s4;
```

StringBuilder capacity

The StringBuilder constructor can take a capacity parameter. Its default is 16. Each time the StringBuilder runs out of capacity, it allocates a new buffer of twice the size of the old buffer, copies the contents of the old buffer to the new one and leaves the old buffer to be garbage collected.

That means that it makes sense to set the capacity of the StringBuilder via the constructor if you have some idea how big it will need to be.

Using Compare for case-insensitive compares

Instead of the following:

```
// ToLower allocates two new strings
if (s1.ToLower() == s2.ToLower())
{
}
```

Use the following:

```
if (string.Compare(s1, s2, true) == 0)
{
}
```

This code takes the current culture into account. A simple byte-by-byte comparison will be a bit faster. To implement this, use the following:

```
if (string.Compare(s1, s2, StringComparison.OrdinalIgnoreCase) == 0)
{
}
```

Using Response.Write buffer

If you use `Response.Write` to send data to the browser, use its internal buffer.

For example, instead of the following:

```
// Concatenation creates intermediate string
Response.Write(s1 + s2);
```

Use the following:

```
Response.Write(s1);
Response.Write(s2);
```

If you build custom controls, use the same technique with the `HtmlTextWriter` class.

Pooling objects over 85 KB

As you saw, frequently allocating and collecting objects over 85 KB is expensive and can lead to fragmentation.

If your site instantiates objects of a class taking over 85 KB in space, consider creating a pool of these objects in one go during application start up, rather than allocating them on the fly.

When figuring out whether an object takes over 85 KB, consider whether it takes a lot of room itself, or merely references other objects that take a lot of room. For example, a byte array with 85 * 1024 = 87040 entries takes 85 KB:

```
byte[]  takes85KB = new byte[87040]; // 85 * 1024 = 87040
```

However, an array of 85 objects each taking 1024 bytes doesn't take that much space, because the array merely holds references to the objects.

Now that we've looked at managed resources, let's have a look at reducing memory used by unmanaged resources.

Unmanaged resources

Some commonly used objects are based on unmanaged resources, such as file handles and database connections. These file handles and connections are scarce resources. When these objects lose all references, the garbage collector will eventually remove them and in the process, release the scarce resources they have in use. However, instead of waiting for the garbage collector, you'll want to release the scarce resources the moment they are no longer in use so that another thread can use them.

IDisposable

To allow your code to do this, these objects implement the interface **IDisposable**. This exposes the method `Dispose()`, which disposes the object. They also often implement a method `Close()` with the same functionality as `Dispose()`, even though `Close()` is not exposed by IDisposable.

If an object implements IDisposable, be sure to call its `Dispose()` method as soon as you can; do not cache these resources.

To make sure that an unmanaged resource is quickly released, even when an exception occurs, you'll normally call `Dispose()` in a final block, as in the following:

```
SqlConnection connection = new SqlConnection(connectionString);
try
{
    // use connection ...
}
finally
{
    connection.Dispose();
}
```

Shorthand for this code is provided by the C# using statement:

```
using (SqlConnection connection = new SqlConnection(connectionString))
{
    // use connection ...
} // connection.Dispose called implicitly
```

There is no need to wait for the end of the `using` statement to dispose the connection. If you call `Dispose()` on an object that has already been disposed, nothing happens. For example:

```
using (SqlConnection connection = new SqlConnection(connectionString))
{
    // use connection ...
    connection.Dispose();
    // long running code that doesn't use the connection ...
} // connection.Dispose is called again implicitly
```

If you create a class that holds objects that implement IDisposable, or derives from a class that implements IDisposable, or that deals with unmanaged objects provided by the operating system, you'll need to implement IDisposable yourself. For more information, visit:

- IDisposable Interface at
  `http://msdn.microsoft.com/en-us/library/system.idisposable.aspx?ppud=4`
- Implementing a Dispose Method at
  `http://msdn.microsoft.com/en-us/library/fs2xkftw.aspx?ppud=4`

Counters

To find out more about the use of unmanaged objects, check these counters with `perfmon`:

Category: .NET CLR Memory	
# of Pinned Objects	The number of pinned objects encountered in the last garbage collection. Pinned objects are used with unmanaged code. The garbage collector cannot move pinned objects in memory, potentially causing fragmentation of the heap.

Category: .NET CLR LocksAndThreads	
# of current logical Threads	Number of current .NET thread objects in the application. If this keeps rising, you keep creating new threads without removing the old threads and their stack frames.

Category: Process	
Private Bytes	The current size, in bytes, of memory that this process has allocated that cannot be shared with other processes. The number of bytes allocated for unmanaged objects equals **Private Bytes - # Bytes in all Heaps** (category **.NET CLR Memory**).

Sessions

Session state allows you to store information for a particular visitor session in between requests. An example of a session is a visitor browsing your site. Session state lets you store information relevant to the session via a dictionary-type syntax:

```
Session["book"] = "ASP.NET Site Performance";
```

Retrieval is just as easy:

```
string bookName = (string)Session["book"];
```

In the default **InProc** mode, the session state information is stored in memory. That's fast, but won't work if you use multiple web servers, because the next request from the same visitor may go to another server. The StateServer and SQL Server modes cater to server farms by storing session state on a central server or database. If the mode is set to something different than InProc, you can find the mode in the `<sessionState>` element in `web.config`.

I'll assume from now on that you are using session state using InProc mode, because it is that mode that takes memory. If it doesn't apply to you, skip this section.

The session state for each individual visitor session is stored in its own bit of memory. To figure out which session state to use, ASP.NET stores a session ID cookie on the browser. You also have the option of storing it in the URL.

There is no definite way for ASP.NET to find out whether the visitor has stopped using your site, so the session state can be removed. To solve that, ASP.NET assumes the session state can be removed after 20 minutes without requests from the visitor, which is configurable. This means that if you keep the default session timeout, whatever you put in the session state will be taking up memory space for at least 20 minutes.

So how much memory does session state use?

- Assume that the average visitor spends 10 minutes on your site. Add the default timeout of 20 minutes to get 30 minutes, during which each session state is active.

- Assume your site receives 100 requests per second, and that each visitor sends five requests while they are active on your site. That means you have 100/5 =20 visitors per second.

- Assuming you start using the session state from the first request, the number of active sessions at any one time will be (session life span of 30 minutes) * (60 seconds per minute) * (20 visitors per second) =36000 sessions.

- Finally, assume you are storing 20 KB in session state for each visitor from the first request in the session.

- Memory used by session state is then (36000 sessions) * (20 KB per session) =720 MB. That is not too bad. However, it does show you'll run into memory shortages if either the number of visitors or the amount of data you store in session state goes up dramatically.

To find the number of active sessions on your site, use `perfmon` to check the following counter in category ASP.NET Applications. Refer to *Chapter 2, Reducing Time to First Byte, Pinpointing bottlenecks* section, *Thread usage* subsection to see how to check a counter.

Category: ASP.NET Applications	
Sessions Active	The current number of sessions currently active.

If you decide that session state is taking too much memory, here are some solutions.

- Reduce session state life time
- Reduce space taken by session state
- Use another session mode
- Stop using session state

Let's go through these one-by-one.

Reducing session state life time

If sessions expire sooner, they take up less space. Here are a few options:

- Reduce the session time-out used by ASP.NET. You can set the timeout in minutes in `web.config`, via the `sessionState` element:

```
<configuration>
  <system.web>
    <sessionState mode="InProc" timeout="20" />
  </system.web>
</configuration>
```

  Also, we can set the session time-out programmatically:

```
Session.Timeout = 20;
```

- Explicitly abandon the session, for example when a visitor logs out:

```
Session.Abandon();
```

Reducing space taken by session state

Try to reduce the size of the state information stored per session:

- Do not store objects that carry overhead. For example, do not store user interface elements or data tables. Instead, store just the information you need.

- Store information that is not session-specific in cache, where it will be shared by all visitors. For example, a list of countries is not session-specific.

- Do not store information from the database in session, but retrieve it for each request. This way, you trade off increased load on the database for reduced memory usage on the web server. This would be attractive if retrieving the data is fast and doesn't happen often, and the data itself takes a lot of memory space.

Using another session mode

If there is no room in memory for session state, you can use SqlServer mode and put it in the database. This saves you memory and as an added bonus, you won't lose your session state when the web server or application pool restarts. But it is much slower and puts a bigger load on the database.

To set up SqlServer mode, follow these steps:

1. Open a command window and navigate to folder `C:\Windows\Microsoft.NET\Framework\v2.0.50727`.

   If you use .NET 4, browse to `C:\Windows\Microsoft.NET\Framework\v4.0.30128`.

2. Execute `aspnet_regsql -E -S localhost -ssadd -sstype p`.

   `-E` says to use a trusted connection. Alternatively, use `-U <login id> -P <password>`.

   `-S` specifies the server.

   `-ssadd` tells it to create support for SqlServer mode.

   Finally, `-sstype p` says to create the necessary tables in a new database `ASPState`, rather than in `tempdb`. If you want another database, use `-sstype c -d <database name>`.

   In addition to creating a new database `ASPState`, it also creates a new job `ASPState_Job_DeleteExpiredSessions`. This runs every minute and cleans up expired sessions.

3. Add a `sessionState` element to `web.config` along these lines:

```
<system.web>
  <sessionState
    mode="SQLServer"
    sqlConnectionString="Data Source=.; Integrated Security=True"
    timeout="20" />
</system.web>
```

The `sqlConnectionString` attribute specifies the database to use. In this case, it is the local database. Do not set the database if you used `-sstype p` with `aspnet_regsql`; otherwise, you will get a runtime error.

4. Now that you are incurring the higher cost of using SqlServer mode instead of InProc mode, specify read-only mode in the page directive of every page that doesn't update session state:

```
<%@ Page EnableSessionState="ReadOnly" %>
```

This reduces the number of trips to the session database from two to one for each page access. For more optimizations, see *Sessions* section in *Chapter 7, Reducing Long Wait Times*.

Stop using session state

In many cases, there is no need to use session state at all. Here are some alternatives:

- Reduce page refreshes by using AJAX-type asynchronous requests. That enables you to store session information on the page itself, such as in user interface elements. This is further discussed in *Chapter 11, Optimizing Forms*, in the *Submitting forms asynchronously* and *AJAX-type grids* sections.

- Store session state in `ViewState`, on the page itself. This makes sense if the size of the session state is not too large, and all page-specific. A disadvantage of `ViewState` is that it takes more bandwidth, and that it is more open to tampering by the visitor. Accessing ViewState is similar to writing to session state:

```
ViewState["data"] = "information";
string information = (string)ViewState["data"];
```

One good reason not to use session state is that it involves sending a session ID in either a cookie or the URL. Either of these options impairs caching. See the *Proxy caching* section in *Chapter 5, Caching*.

Find out more

Here are more online resources:

- Large Object Heap Uncovered
  `http://msdn.microsoft.com/en-us/magazine/cc534993.aspx`
- Notes on the CLR Garbage Collector
  `http://vineetgupta.spaces.live.com/blog/`
  `cns!8DE4BDC896BEE1AD!1104.entry?ppud=4&wa=wsignin1.0&`
  `sa=923517169`

Summary

In this chapter, we first learned about the life cycle of managed objects, including garbage collection, the three generations of objects, and the Large Object Heap.

Then, we saw how to gain insight into our application's memory use using counters and CLR Profiler.

This was followed by ways to reduce memory use by managed objects, such as acquire late / release early, and using the `StringBuilder` to concatenate strings.

We then saw how to reduce memory usage by unmanaged resources, by taking care to dispose them as soon as possible.

Finally, we discussed ways to reduce memory use by sessions.

Now that we've seen how to reduce usage of memory, let's move on to reducing CPU usage.

CPU

Unlike bottlenecks such as memory shortage that can be relatively cheaply addressed by adding hardware to the web server, upgrading or adding CPUs is relatively expensive. That makes it attractive to first try to reduce CPU usage when confronted by a CPU-related bottleneck.

In this chapter, we'll discuss the following:

- Techniques and tools to identify code that require a lot of CPU usage
- Specific ways to reduce CPU usage such as more efficient data access, better use of exceptions, and more efficient data binding

Let's start off with identifying where your code incurs the greatest CPU usage.

Identifying bottlenecks

There are a number of techniques to identify pieces of code with high levels of CPU usage:

- Focus on pieces of code that are executed frequently. Loops, and especially loops within loops, are good candidates. If you sort collections using a class derived from **IComparable**, the code in that class will be very busy. If you retrieve data from a database, each record needs to be processed in turn, using some sort of loop.
- You could instrument your code with lightweight counters, to measure how often each section is executed and how long it takes to execute. Counters are discussed in the *Measuring wait times* section in *Chapter 7, Reducing Long Wait Times*.

- Do some old-style debugging. Run a stress test on your development site, so that it uses a lot of CPU. Take out one half of the code, and see what difference this makes to CPU usage. If CPU usage goes down considerably, the culprit is probably in the half you took out. Keep hacking until you isolate the offending code.

- If you do non-trivial things in your code, have another look at your algorithms. If you use an inefficient algorithm, changing the algorithm will have a much better payoff than any tweaking around the edges.

To measure how long a section of code takes, use the `stopWatch` class, as shown in the following code:

```
using System.Diagnostics;

Stopwatch stopWatch = new Stopwatch();
stopWatch.Start();

// first bit of code ...

stopWatch.Stop();
TimeSpan elapsedTime1 = stopWatch.Elapsed;

stopWatch.Reset();
stopWatch.Start();

// second bit of code ...

stopWatch.Stop();
TimeSpan elapsedTime2 = stopWatch.Elapsed;
```

Tools

Sometimes, the bottleneck is well hidden, making the old school methods shown above less effective. In that case, consider using a profiler tool. These tools instrument your application in order to measure for example, execution time taken per method, which is fine in your development environment, but would slow down your production site. Following are some of the more popular tools at the time of writing:

- **Visual Studio Performance Profiling**: If you are lucky enough to be using Visual Studio 2008 Team Systems Development Edition, or Visual Studio 2010 Ultimate or Premium, you already have access to a powerful performance profiling tool. One of its features is that for each function, it reports how much memory it allocates, how much time it takes on average, and how often it is called. Reports can be exported to CSV and XML files. Another great feature is **Hotpathing**, which shows which areas of your application take the most time for execution.

For a full description of the Visual Studio profiling tool, visit:

- ° Analyzing Application Performance by Using Profiling Tools (VS 2010)
  `http://msdn.microsoft.com/en-us/library/z9z62c29.aspx`
- ° Find Application Bottlenecks with Visual Studio Profiler (VS 2008)
  `http://msdn.microsoft.com/en-us/magazine/cc337887.aspx`

- **ANTS Performance Profiler**: This sophisticated (and expensive) tool shows a live timeline showing CPU usage, heap allocations, and other items you select while using your development site. You can drill down at any particular point in the timeline to see for example ticks or time spent, the stack trace at that time, the source code making up a method, how long each line took, and how often it was used. It can also profile SQL queries and file I/O. You can save the results of a test run for later analysis in ANTS, or save it as an HTML file. For more details, visit `http://www.red-gate.com/products/ants_performance_profiler/`.

- **Eqatec Profiler**: This easy-to-use profiler focuses on CPU usage and de-emphasizes memory usage. It has its own **Application Programming Interface (API)**, allowing you to take a snapshot at a given point in your code, or to prevent a method from being profiled. It supports the .NET Compact Framework. Best of all, at the time of writing, it had a fully functional free edition, which is good if your company doesn't like spending money on tools. For more details, visit `http://www.eqatec.com/tools/profiler/`.

- **Slimtune**: It is an open source profiler and performance analysis/tuning tool for .NET-based applications. Features include remote profiling, real-time results, and multiple plugin-based visualizations. Visit `http://code.google.com/p/slimtune/` for more details.

Data access

Accessing the database is the most expensive part of the processing for most pages. Here you'll see a number of ways to reduce that expense.

Connection pooling

Opening a connection to the database is expensive. Because of this, ASP.NET maintains a pool of open connections. There is a pool per connection string, by Windows identity when integrated security is used, and by whether they are enlisted in a transaction.

When you open a connection, you actually receive a connection from the pool. When you close that connection, it stays open and goes back to the pool, ready for use by another thread.

To make this work efficiently, always use exactly the same connection string for each database you access. If you access one database, have one connection string.

It's easiest to store the connection string in a central location, in `web.config`:

```
<configuration>
    <connectionStrings>
        <add name="ConnectionString" connectionString="....."/>
    </connectionStrings>
</configuration>
```

In your code, retrieve it as follows:

```
using System.Configuration;
...
string connectionString =
    ConfigurationManager.ConnectionStrings[
        "ConnectionString"].ConnectionString;
```

Connection pooling is controlled by these connection string parameters:

Max Pool Size	Maximum size of the connection pool. Defaults to 100. When a connection is requested from the pool and none is available, a new connection is created and added to the pool, unless the maximum pool size has been reached. If the pool is already at maximum size, the request is queued until a connection becomes available.
Min Pool Size	Initial number of connections in the pool when it is created. Defaults to zero. This means that the first few database accesses will be delayed due to the creation of new connections. To prevent that delay, set this parameter to the number of connections you think the pool will grow to during the life of your web application.
Connect Timeout	Time in seconds that a request will wait for a connection before terminating the attempt and generating an error. Defaults to 15 seconds.
Pooling	Switches connection pooling on or off. Defaults to true. Set to false to switch off connection pooling. Read on to know why you would want to do that.

Here is an example of a connection string that sets the minimum pool size:

```
Data Source=10.1.1.5;Initial Catalog=TuneUp;User ID=tuneup;
    Password=fast3rweb!;Min Pool Size=5;
```

What about the Pooling parameter? Why would you want to switch off connection pooling? In short, this is to stop your application from crashing when it leaks connections. Here is how this works.

Consider this code:

```
SqlConnection connection = new SqlConnection(connectionString);
connection.Open();
... code that may throw an exception ...
connection.Close();
```

If the code throws an exception, the connection doesn't get closed. It will eventually get closed by the garbage collector, but that may take a while depending on memory pressures. Meanwhile, your application leaks connections; more and more connections get added to the connection pool.

When the maximum number of connections is reached, incoming requests will start to time out while waiting for a connection, and be terminated. This is not good.

The best way to fix this is to fix your code, so that it closes the connection even when an exception happens:

```
using (SqlConnection connection = new
  SqlConnection(connectionString))
{
    connection.Open();
    ... code that may throw an exception ...
}
```

However, if your best customer is on the phone demanding a solution *now*, you may not have the time to track down the offending code, change it, and install it. In that case, it makes sense to switch off connection pooling so your application stops crashing for now.

If your code rarely throws exceptions, the rate of leakage will be low as well. In that case, you are likely to see intermittent crashes rather than a big drama.

To prevent all this pain, you can keep an eye on the number of connections in the connection pool using the following counter on the database server. If the number of connections keeps going up even though traffic is stable, you may have a leak. Refer to the *Thread usage* subsection of the *Pinpointing bottlenecks* section in *Chapter 2, Reducing Time to First Byte* to see how to check a counter with perfmon.

Category: SQL Server General Statistics	
User Connections	Number of users connected to the system.

DataSet versus List

When you read data from the database, you probably store it into a collection. That way, you can cache it, and pass it on to another layer.

The easiest collection to use is the DataSet—it takes only a few lines to fill and it comes with lots of good features. An alternative is a generic List, which takes more work to fill and doesn't have the good features, but is much lighter. If you don't need the features and CPU cycles are short, how great is the difference?

The test code is just simple standard ADO.NET, so I'll leave it to you to retrieve it from the page *DataAccess.aspx* in the folder *CPU* in the downloaded code bundle. It retrieves 10 records with four columns each from a database, repeating this 100 times. The results below relate to the complete database retrieval, not just the loading of the result set into the collection:

Test	Time taken (in ticks)
100 * loading 10 records/4 fields in DataSet	250500
100 * loading 10 records/4 fields in generic List	202239

If you don't need the features offered by a DataSet, you can save significant CPU cycles by using a generic List instead.

Returning multiple result sets

ADO.NET allows you to receive a number of result sets in one go. Take for example the following stored procedure:

```
CREATE PROCEDURE [dbo].[GetBooksAndAuthors]
AS
BEGIN
  SET NOCOUNT ON;

  SELECT [BookId]
    ,[Title]
    ,[AuthorId]
    ,[Price]
  FROM [dbo].[Book]

  SELECT [AuthorId]
    ,[Name]
    ,[Address]
    ,[Phone]
    ,[Email]
  FROM [dbo].[Author]
END
```

This returns two result sets, one with the book records and the other with the author records. You can access the second result set using `SqlDataReader.NextResult`, like this:

```
using (SqlDataReader reader = cmd.ExecuteReader())
{
    while (reader.Read())
    {
        // read first result set ...
    }

    reader.NextResult();

    while (reader.Read())
    {
        // read second result set ...
    }
}
```

This means that if you need to show multiple result sets on a page, you can get them all in one go rather than one at a time.

The working test code is in the page `MultiTableDataAccess.aspx` in the downloaded code bundle. It retrieves 10 records with four columns, each from two tables, repeating this 100 times. The results on my machine were:

Test	Time taken for total database retrieval (in ticks)	Time taken excluding waiting for response from database (in ticks)
100 * loading 2 result sets of 10 records / 4 fields using 2 separate requests	413770	108961
100 * loading 2 result sets of 10 records / 4 fields using a single request returning 2 result sets	284335	90897

This shows that it is attractive to retrieve all result sets you need in one go, rather than one-by-one. You not only save time spent waiting for the database, but also CPU cycles, worker thread switching delays, and so on, as evidenced by the right-most column.

Sending multiple inserts in one go

You may have a situation where you need to call a stored procedure a variable number of times. For example, you could have a grid where a visitor enters one or more new records, and then clicks a button to save them all in one go in the database. If you have a stored procedure that inserts a record, you would call that stored procedure for each new record to be inserted.

The conventional approach would be to send each call to the stored procedure individually. However, you can also send them all in one go. First, create the SQL with parameters as shown in the following code:

```
const string singleExec = "EXEC dbo.InsertData @Title{0}, @Author{0},
@Price{0};";
StringBuilder sql = new StringBuilder();
for (int j = 0; j < nbrInserts; j++)
{
    sql.AppendFormat(singleExec, j);
}
```

This creates a single string with multiple EXEC statements, separated by a semi-colon (;). To distinguish the parameters for each EXEC, AppendFormat is used to append the sequence number in variable j to the parameter names.

Assigning values to the parameters would look like the following:

```
for (int j = 0; j < nbrInserts; j++)
{
    cmd.Parameters.AddWithValue("@Title" + j.ToString(), ...);
    cmd.Parameters.AddWithValue("@Author" + j.ToString(), ...);
    cmd.Parameters.AddWithValue("@Price" + j.ToString(), ...);
}
Then send all EXEC statements in one go to the database:
cmd.CommandType = CommandType.Text;
cmd.ExecuteNonQuery();
```

Note that the command text contains SQL text (the EXEC statements), not a stored procedure name. So, you use the command type CommandType.Text.

The working test code is in the page `MultiInsert.aspx` in the folder CPU in the downloaded code bundle. It sends four stored procedure calls, repeating this 100 times. The results on my machine were:

Test	Time taken for total database access (in ticks)	Time taken excluding waiting for response from database (in ticks)
100 * sending an individual stored procedure four times (making 400 sends)	3022521	99387
100 * sending four stored procedure calls in one go (making 100 sends)	2096341	54767

This shows that it is attractive to send multiple stored procedure calls in one go, rather than one by one. You not only save time spent waiting for the database, but also CPU cycles, worker thread switching delays, and so on, as evidenced by the right-most column.

Using native data providers

Instead of generic data providers such as `System.Data.OleDb` and `System.Data.ODBC`, use a native provider if you can, such as `System.Data.SqlClient` or `System.Data.OracleClient`. The native providers tend to perform better because there is less abstraction.

Exceptions

Throwing exceptions is expensive. When you throw an exception, first the exception object is created on the heap. Included in the exception object is the call stack, which the runtime has to create. Then the runtime finds the right exception handler and executes it along with any finally blocks that need to be executed as well. Use exceptions only for truly exceptional situations, not for normal program flow.

Revealing the time taken by exceptions

Take for example converting a string to an integer. You can use either `Int32.Parse`, which throws an exception if the conversion failed, or `Int32.TryParse`, which returns a success boolean.

Test code with `Int32.Parse`:

```
for (int i = 0; i < 1000; i++)
{
    int targetInt = 0;
    try
    {
        targetInt = Int32.Parse("xyz");
    }
    catch
    {
    }
}
```

Test code with `Int32.TryParse`:

```
for (int i = 0; i < 1000; i++)
{
    int targetInt = 0;
    if (!Int32.TryParse("xyz", out targetInt))
    {
    }
}
```

On my machine, these were the results:

Test	Time taken (ticks)
`Int32.Parse` — throw 1000 exceptions	1052207
`Int32.TryParse` — no exceptions	1522

This illustrates that you do not want to use exceptions for anything other than true exceptions, which is what they are meant for in the first place.

The `Server.Transfer`, `Response.Redirect` and `Response.End` methods all raise `ThreadAbortException`, unless you use overloads that allow you to prevent this.

Counters

The following counters in category **.NET CLR Exceptions** show exception activity in your site. To see how to access these counters with `perfmon`, see the *Thread usage* subsection of *Pinpointing bottlenecks* section in chapter 2.

Category: .NET CLR Exceptions	
# of Exceps Thrown	The total number of exceptions thrown since the start of the application.
# of Exceps Thrown/sec	The number of exceptions thrown per second.
# of Filters/sec	The number of .NET exception filters executed per second. An exception filter evaluates whether an exception should be handled or not.
# of Finallys/sec	The number of finally blocks executed per second. Only the `finally` blocks that are executed for an exception are counted, not those on normal code paths.
Throw To Catch Depth/sec	The number of stack frames traversed from the frame that threw the .NET exception to the frame that handled the exception per second.

DataBinder.Eval

Controls such as GridView and Repeater work with templates. A popular way to refer to fields within templates uses `DataBinder.Eval`, as shown in the following code:

```
<asp:Repeater ID="rptrEval" runat="server">
    <ItemTemplate>
        <%# Eval("field1")%>
        <%# Eval("field2")%>
        <%# Eval("field3")%>
        <%# Eval("field4")%>
    </ItemTemplate>
</asp:Repeater>
```

However, this uses reflection to arrive at the value of the field. If you have 10 rows with four fields each, you execute `Eval` 40 times.

A much faster way is to refer directly to the class that contains the field:

```
<asp:Repeater ID="rptrCast" runat="server">
    <ItemTemplate>
        <%# ((MyClass)Container.DataItem).field1 %>
        <%# ((MyClass)Container.DataItem).field2 %>
        <%# ((MyClass)Container.DataItem).field3 %>
        <%# ((MyClass)Container.DataItem).field4 %>
    </ItemTemplate>
</asp:Repeater>
```

In this example, I have used class MyClass. If you're binding against a DataTable, you would use "DataRowView".

When binding a List<MyClass> with 10 rows to each Repeater, on my machine the call to Repeater.DataBind() took these many ticks:

Test	Time taken (in ticks)
40 * Eval	5256
40 * cast	353

That's a big difference for a small change in your code.

Garbage collector

If the garbage collector is working overtime, it may consume a lot of CPU cycles. Check the counters shown in *Chapter 3, Memory* to see if this is the case, especially **% Time in GC**. To see how to check a counter in perfmon, refer to the *Pinpointing bottlenecks* section, the *Thread usage* subsection in chapter 2.

Category: .NET CLR Memory	
% Time in GC	The percentage of time spent in the GC since the end of the last collection. A value over 10 percent indicates a high allocation rate, or a high proportion of objects surviving garbage collections.

Threading

If used poorly, threading can consume a lot of CPU cycles needlessly. If your code is multi-threaded, consider the following ways to reduce threading overhead:

- If you use threads to wait for off-box resources such as databases or web services, consider using asynchronous requests instead. These are described in *Chapter 6, Thread Usage*.

- Do not create your own threads. This is very expensive. Instead, use `ThreadPool.QueueUserWorkItem` to get a thread from the thread pool.

- Do not use threads for CPU-intensive tasks. If you have four CPUs, there is no sense in having more than four CPU-intensive tasks.

- Thread switches are expensive. Try to reduce the number of threads running simultaneously.

To get more information about the threads currently running, check these counters in `perfmon`.

Category: Thread	
% Processor Time	Shows for each thread what percentage of processor time it is taking.
Context Switches/sec	Shows for each thread the rate of context switches per second.

StringBuilder

If you need to append a series of strings to another string in a loop, you can save CPU cycles by using a `StringBuilder`. This is because string += concatenations create a new string on the heap, which takes time.

Here is some test code using regular string concatenations:

```
for (int i = 0; i < 1000; i++)
{
    string s = "";
    for (int j = 0; j < 20; j++)
    {
        s += "aabbcc";
    }
}
```

And here is the equivalent using a `StringBuilder`:

```
for (int i = 0; i < 1000; i++)
{
    string s = "";
    StringBuilder sb = new StringBuilder();
    for (int j = 0; j < 20; j++)
    {
        sb.Append("aabbcc");
    }
    s = sb.ToString();
}
```

Both bits of code append a string to another string 20 times. They repeat doing that a 1000 times to get some meaningful numbers. The overhead of creating the `StringBuilder` and getting its contents into a string is contained within the 1000 times loop.

On my machine, the results were:

Test	Time taken (ticks)
1000 * 20 concatenations	29474
1000 * 20 StringBuilder appends	11906

This shows that you can save some CPU cycles by using `StringBuilder`. Bigger advantages are probably reduced memory use and a reduced number of objects on the heap for the garbage collector to process.

Do not use `StringBuilder` if all concatenations happen in one go, such as in the following:

```
string s = s1 + s2 + s3;
```

Regex instantiation

When matching a string against a regular expression, you have a few choices. You can first instantiate a `Regex` object with the regular expression and then call the `IsMatch` method on that object, passing in the string. Also, you can call the static `Regex.IsMatch`, which takes both the regular expression and the string.

If you repeat the same match many times, you will save CPU cycles by instantiating the `Regex` object outside the loop, rather than using the static version of `IsMatch`.

Here is a loop using the static `IsMatch`:

```
for (int i = 0; i < 1000; i++)
{
    bool b = (Regex.IsMatch("The number 1000.", @"\d+"));
}
```

And here its counterpart which instantiates Regex outside the loop:

```
Regex regex = new Regex(@"\d+");
for (int i = 0; i < 1000; i++)
{
    bool b = regex.IsMatch("The number 1000.");
}
```

Here are the results of a typical run:

Test	Time taken (in ticks)
1000 * static IsMatch	21783
1000 * instantiated Regex	14167

If you spend a lot of time matching regular expressions on your site, you could create a static class with regular expression objects. That way, you take the instantiation hit only once during application startup, rather than for each request.

UtcNow

If you compare dates in your site without showing those dates to the visitor, `DateTime.UtcNow` is a lot faster than `DateTime.Now`.

Take this code, which compares against `DateTime.Now` 1000 times:

```
DateTime dt = DateTime.Now;
for (int i = 0; i < 1000; i++)
{
    DateTime dt2 = DateTime.Now;
    bool b = (dt2 > dt);
}
```

The equivalent using `UtcNow` is as follows:

```
DateTime dtu = DateTime.UtcNow;
for (int i = 0; i < 1000; i++)
{
    DateTime dtu2 = DateTime.UtcNow;
    bool b = (dtu2 > dtu);
}
```

Here is how they compare on my machine:

Test	Time taken (ticks)
1000 * Now	3964
1000 * UtcNow	136

Foreach

The C# statement foreach is a convenient way to traverse an enumerable collection, but because it uses an enumerator it is also more expensive than a normal for loop.

The following code uses a trivial foreach loop:

```
int k = 0;
foreach (int j in list)
{
    k = j;
}
```

This code uses a for loop instead:

```
int k = 0;
int listLength = list.Count;
for (int i = 0; i < listLength; i++)
{
    k = list[i];
}
```

For completeness, I also tested a loop that counts backwards to zero, rather than forwards to the list count:

```
int k = 0;
for (int i = list.Count - 1; i >= 0; i--)
{
    k = list[i];
}
```

I used a List<int> with 1000 integers. On my machine, the results were:

Test	Time taken (ticks)
foreach – 1000 List<int> accesses	168
for – 1000 List<int> accesses	80
for backwards - 1000 List<int> accesses	75

This concludes that if you're counting every CPU cycle, you may want to look at tight `foreach` loops with very high numbers of iterations. Looping backwards will give you a very slight performance boost.

Virtual properties

When you declare a property in a class as `virtual`, you allow classes derived from your class to override that property. However, this also slows down access to the property, because the compiler can no longer inline it.

This means that if you read the property a great many times, you can save some CPU cycles by copying it into a local variable and then accessing the local variable.

Take for example this class, which has one `virtual` property:

```
private class MyClass
{
    public virtual int IntProperty { get; set; }
}
```

This code accesses the property a 1000 times:

```
int k = -1;
for (int i = 0; i < 1000; i++)
{
    k = myClass.IntProperty;
}
```

This code copies the property into a local variable:

```
int k = -1;
int j = myClass.IntProperty;
for (int i = 0; i < 1000; i++)
{
    k = j;
}
```

Here are the test results on my machine:

Test	Time taken (ticks)
Access property 1000 times	51
Access local variable 1000 times	19

You won't see this difference for non-virtual properties, because the compiler can inline them.

Avoid unnecessary processing

You don't want to spend a lot of CPU cycles doing work that isn't needed. Here are some ways to avoid that:

- Validate early. Make sure you have all the data you need in the correct form before spending resources processing the data. If you're going to fail, fail early.

- Check whether the visitor is still connected before doing expensive processing. You can do this by checking `Response.IsClientConnected`.

- Check `Page.IsPostBack`, so that you won't regenerate data that you already have in `ViewState`.

Trimming HTTP pipeline

Some of the ASP.NET features are supported by HTTP modules. These modules are in the pipeline of each request whether you use them or not. It makes sense to remove those modules that you don't need, to remove their overhead.

In the `ListHttpModules` folder in the downloaded code bundle, a simple website is present that lists all the modules currently in the pipeline and their types. When you've identified a module you don't need, remove it in `web.config`, as shown in the following:

```
<system.web>
    <httpModules>
        <remove name="RoleManager" />
    </httpModules>
</system.web>
```

Find out more

Here are more online resources:

- 10 Tips for Writing High-Performance Web Applications
  http://msdn.microsoft.com/en-us/magazine/cc163854.aspx?ppud=4

- Improving ASP.NET Performance
  http://msdn.microsoft.com/en-us/library/ms998549.aspx

- Base Class Library Performance Tips and Tricks
  http://msdn.microsoft.com/en-us/magazine/cc163670.aspx

Summary

In this chapter, we first saw how to identify those areas in your application that require the most CPU time.

We then touched on a series of techniques to reduce CPU usage, including retrieving multiple result sets from the database and sending multiple stored procedure calls, improved data binding, and using exceptions only for exceptional circumstances.

In the next chapter, we'll get familiar with caching, a technique that is both easy to use and extremely powerful if used well.

5
Caching

Caching lets you store web pages on the visitor's browser, intermediate proxies, and in server memory. It also lets you store data objects in server memory. This way, there is no need to regenerate these items for every individual web page request. As a result, you improve responsiveness and reduce the load on the CPU and database.

ASP.NET's caching feature is very easy-to-use, requiring only a simple line to cache a web page. Server memory is cheap, and browser and proxy memory cost you nothing. That makes caching a low cost, high-payoff way to improve performance.

This chapter takes you through the five types of caching, and shows how to use them:

- **Browser caching**: Lets you store files in the browser cache itself, so that there is no need for the browser to request them over the Internet.
- **Proxy caching**: Lets you store files in the proxy computers that responses from the server travel through as they make their way over the Internet.
- **Output caching**: Lets you cache `.aspx` pages on the web server. This way, they don't have to be regenerated, saving CPU usage and load on the database.
- **IIS-based caching**: Uses high-performance caches built into IIS.
- **Data caching**: Used to cache individual objects.

Let's start with browser caching.

Browser caching

The server can ask the browser to cache content on the client machine through the cache-control response header. Having your files cached on the browser has the following advantages:

- **Quick file retrieval**: No need for the browser to access the Internet
- **Reduced bandwidth costs and reduced processing load on the server**: Fewer requests sent by the browser
- **Great scalability**: The greater the traffic, the greater number of browsers caching your data

It also comes with a few disadvantages:

- **Unpredictable life span**: Because other websites compete for the same cache space, the browser can evict your files anytime.
- **Outdated content**: There is no way to update the browser cache if a file is changed on the server. For images, JavaScript, and CSS files, you can solve this by including a version number in the filename, as described in *Chapter 12, Reducing Image Load Times* and *Chapter 13, Improving JavaScript Loading*.
- **Security risk**: Because the file is stored on the visitor's computer, an unauthorized person could read the file if they have access to that computer.

OutputCache directive

To enable browser caching of a page, add the OutputCache directive at the top of the .aspx page:

```
<%@ Page ... %>
<%@ OutputCache Duration="300" Location="Any" VaryByParam="None" %>
```

This causes the server to include these headers in the response to the browser:

```
Cache-Control: public, max-age=300
Expires: <date and time>
```

This tells the browser and intermediate proxies that they can cache the response for up to 300 seconds. Whether they actually do so is up to them; there are no guarantees here. Proxy caching is discussed later in the chapter in the *Proxy caching* section.

The attribute VaryByParam is required. If you forget to put it in, you'll get a compile error. Later in the chapter, we'll see what VaryByParam does in the *Output caching* section.

Any is not the only possible value for Location. Following is the full list:

Location value	Where file may be cached	When to use
Any	Server, browser, and intermediate proxies	Always, unless you have specific reasons not to, as listed in the following rows.
None	Nowhere	Critical that only the latest version of the file be used.
Client	Browser only	No memory available on the server for caching or the page is highly specific to the visitor, making server caching unattractive. Proxy caching cannot be used for security reasons (see the *Proxy caching* section).
DownStream	Browser and proxies	No memory available on the server or the file is highly specific to the visitor, and the consequences of it being sent to the wrong visitor by the proxy are low.
Server	Server only	Tight control required over what version of the file is used by the browser.
ServerAndClient	Server and browser	Proxy caching cannot be used for security reasons.

This shows that if you set Location to Client or ServerAndClient, you disable proxy caching. This results in a "private" Cache-Control response header that tells proxies not to cache the file:

```
Cache-Control: private, max-age=300
Expires: <date and time>
```

We'll discuss proxy and server caching shortly. But first, let's have a quick look at how to control caching in code instead of via a directive.

Enabling caching in code

You can enable browser caching in code as well, as shown in the following code:

```
Response.Cache.SetMaxAge(new TimeSpan(0, 5, 0));
Response.Cache.SetCacheability(HttpCacheability.Public);
```

To suppress caching on the server, use the following:

```
Response.Cache.SetNoServerCaching();
```

Use `HttpCacheability.Private` to stop proxies from caching the page:

```
Response.Cache.SetCacheability(HttpCacheability.Private);
```

Disabling caching in code

To completely disable caching, use the following:

```
Response.Cache.SetCacheability(HttpCacheability.NoCache);
```

Proxy caching

Requests and responses may pass through proxies on their way between server and browser. These proxies have the ability to cache content, which can then be used to serve requests from other visitors. For example, your ISP may use a proxy to cache content. Hence, it needs to send fewer requests over the Internet, as shown in the diagram below:

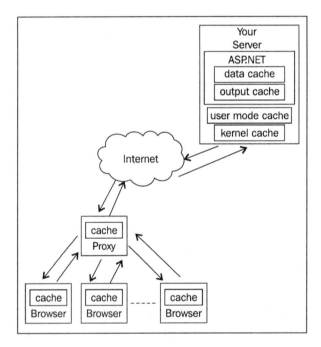

Having a proxy cache a response for you gives the following advantages:

- If a proxy caches your file while it is travelling to one visitor, it can then serve that file in response to a request from an unrelated visitor as well. Double the fun for the same price!

- Faster file retrieval—the browser tends to be geographically closer to the proxy than to your web server.

- As with browser caching, reduced load on the web server, reduced bandwidth costs, and great scalability.

However, you'll incur these disadvantages as well:

- Security risk—the proxy could send visitor-specific data to an unrelated visitor

- Proxies often do not cache files with a query string (discussed later in the chapter)

- Cannot be used with responses that set a cookie (discussed later in the chapter)

- As with browser caching, the proxy may evict your file anytime from cache, and you can't update the proxy cache if a file is changed on the server

In the *Browser caching* section, we already saw how to enable proxy caching using the `OutputCache` directive. For example:

```
<%@ OutputCache Duration="300" Location="Any"
  VaryByParam="None" %>
```

This caches the page on the browser, proxies, and the server. We would set `Location` to `Downstream` to only cache on the browser and proxies, but not on the server.

Caching different versions of the same page

Your site may serve different versions of a page, based on a request header. For example, you could send English text when you receive a request with the header:

```
Accept-Language: en-US
```

You could send the German version when you receive:

```
Accept-Language: de-DE
```

Now imagine one of the pages you sent to a German visitor is cached by a proxy. If the proxy then receives a request for that same page (based on URL) from an English speaker, the proxy will happily serve the German page from its cache. You now have an English speaking visitor staring at a page in German. This is interesting, but is not the desired result.

The solution is to tell the proxy that both the URL and the `Accept-Language` request header must match before it sends the page from its cache. You can do that by sending a `Vary` header in the response from the server, as follows:

```
Vary: Accept-Language
```

You can get ASP.NET to send that header by including `VaryByHeader` in the `OutputCache` directive:

```
<%@ OutputCache Duration="300" Location="Any" VaryByParam="None"
    VaryByHeader="Accept-Language" %>
```

You can also set it in code:

```
Response.Cache.VaryByHeaders["Accept-Language"] = true;
```

Finally, a big gotcha! IIS has the ability to compress your responses, creating massive savings on bandwidth and transfer times (see *Chapter 10, Compression*). However, when you switch on dynamic file compression so that IIS compresses your `.aspx` files, IIS overwrites your `Vary` header with its own:

```
Vary: Accept-Encoding
```

It does this to ensure that compressed content is not sent to a visitor who can't decompress the content. That's a good reason, but it could have combined your `Vary` header with its own, which it doesn't. There is no real way around this. If you vary your responses based on a request header and also use dynamic compression, don't use proxy caching—set Location to `Client`, `Server`, or `ServerAndClient`.

Cookies

Cookies and proxy caching don't mix well. Here is the issue.

When you set a cookie on the server, it sends a `Set-Cookie` response header along with the page to the browser, as shown:

```
Set-Cookie: MyCookie=LanguagePreference=Dutch; path=/
```

Afterwards, the browser returns the cookie to your server in each request in the Cookie request header, until the cookie expires:

```
Cookie: MyCookie=LanguagePreference=Dutch
```

When proxies cache a page, they also cache the response headers. The problem is that cookies tend to be very visitor-specific, and so shouldn't be sent to the other visitors. Remember that the first time you store something in session state, ASP.NET sets a cookie with the session ID. Also, when a user successfully logs into your site, ASP.NET sets a cookie to remember that the user is logged in.

Some proxies don't cache pages with a `Set-Cookie` header. However in general, you can't be sure about the behavior of the unknown proxies your responses travel through.

Because of this, do not allow proxy caching when you set a cookie. Instead, set `Location` to `Client`, `Server` or `ServerAndClient`. Also, try not to set a cookie on every request but only when strictly needed, so that you don't miss out on proxy caching more than necessary.

Removing query string from URL

Many proxies will not cache your response if the URL contains a `?`, indicating that it contains a query string. That makes sense from the proxy's point of view—a page called `default.aspx` probably has a higher chance of being requested again than `default.aspx?id=55`. The proxy needs to use its limited cache space efficiently.

To get around this, instead of `default.aspx?id=55` you could use for example, `default/55.aspx`. To make that work, you'd need to translate these new URLs when they reach your application back to the old form, so that the rest of the application can process them.

If you use the classes in the `System.Web.Routing` namespace to map incoming URLs onto handlers, you can easily accomplish this by updating your routing; same goes if you use ASP.NET MVC. Otherwise, you can use either of the following two ways:

- Using the `URLRewrite` extension to IIS 7 (easiest)
- Using the `RewritePath` method in `Global.asax`

URLRewrite extension to IIS 7

The `URLRewrite` extension allows you to include rewrite rules in `web.config`.

First, install the URL Rewriting module for IIS 7, which is available at `http://www.iis.net/download/URLRewrite`.

Then, add the following to your `web.config` (folder `UrlRewriting` in the downloaded code bundle):

```
<configuration>
...
  <system.webServer>
    <rewrite>
      <rules>
        <rule name="restore query string">
          <match url="(.*)/(\d+)\.aspx$" />
          <action type="Rewrite" url="{R:1}.aspx?id={R:2}" />
        </rule>
      </rules>
    </rewrite>
  </system.webServer>
...
</configuration>
```

This rule matches all URLs against the regular expression `(.*)/(\d+)\.aspx$`. The two sections between brackets are capture groups. If the URL matches, the URL is rewritten into `{R:1}.aspx?id={R:2}`. `{R1}` will contain the contents of the first group `(.*)`, while `{R:2}` will contain the contents of the second group `(\d+)`. If you apply this against `default/55.aspx`, you'll see that it works nicely.

RewritePath method in Global.asax

If you use IIS 6, or if installing the `URLRewrite` extension is not an option, you can use the `RewritePath` method in the `Application_BeginRequest` handler in `Global.asax` (folder `UrlRewriting` in the downloaded code bundle):

1. First, add a `Global.asax` file to your website if there isn't one already: In Visual Studio, right-click on your website, choose **Add New Item**, select the **Global Application Class** icon, and click on the **Add** button.

2. Then, add the following code to `Global.asax`:

```
private void Application_BeginRequest(
  Object source, EventArgs e)
{
  HttpApplication application = (HttpApplication)source;
  HttpContext context = application.Context;

  string rawUrl = context.Request.RawUrl;
  string newUrl = Regex.Replace(rawUrl, @"/(\d+)\.aspx$",
    @".aspx?id=$1");
  context.RewritePath(newUrl, false);
}
```

3. The `Application_BeginRequest` event handler executes each time a request comes in. It reads the original URL such as `http://mydomain.com/default/55.aspx` from `context.Request.RawUrl`, and then does a regular expression replace to arrive at the new URL `http://mydomain.com/default.aspx?id=55`. The `replace` statement checks whether there is a string of the form `/<number>.aspx` at the end of the URL and if there is, replaces it with `.aspx?id=<number>`.

That's all there is to it, except for one thing — resetting the action attribute of any form tags on your pages, which is explained in the next section.

Resetting the form action attribute

ASP.NET pages tend to post back to themselves, meaning that they have an HTML form tag with the action attribute set to the URL of the page itself. Now that the URL has been rewritten to internal format, ASP.NET sets the action attribute to that internal URL. In this case, that's not a problem — when the rewriter code above gets a URL of the form `default.aspx?id=55`, it doesn't match the regular expression. So, it lets it through without changes and your form continues to work.

However, just in case you need to set the action attribute of the form tag to the original URL (such as `/default/55.aspx`), follow these steps:

1. First derive a new control from `HtmlForm`. Let's call it `RawUrlForm`.

2. Then override its `RenderAttributes` method, so that it sets the `Action` attribute to the original URL (folder `UrlRewriting` in the downloaded code bundle):

```
using System.Web.UI;
using System.Web.UI.HtmlControls;

public class RawUrlForm : HtmlForm
{
  protected override void RenderAttributes(HtmlTextWriter writer)
  {
    this.Action = Page.Request.RawUrl;
    base.RenderAttributes(writer);
  }
}
```

3. You could store your new ASP.NET form control in the `App_Code` folder or in a separate project.

4. Now edit `web.config` to tell ASP.NET to use this new control in place of `HtmlForm`. That way, when it generates a form tag, it automatically uses your new control instead of `HtmlForm`, and there is no need to change your HTML:

```
<pages>
  <tagMapping>
    <add tagType="System.Web.UI.HtmlControls.HtmlForm"
      mappedTagType="RawUrlForm" />
  </tagMapping>
</pages>
```

Output caching

Output caching lets you cache entire pages or sections of pages on the server itself. It gives you the following advantages:

- Flexibility: Supports caching different versions of files, by query string variable, request header, or a custom variable.

- Allows caching of parts of a page.

- Life span of cached items is relatively predictable—no competition for cache space by other websites. This may not apply if you use shared hosting, where many websites use the same web server.

It comes with the following disadvantages as well:

- Not really suitable for caching visitor-specific pages because this would mean storing many pages with low hit rates.

- Uses server memory.

- No caching across servers because the cache is all in server memory. In a web farm, each server has its own cache. This means that each file is duplicated over multiple web servers' caches, taking more memory than needed and leading to possible inconsistencies between the versions in each cache.

- If the application pool recycles or the web server restarts, the cache content disappears.

You can solve the last two disadvantages by placing the cache on separate caching servers. To do this, consider packages such as **Memcached** (http://memcached. org) and Windows Server **AppFabric** (http://msdn.microsoft.com/en-us/ windowsserver/ee695849.aspx). Alternatively, you could implement an output cache provider, as described in the *Output cache provider* section later on.

Debugging

When a piece of content is served from cache, any code behind used to produce that content isn't executed, which is good. Keep this in mind though when you are debugging that code behind. If your code behind doesn't get executed, your breakpoints don't get hit.

Cookies

ASP.NET disables all output caching if you set a cookie, to make sure the cookie isn't sent to the wrong visitor. Since setting cookies and proxy caching also don't go together (see the *Proxy caching* section) performance-wise, you'll want to keep setting cookies to a minimum.

What to cache and what not to cache

Because output caching takes memory and memory is finite, you should carefully consider what to cache and what not to cache. In general, it is worthwhile to cache the following types of content:

- Content that is requested frequently, enabling you to serve more requests from cache before the cache entry needs to be refreshed. This favors content that is only updated infrequently, or where serving stale content is not a major problem.
- Content that is expensive to generate.
- Content that takes little room in cache.

That makes your home page a prime candidate, because it is probably your busiest page. It may also include category pages on an e-commerce site or a page showing reports because it is expensive to produce.

On the other hand, user-specific content will be retrieved only by a single user. If you have thousands of product pages, caching each of them may not be worthwhile. Responses to postbacks should not be cached because they depend on the values in a POST request.

Enabling output caching

Enabling output caching works the same way as enabling browser caching and proxy caching — by including the OutputCache directive at the top of the page. We've already seen this when we discussed browser caching and proxy caching, but I'll repeat it here for completeness:

```
<%@ Page ... %>
<%@ OutputCache Duration="300" Location="Any" VaryByParam="None" %>
```

This sets the expiry time to 300 seconds or five minutes. If your page is more static than that, make it longer.

Setting Location to Any enables caching on the server, the browser, and in proxies. To only cache on the server, set Location to Server. To only cache on the server and the client, but not on proxies, set Location to ServerAndClient.

Output cache example

You can make sure that the cache works using this simple page which shows the time it was generated (in the downloaded code bundle in the folder Caching):

```
<%@ Page Language="C#" AutoEventWireup="true" CodeFile="CachedTime.
aspx.cs" Inherits="CachedTime" %>
<%@ OutputCache Duration="10" Location="Any" VaryByParam="None" %>
<%= DateTime.Now.ToString() %>
```

This uses a 10-second cache, so you don't have to wait for five minutes for the page to expire from cache. If you refresh the page, you'll find that it only shows a new time once every 10 seconds.

VaryByParam

The OutputCache directive you saw so far doesn't take query strings into account. Take for example the code for the page CachedQueryString.aspx (in the downloaded code bundle in the folder Caching):

```
<%@ Page Language="C#" %>
<%@ OutputCache Duration="10" Location="Any" VaryByParam="None" %>
<%= Request.QueryString["id"] %>
```

This shows the content of the query string id. However, because the cache does not take the query string into account, if you request CachedQuery.aspx?id=1 and then CachedQuery.aspx?id=2, it will still show 1, even though you specified 2.

To solve this, use `VaryByParam` in the `OutputCache` directive to tell ASP.NET to cache a version of the page for each value of query string parameter `id`:

```
<%@ OutputCache Duration="10" Location="Any" VaryByParam="id" %>
```

If your page uses multiple query string parameters, separate them with semicolons:

```
<%@ OutputCache Duration="10" Location="Any" VaryByParam="id;location"
%>
```

You could also use an asterisk to tell ASP.NET to look at all the parameters, irrespective of their names:

```
<%@ OutputCache Duration="10" Location="Any" VaryByParam="*" %>
```

VaryByHeader

Your page could be dependent on a request header instead of, or as well as, a query string parameter. To store different versions based on a request header, use `VaryByHeader`, as follows:

```
<%@ OutputCache Duration="10" Location="Any"
   VaryByHeader="Accept-Language" VaryByParam="None" %>
```

You'll find a full list of HTTP request headers at:

- HTTP Request fields
  http://www.w3.org/Protocols/HTTP/HTRQ_Headers.html

VaryByCustom

Suppose you want to cache on something that is not a query string parameter or a request header? To see how to do this, let's have a page that is cached by weekday.

First add a `VaryByCustom` attribute to the `OutputCache` directive, with our new weekday value:

```
<%@ OutputCache Duration="300" Location="Any" VaryByCustom="weekday"
VaryByParam="None"  %>
```

Obviously, ASP.NET doesn't know how to interpret `weekday`. To find out, it will call method `GetVaryByCustomString` in `Global.asax`. Override that method, and when ASP.NET calls it to find out about `weekday`, return a string with the day of the week. ASP.NET will then cache a version of the page for each different string that you return—one version for Monday, one for Tuesday, and so on:

```
public override string GetVaryByCustomString(HttpContext context,
string custom)
{
    if (custom == "weekday")
    {
        return DateTime.Now.DayOfWeek.ToString();
    }
    else
    {
        return base.GetVaryByCustomString(context, custom);
    }
}
```

 Note that ASP.NET doesn't care about the actual contents of the string, as long as there is a unique string for each version of the page that needs to be cached.

VaryByCustom by browser

Because so many pages have browser-specific content and therefore need to be cached by browser type, `VaryByCustom` recognizes "browser" out of the box, without you having to implement `GetVaryByCustomString`:

```
<%@ Page Language="C#" AutoEventWireup="true" %>
<%@ OutputCache Duration="300" Location="Any" VaryByCustom="browser"
VaryByParam="None"  %>
<%= Request.UserAgent %>
```

This uses the browser name and the major version number to differentiate among browsers.

You can combine `VaryByParam`, `VaryByHeader`, and `VaryByCustom`. Do keep track of all the versions of that one page you potentially create this way, and how much space they will take in cache.

Fragment caching

To cache only parts of a page, put those parts in user controls and then cache those user controls. You cache a user control by including the `OutputCache` directive at the top of the user control, along the same lines as caching a page, as shown:

```
<%@ Control Language="C#" %>
<%@ OutputCache Duration="10" VaryByParam="None"  %>
Cached user control: <%= DateTime.Now.ToString() %>
```

You can't use `Location` in the `OutputCache` directive in a user control.

You use a cached user control the exact same way as a non-cached user control. However, if the user control exposes properties to your page, those will not be accessible when the user control is served from cache.

To see how this works, run this page. It isn't cached itself, but uses the user control shown above, which is cached:

```
<%@ Page Language="C#" AutoEventWireup="true"
  CodeFile="CachedFragment.aspx.cs" Inherits="CachedFragment" %>
<%@ Register TagPrefix="uc" TagName="CachedTimeUserControl"
  Src="~/CachedTimeUserControl.ascx" %>
<html xmlns="http://www.w3.org/1999/xhtml">
  <head runat="server">
  </head>
  <body>
    <form id="form1" runat="server">
    <div>
      Non-Cached main page: <%= DateTime.Now.ToString() %>
      <br />
      <uc:CachedTimeUserControl runat="server">
      </uc:CachedTimeUserControl>
    </div>
    </form>
  </body>
</html>
```

If you run this page, you'll find that the time generated on the main page is updated each time you refresh the page, while the time generated by the user control is updated only every 10 seconds when it expires from cache.

If you use a particular user control on multiple pages, the user control is cached per page. That makes sense—a user control on page1.aspx may have different output than the same user control on page2.aspx. However, if the output is the same regardless of the page the user control is on, use the Shared attribute on the OutputCache directive so that the user control is cached just once, as shown in the following code:

```
<%@ OutputCache Duration="300" VaryByParam="None" Shared="true"%>
```

Post-cache substitution

Post-cache substitution (or "Donut" caching) is the inverse of Fragment Caching. Instead of having cached bits on an otherwise non-cached page, it features a cached page with non-cached bits. Here is how it works.

You make the page cached as normal, with an OutputCache directive.

Then, at the point in your page where you want to place the non-cached content, place a substitution control. This takes a static method that will be called when the page is generated normally and also when retrieved from cache. The static method returns a string, which is inserted at the location of the Substitution control:

```
<asp:Substitution MethodName="GetSubstitutedTime" runat="server"/>
```

When the static method is called by the runtime, it passes in the HttpContext with information about the request. It can't rely on the Page object, life cycle events, or other controls because there won't be any when the page is being retrieved from cache:

```
private static string GetSubstitutedTime(HttpContext context)
{
  return DateTime.Now.ToString();
}
```

If you need to execute code for each request such as logging the request, you could run that code as part of a post-cache substitution.

Output cache provider

In ASP.NET 3.5 and earlier, there was no way to change the way cache items were being stored. ASP.NET always stored them in local web server memory and that was it.

ASP.NET 4 changed this by allowing you to write your own output cache provider. This works along the same lines as for example the membership provider—add your chosen provider to your project, and enable it in web.config. All the output caching will now be handled by the new provider. This enables you to for example, store cache items on disk, or to store them on other servers. You can specify which provider to use per request; so if you want to store cache items on disk only for particular pages, you can.

In this section, we'll see how to build an output cache provider, and how to use it on your website. Because this feature was introduced with ASP.NET 4, you will need Visual Studio 2010 Express (free) or better to make this work.

Creating an output cache provider

An output cache provider is simply a class derived from OutputCacheProvider. You can store that class in a separate class library project, or in the App_Code folder of your website. In the class, you override four methods: Set, Add, Get, and Remove (we'll see how in a moment). This means that an output cache provider has the following outline:

```
using System.Web.Caching;

public class FileCacheProvider : OutputCacheProvider
{
    public override void Set(string key, object item, DateTime expiry)
{ ... }
    public override object Add(string key, object item, DateTime
expiry) { ... }
    public override object Get(string key) { ... }
    public override void Remove(string key) { ... }
}
```

Let's go through each of the four methods to be implemented. You'll find a working example of an output provider in the downloaded code bundle in the folder OutputCacheProvider, project OutputCacheProviderSample.

Set

This method is tasked with storing an item under a given key. It also receives a UTC date/time after which the item is no longer valid. This expiry time needs to be stored with the item, so that it can be checked when the item is retrieved. If an item with the given key already exists in cache, its contents and expiry need to be overwritten.

Get

This method simply retrieves the item with a given key from cache and returns its content. If the item doesn't exist or if it has expired, Get returns null.

Add

This method is a bit like `Set`, but with a twist. If the item doesn't exist yet in cache, it is stored, and is also returned by the method. However, if the item already exists in cache, it is left alone and the item that was already in cache is returned.

Remove

As the name indicates, this method is tasked with removing the item with the given key from cache.

Now that you know how to create an output cache provider, let's see how to use it in your site.

Using an output cache provider

You tell ASP.NET about a new output cache provider the same way as with other providers—by adding it to a list of providers in `web.config`, as shown in the following code:

```
<configuration>
  <system.web>
  ...
    <caching>
      <outputCache defaultProvider="FileCache">
        <providers>
          <add name="FileCache" type="OutputCacheProviderSample.
FileCacheProvider, OutputCacheProviders" />
        </providers>
      </outputCache>
    </caching>
  ...
  </system.web>
</configuration>
```

This tells ASP.NET to use the provider implemented in class `FileCacheProvider` which is part of namespace `OutputCacheProviderSample`, and which can be found in assembly `OutputCacheProviders`. If you put the class in `App_Code`, you can omit the assembly.

By setting attribute `defaultProvider` to the name of the new provider, you ensure ASP.NET uses this new provider by default to provide output caching.

What if you want to use the new provider only with certain pages or user controls? There are three aspects to this:

- Configure the new provider in `web.config`, but use ASP.NET's built-in provider by default

- Use the new provider for particular pages
- Use the new provider for particular user controls

Firstly in the `web.config` entry we just saw, set default provider to `AspNetInternalProvider`, ASP.NET's built-in provider:

```
<outputCache defaultProvider="AspNetInternalProvider">
  <providers>
    <add name="FileCache"
      type="OutputCacheProviderSample.FileCacheProvider,
      OutputCacheProviderSample" />
  </providers>
</outputCache>
```

To select an output cache provider based on the filename in the incoming request, override method `GetOutputCacheProviderName` in `Global.asax`, as follows (file `Global.asax`, folder `OutputCacheProvider` in the downloaded code bundle):

```
public override string GetOutputCacheProviderName
  (HttpContext context)
{
    if (context.Request.Path.EndsWith("CachedWeekday.aspx"))
        return "FileCache";
    else
        return base.GetOutputCacheProviderName(context);
}
```

This code tells ASP.NET to use the `FileCache` provider (as configured in `web.config`) when the path of the incoming request ends in `CachedWeekday.aspx`. Otherwise, it calls the base method to return the name of the default provider. The path of the request is the requested URL minus the domain name and the query string.

Interestingly, specifying a custom output cache provider is much easier for user controls—simply add the `providerName` attribute to the `OutputCache` directive:

```
<%@ OutputCache Duration="10" VaryByParam="None"
  ProviderName="FileCache"  %>
```

Sadly, you can't do this for pages; it is only for user controls.

Kernel caching and IIS 7 output caching

When you enable output caching on the server, you also enable kernel caching and IIS 7 output caching. Output caching was introduced in IIS 7, while IIS 6 already supported kernel caching. Serving a request from these caches is faster than serving from the ASP.NET output cache, because they are built into IIS itself. Here is how this works.

When a new request arrives at the web server, it is initially processed by `http.sys`, a kernel driver. This driver first tries to serve the request from the kernel cache. If it can't, it sends the request to a port that an IIS thread listens to. This IIS thread then tries to serve the request from the IIS 7 output cache. If it can't, it hands the request on to ASP.NET, which activates another thread to actually process the request. ASP.NET tries to serve the request from its own cache, and if it can't, it generates the output. The resulting output is sent to a third thread, which sends it to the browser.

This means that when a file is served from kernel cache, you save three thread switches and the need to switch to user mode. This makes serving a file from kernel cache very fast. IIS 7 output caching does require a thread switch and a switch to user mode. So it is not as fast, but is still faster than ASP.NET caching. Because of the switch to user mode, it is also referred to as user mode caching.

Configuring IIS caching

You already saw that kernel caching and IIS 7 output caching are enabled when server caching is enabled in the `OutputCache` directive. However, if you generate for example, a PNG file using an HTTP Handler, there will be no `OutputCache` directive. You can get around this by configuring the caches in IIS manager:

To configure IIS 7 output caching:

1. Start IIS manager. In Vista, click **Start | Control Panel**. Search "admin" and double-click on **Internet Information Services (IIS) Manager**.

2. Select the server or site you want to manage.

3. In the center pane, double-click on the **Output Caching** icon.

4. In the right-hand column, click on **Add**. The **Add Cache Rule** dialog will open.

5. You'll find that IIS 7 output caching is referred to here as user mode caching. For both types of caching, you can specify extensions of files to be cached, their expiry timeout, and whether to use file change notification. IIS 7 output caching also allows you to cache files based on query string variables and HTTP headers. Click on the **Advanced** button to access this feature.

6. Click on **OK**.

Limitations of kernel caching

Kernel caching is fast, so you want it to cache your files. Unfortunately, there is a long list of limitations that stop `http.sys` from caching a response in kernel cache. The most important are:

- Dynamic compression cannot be used for the response; static compression is ok. Compression is discussed in *Chapter 10, Compression*.

- The response cannot be accessed as a default document, making it unlikely that your home page gets cached. So if someone visits `http://mydomain.com` without typing a filename, the response won't go into kernel cache. If they visit `http://mydomain.com/default.aspx` instead, it can get cached, depending on the other limitations.

- The request cannot contain a query string. Of course, you could try to get around this by rewriting the URL as you saw in the section on proxy caching. This won't work though because of the following limitation:

  If you use `VaryByParam` or `VaryByHeaders` in the `OutputCache` directive of a file, it won't go into kernel cache. And if you don't use `VaryByParam`, the ASP.NET cache will store only one version of the file, without taking the query string parameter into account. ASP.NET caching looks at the rewritten URL, not the original URL.

Other more exotic conditions that will stop a response from being cached are at:

- Reasons content is not cached by HTTP.sys in kernel at `http://support.microsoft.com/kb/817445`

Checking the contents of the kernel cache

To see the contents of the kernel cache, run the `netsh` program from the following command line:

```
netsh http show cachestate
```

Note that a response will not be immediately cached, even if it is eligible. It will be cached only if it is frequently hit. The default threshold for this is two times or more per 10 seconds.

Data caching

Data caching is aimed at caching individual objects using code in your code behind, rather than caching pages or user controls via page directives. It lets you store key-value pairs in cache on the server. These pairs are then accessible for all requests to the same website. However, as you saw in the section about output caching, if you have a web farm with multiple servers, each server has access only to its own cache. It is very flexible—you can specify expiry times, priorities, and dependencies on other items such as files or database objects.

We'll discuss more advanced topics such as database dependencies in a moment; first, let's see how to introduce data caching in your code.

Basic use

As you saw, you access the cache as a dictionary. The simplest way to add something to the cache is to assign an object to a key name:

```
Cache["key"] = myObject;
```

Retrieving an item goes along the same lines:

```
MyObject myObject = (MyObject)Cache["key"];
```

The cache stores items as objects. So, when you retrieve an item, you need to cast it to the right type.

When you retrieve an object, you really retrieve a reference to the object in cache. That means that the object is shared among the threads executing requests. Make sure that the object is thread-safe, or make a deep copy of it after you have retrieved it.

An item is not guaranteed to be in cache, because it can be removed by the cache manager due to memory pressures. If the item you request is not in cache, you will receive null. As a result, retrieving an item from cache tends to follow this pattern:

```
MyObject myObject = (MyObject)Cache["key"];
if (myObject == null)
{
    myObject = new MyObject();

    // Load data into myObject ...

    Cache["key"] = myObject;
}
```

An issue is that the Cache is accessed by multiple threads executing requests. Single operations on the Cache are thread-safe, but not a sequence like this. While one thread is loading data into myObject, another thread could come along, find myObject missing and start loading data as well. Use locking to prevent this:

```
public Object lockObject = new Object();
...
lock (lockObject)
{
  MyObject myObject = (MyObject)Cache["key"];
  if (myObject == null)
  {
    myObject = new MyObject();
    // Load data into myObject ...
    Cache["key"] = myObject;
  }
}
```

Remember that the Cache gives you a reference to the cached item, which can disappear even while your code is running. Avoid writing the code such as the following:

```
// Don't do this
MyObject myObject = (MyObject)Cache["key"];

// Lengthy operation ...

// Access myObject as retrieved from cache
string s = myObject.data;
```

Expiry

ASP.NET lets you set an absolute expiry time for a cached item. It also supports sliding expiration, where an item that hasn't been retrieved for some time is removed.

To store an item in cache with an absolute expiry time of 30 minutes from now, use the Insert method, like this:

```
using System.Web.Caching;

Cache.Insert(
    "key", myObject, null,
    DateTime.Now.AddMinutes(30), Cache.NoSlidingExpiration);
```

To use a sliding expiry of 30 minutes instead, where the item is removed when it hasn't been used for over 30 minutes, use the following:

```
Cache.Insert(
    "key", myObject, null,
    Cache.NoAbsoluteExpiration, TimeSpan.FromMinutes(30));
```

Priority

Some items are more expensive to create than others. To reflect this, you can assign a priority to an item. When there are memory pressures, lower priority items will be removed before higher priority items.

There are six priority levels: Low, BelowNormal, Normal, AboveNormal, High, and NotRemovable. When no priority is assigned, an item has priority Normal by default.

To set a priority when adding items to cache, you use a different overload of the Insert method:

```
Cache.Insert(
  "key", expensiveObject, null,
  Cache.NoAbsoluteExpiration, Cache.NoSlidingExpiration,
  CacheItemPriority.AboveNormal,
  null);
```

File dependencies

When inserting an item in the cache, you can specify that the item is dependent on some other item, file, or database item. The result is that if the other item changes, the cached item is automatically removed. This is perfect for cached files and cached database records, because this makes it easy to prevent the cached item from getting outdated.

In this section, you'll see how to create a file dependency. The next section shows how to do a database dependency.

To create a file dependency, create a CacheDependency object based on the physical path to the file, and pass it to Cache.Insert:

```
using System.Web.Caching;
CacheDependency cd = new CacheDependency(filePath);
Cache.Insert(key, fileContent, cd);
```

This creates a dependency based on the file with the given `filePath`. When the operating system changes that file, the item will be removed from cache. That way, the next time your code tries to access the cached item, it will find it isn't, causing it to reload the file. You can combine expiry times and priorities with cache dependencies by using another overload of `Cache.Insert`.

Database dependencies

Database dependencies are more complicated to use than file dependencies. The reason is that while with file dependencies, it is obvious which item to track for changes (the file itself), with database dependencies the item to track is a table. And to figure out which table that is, the query that produced the data needs to be analyzed. As you can imagine, that's no mean feat. As a result, there are a lot of restrictions on the queries you can use. Some database configuration is also involved.

When the database executes a command that may change the data that was returned from the query, it signals the web server, which then removes the cached item. That command doesn't have to come from this web server; any command from any source that affects the data will do.

Obviously there is some overhead associated with this, which is another reason to only cache database items that do not change often.

The database dependency feature you'll see here is supported by SQL Server 2005 and later. SQL Server 2000 does support database dependencies, but in a different and more complex manner which is not described in this book.

You can use database dependencies with both ad hoc queries and stored procedures. If you use a stored procedure when the following discussion refers to a query, that would be the query in your stored procedure.

Restrictions on queries

Only a small subset of queries can be used with database dependencies. If you go beyond that subset, the dependency will always remove the cached item, whether the data was changed or not. Here are the most important restrictions:

- You can only use a single `SELECT` statement or a stored procedure that contains a single `SELECT` statement.
- If you use a stored procedure, both `ANSI_NULLS` and `QUOTED_IDENTIFIER` must be `ON` when you create the procedure.
- Also, do not use `SET NOCOUNT ON` in the stored procedure body. Also, don't use `TRY CATCH` or `RETURN` either.

- Do not use SELECT *. Specifically state all column names.
- Use two-part table names, such as dbo.Books. Do not include the database name in the table name.
- No computed columns.
- No aggregate expressions. COUNT_BIG and SUM are allowed if you use GROUP BY, but SUM cannot be used on a nullable column. No HAVING, CUBE, or ROLLUP.
- You cannot reference views, system tables, derived tables, temporary tables, or table variables.
- The query must not have comparisons or expressions with double/real data types.
- You cannot use TOP.

Here are more restrictions:

- No unnamed columns or duplicate column names.
- A projected column in the SELECT query that is used as a simple expression must not appear more than once.
- Do not use PIVOT or UNPIVOT operators.
- Do not use UNION, INTERSECT or EXCEPT. Do not use DISTINCT, COMPUTE or COMPUTE BY, or INTO either.
- Do not reference server global variables.
- The query must not contain subqueries, outer joins, or self-joins.
- You cannot use the types text, ntext, and image.
- The query must not use the CONTAINS or FREETEXT full-text predicates.
- The query must not use rowset functions, including OPENROWSET and OPENQUERY.
- Do not use any nondeterministic functions, including ranking and windowing functions.
- The query must not include FOR BROWSE information.
- The query must not reference a queue.
- The query must not contain conditional statements that cannot change and cannot return results (for example, WHERE 1=0).
- The query can not specify READPAST locking hint.
- The query must not reference any Service Broker QUEUE.
- Do not reference synonyms.

Here is an example of a stored procedure that you CAN use:

```
SET ANSI_NULLS ON
GO
SET QUOTED_IDENTIFIER ON
GO
CREATE PROCEDURE GetData
AS
BEGIN
  --Do NOT use SET NOCOUNT ON;
  SELECT [BookId], [Title], [Author], [Price]
    FROM [dbo].[Book]
END
GO
```

If the database dependencies feature will still work for you, take these steps to implement it:

1. Start the SQL Server Service Broker.

2. Start the listening service in your site.

3. Create the dependency when inserting an item in cache.

You'll find working sample code in the downloaded code bundle in the folder DatabaseDependency. To set up the required database, first run file tuneup. database.sql and then book.table.sql against your database. Change the connection string in web.config, so that it uses your own database server.

Starting the Service Broker

For database dependencies to work, you need to have the SQL Server Service Broker running on the database server:

1. Restart the database server to make sure that there are no sessions open to the database, including the ones from Visual Studio.

2. Run these commands (replace TuneUp with your database name):

   USE TuneUp

   ALTER DATABASE TuneUp SET ENABLE_BROKER WITH ROLLBACK IMMEDIATE

Starting the listening service

Before your site can use database dependencies, it needs to start the listening service. This needs to be done only once, making `Application_Start` in `Global.asax` a good place:

```
<%@ Application Language="C#" %>
<%@ Import Namespace="System.Data.SqlClient" %>
<%@ Import Namespace="System.Web.Configuration" %>

<script runat="server">

  void Application_Start(object sender, EventArgs e)
  {
    // Code that runs on application startup
    string connectionString = ...;
    SqlDependency.Start(connectionString);
  }
</script>
```

Creating the dependency

Finally, the code that actually creates the dependency and inserts an item into cache goes along the same lines as implementing a file dependency. However, instead of a filename, you use a `SqlCommand` object and instead of a `CacheDependency`, you use a `SqlCacheDependency` object. The result looks as follows:

```
using (SqlCommand cmd = new SqlCommand(sql, connection))
{
  using (SqlDataAdapter adapter = new SqlDataAdapter(cmd))
  {
    SqlCacheDependency cd = new SqlCacheDependency(cmd);
    dataSet = new DataSet();
    adapter.Fill(dataSet);
    Cache.Insert("key", dataSet, cd);
  }
}
```

This example code fills a dataset from the database and then caches that dataset using a database dependency to make sure the dataset is removed from cache when the underlying data in the database changes. As you can see, the `SqlCacheDependency` is used here in the same way as the `CacheDependency` was in the *File dependencies* section, except that instead of a filepath, it uses the `SqlCommand` object that is used to retrieve the data. Finally, you don't have to use a dataset to use database dependencies; you can use for example, `SqlDataReader` as well.

Item removed callback

You can have ASP.NET call a callback method when an item expires. To make that happen, pass a delegate with the callback method to the `Insert` method, along these lines:

```
private void ItemRemovedCallback(
    string itemKey, object itemValue,
    CacheItemRemovedReason cacheItemRemovedReason) { ... }

Cache.Insert(
    "key", expensiveObject, null,
    Cache.NoAbsoluteExpiration, Cache.NoSlidingExpiration,
    CacheItemPriority.Default,
    new CacheItemRemovedCallback(ItemRemovedCallback));
```

When the item is removed from cache, method `ItemRemovedCallback` is called. As you see here, the callback method receives the key of the removed item, its value and the reason why it was removed. The possible values for `CacheItemRemovedReason` are as follows:

Value	Description
Removed	Removed by a call to `Cache.Remove` or by a call to `Cache.Insert` that replaced this item.
Expired	The item expired because of its absolute or sliding expiration policy.
Underused	Removed because ASP.NET needed to free up memory, and decided this item had the lowest priority.
DependencyChanged	Removed because a dependency associated with the item changed.

Things to keep in mind

Before you rush off and implement an item removed callback method, keep in mind the following:

- Items may expire independent of incoming requests. This means that while your item removed callback method runs, it can't rely on there being a request context, and so `HttpContext.Current` may be null. For this reason, if you need to access the cache in your callback, use `HttpRuntime.Cache` instead of `HttpContext.Current.Cache`.

- The callback method should be static. If it is an instance method of an object, the garbage collector won't clean up the object because the cache item refers to it.

- The callback method will be called not only when the item is completely removed from cache, but also when it gets replaced. During a replace, the old item is first removed and then the new item is inserted.

In the downloaded code bundle in the folder `ItemRemovedCallback`, you'll find a working example of an item removed callback method.

Optimal use of server cache

You will want to make sure that you make optimal use of the cache. Otherwise you don't achieve the savings in responsiveness, CPU usage, and database load that you could have.

You can use the cache-related counters made available by ASP.NET to see how well the cache is being used. If you use output caching, check:

Category: ASP.NET Applications	
Output Cache Hit Ratio	The percentage of total output cache requests that were serviced from the output cache.
Output Cache Hits	Total number of output cache hits.
Output Cache Misses	Total number of output cache misses.
Output Cache Entries	Total number of items in the output cache.
Output Cache Turnover Rate	The number of additions and removals to and from the output cache per second.

If you use data caching, check the following counters:

Category: ASP.NET Applications	
Cache API Hit Ratio	The percentage of total data cache requests that were serviced from the data cache.
Cache API Hits	Total number of data cache hits.
Cache API Misses	Total number of data cache misses.
Cache API Entries	Total number of items in the data cache.
Cache API Turnover Rate	The number of additions and removals to and from the data cache per second.

When interpreting the numbers, keep the following in mind:

- With sufficient memory, you want the hit ratio to be over 80 percent
- The greater the total number of items in the cache, the more memory you are using to achieve your hit ratio, and the more vulnerable you are to memory shortages
- The greater the number of additions and removals to and from the cache per second, the more resources you are spending on regenerating information

To experiment with these counters, get the website in the `MemoryBound_CacheTest` folder in the downloaded code bundle and load test it. To see how to do a load test, refer to *Chapter 14, Load Testing*.

Find out more

Here are more online resources:

- ASP.NET Caching at
  `http://msdn.microsoft.com/en-us/library/xsbfdd8c.aspx`
- ASP.NET Caching: Techniques and Best Practices at
  `http://msdn.microsoft.com/en-us/library/aa478965.aspx`
- Top 10 Performance Improvements in IIS 7.0 at
  `http://technet.microsoft.com/en-us/magazine/2008.09.iis.aspx#id0110054`
- The "Reluctant Cache" Pattern at
  `http://weblogs.asp.net/gavinjoyce/pages/The-Reluctant-Cache-Pattern.aspx`
- HTTP 1/1 definition, section 14 Header Field Definitions at
  `http://www.w3.org/Protocols/rfc2616/rfc2616-sec14.html`
- ASP.NET Routing… Goodbye URL rewriting? at
  `http://chriscavanagh.wordpress.com/2008/03/11/aspnet-routing-goodbye-url-rewriting/`
- Configuring Output Caching in IIS 7 at
  `http://technet.microsoft.com/en-us/library/cc732475(WS.10).aspx`
- Extensible Output Caching with ASP.NET 4 (VS 2010 and .NET 4.0 Series) at
  `http://weblogs.asp.net/scottgu/archive/2010/01/27/extensible-output-caching-with-asp-net-4-vs-2010-and-net-4-0-series.aspx`
- OutputCacheProvider Class at
  `http://msdn.microsoft.com/en-us/library/system.web.caching.outputcacheprovider.aspx`

- outputCache Element for caching at
  http://msdn.microsoft.com/en-us/library/ms228124.aspx

- Response caching in IIS7 at
  http://blogs.iis.net/ksingla/archive/2006/11/16/caching-in-iis7.aspx

- Walkthrough: IIS 7.0 Output Caching at
  http://learn.iis.net/page.aspx/154/walkthrough-iis-70-output-caching/

- Caching <caching> at
  http://www.iis.net/ConfigReference/system.webServer/caching

Summary

In this chapter, we learned how to use caching to trade memory usage for a reduction in the time taken to generate a page.

We first saw how to ask browsers and proxies to cache our pages and how they provide a (limited) free lunch by providing cache memory that's not only free to us, but close to the visitor as well. While discussing proxy caching, we learned about some security issues and saw that proxy caching doesn't mix with query strings and setting cookies.

Then we looked at output caching, where entire pages or parts of pages are cached on the web server. We saw how to cache different versions of each page based on query string parameters, HTTP headers, or even custom variables. Fragment caching and post-cache substitution were discussed as ways to cache part of a page, while the rest is regenerated for each request. We also looked at implementing your own output cache provider, and two more caching features built into IIS 7: IIS 7 output caching (also known as user mode caching) and kernel caching.

Finally, we discussed data caching, which allows us to store individual objects in cache rather than pages. We saw how to set the priority and expiry time of each item. Dependencies on other cache items were discussed, as were file and database dependencies. We also saw how to use item removed callbacks to log the expiry of a cache item.

Finally, we looked at various counters that show how well the cache is being used.

In the next chapter, we'll see how to reduce the chance of requests being delayed because of a lack of IIS worker threads, by making more efficient use of those threads.

6
Thread Usage

When your site accesses a file or an off-box resource such as the database or a web service, the thread executing the request is blocked while it waits for the resource to respond. You now have a thread doing nothing, while there may be requests waiting for a thread to become available.

You can solve this by using asynchronous methods to access files and off-box resources. Instead of blocking a thread, these methods release the thread when they start waiting, so that it can then be used by another request. When the resource becomes available, a new thread is acquired from the thread pool to continue processing.

This chapter shows how to convert synchronous code that blocks the thread to asynchronous code. Each example will first describe the synchronous version, and then we'll see how to make it asynchronous. Specifically, you will learn:

- How to convert the code that accesses web services
- How to convert the code that accesses the database, including how to build an asynchronous data layer
- How to convert the code that accesses files
- How to change thread-related configuration settings and page timeouts

Asynchronous web service access

To see how to access a web service asynchronously, we'll work through an example based on accessing the "USA Weather Forecast" web service provided by http://www.webservicex.net. One of its methods takes a US ZIP code, and returns a weather forecast for that location.

Synchronous version

Before tackling the asynchronous version, we'll quickly look at the standard synchronous way of accessing this service. You'll find the code in the code bundle in the folder ThreadStarvation_WebService_Sync.

1. Add the web service to your website. Right-click on the website and choose **Add Web Reference**. In the **URL** field, enter the URL of the web service:

   ```
   http://www.webservicex.net/WeatherForecast.asmx?WSDL
   ```

   Note the description of the web service and its namespace:

   ```
   net.webservicex.www.
   ```

   Click on the **Add Reference** button to add the web reference.

2. Add a using statement to your code behind file to include the namespace provided by the web service:

   ```
   using net.webservicex.www;
   ```

3. To actually use the web service, instantiate the proxy class WeatherForecast that was automatically generated when you created the web reference:

   ```
   WeatherForecast weatherForecast = new WeatherForecast();
   ```

4. Then call the method to get the weather forecast based on a ZIP code:

   ```
   WeatherForecasts weatherForecasts =
     weatherForecast.GetWeatherByZipCode(zip);
   ```

5. If you open http://www.webservicex.net/WeatherForecast. asmx?WSDL, you'll see that the WeatherForecasts class returned by the GetWeatherByZipCode method contains a list of days, with their forecasts. You can show that list using a simple Repeater control, as follows:

   ```
   rpWeatherDetails.DataSource = weatherForecasts.Details;
   rpWeatherDetails.DataBind();
   ```

   Following is the matching Repeater on the .aspx page:

   ```
   <asp:Repeater ID="rpWeatherDetails" runat="server">
    <ItemTemplate>
   <p>
       <b><%# DataBinder.Eval(Container.DataItem, "Day")%></b><br />
       Min Temperature:
        <%# DataBinder.Eval(Container.DataItem,
   "MinTemperatureF")%>F,
       Max Temperature:
        <%# DataBinder.Eval(Container.DataItem, "MaxTemperatureF")%>F
   </p>
   </ItemTemplate>
   </asp:Repeater>
   ```

That's pretty simple. Now, it's time to translate this to the asynchronous version.

Asynchronous version

You'll find the code for the asynchronous version in the code bundle downloaded in folder `ThreadStarvation_WebService_Async`.

Firstly, in the `.aspx` file, set `Async="true"` and set `AsyncTimeout` to a timeout in seconds in the `Page` directive. If there is no response within that timeout, the runtime will call a timeout event handler that you define; we'll see how to do that later on.

```
<%@ Page Language="C#" Async="true" AsyncTimeout="30"
  AutoEventWireup="true"  CodeFile="Default.aspx.cs"
  Inherits="_Default" %>
```

If you have multiple asynchronous tasks on the page, the timeout applies to every one of them.

Instead of setting the timeout in the `Page` directive, you can set it programmatically as follows:

```
Page.AsyncTimeout = TimeSpan.FromSeconds(30);
```

Secondly, in the code behind, register a `PageAsyncTask` object. The constructor of this object takes the `BeginAsync` method that will start the web service access. The runtime will not call this right after registration, but only after the pre-render page event. The constructor also takes the `EndAsync` handler that is called when the operation finishes, and the `TimeoutAsync` handler that is called when a timeout happens.

You can use the fourth parameter of the constructor to pass extra data to the `BeginAsync` method. Finally, if you want to execute a series of tasks in parallel, register them one-by-one and set the fifth parameter of the constructor to `true`:

```
protected void Page_Load(object sender, EventArgs e)
{
  PageAsyncTask pageAsyncTask =
  new PageAsyncTask(BeginAsync, EndAsync, TimeoutAsync,
    null, false);

  RegisterAsyncTask(pageAsyncTask);
}
```

You would typically do this registration in the Page Load handler, or an event handler.

What if you need to register a task after the pre-render event? What about registering a task based on the results of some other task? For these late registrations, use the `ExecuteRegisteredAsyncTasks` page method. This will manually run all registered tasks that have not yet been started.

In the `BeginAsync` method, first instantiate the proxy class `WeatherForecast` that was automatically generated when you created the web reference. Then call the `Begin..` version of the `GetWeatherByZipCode` web service method. This was automatically generated by Visual Studio when you added the web reference.

In addition to the regular `GetWeatherByZipCode` ZIP parameter, `BeginGetWeatherByZipCode` also takes the callback method passed in to `BeginAsync`, and an object with extra data. The extra data will be passed on to `EndAsync` by the runtime. Here, it is used to pass on the `weatherForecast` proxy object, so `EndAsync` can use it to call `EndGetWeatherByZipCode`:

```
private IAsyncResult BeginAsync(object sender, EventArgs e,
  AsyncCallback cb, object extraData)
{
  WeatherForecast weatherForecast = new WeatherForecast();
  IAsyncResult asyncResult =
  weatherForecast.BeginGetWeatherByZipCode(zip, cb,
  weatherForecast);

  return asyncResult;
}
```

In the `EndAsync` method, first retrieve the `weatherForecast` proxy that was passed on by `BeginAsync` via the extra data. Then call the `End..` version of the `GetWeatherByZipCode` web service method to retrieve the actual weather forecast. Finally process the weather forecast by binding it to a repeater, the same way as in the synchronous version:

```
private void EndAsync(IAsyncResult asyncResult)
{
  object extraData = asyncResult.AsyncState;
  WeatherForecast weatherForecast = (WeatherForecast)extraData;

  WeatherForecasts weatherForecasts =
  weatherForecast.EndGetWeatherByZipCode(asyncResult);

  rpWeatherDetails.DataSource = weatherForecasts.Details;
  rpWeatherDetails.DataBind();
}
```

Finally, the `TimeoutAsync` method responds to a timeout, for example by warning the visitor or by throwing an exception. This receives the same extra data as the `EndAsync` method, so you still have access to whatever extra data you passed to the `Begin..` method in the `BeginAsync` method:

```
private static void TimeoutAsync(IAsyncResult asyncResult)
{
  // Timeout processing
}
```

> **WARNING**
>
> Keep in mind that if a timeout happens, `EndAsync` doesn't get called, only `TimeoutAsync` is called. This means that if there still are resources to be released such as a database connection, you need to do that here.

There you have your asynchronous version. This style of programming is obviously different from the normal synchronous way. Firstly, the operation gets started only in the `BeginAsync` method after the pre-render event, rather than in the Page Load handler. Instead of writing code to process the results right after calling the web service method, processing takes place in a second method `EndAsync`. Essentially, you're handling events, rather than writing a sequential code.

Having asynchronous code to access web services is nice, but you'll probably more often use asynchronous code to access a database via a data access layer. Let's see how to build such an asynchronous data access layer.

Asynchronous data access layer

You'll find the code for the asynchronous data access layer in the downloaded code bundle, in the folder `ThreadStarvation_Db_Async`. A synchronous version is in folder `ThreadStarvation_Db_Sync`. Use the SQL scripts `tuneup.database.sql` and `book.table.sql` to create the database and books table used in the code. Don't forget to modify the connection string in `web.config` so that it uses your database server.

Usage

To keep it simple, the asynchronous data layer will access one database table containing books, and it will support only one method, which gets a book by its `bookId`. Given the overall structure, it should be easy to extend this layer and modify it for your own needs.

Don't forget to set `Async="true"` and set `AsyncTimeout` to a timeout in seconds in the `Page` directive of each page where you use asynchronous operations:

```
<%@ Page Language="C#" Async="true" AsyncTimeout="30"
  AutoEventWireup="true"  CodeFile="Default.aspx.cs"
  Inherits="_Default" %>
```

A typical bit of code accessing the asynchronous data layer will look like the following:

```
DataAccessAsync.Books.GetById(bookId, delegate(BookDTO bookDTO)
{
  // This anonymous method will be called when the
  // operation has been completed.
  Label1.Text = string.Format(
    "Id: {0}, Title: {1}, Author: {2}, Price: {3}",
    bookDTO.Id, bookDTO.Title, bookDTO.Author,
    bookDTO.Price);
},
delegate()
{
  // This anonymous method will be called when a timeout happens.
  Label1.Text = "Timeout happened";
});
```

The `GetById` data access method registers the task of retrieving a book based on its book ID. It takes the book ID, a method that will be called when the data has been retrieved, and a method that will be called when a timeout happens. Instead of defining separate methods somewhere else and then passing them in, this code passes in anonymous methods to keep everything in one place.

The method that is called when the data has been retrieved takes a `BookDTO` object with the book's details. It is the job of the data layer to retrieve that object from the database.

Implementation

The `GetById` method sits in the class `Books`, in the `DataAccessAsync` project. As just shown, it takes the book ID, a method to be called when the book has been retrieved, and a method to be called when a timeout happened:

```
public delegate void OnFinishedGetByIdDelegate(BookDTO bookDTO);
public delegate void NoParamsDelegate();

public static void GetById(int bookId,
OnFinishedGetByIdDelegate onFinished, NoParamsDelegate onTimedOut)
{
```

In the web service example, we saw how you can pass extra data on to the `BeginAsync` method. We'll use that here to pass on parameters such as the book ID. Because there are three parameters and only one extra data object, the code defines an `AsyncData` class that can hold all the parameters; we'll get to that in a moment. Here, the method `AsyncDataForGetById` creates an `AsyncData` object and fills it with the parameters:

```
AsyncData asyncData = AsyncDataForGetById(bookId, onFinished,
    onTimedOut);
```

Create the `PageAsyncTask` to be registered the same way you saw in the web service example. Pass in the `asyncData` object as the extra data:

```
PageAsyncTask pageAsyncTask = new PageAsyncTask(BeginAsync,
    EndAsync, TimeoutAsync, asyncData, false);
```

Finally, register the `PageAsyncTask`. To call `RegisterAsyncTask`, you first need the `Page` object, which is not readily available in this class project. However, you can retrieve it from the current context, because the `Page` object is actually the handler for the current request:

```
    Page currentPage;
    currentPage = (Page)System.Web.HttpContext.Current.Handler;
    currentPage.RegisterAsyncTask(pageAsyncTask);
}
```

As you just saw, the `AsyncData` class is used to carry parameters via the extra data parameter of `BeginAsync`. To make it more generally useful beyond just the "get book by ID" operation, its `onFinished` property is simply an object, rather than `OnFinishedGetByIdDelegate`. Likewise, instead of a book ID property, it carries the SQL command text and parameters to be sent to the database. Finally, we need an `SqlCommand` property, because `BeginAsync` will generate an `SqlCommand` object to start the retrieval and then pass it on to `EndAsync` to finish the same operation:

```
private class AsyncData
{
  public object onFinished { get; set; }
  public NoParamsDelegate onTimedOut { get; set; }
  public string commandText { get; set; }
  public List<SqlParameter> parameters { get; set; }
  public SqlCommand command { get; set; }
}
```

`AsyncData` is for general use, whereas the `AsyncDataForGetById` method is specific to the "get by ID" operation. It creates an `AsyncData` object based on the parameters passed in to `GetById`. It sets the SQL command text and matching parameters to retrieve a book with the given book ID. Finally, it returns the newly created `AsyncData` object:

```
private static AsyncData AsyncDataForGetById(
   int bookId, OnFinishedGetByIdDelegate onFinished,
   NoParamsDelegate onTimedOut)
{
   AsyncData asyncData = new AsyncData();
   asyncData.onFinished = onFinished;
   asyncData.onTimedOut = onTimedOut;

   asyncData.commandText =
   "SELECT BookId, Author, Title, Price
     FROM dbo.Book WHERE BookId=@BookId; ";

   List<SqlParameter> parameters = new List<SqlParameter>();
   parameters.Add(new SqlParameter("@BookId", bookId));
   asyncData.parameters = parameters;

   return asyncData;
}
```

You'll recognize `BeginAsync` from the web service example:

```
private static IAsyncResult BeginAsync(
   object sender, EventArgs e, AsyncCallback cb, object extraData)
{
```

The `extraData` parameter has the `AsyncData` object with all the parameters. It was passed in to the `PageAsyncTask` constructor:

```
AsyncData asyncData = (AsyncData)extraData;
```

Create a connection object and a command object. Copy the parameter that was created in method `AsyncDataForGetById` to the command. Use a loop here, so that this same code can be used with any future operations that use multiple parameters:

```
string connectionString = ConfigurationManager.ConnectionStrings
   ["ConnectionString"].ConnectionString;
SqlConnection connection = new SqlConnection(connectionString);
connection.Open();

SqlCommand command = new SqlCommand
   (asyncData.commandText, connection);
```

```
foreach (SqlParameter sqlParameter in asyncData.parameters)
{
  command.Parameters.Add(sqlParameter);
}
```

Store the command in the `AsyncData` object. That way, the command will reach `EndAsync` along with the other parameters:

```
asyncData.command = command;
```

Use the asynchronous version of `ExecuteReader`, called `BeginExecuteReader`. Similar to the `Begin..` method in the web service example, this takes the callback method passed into `BeginAsync`, and the `AsyncData` object with the parameters. When the runtime calls `EndAsync`, it will pass on the `AsyncData` object to `EndAsync`.

```
IAsyncResult asyncResult =
  command.BeginExecuteReader(cb, asyncData);
return asyncResult;
}
```

`EndAsync` too will be familiar from the web service example. Its first action is to retrieve the `AsyncData` object:

```
private static void EndAsync(IAsyncResult asyncResult)
{
  object extraData = asyncResult.AsyncState;
  AsyncData asyncData = (AsyncData)extraData;
```

Retrieve the command object that was created by `BeginAsync`. Use a `using` construct, so that it will be properly disposed when we're done:

```
using (SqlCommand command = (SqlCommand)asyncData.command)
{
```

Use a second `using` construct to make sure the connection is disposed at the end as well:

```
using (command.Connection)
{
```

Call `EndExecuteReader` to retrieve the `reader` representing the data from the database. Again use `using`, to dispose the reader automatically:

```
using (SqlDataReader reader =
  command.EndExecuteReader(asyncResult))
{
```

Processing the `reader` is specific to the actual operation. This example reads a book, but other operations might include reading a set of books, or reading some other type of object. To find out which operation is being executed, look at the type of `asyncData.onFinished`. If it is `OnFinishedGetByIdDelegate`, you know we're going to read a single book.

```
// GetbyId specific processing
OnFinishedGetByIdDelegate onFinishedGetById =
asyncData.onFinished as OnFinishedGetByIdDelegate;

if (onFinishedGetById != null)
{
```

This is just standard coding. Read the `BookDTO` object from the reader:

```
BookDTO bookDTO = null;
if (reader.Read())
{
  bookDTO =new BookDTO(Convert.ToInt32(reader["BookId"]),
    reader["Author"].ToString(),
    reader["Title"].ToString(),
    Convert.ToDecimal(reader["Price"]));
}
```

The delegate `onFinishedGetById` contains the method to be called when the data from the database is available, as originally passed on to `GetById`. Call it, now that we have the data:

```
        onFinishedGetById(bookDTO);
      }
    }
  }
}
}
```

Finally, implement the `TimeoutAsync` method:

```
private static void TimeoutAsync(IAsyncResult asyncResult)
{
```

Retrieve the `AsyncData` object with the parameters, the same way as with the `EndAsync` method:

```
object extraData = asyncResult.AsyncState;
AsyncData asyncData = (AsyncData)extraData;
```

Get the command object from the `AsyncData` object. Now dispose the connection and then the command object itself:

```
SqlCommand command = (SqlCommand)asyncData.command;
command.Connection.Dispose();
command.Dispose();
```

Finally, execute the delegate `onTimedOut` that was originally passed to the `GetById` method:

```
if (asyncData.onTimedOut != null)
{
  asyncData.onTimedOut();
}
}
```

This is all the code. To make it work, add `Async=True` to the connection string in `web.config` to allow asynchronous database operations:

```
<connectionStrings>
  <add name="ConnectionString"
    connectionString="Data Source=MPERDECK-PC;
    Initial Catalog=TuneUp;User ID=tuneup;
    Password=fast3rweb!;  Async=True;"/>
</connectionStrings>
```

There you have it; a simple, but functional asynchronous data layer. You could improve on this quite a bit, for example by factoring out the `BeginAsync`, `EndAsync`, and `TimeoutAsync` method to a common base class to make it easier to add operations on different types of objects, rather than just books. Another improvement would be to expose the `executeInParallel` parameter to the `PageAsyncTask` constructor via another parameter to `GetById`. That would make it easy to execute database retrieval in parallel with a web service request.

Performance testing

So how much difference does asynchronous processing make? This all depends on whether you use IIS 6, IIS 7 classic mode or IIS 7 integrated mode, your hardware, the workload, and so on. Load tests of both the synchronous and asynchronous database code running under IIS 7 integrated mode showed throughput per second for the asynchronous version to be at least five times higher than that of the synchronous version.

You can run these tests yourself with the free load testing tool **WCAT**, using the following items in the code bundle downloaded for the book (turn to *Chapter 14, Load Testing* to see how to set up such a load test):

folder `ThreadStarvation_Db_Async`	Complete test site for the asynchronous data layer you just saw.
folder `ThreadStarvation_Db_Sync`	Synchronous version of the above mentioned project.
`settings.ubr`	WCAT settings file. Modify to set your own server.
`testdefault_scenario.ubr`	WCAT scenario file.
`runwcat_testdefault.bat`	Runs WCAT with the previously-mentioned settings and scenario files.

After the synchronous and asynchronous runs, check the throughput, as reported in the WCAT `log.xml` file.

Asynchronous generic handlers

When you use AJAX-type asynchronous requests from your page to retrieve data from the database, you would want to use an `.ashx` generic handler or maybe a web service to process that request, rather than a full-blooded `.aspx` page. This will save you the overhead of the full page life cycle.

Accessing a database asynchronously from a generic handler is different from doing the same from a page. Let's see how this works.

Synchronous version

Firstly, let's have a quick look at a synchronous generic handler. We'll then work that into its asynchronous counterpart using the asynchronous data access layer we just saw.

You'll find the code in the downloaded code bundle in the folder `ThreadStarvation_Db_Sync`, file `Handler.ashx`.

To add a generic handler to your website, right-click on the website, choose **Add New Item**, and choose **Generic Handler**. Enter a filename and click on the **Add** button.

The full synchronous handler is shown below. It is simply a class derived from
`IHttpHandler`. There is one method doing all the work: `ProcessRequest`. It gets the
book ID from the query string, and then calls `DataAccess.Books.GetById` to get the
book with that ID from the database, returning a `BookDTO` object. Finally, it processes
the `BookDTO` into a string and writes that string back to the browser:

```csharp
<%@ WebHandler Language="C#" Class="Handler" %>

using System;
using System.Web;
using DataTransferObjects;

public class Handler : IHttpHandler {

    public void ProcessRequest (HttpContext context)
    {
        int bookId = Convert.ToInt32(context.Request.
QueryString["id"]);
        string response;

        BookDTO bookDTO = DataAccess.Books.GetById(bookId);
        response =
            string.Format(
                "Id: {0}, Title: {1}, Author: {2}, Price: {3}",
                bookDTO.Id, bookDTO.Title, bookDTO.Author, bookDTO.
Price);

        context.Response.ContentType = "text/plain";
        context.Response.Write(response);
    }

    public bool IsReusable {
        get {
            return false;
        }
    }
}
```

That was simple. Now, let's see how the asynchronous version works.

Asynchronous version

There are two differences between a synchronous generic handler and its asynchronous counterpart:

- The asynchronous handler class derives from `IHttpAsyncHandler` rather than `IHttpHandler`.

- Instead of implementing a single `ProcessRequest` method, you implement two methods: `BeginProcessRequest` and `EndProcessRequest`. Because `IHttpAsyncHandler` derives from `IHttpHandler`, `ProcessRequest` is still there, but there is no need to implement it.

This means that your asynchronous handler looks like the following:

```
<%@ WebHandler Language="C#" Class="Handler" %>

using System;
using System.Web;

public class Handler : IHttpAsyncHandler
{
  public IAsyncResult BeginProcessRequest(HttpContext context,
    AsyncCallback cb, object extraData)
  {
    // Begin asynchronous operation ...
  }

  public void EndProcessRequest(IAsyncResult result)
  {
    // End asynchronous operation ...
  }

  public void ProcessRequest(HttpContext context)
  {
    throw new NotImplementedException();
  }

  public bool IsReusable {
  get {
    return false;
  }
  }
}
```

Look closely at the parameters of `BeginProcessRequest` and `EndProcessRequest`. `BeginProcessRequest` returns an `IAsyncResult` and takes the same context parameter as the synchronous `ProcessRequest` did, plus a callback method and an extra data object. This matches other `Begin..` methods, such as the one you saw in the web service example, and the `BeginExecuteReader` in the asynchronous data layer. `EndProcessRequest` meanwhile takes an `IAsyncResult` object, just as the other `End..` methods, such as `EndExecuteReader` in the asynchronous data layer.

What it comes down to is that there is no need to register `BeginAsync` and `EndAsync` as there was in the other examples. We'll need to extend the asynchronous data layer a bit, to provide a lower-level interface. Also, there is no support for handling timeouts.

Our implementation of `BeginProcessRequest` takes a callback method and needs to return an `IAsyncResult` object. The `BeginAsync` method that you saw in the asynchronous data layer will return the `IAsyncResult` object we need, and it takes the callback method. We'll have to build an `AsyncData` object though to pass parameters such as the book id to `BeginAsync`.

Our implementation of `EndProcessRequest`, meanwhile, gets an `IAsyncResult` parameter. So to finish processing, it only needs to call `EndAsync`, which we saw in the asynchronous data layer, too.

Because `BeginAsync` and `EndAsync` are very low level, we won't call them here directly, but create wrapper methods `BeginGetById` and `EndGetById`.

This all means that when we're done, we'll be able to write code like the following in the handler:

```
public IAsyncResult BeginProcessRequest(HttpContext context,
  AsyncCallback cb, object extraData)
{
  int bookId = Convert.ToInt32(context.Request.QueryString["id"]);
  return DataAccessAsync.Books.BeginGetById(cb, bookId,
    delegate(BookDTO bookDTO)
  {
    // This anonymous method will be called when
    // the GetById operation has been completed.
    string response =
    string.Format("Id: {0}, Title: {1}, Author: {2},
      Price: {3}",bookDTO.Id, bookDTO.Title, bookDTO.Author,
      bookDTO.Price);

    context.Response.ContentType = "text/plain";
    context.Response.Write(response);
  });
}

public void EndProcessRequest(IAsyncResult result)
{
  DataAccessAsync.Books.EndGetById(result);
}
```

Implementation

Here is the code for the wrapper methods `BeginGetById` and `EndGetById`. You'll find them in the downloaded code bundle in the folder `ThreadStarvation_Db_Async`, file `Books.cs`, with the rest of the asynchronous data layer.

`BeginGetById` takes the same parameters as `GetById`, the method used for web pages, except for the timeout handler. It also gets the callback method. It's now simply a matter of building an `AsyncData` object using the `AsyncDataForGetById` method. Pass that and the callback method to `BeginAsync`, and return the `IAsyncResult` that `BeginAsync` returns:

```
public static IAsyncResult BeginGetById(AsyncCallback cb,
  int bookId, OnFinishedGetByIdDelegate onFinished)
{
  AsyncData asyncData =
  AsyncDataForGetById(bookId, onFinished, null);

  return BeginAsync(null, null, cb, asyncData);
}
```

`EndGetById` is even simpler:

```
public static void EndGetById(IAsyncResult asyncResult)
{
  EndAsync(asyncResult);
}
```

Performance testing

You can see the difference in performance between the asynchronous handler and the synchronous handler by running a load test, using the following items in the downloaded code bundle (turn to chapter 14 to see how to set up a load test):

folder `ThreadStarvation_Db_Async`	Holds the complete test site for the asynchronous data layer, including the asynchronous handler.
folder `ThreadStarvation_Db_Sync`	Synchronous version of the above mentioned project, including the synchronous handler we looked at before getting to the asynchronous handler.
`settings.ubr`	WCAT settings file. Modify to set your own server.
`testhandler_scenario.ubr`	WCAT scenario file.
`runwcat_testhandler.bat`	Runs WCAT with the settings and scenario files given above.

After the synchronous and asynchronous runs, check the throughput as reported in the WCAT `log.xml` file.

Asynchronous file writes

We've now seen how to asynchronously access the database and a web service. Another area where asynchronous coding may bring performance benefits is writing files to disc after they have been uploaded using the `FileUpload` control.

Synchronous version

You'll find this code in the downloaded code bundle in the folder `ThreadStarvation_FileWrite_Sync`. When you open the website in Visual Studio, you'll find that it stores uploaded files in a folder `images`. When you publish the website, to enable the website to write files into that folder, give user **IIS_IUSRS** modify permission to that folder:

1. Right-click on the images folder. Click on **Properties | Security | Edit**.

2. Select **IIS_IUSRS** in upper-pane (add it if it isn't shown).

3. Check the **Allow** checkbox in the **Modify** row and click on **OK**.

Using a `FileUpload` control synchronously is pretty easy. You put it on a `.aspx` page, together with a button to initiate the actual upload and a label control for error messages, shown as follows:

```
<p>
  Select a file:
    <asp:FileUpload ID="FileUpload1" runat="server" />
</p>
<p>
  <asp:Label ID="Label1" runat="server"></asp:Label>
</p>
<p>
  <asp:Button ID="btnUpload" runat="server" Text="Upload"
    OnClick="btnUpload_Click" />
</p>
```

The button-click handler first checks whether the visitor actually entered a filename in the upload control. If he did, it then saves the file with the `SaveAs` method exposed by `FileUpload`:

```
protected void btnUpload_Click(object sender, EventArgs e)
{
  if (!FileUpload1.HasFile)
  {
    Label1.Text = "No file specified.";
    return;
  }

  string fileName = FileUpload1.FileName;
  FileUpload1.SaveAs(Server.MapPath(@"images\" + fileName));
}
```

Let's see how this translates to the asynchronous version.

Asynchronous version

You'll find this code in the downloaded code bundle, in the folder `ThreadStarvation_FileWrite_Async`.

Writing a file asynchronously is similar to implementing other types of asynchronous code. First, be sure to include `Async="true"` in the `Page` directive:

```
<%@ Page Language="C#" Async="true" AutoEventWireup="true"
  CodeFile="Default.aspx.cs" Inherits="_Default" %>
```

Now turn to the code behind. Unfortunately, there is no asynchronous version of the `SaveAs` method, so we'll have to take the buffer holding the contents of the file and write that asynchronously to a file on disk.

Because the file write is initiated in `BeginAsync`, we'll need a class to hold the file details so that they can be passed to `BeginAsync` as a single object:

```
public class FileWriteData
{
  public byte[] fileBytesBuffer { get; set; }
  public int bufferLength { get; set; }
  public string fileName { get; set; }
  public FileStream fs { get; set; }
}
```

After the visitor has entered a file in the upload control, they'll click a button to send it to server. The click handler for that button is shown in the following code.

The first bit of the handler checks whether the visitor actually selected a file:

```
protected void btnUpload_Click(object sender, EventArgs e)
{
  if (!FileUpload1.HasFile)
  {
    Label1.Text = "No file specified.";
    return;
  }
```

Now, gather all the file details in a FileWriteData object:

```
FileWriteData fwd = new FileWriteData();
fwd.fileBytesBuffer = FileUpload1.FileBytes;
fwd.bufferLength = FileUpload1.PostedFile.ContentLength;
fwd.fileName = FileUpload1.FileName;
```

Finally, register the PageAsyncTask, passing in the FileWriteData object:

```
    PageAsyncTask pageAsyncTask =
    new PageAsyncTask(BeginAsync, EndAsync, null, fwd, false);

    RegisterAsyncTask(pageAsyncTask);
}
```

The BeginAsync method works along the usual lines. First, retrieve the FileWriteData object with the file information. Then, create the object that is going to do the actual work; in this case a FileStream. Let's give it a buffer of 64 KB, to match the NTFS internal buffer size. Be sure to set the last parameter useAsync to true. Because Windows won't do an asynchronous write if that means extending an existing file, use SetLength to give the file its final size upfront. Store the FileStream in the FileWriteData object, so that EndAsync can later access it to finalize the file write. Finally, call the asynchronous version of the write method, BeginWrite, to initiate the file write:

```
private IAsyncResult BeginAsync(object sender, EventArgs e,
  AsyncCallback cb, object extraData)
{
  FileWriteData fwd = (FileWriteData)extraData;

  FileStream fs =
  new FileStream(Server.MapPath(@"images\" + fwd.fileName),
    FileMode.OpenOrCreate, FileAccess.Write, FileShare.Write,
    64 * 1024, true);
```

```
    fs.SetLength(fwd.bufferLength);
    fwd.fs = fs;

    IAsyncResult asyncResult = fs.BeginWrite(fwd.fileBytesBuffer, 0,
      fwd.bufferLength, cb, fwd);
    return asyncResult;
}
```

As expected, the `EndAsync` method first retrieves the `FileWriteData` object. It then calls `EndWrite` to finish the write operation, closes the file, and disposes the `FileStream` via the `using` statement. Finally, it tells the visitor that the file was saved:

```
private void EndAsync(IAsyncResult asyncResult)
{
    object extraData = asyncResult.AsyncState;
    FileWriteData fwd = (FileWriteData)extraData;

    using (FileStream fs = fwd.fs)
    {
      fs.EndWrite(asyncResult);
      fs.Close();
    }

    Label1.Text = "File saved.";
}
```

That concludes the asynchronous implementation. Reading a file follows a similar pattern, using the Stream methods `BeginRead` and `EndRead`.

A word of caution

Be careful with asynchronous file reads and writes. Because asynchronous I/O carries some overhead such as giving up the running thread and getting it back later, using asynchronous I/O with small files can make your site slower instead of faster. Find out what file sizes normally get uploaded to the site, and then load test your new version with some typically-sized files.

Asynchronous file reads and writes are not always carried out asynchronously. Reads and writes using compressed filesystems and writes to encrypted files are always done synchronously. As we saw while we discussed the code, writes that result in extending a file will be synchronous as well—you can get around this by using `FileStream.SetLength` to give the file its final length upfront. To see whether a task was executed synchronously or asynchronously, check the `IAsyncResult.CompletedSynchronously` flag in `EndAsync`, as shown in the following code:

```
private void EndAsync(IAsyncResult asyncResult)
{
    bool completedSynchronously =
      asyncResult.CompletedSynchronously;
```

Asynchronous web requests

It is fairly uncommon for a website to load other web pages using code on the server-side, so an example of this is not included here. As an alternative to reading web pages for each request, you could improve performance dramatically by caching the pages (refer to *Chapter 5, Caching*), or by having a separate program to read the pages periodically and store them in the database.

If you still want to load other web pages while processing a request, you'll find a good example at `http://msdn.microsoft.com/en-us/library/system.net.webrequest.begingetresponse.aspx`.

We've now seen how to change your code to use the existing threads more efficiently. You can also make configuration changes to modify the maximum number of threads. Let's see how that's done.

Configuration changes

If you have a lot of free CPU and memory on your server, it may be worthwhile to tweak the maximum number of threads executing requests.

Keep in mind that the runtime conservatively manages the number of threads used to execute requests. Hence, even if you increase the maximum number of threads, that may not lead to more threads being used.

WARNING

Be careful here. You can spend a lot of time on this and end up doing more harm than good. Load test your solution before taking it into production (chapter 14 shows how to do load testing).

IIS 6, IIS 7 Classic Mode

In IIS 6 and IIS 7 when using the classic pipeline mode, the maximum number of threads is determined by the following formula:

Maximum threads = (`maxWorkerThreads` * number of CPUs) – `minFreeThreads`

Number of CPUs here refers to the number of processor cores in your server. So a computer with a single E8400 Intel Core 2 Duo, which has two cores, is considered to have two CPUs.

`maxWorkerThreads` is an attribute of the `processModel` element in `machine.config`:

```
<processModel maxWorkerThreads="20" .... >
```

`minFreeThreads` is an attribute of the `httpRuntime` element in `machine.config`:

```
<httpRuntime minFreeThreads="8"  .... >
```

I/O-related configuration

If you make a lot of calls to web services or access lots of other websites, the following settings could be relevant to you:

- `maxIoThreads`: It is the maximum number of I/O threads to use for the process per CPU in the thread pool. It must be greater than or equal to `minFreeThread`.

  ```
  <processModel maxIoThreads="20" ... >
  ```

- `maxconnection`: It determines how many connections can be made to a specific IP address from the application pool.

  For example, this configuration allows four connections to `http://www.example.com` and two connections to the other addresses:

  ```
  <configuration>
    <system.net>
      <connectionManagement>
        <add address = "http://www.example.com" maxconnection =
          "4" />
        <add address = "*" maxconnection = "2" />
      </connectionManagement>
    </system.net>
  </configuration>
  ```

ASP.NET 2.0

During the life span of .NET 1.1, Microsoft concluded that the default settings for a number of the attributes shown in the previous section were too low for most sites because those settings kept the maximum number of threads below what could be handled by the server hardware at the time. In response, in ASP.NET 2.0 the `autoConfig` attribute was introduced to give those attributes higher defaults:

```
<processModel autoConfig="true"/>
```

When `true`, `autoConfig` makes the following changes to your configuration at runtime:

- Sets `maxWorkerThreads` and `maxIoThreads` to 100
- Sets `maxconnection` to 12 * number of CPUs
- Sets `minFreeThreads` to 88 * number of CPUs
- Sets `minWorkerThreads` to 50

This effectively limits the number of concurrently executing requests per CPU to 12, which is fine for most sites. However, if you have synchronous code that does a lot of waiting for the database, web services, and so on, you can set `autoConfig` to `false` and make your own changes. Test your changes before making them live.

IIS 7 integrated mode

When using integrated mode, the maximum number of requests executed in parallel is no longer set by the configuration shown in the previous sections. Instead, it is determined by the following settings:

- `maxConcurrentRequestsPerCPU`: It limits the number of requests executing per CPU, even if more threads are available. It's set to 12 by default in .NET 3.5 and its previous versions, and to 5000 in .NET 4. If it is set to zero, there is no limit.

- `maxConcurrentThreadsPerCPU`: It limits the number of threads used per CPU to process requests. No limit if set to zero, which is also the default.

One of these two needs to be zero, and the other one non-zero.

Before .NET 3.5 SP1, if you wanted to change these settings, you had to add DWORD keys with the same names in the registry to HKEY_LOCAL_MACHINE\SOFTWARE\ Microsoft\ASP.NET\2.0.50727.0.

In .NET 3.5 SP1 and later, you can add these settings to `aspnet.config`, which lives in C:\Windows\Microsoft.NET\Framework\v2.0.50727 or C:\Windows\ Microsoft.NET\Framework\v4.0.30128:

```
<system.web>
  <applicationPool maxConcurrentRequestsPerCPU="12"
    maxConcurrentThreadsPerCPU="0" requestQueueLimit="5000"/>
</system.web>
```

As we saw, in .NET 4, the default of `maxConcurrentRequestsPerCPU` is 5000, which means that it doesn't impose a real limit any more.

With `maxConcurrentRequestsPerCPU` set to 5000 and `maxConcurrentThreadsPerCPU` set to zero, the maximum number of threads executing requests is now effectively the number of threads in the thread pool. From ASP.NET 2.0 onwards, that limit is 100 threads per CPU, so on a dual core machine, you get 200 threads.

To increase that limit, set the `SetMaxThreads` property exposed by the ThreadPool object in namespace `System.Threading`.

> **WARNING**
> Be careful with this. Having more running threads mean more task-switching overhead.

Maximum queue size

When requests come in faster than can be processed, they queue up. If the queue gets too long, ASP.NET begins returning "503—Server Too Busy" errors to new requests.

The maximum queue size is set via the `requestQueueLimit` attribute in the `ProcessModelSection` element in `machine.config`:

```
<processModel requestQueueLimit ="5000" … >
```

Setting timeouts aggressively

If some of your pages access an external resource synchronously such as a web service and the external resource slows down dramatically, then those pages will start timing out. This is good, because otherwise they keep blocking the thread.

However, the default timeout is 110 seconds in .NET 2.0 or higher, and 90 seconds in .NET 1.0 and 1.1. On a busy site with requests waiting for threads to become available, having threads blocked for 110 seconds may be too long.

Setting the timeout to, for example 30 seconds, may not result in many more timeouts, while you get better use of the available threads.

Timeouts are set in `web.config`, via the `executionTimeout` attribute of element `httpRuntime`:

```
<system.web>
  <httpRuntime executionTimeout="30" />
</system.web>
```

You can also set timeouts per page as follows:

```
<configuration>
  . . .
  <location path="Page.aspx">
    <system.web>
      <httpRuntime executionTimeout="30" />
    </system.web>
  </location>
  . . .
</configuration>
```

Alternatively, you can access external resources asynchronously. In the preceding sections, you saw how to implement timeouts when you do that.

Find out more

Following are some more online resources:

- ASP.NET Thread Usage on IIS 7.0 and 6.0
  `http://blogs.msdn.com/b/tmarq/archive/2007/07/21/asp-net-thread-usage-on-iis-7-0-and-6-0.aspx`

- <applicationPool> Element (Web Settings)
  `http://msdn.microsoft.com/en-us/library/dd560842.aspx`

- Performing Asynchronous Work, or Tasks, in ASP.NET Applications
  `http://blogs.msdn.com/b/tmarq/archive/2010/04/14/performing-asynchronous-work-or-tasks-in-asp-net-applications.aspx`

- Asynchronous Pages in ASP.NET 2.0
  `http://msdn.microsoft.com/en-us/magazine/cc163725.aspx`

Summary

In this chapter, we focused on converting synchronous code, which blocks the current thread, to asynchronous code, that releases the thread while waiting for an off-box operation to complete. This makes more threads available to IIS to process requests.

We first saw how to convert synchronous access of a web service to asynchronous access. Then we looked at the more complex case of asynchronously accessing a database, including an asynchronous data layer, and then applied this to both, a regular web page and a generic handler. We then learned how to write a file asynchronously.

This chapter also discussed configuring the server in relation to the threads it uses to process requests, and wrapped up by looking at changing page timeouts to free resources as soon as possible.

In the next chapter, we'll find out how to measure wait times for external resources such as web services and locks. We'll also see how to reduce those wait times.

7
Reducing Long Wait Times

If the server is not running out of memory, CPU capacity, or threads and requests are still taking long to complete, chances are that the server has to wait too long for off-box resources, such as the database.

In this chapter, we'll cover the following topics:

- How to measure the wait times for each off-box resource using custom counters
- Waiting concurrently instead of sequentially
- Improving session state performance
- Reducing thread-locking delays

One major source of delays is database access, which is discussed in *Chapter 8, Speeding up Database Access*.

Measuring wait times

We can use a number of ways to find out which external requests are most frequent and how long the site has to wait for a response:

- Run the code in the debugger with breakpoints around each external request. This will give you a quick hint of which external request is the likely culprit. However, you wouldn't do this in a production environment, as it only gives you information for a few requests.
- Use the **Trace** class (in the namespace `System.Diagnostics`) to trace how long each request takes. This will give you a lot of detailed information. However, the overhead incurred by processing all the trace messages may be too high to use in a production environment, and you would have to somehow aggregate the trace data to find which requests are the most frequent and take the longest.

- Build performance counters into your code that record the frequency of each request and the average wait time. These counters are light-weight, and hence, can be used in a production environment. Also, you can readily access them via `perfmon`, along with the counters provided by ASP.NET, SQL Server, and so on that you have already come across.

The remainder of this section focuses on performance counters, because debugging and tracing are well-covered in general ASP.NET programming books. Also, performance counters are a convenient way to keep an eye on off-box requests on a day-to-day basis instead of as a one-off.

Windows offers you 28 types of performance counters to choose from. Some of these are esoteric, others extremely useful. For example, you can measure the rate per second that a request is made, and the average time in milliseconds that the site waits for a response. Adding your own custom counters is easy, and you can see their real-time values in `perfmon`, along with that of the built-in counters.

The runtime overhead of counters is minimal. You have already come across some of the hundreds of counters published by ASP.NET, SQL Server, and Windows itself. Even if you add a lot of counters, CPU overhead would be well under one percent.

Because going into all 28 types of counters would probably take another book, this section describes only three commonly used counters: simple number, rate per second, and time. A list of all types of counters with examples of their use is available at `http://msdn.microsoft.com/en-us/library/system.diagnostics.performancecountertype.aspx?ppud=4`.

To use the counters, you need to follow these three steps:

1. Create custom counters.
2. Update them in your code.
3. See their values in `perfmon`.

Creating custom counters

In this example, we'll put counters on a page that simply waits for one second to simulate waiting for an external resource.

Windows allows you to group counters into categories. We'll create a new category "Test Counters" for the new counters.

Here are the actual counters we'll put on the page. They are of the three types that you'll use most often.

Counter Name	Counter Type	Description
Nbr Page Hits	NumberOfItems64	64 bit counter, counting the total number of hits on the page since the website started.
Hits/second	RateOfCountsPerSecond32	Hits per second
Average Wait	AverageTimer32	Time taken by the resource. Inspite of the name, it is used here to simply measure an interval, not an average.
Average Wait Base*	AverageBase	Utility counter required by Average Wait.

*The text says there are three counters, but the table lists four. Why? The last counter, Average Wait Base, doesn't provide information on its own, but helps to compute the value of counter Average Wait. Later on, we'll see how this works.

There are two ways to create the "Test Counters" category and the counters themselves:

- **Using Visual Studio**: This is relatively quick, but if you want to apply the same counters to for example your development and production environments, you'll have to enter the counters separately in each environment

- **Programmatically**: Because this involves writing code, it takes a bit longer upfront, but makes it easier to apply the same counters to multiple environments and to place the counters under source control

Creating counters with Visual Studio

To create the counters in Visual Studio:

1. Make sure you have administrative privileges or are a member of the Performance Monitor Users group.

2. Open Visual Studio.

3. Click on the **Server Explorer** tab.

4. Expand **Servers**.

5. Expand your machine.

6. Right-click on **Performance Counters** and choose **Create New Category**.

7. Enter **Test Counters** in the **Category Name** field.

8. Click on the **New** button for each of the four counters to add, as listed in the table you saw earlier. Be sure to add the **Average Wait Base** counter right after **Average Wait**, to properly associate the two counters.

9. Click on **OK** when you're done.

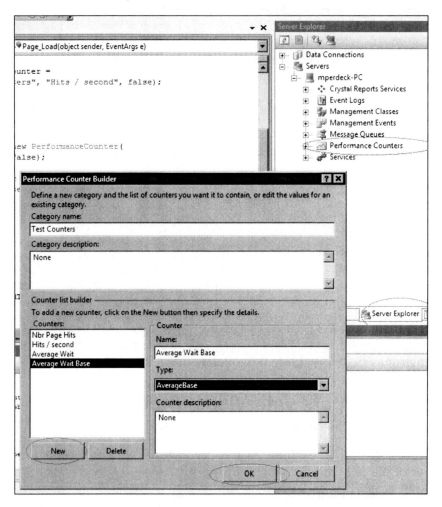

This technique is easy. However, you'll need to remember to add the same counters to the production machine when you release new code with new custom counters. Writing a program to create the counters is more work initially, but gives you easier maintenance in the long run. Let's see how to do this.

Creating counters programmatically

From a maintenance point of view, it would be best to create the counters when the web application starts, in the `Global.asax` file. However, you would then have to make the account under which the application pool runs part of the Performance Monitor Users group.

An alternative is to create the counters in a separate console program. An administrator can then run the program to create the counters on the server. Here is the code (in the folder `CountersDemo` in the downloaded code bundle for the chapter):

```
using System;
using System.Diagnostics;

namespace CreateCounters
{
  class Program
  {
    static void Main(string[] args)
    {
```

To create a group of counters, you create each one in turn, and add them to a `CounterCreationDataCollection` object:

```
CounterCreationDataCollection ccdc = new
   CounterCreationDataCollection();
```

Create the first counter, `Nbr Page Hits`. Give it a short help message and the counter type. Now, add it to the `CounterCreationDataCollection` object:

```
CounterCreationData ccd = new CounterCreationData
  ("Nbr Page Hits", "Total number of page hits",
   PerformanceCounterType.NumberOfItems64);
ccdc.Add(ccd);
```

Add the second, third, and fourth counters along the same lines:

```
ccd = new CounterCreationData("Hits / second",
  "Total number of page hits / sec",
   PerformanceCounterType.RateOfCountsPerSecond32);
ccdc.Add(ccd);

ccd = new CounterCreationData("Average Wait",
  "Average wait in seconds",
   PerformanceCounterType.AverageTimer32);
ccdc.Add(ccd);

ccd = new CounterCreationData("Average Wait Base", "",
   PerformanceCounterType.AverageBase);
ccdc.Add(ccd);
```

Now, it's time to take the `CounterCreationDataCollection` object and make it into a category. Because you'll get an exception when you try to create a category that already exists if there already is a category with the same name, delete it now. Because you can't add new counters to an existing category, there is no simple work-around for this:

```
if (PerformanceCounterCategory.Exists("Test Counters"))
{
   PerformanceCounterCategory.Delete("Test Counters");
}
```

Finally, create the `Test Counters` category. Give it a short help message, and make it a single instance. You can also make a category multi-instance, which allows you to split the category into instances. Also, pass in the `CounterCreationDataCollection` object with all the counters. This creates the complete category with all your counters in one go, as shown in the following code:

```
      PerformanceCounterCategory.Create("Test Counters",
         "Counters for test site",PerformanceCounterCategoryType.
         SingleInstance,ccdc);
     }
   }
}
```

Now that you know how to create the counters, let's see how to update them in your code.

Updating counters in your code

To keep things simple, this example uses the counters in a page that simply waits for a second to simulate waiting for an external resource:

```
using System;
using System.Diagnostics;

public partial class _Default : System.Web.UI.Page
{
   protected void Page_Load(object sender, EventArgs e)
   {
```

First, increment the `nbrPageHits` counter. To do this, create a `PerformanceCounter` object, attaching it to the `nbrPageHits` counter in the `Test Counters` category. Then, increment the `PerformanceCounter` object:

```
PerformanceCounter nbrPageHitsCounter =
new PerformanceCounter("Test Counters", "Nbr Page Hits", false);
nbrPageHitsCounter.Increment();
```

Now, do the same with the Hits/second counter. Because you set its type to RateOfCountsPerSecond32 when you generated it in the console program, the counter will automatically give you a rate per second when viewed in perfmon:

```
PerformanceCounter nbrPageHitsPerSecCounter =
    new PerformanceCounter("Test Counters", "Hits / second", false);
nbrPageHitsPerSecCounter.Increment();
```

To measure how long the actual operation takes, create a Stopwatch object, and start it:

```
Stopwatch sw = new Stopwatch();
sw.Start();
```

Execute the simulated operation:

```
// Simulate actual operation
System.Threading.Thread.Sleep(1000);
```

Stop the stopwatch:

```
sw.Stop();
```

Update the Average Wait counter and the associated Average Wait Base counter to record the elapsed time in the stopwatch.

```
    PerformanceCounter waitTimeCounter = new
        PerformanceCounter("Test Counters", "Average Wait", false);
    waitTimeCounter.IncrementBy(sw.ElapsedTicks);
    PerformanceCounter waitTimeBaseCounter = new
        PerformanceCounter("Test Counters", "Average Wait Base",
        false);
    waitTimeBaseCounter.Increment();
  }
}
```

Now that we've seen how to create and use the most commonly used counters, it's time to retrieve their values.

Viewing custom counters in perfmon

You saw how to access performance counters in *Chapter 2, Reducing Time to First Byte* in the *Pinpointing bottlenecks* section, the *Thread usage* subsection. Accessing your custom counters goes the same way:

1. On the server, run `perfmon` from the command prompt. To open the command prompt on Vista, click on **Start | All Programs | Accessories | Command Prompt**. This opens the monitor window.

2. Expand **Monitoring Tools** and click on **Performance Monitor**.

3. Click on the green "plus" sign.

4. In the **Add Counters** dialog, scroll down to your new **Test Counters** category.

5. Expand that category and add your new counters. Click on **OK**.

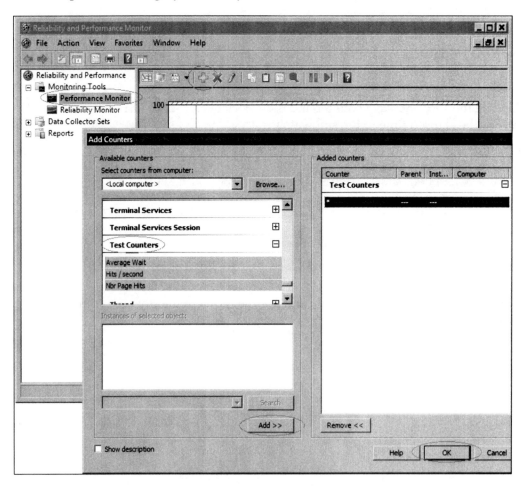

6. To see the counters in action, run a load test as described in chapter 14. If you use WCAT, you could use files `runwcat_testcounters.bat` and `testcounters_scenario.ubr` from the downloaded code bundle.

Now that you have seen how to measure wait times, let's turn to a number of ways to reduce those wait times.

Waiting concurrently

If your site needs to wait for responses from multiple external resources, and those requests are not dependent on each other, initiate those requests in one go and wait for all responses in parallel instead of one after the other. If you need information from three web services, each taking five seconds to respond, you'll now wait for five seconds only, instead of 3*5=15 seconds.

You can easily implement this using asynchronous code, as discussed in *Chapter 6, Thread Usage* in the *Asynchronous web service access* section, the *Asynchronous version* subsection. When you register each asynchronous task, pass `true` in the `executeInParallel` parameter of the `PageAsyncTask` constructor, as shown in the following code:

```
bool executeInParallel = true;
PageAsyncTask pageAsyncTask =
    new PageAsyncTask(BeginAsync, EndAsync, null, null,
executeInParallel);
RegisterAsyncTask(pageAsyncTask);
```

Retrieving multiple result sets from the database

ADO.NET allows you to retrieve multiple result sets from the database, instead of retrieving them one-by-one. This was further described in *Chapter 4, CPU* in the *Data access* section, the *Returning multiple result sets* subsection.

Reducing overhead by using off-box session modes

If you use session state on a server farm, you probably use StateServer or SqlServer mode rather than InProc mode, because requests coming from the one visitor may be processed at different servers.

This means that when a request starts being processed, ASP.NET retrieves the current session state from the StateServer or the SQL Server database, and de-serializes it so that your code can work with it. Then, towards the end of the life cycle of the page, the session state is serialized again and stored in the StateServer or the SQL Server database. As part of this, ASP.NET updates the last update time of the session, so that it can expire the session if it hasn't been used for too long. If you use SqlServer mode, this all means two trips to the database per request.

A few ways to reduce all this overhead are discussed in the following sections.

Reducing trips to the database

You can reduce the number of trips to the database by setting `EnableSessionState` in the `Page` directive to `True`, as shown:

```
<%@ Page EnableSessionState="True" ... %>
```

`EnableSessionState` takes these values:

- `True`: It is the default value; you get both trips to the database.
- `False`: It disables access to session state on the page and prevents the initial read. However, to prevent session expiry, the session state in the store will still be marked as accessed towards the end of the page life cycle. Hence, you wind up with just one trip to the database.
- `ReadOnly`: This value makes the session state read-only. When page processing starts, the session state is still retrieved and deserialized. However, towards the end of the page life cycle, there is no update of the session state. This means you wind up with just one trip to the database. An added advantage is that this mode uses only read locks, enabling multiple read-only requests to access the session state concurrently. As a result, it prevents lock contention when multiple files are processed for the same visitor.

Setting EnableSessionState

As you saw, you can set `EnableSessionState` in the `Page` directive:

```
<%@ Page EnableSessionState="ReadOnly" %>
```

You can also set it on a site-wide basis in `web.config`:

```
<configuration>
    <system.web>
        <pages enableSessionState="ReadOnly" />
    </system.web>
</configuration>
```

You can then override this default state in the `Page` directive of each page.

Reducing serialization and transfer overhead

In addition to reducing the number of trips to the database, it makes sense to reduce serialization and transfer overhead to save time and CPU usage.

Instead of storing an object with multiple fields in one go in Session, store its individual fields. This has the following advantages:

- Serializing .NET Framework primitive types such as String, Boolean, DateTime, TimeSpan, Int16, Int32, Int64, Byte, Char, Single, Double, Decimal, SByte, UInt16, UInt32, UInt64, Guid, and IntPtr is very quick and efficient. Serializing object types however, uses the BinaryFormatter, which is much slower.

- It allows you to access only those individual fields that really need to be accessed. Fields that do not get accessed do not get updated in the session store, saving serialization and transfer overhead.

Suppose you use objects of this class (page `Original.aspx.cs` in folder `LongWaitTimes_ReduceSessionSerializatonOverhead` in the code bundle downloaded):

```
[Serializable]
private class Person
{
    public string FirstName { get; set; }
    public string LastName { get; set; }
}
```

You would retrieve and store this in Session as shown:

```
// Get object from session
Person myPerson = (Person)Session["MyPerson"];

// Make changes
myPerson.LastName = "Jones";

// Store object in session
Session["MyPerson"] = myPerson;
```

This will use the BinaryFormatter to deserialize/serialize the entire `myPerson` object and transfer it in its entirety from/to the session store.

Now look at the alternative (page `Improved.aspx.cs` in folder `LongWaitTimes_`
`ReduceSessionSerializatonOverhead` in the downloaded code bundle):

```
private class SessionBackedPerson
{
  private string _id;
  public SessionBackedPerson(string id)
  {
    _id = id;
  }

  private string _firstName;
  public string FirstName
  {
    get
    {
      _firstName = HttpContext.Current.Session[_id +
        "_firstName"].ToString();
      return _firstName;
    }

    set
    {
      if (value != _firstName)
      {
        _firstName = value;
        HttpContext.Current.Session[_id + "_firstName"] = value;
      }
    }
  }

  private string _lastName;
  public string LastName
  {
    get
    {
      _lastName = HttpContext.Current.Session[_id +
        "_lastName"].ToString();
      return _lastName;
    }

    set
    {
      if (value != _lastName)
      {
        _lastName = value;
        HttpContext.Current.Session[_id + "_lastName"] = value;
      }
    }
  }
}
```

This class takes care of storing its own individual properties in Session. Because of this, it needs to know its ID when it is constructed, so that it can construct a unique session key. When setting a property value, the Session object is only accessed when the new value is actually different from the old value.

As a result, this solution only stores individual primitives that are quick to serialize, rather than the entire object. It also only updates those fields in Session that have actually been updated.

Working with this new class requires changing the page code. Instead of retrieving an object from Session, the code needs to simply instantiate a new object, passing in the ID to the constructor. Then when the code updates any properties, they are stored in Session right away, with no need to store the entire object in Session at the end:

```
protected void Page_Load(object sender, EventArgs e)
{
    SessionBackedPerson myPerson = new SessionBackedPerson("myPers
on");

    // Update object, and session, in one go.
    // Only touch LastName, not FirstName.
    myPerson.LastName = "Jones";
}
```

We've now seen a number of ways to reduce the cost of sessions. But what about getting rid of them altogether? Refer to the next section for more about that option.

Cutting your dependence on sessions

The great advantage of session state is that it lives on the server, so is more difficult to access or modify by unauthorized people. However, if this is not an issue, here are some options to get rid of session state and its overhead in your pages:

- If you are not keeping a lot of session data, use simple cookies instead.
- Store session data in ViewState. This requires more bandwidth but reduces database traffic.
- Use AJAX-style asynchronous callbacks on your pages instead of full-page refreshes, so that you can keep session information on the page. This is further discussed in *Chapter 11, Optimizing Forms*.

Thread locking

If you use locking to ensure only a single thread can access a given resource, some threads may have to wait for a lock to become available.

To see if this is an issue, use perfmon to check the following counters, all in category **.NET CLR LocksAndThreads** (to see how to do this, refer to the *Pinpointing bottlenecks* section, the *Thread usage* subsection in chapter 2):

Category: .NET CLR LocksAndThreads	
Contention Rate/sec	The rate at which the runtime tries to get a managed lock, and fails to do so.
Current Queue Length	Last recorded number of threads waiting to get a managed lock.

If you consistently have threads failing to get a managed lock, you are looking at a source of delays. You can consider the following ways to reduce these delays:

- Minimize the duration of locks
- Use granular locks
- Use `System.Threading.Interlocked`
- Use `ReaderWriterLock`

Minimizing the duration of locks

Acquire locks on shared resources just before you access them, and release them immediately after you are finished with them. By limiting the time each resource is locked, you minimize the time threads need to wait for resources to become available.

Using granular locks

If you use the C# lock statement, or the Monitor object, lock as small an object as possible.

Take for example the following code:

```
lock (protectedObject)
{
    // protected code
}
```

This is shorthand for the following code:

```
try
{
    Monitor.Enter(protectedObject);

    // protected code ...
}
finally
{
    Monitor.Exit(protectedObject);
}
```

 Note that `Monitor.Enter` effectively locks the given object `protectedObject`. Because only a single thread can lock the object, this has the result of allowing only a single thread to execute the protected code.

This works well, as long as the object that is locked is solely related to the protected code. Only lock on private or internal objects. Otherwise, some unrelated code might try to lock on the same object to protect some other bit of code, leading to unnecessary delays. For example, do not lock on `this`:

```
lock (this)
{
    // protected code ...
}
```

Instead, lock on a private object:

```
private readonly object privateObject = new object();

public void MyMethod()
{
    lock (privateObject)
    {
        // protected code ...
    }
}
```

If you are protecting static code, do not lock on the class type:

```
lock (typeof(MyClass))
{
    // protected code ...
}
```

Instead, use a static object:

```
private static readonly object privateStaticObject = new object();

public void MyMethod()
{
    lock (privateStaticObject)
    {
        // protected code ...
    }
}
```

Using System.Threading.Interlocked

If your protected code simply increments or decrements an integer, adds one integer to another, or exchanges two values, consider using the `System.Threading.Interlocked` class instead of lock. `Interlocked` executes a lot faster than lock, so should result in less waiting for locks.

For example, instead of the following:

```
lock (privateObject)
{
    counter++;
}
```

Use the following:

```
Interlocked.Increment(ref counter);
```

Using ReaderWriterLock

If most threads accessing a protected object read only that object, and relatively few threads update the object, consider using a `ReaderWriterLock`. This allows multiple readers to access the protected code, but only a single writer to access it.

Acquiring a reader lock

When using a `ReaderWriterLock`, you declare the `ReaderWriterLock` at the class level:

```
static ReaderWriterLock readerWriterLock = new ReaderWriterLock();
```

Then to acquire a reader lock within a method, call `AcquireReaderLock`. You can give this a timeout. When a timeout occurs, an `ApplicationException` is thrown. To release the lock, call `ReleaseReaderLock`. Be sure to only release the lock if you actually have the lock, that is, you didn't suffer a timeout, otherwise an `ApplicationException` is thrown.

```
try
{
   readerWriterLock.AcquireReaderLock(millisecondsTimeout);

   // Read the protected object
}
catch (ApplicationException)
{
   // The reader lock request timed out.
}
finally
{
   // Ensure that the lock is released, provided there was no
   // timeout.
   if (readerWriterLock.IsReaderLockHeld)
   {
     readerWriterLock.ReleaseReaderLock();
   }
}
```

Acquiring a writer lock

Using a writer lock goes along the same lines. Acquire a writer lock by calling `AcquireWriterLock`. When you're done with it, call `ReleaseWriterLock`, making sure you actually had the lock:

```
try
{
   readerWriterLock.AcquireWriterLock(millisecondsTimeout);
   // Update the protected object
}
catch (ApplicationException)
{
   // The writer lock request timed out.
}
```

```
finally
{
  // Ensure that the lock is released, provided there was no
  // timeout.
  if (readerWriterLock.IsWriterLockHeld)
  {
    readerWriterLock.ReleaseWriterLock();
  }
}
```

If your code holds a reader lock and then decides that it needs to update the protected object, it can either release the reader lock and acquire a writer lock, or call the UpgradeToWriterLock method. You can also downgrade from a writer lock to a reader lock using DowngradeFromWriterLock, allowing the waiting reader threads to start reading.

Alternating readers and writers

While it is fine for multiple threads to read the protected object simultaneously, a thread that updates the protected object needs exclusive access. That way, while the thread is updating the object, no other threads can read or update that same object. To implement this, threads waiting for reader locks and threads waiting for writer locks sit in separate queues. When a writer releases its lock, all threads waiting for a reader lock have their locks granted and proceed through the protected code. When they have all released their reader locks, the next thread waiting for a writer lock has its lock granted. This way, the protected code is executed alternately by reader and writer threads.

To make sure that writer threads are not locked indefinitely by a constant stream of reading threads, if a new thread tries to acquire a reader lock while other reading threads are already executing the protected code, the new thread has to wait until the next writer thread has finished. Obviously, if there is no thread waiting for a writer lock, the new reader thread has its lock granted right away.

All of this is depicted in the following diagram:

Optimizing disk writes

If your site creates many new files on disk, such as files uploaded by visitors, consider these performance improvements:

- Avoid head seeks
- Use `FileStream.SetLength` to avoid fragmentation
- Use 64 K buffers
- Disable 8.3 filenames

Avoiding head seeks

Writing bytes sequentially without moving the read/write head happens much faster than random access. If you are only writing the files and not reading them, try writing them on a dedicated disk drive using a single dedicated thread. That way, other processes won't move the read/write head on the drive.

Using FileStream.SetLength to avoid fragmentation

If multiple threads write files at the same time, space used for those files will become interleaved, leading to instant fragmentation.

To prevent this, use the `FileStream.SetLength` method to reserve enough space for the file before you start writing.

If you use the ASP.NET `FileUpload` control to receive files from a visitor, it can give get the length of a file as shown:

```
int bufferLength = FileUpload1.PostedFile.ContentLength;
```

Using 64 K buffers

The NTFS file system uses an internal buffer of 64 KB. The `FileStream` constructor allows you to set the buffer size for file writes. By setting the `FileStream` buffer size to 64 KB, you bypass both the internal `FileStream` buffer and the NTFS buffer, which can result in higher performance.

Disabling 8.3 filenames

To retain backwards compatibility with MS-DOS, the NTFS file system maintains an 8.3 filename for each file or directory. This creates some overhead, because the system has to make sure that the 8.3 filename is unique, and so has to check the other names in the directory. You would have to have over 20,000 files in a single directory though for this to become significant.

Before disabling 8.3 filenames, make sure there are no applications on your system that rely on these names. Test the change first on a test system with the same operating system as the operational system.

To disable 8.3 filenames, execute this from the command prompt (after you back up the registry.):

```
fsutil behavior set disable8dot3
```

Because this changes the registry, you need to restart the machine for this to take effect.

Find out more

Here are more online resources:

- Why Disabling the Creation of 8.3 DOS File Names Will Not Improve Performance. Or Will It?
  `http://blogs.sepago.de/helge/2008/09/22/why-disabling-the-creation-of-83-dos-file-names-will-not-improve-performance-or-will-it/`

- Fast, Scalable, and Secure Session State Management for Your Web Applications
  `http://msdn.microsoft.com/en-us/magazine/cc163730.aspx`

- Performance Counter Type Reference
  `http://www.informit.com/guides/content.aspx?g=dotnet&seqNum=253`

Summary

In this chapter, we first saw how to implement performance counters to keep track of the frequency and response times of off-box requests. We then discussed a number of ways to reduce wait times. These included waiting concurrently instead of sequentially, reducing the overhead of session state kept on a state server or database server, minimizing delays due to thread locking and optimizing disk writes. We also had a quick look at disabling 8.3 filenames.

In the next chapter, we'll move into DBA territory and see how to speed up database accesses, including applying the correct indexes and identifying and optimizing expensive queries.

8
Speeding up Database Access

In many websites, database access is the most expensive part of producing a web page. This chapter shows how to identify the most common sources of delays and how to resolve them.

SQL Server is a very large subject in itself. Rather than attempting to cover all aspects of SQL Server database access, this chapter focuses on those areas where you are likely to gain the biggest payoffs.

It consists of two major sections:

- The *Pinpointing bottlenecks* section shows how to pinpoint and prioritize a number of common bottlenecks, so that you can spend your time where it counts the most. These bottlenecks include:
    - Missing indexes
    - Expensive queries
    - Locking
    - Execution plan reuse
    - Fragmentation
    - Memory
    - Disk
    - CPU

The *Fixing bottlenecks* section then shows how to actually fix each of the bottlenecks you prioritized in the previous section.

Pinpointing bottlenecks

In this section, we'll identify the biggest bottlenecks. In the next section, we'll see how to fix the bottlenecks we identified here.

Missing indexes and expensive queries

You can greatly improve the performance of your queries by reducing the number of reads executed by those queries. The more reads you execute, the more potentially you stress the disk, CPU, and memory. Secondly, a query reading a resource normally blocks another query from updating that resource. If the updating query has to wait while holding locks itself, it may then delay a chain of other queries. Finally, unless the entire database fits in memory, each time data is read from disk, other data is evicted from memory. If that data is needed later, it then needs to be read from the disk again.

The most effective way to reduce the number of reads is to create sufficient indexes on your tables. Just as an index in a book, an SQL Server index allows a query to go straight to the table row(s) it needs, rather than having to scan the entire table. Indexes are not a cure-all though—they do incur overhead and slow down updates, so they need to be used wisely.

In this section, we'll see:

- How to identify missing indexes that would reduce the number of reads in the database

- How to identify those queries that create the greatest strain, either because they are used very often, or because they are just plain expensive

- How to identify superfluous indexes that take resources but provide little benefit

Missing indexes

SQL Server allows you to put indexes on table columns, to speed up WHERE and JOIN statements on those columns. When the query optimizer optimizes a query, it stores information about those indexes it would have liked to have used, but weren't available. You can access this information with the **Dynamic Management View (DMV)** dm_db_missing_index_details (indexesqueries.sql in the downloaded code bundle):

```
select d.name AS DatabaseName, mid.*
from sys.dm_db_missing_index_details mid
join sys.databases d ON mid.database_id=d.database_id
```

The most important columns returned by this query are:

Column	Description
DatabaseName	Name of the database this row relates to.
equality_columns	Comma-separated list of columns used with the equals operator, such as: column=value
inequality_columns	Comma-separated list of columns used with a comparison operator other than the equals operator, such as: column>value
included_columns	Comma-separated list of columns that could profitably be included in an index. Included columns will be discussed in the *Fixing bottlenecks* section, *Missing indexes* subsection.
statement	Name of the table where the index is missing.

This information is not persistent—you will lose it after a server restart.

An alternative is to use **Database Engine Tuning Advisor**, which is included with SQL Server 2008 (except for the Express version). This tool analyzes a trace of database operations and identifies an optimal set of indexes that takes the requirements of all queries into account. It even gives you the SQL statements needed to create the missing indexes it identified.

The first step is to get a trace of database operations during a representative period. If your database is the busiest during business hours, then that is probably when you want to run the trace:

1. Start SQL Profiler. Click on **Start | Programs | Microsoft SQL Server 2008 | Performance Tools | SQL Server Profiler**.

2. In SQL Profiler, click on **File | New Trace**.

3. Click on the **Events Selection** tab.

4. You want to minimize the number of events captured to reduce the load on the server. Deselect every event, except **SQL:BatchCompleted** and **RPC:Completed**. It is those events that contain resource information for each batch, and so are used by Database Engine Tuning Advisor to analyze the workload. Make sure that the **TextData** column is selected for both the events.

5. To capture events related only to your database, click on the **Column Filters** button. Click on **DatabaseName** in the left column, expand **Like** in the right-hand pane, and enter your database name. Click on **OK**.

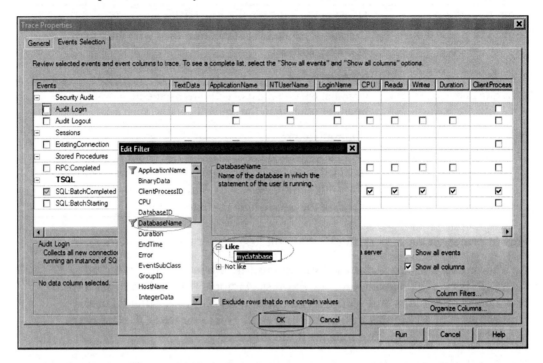

6. To further cut down the trace and only trace calls from your website, put a filter on **ApplicationName**, so only events where this equals ".Net SqlClient Data Provider" will be recorded.

7. Click on the **Run** button to start the trace. You will see batch completions scrolling through the window. At any stage, you can click on **File | Save** or press *Ctrl + S* to save the trace to a file.

8. Save the template so that you don't have to recreate it next time. Click on **File | Save As | Trace Template**. Fill in a descriptive name and click on **OK**. Next time you create a new trace by clicking on **File | New Trace**, you can retrieve the template from the **Use the template** drop-down.

    Sending all these events to your screen takes a lot of server resources. You probably won't be looking at it all day anyway. The solution is to save your trace as a script and then use that to run a background trace. You'll also be able to reuse the script later on.

9. Click on **File | Export | Script Trace Definition | For SQL Server 2005 – 2008**. Save the file with a `.sql` extension. You can now close SQL Server Profiler, which will also stop the trace.

10. In SQL Server Management Studio, open the `.sql` file you just created. Find the string `InsertFileNameHere` and replace it with the full path of the file where you want the log stored. Leave off the extension; the script will set it to `.trc`. Press *Ctrl + S* to save the `.sql` file.

11. To start the trace, press *F5* to run the `.sql` file. It will tell you the trace ID of this trace.

12. To see the status of this trace and any other traces in the system, execute the following command in a query window:

```
select * from ::fn_trace_getinfo(default)
```

Find the row with property 5 for your trace ID. If the value column in that row is 1, your trace is running. The trace with trace ID 1 is a system trace.

13. To stop the trace after it has captured a representative period, assuming your trace ID is two, run the following command:

```
exec sp_trace_setstatus 2,0
```

To restart it, run:

```
exec sp_trace_setstatus 2,1
```

14. To stop and close it so that you can access the trace file, run:

```
exec sp_trace_setstatus 2,0
exec sp_trace_setstatus 2,2
```

Now, run Database Engine Tuning Advisor:

1. Start SQL Profiler. Click on **Start | Programs | Microsoft SQL Server 2008 | Performance Tools | Database Engine Tuning Advisor**.

2. In the Workload area, select your trace file. In the **Database for workload analysis** drop-down, select the first database you want to be analyzed.

3. Under **Select databases and tables to tune**, select the databases for which you want index recommendations.

4. Especially with a big trace, Database Engine Tuning Advisor may take a long time to do its analysis. On the **Tuning Options** tab, you can tell it when to stop analyzing. This is just a limit; if it is done sooner, it will produce results as soon as it is done.

5. To start the analysis, click on the **Start Analysis** button in the toolbar.

Keep in mind that Database Engine Tuning Advisor is just a computer program. Consider its recommendations, but make up your own mind. Be sure to give it a trace with a representative workload, otherwise its recommendations may make things worse rather than better. For example, if you provide a trace that was captured at night when you process few transactions but execute lots of reporting jobs, its advice is going to be skewed towards optimizing reporting, not transactions.

Expensive queries

If you use SQL Server 2008 or higher, you can use the activity monitor to find the recently-executed expensive queries. In SSMS, right-click on your database server (normally in the top, left corner of the window) and choose **Activity Monitor**.

You can get a lot more information by using the DMV dm_exec_query_stats. When the query optimizer creates the execution plan for a query, it caches the plan for reuse. Each time a plan is used to execute a query, performance statistics are kept. You can access those statistics with dm_exec_query_stats (indexesqueries.sql in the downloaded code bundle):

```
SELECT
  est.text AS batchtext,
  SUBSTRING(est.text, (eqs.statement_start_offset/2)+1,
    (CASE eqs.statement_end_offset WHEN -1
    THEN DATALENGTH(est.text)
    ELSE eqs.statement_end_offset END -
    ((eqs.statement_start_offset/2) + 1))) AS querytext,
  eqs.creation_time, eqs.last_execution_time, eqs.execution_count,
  eqs.total_worker_time, eqs.last_worker_time,
  eqs.min_worker_time, eqs.max_worker_time,
  eqs.total_physical_reads, eqs.last_physical_reads,
  eqs.min_physical_reads, eqs.max_physical_reads,
  eqs.total_elapsed_time, eqs.last_elapsed_time,
  eqs.min_elapsed_time, eqs.max_elapsed_time,
  eqs.total_logical_writes, eqs.last_logical_writes,
  eqs.min_logical_writes, eqs.max_logical_writes,
  eqs.query_plan_hash
FROM
  sys.dm_exec_query_stats AS eqs
  CROSS APPLY sys.dm_exec_sql_text(eqs.sql_handle) AS est
ORDER BY eqs.total_physical_reads DESC
```

A limitation of this DMV is that when you run it, not all queries that have run since the last server restart will have a plan in cache. Some plans may have expired due to lack of use. Plans that were very cheap to produce, but not necessarily cheap to run, may not have been stored at all. And if a plan has been recompiled, the statistics only apply for the period since recompilation.

Another limitation is that this query is only suitable for stored procedures. If you use ad hoc queries, the parameters are embedded in the query. This causes the query optimizer to produce a plan for each set of parameters, unless the query has been parameterized. This is further discussed in the *Execution plan reuse* section.

To get around this, `dm_exec_query_stats` returns a column `query_plan_hash` which is the same for each query that has the same execution plan. By aggregating on this column using `GROUP BY`, you can get aggregate performance data for queries that share the same logic.

The query returns the following information:

Column	Description
batchtext	Text of the entire batch or stored procedure containing the query.
querytext	Text of the actual query.
creation_time	Time that the execution plan was created.
last_execution_time	Last time the plan was executed.
execution_count	Number of times the plan was executed after it was created. This is not the number of times the query itself was executed; its plan may have been recompiled at some stage.
total_worker_time	Total amount of CPU time in microseconds that was consumed by executions of this plan since it was created.
last_worker_time	CPU time in microseconds that was consumed the last time the plan was executed.
min_worker_time	Minimum CPU time in microseconds that this plan has ever consumed during a single execution.
max_worker_time	Maximum CPU time in microseconds that this plan has ever consumed during a single execution.
total_physical_reads	Total number of physical reads performed by executions of this plan since it was compiled.
last_physical_reads	Number of physical reads performed the last time the plan was executed.
min_physical_reads	Minimum number of physical reads that this plan has ever performed during a single execution.
max_physical_reads	Maximum number of physical reads that this plan has ever performed during a single execution.
total_logical_writes	Total number of logical writes performed by executions of this plan since it was compiled.
last_logical_writes	Number of logical writes performed the last time the plan was executed.

Column	Description
min_logical_writes	Minimum number of logical writes that this plan has ever performed during a single execution.
max_logical_writes	Maximum number of logical writes that this plan has ever performed during a single execution.
total_elapsed_time	Total elapsed time in microseconds for completed executions of this plan.
last_elapsed_time	Elapsed time in microseconds for the most recently completed execution of this plan.
min_elapsed_time	Minimum elapsed time in microseconds for any completed execution of this plan.
max_elapsed_time	Maximum elapsed time in microseconds for any completed execution of this plan.

An alternative to using dm_exec_query_stats is to analyze the trace you made with SQL Server Profiler. After all, this contains performance data for every completed batch. A batch corresponds to a stored procedure or a query if you use ad hoc queries.

To investigate this a bit further, load the trace file into a table. You can use Profiler to do this:

1. Start SQL Profiler. Click on **Start | Programs | Microsoft SQL Server 2008 | Performance Tools | SQL Server Profiler**.

2. To open the trace file, click on **File | Open | Trace File**, or press *Ctrl + O*. If you want, you can now analyze the trace in the profiler.

3. To save the trace to a table, click on **File | Save As | Trace Table**. If the table you specify does not yet exist, the profiler will create it.

Alternatively, use fn_trace_gettable, shown as follows (indexesqueries.sql in the downloaded code bundle):

```
SELECT * INTO newtracetable
FROM ::fn_trace_gettable('c:\trace.trc', default)
```

The most obvious way to find the most expensive queries or stored procedures is to aggregate the performance data in the table by query or stored procedure, using GROUP BY. However, when you have a look at the TextData column in the table with trace results, you'll find that all queries or stored procedure calls are listed with actual parameter values. To aggregate them, you'll have to filter out those values.

If you send stored procedure calls to the database, good for you. In that case, it isn't too hard to remove the parameters, because they always come after the stored procedure name. In the file processtrace.sql in the downloaded code bundle, you will find an SQL script that does exactly the same thing. It also then aggregates the performance data per stored procedure (stored procedures are discussed further in the *Fixing bottlenecks* section, *Execution plan reuse* subsection).

If you send ad hoc queries, removing the variable bits of the queries will be a lot more difficult, because their locations are different for each query. The following resources may make your job a bit easier:

- SQL Nexus Tool—Recommended free tool that helps find the most expensive queries, available at http://sqlnexus.codeplex.com/
- Trace-scrubbing Tools available at http://msdn.microsoft.com/en-us/library/aa175800(sql.80).aspx

Once you've identified the most expensive queries, you can find out whether adding indexes would speed up their execution.

1. Open a query window in SSMS.
2. From the **Query** menu, choose **Include Actual Execution Plan** or press *Ctrl + M*.
3. Copy an expensive query in the query window and execute it. Above the results pane, you will see a tab **Execution plan**. Click on that tab.
4. If the query optimizer found that an index was missing, you will see a message in green.
5. For more information, right-click in the lower pane and choose **Show Execution Plan XML**. In the XML, look for the **MissingIndexes** element.

If you identified missing indexes, refer to the *Missing indexes* subsection in the *Fixing bottlenecks* section to see how indexes work and how to create them.

If you found any particularly expensive queries, refer to the *Expensive queries* subsection in the *Fixing bottlenecks* section.

Unused indexes

A drawback of indexes is that they need to be updated when the data itself is updated, causing delays. They also take storage space. If an index slows down updates but is hardly used for reading, you're better off dropping it.

Use the DMV `dm_db_index_usage_stats` to get usage information on each index (`indexesqueries.sql` in downloaded code bundle) as shown:

```
SELECT d.name, t.name, i.name, ius.*
FROM sys.dm_db_index_usage_stats ius
JOIN sys.databases d ON d.database_id = ius.database_id
JOIN sys.tables t ON t.object_id = ius.object_id
JOIN sys.indexes i ON i.object_id = ius.object_id AND i.index_id =
ius.index_id
ORDER BY user_updates DESC
```

This gives you the name, table, and database of each index that has seen activity since the last server restart, and the number of updates and reads since the last server restart.

Column `user_updates`, in particular, shows the number of updates caused by `INSERT`, `UPDATE`, or `DELETE` operations. If this is high in relation to the number of reads, consider dropping the index, as shown in the following code:

```
DROP INDEX IX_Title ON dbo.Book
```

You may see clustered indexes being updated. In the *Missing indexes* subsection in the *Fixing bottlenecks* section, we'll see how the table itself is a part of the clustered index, which means that any table update is also an update of the clustered index.

Locking

In a database with lots of queries executing, some queries may try to access the same resource, such as a table or index. You wouldn't want one query to read a resource while another is updating it; otherwise, you could get inconsistent results.

To stop a query from accessing a resource, SQL Server locks the resource. This will inevitably lead to some delays as queries wait for a lock to be released. To find out whether these delays are excessive, check the following performance counters on the database server with `perfmon` (you saw how to do this in *Chapter 2, Reducing Time to First Byte* in the *Pinpointing bottlenecks* section, *Thread usage* subsection):

Category: SQLServer:Latches	
Total Latch Wait Time (ms)	Total wait time in milliseconds for latches in the last second.

Category: SQLServer:Locks	
Lock Timeouts/sec	Number of lock requests per second that timed out. This includes requests for NOWAIT locks.
Lock Wait Time (ms)	Total wait time in milliseconds for locks in the last second.
Number of Deadlocks/sec	Number of lock requests per second that resulted in a deadlock.

A high number for **Total Latch Wait Time** (ms) indicates that SQL Server is waiting too long for its own synchronization mechanism. **Lock Timeouts/sec** should be zero during normal operation and **Lock Wait Time** (ms) very low. If they are not, queries keep waiting for too long for the locks to be released.

Finally, **Number of Deadlocks/sec** should be zero. If not, you have queries waiting on each other to release a lock, preventing either to move forward. SQL Server eventually detects this condition and resolves it by rolling back one of the queries, which means wasted time and wasted work.

If you find locking issues, refer to the *Locking* subsection in the *Fixing bottlenecks* section, to see how to determine which queries cause excessive lock wait times, and how to fix the problem.

Execution plan reuse

Before a query is executed, the SQL Server query optimizer compiles a cost-effective execution plan. This takes many CPU cycles. Because of this, SQL Server caches the execution plan in memory, in the plan cache. It then tries to match incoming queries with those that have already been cached.

In this section, you'll see how to measure how well the plan cache is being used. If there is room for improvement, refer to the *Execution plan reuse* subsection in the *Fixing bottlenecks* section to learn how to fix this.

Performance counters

Start by checking the following performance counters on the database server with perfmon (you saw how to do this in *Chapter 2, Reduce Time to First Byte, Pinpointing bottlenecks* section, *Thread usage* subsection):

Category: Processor (_Total)	
% Processor Time	The percentage of elapsed time that the processor is busy.

Category: SQL Server:SQL Statistics	
SQL Compilations/sec	Number of batch compiles and statement compiles per second. Expected to be very high initially after server startup.
SQL Re-Compilations/sec	Number of recompiles per second.

These counters will show high values at server startup as every incoming query needs to be compiled. The plan cache sits in memory, so doesn't survive a restart. During normal operation, you would expect compilations per second to be less than 100, and re-compilations per second to be close to zero.

dm_exec_query_optimizer_info

Alternatively, you could look at the time spent by the server on optimizing queries. Because query optimizations are heavily CPU-bound, almost all the time is spent by a CPU on this.

The **Dynamic Management View (DMV)** `sys.dm_exec_query_optimizer_info` gives you the number of query optimizations since the last server restart, and the elapsed time in seconds it took on average to complete them (`executionplan.sql` in the downloaded code bundle):

```
SELECT
   occurrence AS [Query optimizations since server restart],
   value AS [Avg time per optimization in seconds],
   occurrence * value AS [Time spend optimizing since server
     restart in seconds]
FROM sys.dm_exec_query_optimizer_info
WHERE counter='elapsed time'
```

Run this query, wait for a while, and then run it again to find the time spent on optimizing in that period. Be sure to measure the time between the runs, so that you can work out what proportion of time the server spends on optimizing queries.

sys.dm_exec_cached_plans

The DMV `sys.dm_exec_cached_plans` provides information on all execution plans in the plan cache. You can combine this with the DMV `sys.dm_exec_sql_text` to find out how often the plan for a given query has been reused. If you get little reuse for an otherwise busy query or a stored procedure, you are getting too little benefit out of the plan cache (`executionplan.sql` in downloaded code bundle):

```
SELECT ecp.objtype, ecp.usecounts, ecp.size_in_bytes,
   REPLACE(REPLACE(est.text, char(13), ''), char(10), ' ') AS querytext
FROM sys.dm_exec_cached_plans ecp
cross apply sys.dm_exec_sql_text(ecp.plan_handle) est
WHERE cacheobjtype='Compiled Plan'
```

The column `objtype` is `Proc` for stored procedures and `Adhoc` for ad hoc queries, while the field `usecounts` shows how often a plan has been used.

In the *Missing indexes and expensive queries* section, you saw how to identify busy queries and stored procedures.

Fragmentation

The data and indexes in a database are organized on disk in 8-KB pages. A page is the smallest unit that SQL Server uses to transfer data to or from disk.

When you insert or update data, a page may run out of room. SQL Server then creates another page, and moves half of the contents of the existing page to the new page. That leaves free space not only in the new page, but in the original page as well. That way, if you keep inserting or updating data in the original page, it doesn't split again and again.

This means that after many updates, inserts, and deletes as well, you'll wind up with lots of pages that are partially empty. This takes more disk space than needed, but more importantly also slows down reading, because SQL Server now has to read more pages to access data. The pages may also wind up in a different physical order on disk than the logical order in which SQL Server needs to read them. As a result, instead of simply reading each page sequentially right after each other, it needs to wait for the disk head to reach the next page, hence more delays.

To establish the level of fragmentation for each table and index in your database, use the `dm_db_index_physical_stats` DMV (`fragmentation.sql` in the downloaded code bundle):

```
DECLARE @DatabaseName sysname
SET @DatabaseName = 'mydatabase' --use your own database name

SELECT o.name AS TableName, i.name AS IndexName, ips.index_type_desc,
  ips.avg_fragmentation_in_percent, ips.page_count, ips.fragment_
count,
  ips.avg_page_space_used_in_percent
FROM sys.dm_db_index_physical_stats(
  DB_ID(@DatabaseName),
  NULL, NULL, NULL, 'Sampled') ips
JOIN sys.objects o ON ips.object_id = o.object_id
JOIN sys.indexes i ON (ips.object_id = i.object_id) AND (ips.index_id
= i.index_id)
WHERE (ips.page_count >= 7) AND (ips.avg_fragmentation_in_percent >
20)
ORDER BY o.name, i.name
```

This gives you all the tables and indexes that take over seven pages and that are more than 20 percent fragmented. Tables and indexes taking less than seven pages tend to show high levels of fragmentation because of the way SQL Server organizes them on disk—there is little point in defragmenting them. Also, fragmentation below 20 percent is not really an issue.

When you see index type CLUSTERED INDEX in an entry, it really refers to the actual table, because the table is a part of the clustered index. Index type HEAP refers to a table without a clustered index.

If you find any tables or indexes that are over 20 percent fragmented and take over seven pages, refer to the *Fragmentation* subsection in the *Fixing bottlenecks* section to see how to resolve this.

Memory

To see if lack of memory is slowing down the database server, check the following counters in perfmon:

Category: Memory	
Pages/sec	When the server runs out of memory, it stores information temporarily on disk, and then later reads it back when needed, which is very expensive. This counter indicates how often this happens.

Category: SQL Server:Buffer Manager	
Page Life Expectancy	Number of seconds a page will stay in the buffer pool without being used. The greater the life expectancy, the greater the chance that SQL Server will be able to get a page from memory instead of having to read it from disk.
Buffer cache hit ratio	Percentage of pages that were found in the buffer pool, without having to read from disk.

If **Pages/sec** is consistently high or **Page Life Expectancy** is consistently low, say below 300, or **Buffer cache hit ratio** is consistently low, say below 90 percent, SQL Server may not have enough memory. This will lead to excessive disk I/O, causing a greater stress on the CPU and disk.

Refer to the *Memory* subsection in the *Fixing bottlenecks* section to see how to fix this issue.

Disk usage

SQL Server is heavily disk-bound, so solving disk bottlenecks can make a big difference. If you found memory shortages in the previous section, fix those first, because a memory shortage can lead to excessive disk usage in itself. Otherwise check the following counters to see if there is a disk bottleneck for some other reason:

Categories: PhysicalDisk and LogicalDisk	
% Disk Time	Percentage of elapsed time that the selected disk was busy reading or writing.
Avg. Disk Queue Length	Average number of read and write requests queued during the sample interval.
Current Disk Queue Length	Current number of requests queued.

If % **Disk Time** is consistently over 85 percent, the disk system is stressed.

Avg. Disk Queue Length and **Current Disk Queue Length** refer to the number of tasks that are queued at the disk controller or are being processed. You want to see a counter value of two or less. If you use a RAID array where the controller is attached to several disks, you want to see counter values of two times the number of individual disks or less.

Refer to the *Disk usage* subsection in the *Fixing bottlenecks* section to fix disk issues.

CPU

If you found memory or disk issues in the previous sections, fix those first because they will stress the CPU as well. Otherwise, check the following counters to see whether the CPU is stressed for another reason:

Category: Processor	
% Processor Time	Proportion of time that the processor is busy.

Category: System	
Processor Queue Length	Number of threads waiting to be processed.

If % **Processor Time** is consistently over 75 percent, or **Processor Queue Length** is consistently greater than two, the CPU is probably stressed. Refer to the *CPU* subsection in the *Fixing bottlenecks* section to resolve this.

Fixing bottlenecks

Now that you have pinpointed the bottlenecks to prioritize, skip to the appropriate subsection to find out how to fix those bottlenecks.

Missing indexes

Just as using an index in a book to find a particular bit of information is often much faster than reading all pages, SQL Server indexes can make finding a particular row in a table dramatically faster by cutting down the number of read operations.

This section first discusses the two types of indexes supported by SQL Server: clustered and non-clustered. It also goes into included columns, a feature of non-clustered indexes. After that, we'll look at when to use each type of index.

Clustered index

Take the following table (`missingindexes.sql` in the downloaded code bundle):

```
CREATE TABLE [dbo].[Book](
    [BookId] [int] IDENTITY(1,1) NOT NULL,
    [Title] [nvarchar](50) NULL,
    [Author] [nvarchar](50) NULL,
    [Price] [decimal](4, 2) NULL)
```

Because this table has no clustered index, it is called a heap table. Its records are unordered, and to get all books with a given title, you have to read all the records. It has a very simple structure:

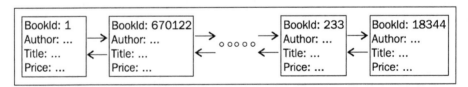

Let's see how long it takes to locate a record in this table. That way, we can compare against the performance of a table with an index.

To do that in a meaningful way, first insert a million records into the table (code to do this is in `missingindexes.sql` in the downloaded code bundle).

Tell SQL Server to show I/O and timing details of each query we run:

```
SET STATISTICS IO ON
SET STATISTICS TIME ON
```

Also, before each query, flush the SQL Server memory cache:

```
CHECKPOINT
DBCC DROPCLEANBUFFERS
```

Now, run the query below with a million records in the Book table:

```
SELECT Title, Author, Price FROM dbo.Book WHERE BookId = 5000
```

The results on my machine are: reads: 9564, CPU time: 109 ms, elapsed time: 808 ms.

SQL Server stores all data in 8-KB pages. This shows that it read 9564 pages, that is, the entire table.

Now, add a clustered index:

```
ALTER TABLE Book
ADD CONSTRAINT [PK_Book] PRIMARY KEY CLUSTERED ([BookId] ASC)
```

This puts the index on column BookId, making WHERE and JOIN statements on BookId faster. It sorts the table by BookId and adds a structure called a **B-tree** to speed up access:

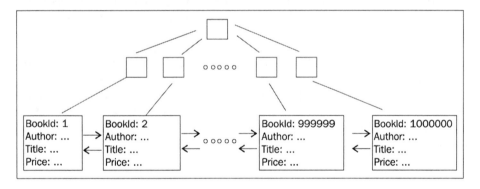

BookId is now used the same way as a page number in a book. Because the pages in a book are sorted by page number, finding a page by page number is very fast.

Now, run the same query again to see the difference:

```
SELECT Title, Author, Price FROM dbo.Book WHERE BookId = 5000
```

The results are: reads: 2, CPU time: 0 ms, elapsed time: 32 ms.

The number of reads of 8-KB pages has gone from 9564 to 2, CPU time from 109ms to less than 1 ms, and elapsed time from 808 ms to 32 ms. That's a dramatic improvement.

Non-clustered index

Now let's select by `Title` instead of `BookId`:

```
SELECT Title, Author FROM dbo.Book WHERE Title = 'Don Quixote'
```

The results are: reads: 9146, CPU time: 156 ms, elapsed time: 1653 ms.

These results are pretty similar to what we got with the heap table, which is no wonder, seeing that there is no index on `Title`.

The solution obviously is to put an index on `Title`. However, because a clustered index involves sorting the table records on the index field, there can be only one clustered index. We've already sorted on `BookId`, and the table can't be sorted on `Title` at the same time.

The solution is to create a non-clustered index. This is essentially a duplicate of the table records, this time sorted by `Title`. To save space, SQL Server leaves out the other columns, such as `Author` and `Price`. You can have up to 249 non-clustered indexes on a table.

Because we still want to access those other columns in queries though, we need a way to get from the non-clustered index records to the actual table records. The solution is to add the `BookId` to the non-clustered records. Because `BookId` has the clustered index, once we have found a `BookId` via the non-clustered index, we can use the clustered index to get to the actual table record. This second step is called a key lookup.

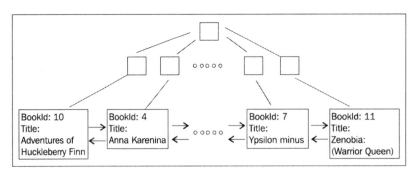

Why go through the clustered index? Why not put the physical address of the table record in the non-clustered index record? The answer is that when you update a table record, it may get bigger, causing SQL Server to move subsequent records to make space. If non-clustered indexes contained physical addresses, they would all have to be updated when this happens. It's a tradeoff between slightly slower reads and much slower updates. If there is no clustered index or if it is not unique, then non-clustered index records do have the physical address.

To see what a non-clustered index will do for us, first create it as follows:

```
CREATE NONCLUSTERED INDEX [IX_Title] ON [dbo].[Book]([Title] ASC)
```

Now, run the same query again:

```
SELECT Title, Author FROM dbo.Book WHERE Title = 'Don Quixote'
```

The results are: reads: 4, CPU time: 0 ms, elapsed time: 46 ms.

The number of reads has gone from 9146 to 4, CPU time from 156 ms to less than 1 ms, and elapsed time from 1653 ms to 46 ms. This means that having a non-clustered index is not quite as good as having a clustered index, but still dramatically better than having no index at all.

Included columns

You can squeeze a bit more performance out of a non-clustered index by cutting out the key lookup—the second step where SQL Server uses the clustered index to find the actual record.

Have another look at the test query—it simply returns `Title` and `Author`. `Title` is already present in the non-clustered index record. If you were to add `Author` to the non-clustered index record as well, there would be no longer any need for SQL Server to access the table record, enabling it to skip the key lookup. It would look similar to the following:

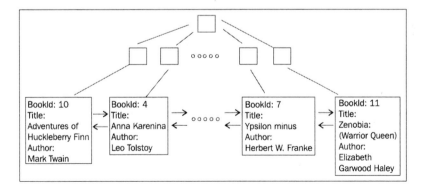

This can be done by including `Author` in the non-clustered index:

```
CREATE NONCLUSTERED INDEX [IX_Title] ON [dbo].[Book]([Title] ASC)
INCLUDE(Author)
WITH drop_existing
```

Now, run the query again:

```
SELECT Title, Author FROM dbo.Book WHERE Title = 'Don Quixote'
```

The results are: reads: 2, CPU time: 0 ms, elapsed time: 26 ms.

The number of reads has gone from 4 to 2, and elapsed time from 46 ms to 26 ms; that's almost 50 percent improvement. In absolute terms, the gain isn't all that great, but for a query that is executed very frequently, this may be worthwhile. Don't overdo this—the bigger you make the non-clustered index records, the fewer fit on an 8-KB page, forcing SQL Server to read more pages.

Selecting columns to give an index

Because indexes do create overhead, you want to carefully select the columns to give indexes. Before starting the selection process, keep the following in mind:

- Putting a Primary Key on a column by default gives it a clustered index (unless you override the default). So, you may already have many columns in your database with an index. As you'll see later in the *When to use a clustered index* section, putting the clustered index on the ID column of a record is almost always a good idea.
- Putting an index on a table column affects all queries that use that table. Don't focus on just one query.
- Before introducing an index on your live database, test the index in development to make sure it really does improve performance.

Let's look at when and when not to use an index, and when to use a clustered index.

When to use an index

You can follow this decision process when selecting columns to give an index:

- Start by looking at the most expensive queries. You identified those in the *Pinpointing bottlenecks* section, *Missing indexes and expensive queries* subsection. There, you also saw indexing suggestions generated by Database Engine Tuning Advisor.

- Look at putting an index on at least one column involved in every JOIN.

- Consider columns used in ORDER BY and GROUP BY clauses. If there is an index on such a column, than SQL Server doesn't have to sort the column again because the index already keeps the column values in sorted order.

- Consider columns used in WHERE clauses, especially if the WHERE will select a small number of records. However, keep in mind the following:

  ° A WHERE clause that applies a function to the column value can't use an index on that column, because the output of the function is not in the index. Take for example the following:

    ```
    SELECT Title, Author FROM dbo.Book
      WHERE LEFT(Title, 3) = 'Don'
    ```

    Putting an index on the Title column won't make this query any faster.

  ° Likewise, SQL Server can't use an index if you use LIKE in a WHERE clause with a wild card at the start of the search string, as in the following:

    ```
    SELECT Title, Author FROM dbo.Book
      WHERE Title LIKE '%Quixote'
    ```

    However, if the search string starts with constant text instead of a wild card, an index can be used:

    ```
    SELECT Title, Author FROM dbo.Book
      WHERE Title LIKE 'Don%'
    ```

- Consider columns that have a UNIQUE constraint. Having an index on the column makes it easier for SQL Server to check whether a new value would not be unique.

- The MIN and MAX functions benefit from working on a column with an index. Because the values are sorted, there is no need to go through the entire table to find the minimum or maximum.

- Think twice before putting an index on a column that takes a lot of space. If you use a non-clustered index, the column values will be duplicated in the index. If you use a clustered index, the column values will be used in all non-clustered indexes. The increased sizes of the index records means fewer fit in each 8-KB page, forcing SQL Server to read more pages. The same applies to including columns in non-clustered indexes.

When not to use an index

Having too many indexes can actually hurt performance. Here are the main reasons not to use an index on a column:

- The column gets updated often
- The column has low specificity, meaning it has lots of duplicate values

Let's look at each reason in turn.

Column updated often

When you update a column without an index, SQL Server needs to write one 8-KB page to disk, provided there are no page splits.

However, if the column has a non-clustered index, or if it is included in a non-clustered index, SQL Server needs to update the index as well, so it has to write at least one additional page to disk. It also has to update the B-tree structure used in the index, potentially leading to more page writes.

If you update a column with a clustered index, the non-clustered index records that use the old value need to be updated too, because the clustered index key is used in the non-clustered indexes to navigate to the actual table records. Secondly, remember that the table records themselves are sorted based on the clustered index. If the update causes the sort order of a record to change, that may mean more writes. Finally, the clustered index needs to keep its B-tree up-to-date.

This doesn't mean you cannot have indexes on columns that get updated; just be aware that indexes slow down updates. Test the effect of any indexes you add.

If an index is critical but rarely used, for example only for overnight report generation, consider dropping the index and recreating it when it is needed.

Low specificity

Even if there is an index on a column, the query optimizer won't always use it. Remember, each time SQL Server accesses a record via an index, it has to go through the index structure. In the case of a non-clustered index, it may have to do a key lookup as well. If you're selecting all books with price $20, and lots of books happen to have that price, than it might be quicker to simply read all book records rather than going through an index over and over again. In that case, it is said that the $20 price has low specificity.

You can use a simple query to determine the average selectivity of the values in a column. For example, to find the average selectivity of the `Price` column in the `Book` table, use (`missingindexes.sql` in downloaded code bundle):

```
SELECT
  COUNT(DISTINCT Price) AS 'Unique prices',
  COUNT(*) AS 'Number of rows',
  CAST((100 * COUNT(DISTINCT Price) / CAST(COUNT(*) AS REAL))
    AS nvarchar(10)) + '%' AS 'Selectivity'
FROM Book
```

If every book has a unique price, selectivity will be 100 percent. However, if half the books cost $20 and the other half $30, then average selectivity will be only 50 percent. If the selectivity is 85 percent or less, an index is likely to incur more overhead than it would save.

Some prices may occur a lot more often than other prices. To see the specificity of each individual price, you would run (`missingindexes.sql` in downloaded code bundle):

```
DECLARE @c real
SELECT @c = CAST(COUNT(*) AS real) FROM Book
SELECT
  Price,
  COUNT(BookId) AS 'Number of rows',
  CAST((1 - (100 * COUNT(BookId) / @c))
    AS nvarchar(20)) + '%' AS 'Selectivity'
FROM Book
GROUP BY Price
ORDER BY COUNT(BookId)
```

The query optimizer is unlikely to use a non-clustered index for a price whose specificity is below 85 percent. It figures out the specificity of each price by keeping statistics on the values in the table.

When to use a clustered index

You saw that there are two types of indexes, clustered and non-clustered, and that you can have only one clustered index. How do you determine the lucky column that will have the clustered index?

To work this out, let's first look at the characteristics of a clustered index against a non-clustered index:

Characteristic	Clustered index compared to a non-clustered index
Reading	Faster: Because there is no need for key lookups. No difference if all the required columns are included in the non-clustered index.
Updating	Slower: Not only the table record, but also all non-clustered index records potentially need to be updated.
Inserting/Deleting	Faster: With a non-clustered index, inserting a new record in the table means inserting a new record in the non-clustered index as well. With a clustered index, the table is effectively part of the index, so there is no need for the second insert. The same goes for deleting a record.
	On the other hand, when the record is inserted at any place in the table but the very end, the insert may cause a page split where half the content of the 8-KB page is moved to another page. Having a page split in a non-clustered index is less likely, because its records are smaller (they normally don't have all columns that a table record has), so more records fit on a page.
	When the record is inserted at the end of the table, there won't be a page split.
Column Size	Needs to be kept short and fast – Every non-clustered index contains a clustered index value, to do the key lookup. Every access via a non-clustered index has to use that value, so you want it to be fast for the server to process. That makes a column of type `int` a lot better to put a clustered index on than a column of type `nvarchar(50)`.

If only one column requires an index, this comparison shows that you'll probably want to give it the clustered index rather than a non-clustered index.

If multiple columns need indexes, you'll probably want to put the clustered index on the primary key column:

- **Reading**: The primary key tends to be involved in a lot of `JOIN` clauses, making read performance important.
- **Updating**: The primary key should never or rarely get updated, because that would mean changing referring foreign keys as well.

- **Inserting/Deleting**: Most often you'll make the primary key an IDENTITY column, so each new record is assigned a unique, ever increasing number. This means that if you put the clustered index on the primary key, new records are always added at the end of the table. When a record is added at the end of a table with a clustered index and there is no space in the current page, the new record goes into a new page but the rest of the data in the current page stays in the page. In other words, there is no expensive page split.

- **Size**: Most often, the primary key is of type int, which is short and fast.

Indeed, when you set the primary key on a column in the SSMS table designer, SSMS gives that column the clustered index by default, unless another column already has the clustered index.

Maintaining indexes

Do the following to keep your indexes working efficiently:

- **Defragment indexes**: Repeated updates cause indexes and tables to become fragmented, decreasing performance. To measure the level of fragmentation and to see how to defragment indexes, refer to the *Pinpointing bottlenecks* section, *Fragmentation* subsection.

- **Keep statistics updated**: SQL Server maintains statistics to figure out whether to use an index for a given query. These statistics are normally kept up-to-date automatically, but this can be switched off. If you did, make sure statistics are kept up-to-date.

- **Remove unused indexes**: As you saw, indexes speed up read access, but slow down updates. To see how to identify unused indexes, see the *Missing indexes and expensive queries* subsection in the *Pinpointing bottlenecks* section.

Expensive queries

It makes sense to try and optimize those queries that are most expensive because they are used heavily, or because each single execution is just plain expensive. You already saw how to identify and create missing indexes. Here are some more ways to optimize your queries and stored procedures.

Cache aggregation queries

Aggregation statements such as COUNT and AVG are expensive, because they need to access lots of records. If you need aggregated data for a web page, consider caching the aggregation results in a table instead of regenerating them for each web page request. Provided you read the aggregates more often than you update the underlying columns, this will reduce your response time and CPU usage. For example, this code stores a COUNT aggregate in a table Aggregates:

```
DECLARE @n int
SELECT @n = COUNT(*) FROM dbo.Book
UPDATE Aggregates SET BookCount = @n
```

You could update the aggregations whenever the underlying data changes using a trigger or as part of the stored procedure that makes the update. You could also recalculate the aggregations periodically with a SQL Server Job. See how to create such a job at:

- How to: Create a Transact-SQL Job Step (SQL Server Management Studio)
  http://msdn.microsoft.com/en-us/library/ms187910.aspx

Keeping records short

Reducing the amount of space taken per table record speeds up access. Records are stored in 8-KB pages on disk. The more records fit on a page, the fewer pages SQL Server needs to read to retrieve a given set of records.

Here are ways to keep your records short:

- Use short data types. If your values fit in a 1 byte TinyInt, don't use a four-byte Int. If you store simple ASCII characters, use varchar(n) which uses one byte per character, instead of nvarchar(n) which uses two. If you store strings of fixed length, use char(n) or nchar(n) instead of varchar(n) or nvarchar(n), saving two bytes of length field.

- Consider storing large, rarely-used columns off-row. Large object fields such as nvarchar(max), varchar(max), varbinary(max), and XML fields are normally stored in row if smaller than 8000 bytes, and replaced by a 16-bit pointer to an off-row area if larger than 8000 bytes. Storing off-row means that accessing the field takes at least two reads instead of one, but also makes for a much shorter record, which may be desirable if the field is rarely accessed. To force large object fields in a table to be always off-row, use:

  ```
  EXEC sp_tableoption 'mytable', 'large value types out of row',
   '1'
  ```

- Consider vertical partitioning. If some columns in a table are much more frequently accessed than others, put the rarely-accessed columns in a separate table. Access to the frequently-used columns will be faster, at the expense of having to JOIN to the second table when it does get used.

- Avoid repeating columns. For example, don't do the following:

AuthorId	Author	Country	Book Title 1	Book Title 2
1	Charles Dickens	United Kingdom	Oliver Twist	The Pickwick Papers
2	Herman Melville	United States	Moby-Dick	
3	Leo Tolstoy	Russia	Anna Karenina	War and Peace

This solution not only creates long records, but also makes it hard to update book titles, and makes it impossible to have more than two titles per author. Instead, store the book titles in a separate book table, and include an AuthorId column that refers back to the Book's author.

- Avoid duplicate values. For example, don't do the following:

BookId	Book Title	Author	Country
1	Oliver Twist	Charles Dickens	United Kingdom
2	The Pickwick Papers	Charles Dickens	United Kingdom
3	Moby-Dick	Herman Melville	United States
4	Anna Karenina	Leo Tolstoy	Russia
5	War and Peace	Leo Tolstoy	Russia

Here the author's name and country are duplicated for each of their books. In addition to resulting in long records, updating author details now requires multiple record updates and an increased risk of inconsistencies. Store authors and books in separate tables, and have the book records refer back to their Author records.

Considering denormalization

Denormalization is essentially the reverse of the last two points in the previous section—avoid repeating columns and avoid duplicate values.

The issue is that while these recommendations improve update speed, consistency, and record sizes, they do lead to data being spread across tables, meaning more JOINs.

For example, say you have 100 addresses spread over 50 cities, with the cities stored in a separate table. This will shorten the address records and make updating a city name easier, but also means having to do a JOIN each time you retrieve an address. If a city name is unlikely to change and you always retrieve the city along with the rest of the address, than you may be better off including the city name in the address record itself. This solution implies having repeated content (the city name), but on the other hand, you'll have one less JOIN.

Being careful with triggers

Triggers can be very convenient, and great for data integrity. On the other hand, they tend to be hidden from view of developers, so they may not realize that an additional INSERT, UPDATE, or DELETE carries the overhead of a trigger.

Keep your triggers short. They run inside the transaction that caused them to fire, so locks held by that transaction continue to be held while the trigger runs. Remember that even if you do not explicitly create a transaction using BEGIN TRAN, each individual INSERT, UPDATE, or DELETE creates its own transaction for the duration of the operation.

When deciding what indexes to use, don't forget to look at your triggers as well as your stored procedures and functions.

Using table variables for small temporary result sets

Consider replacing temporary tables in your stored procedures with table variables.

For example, instead of writing the following:

```
CREATE TABLE #temp (Id INT, Name nvarchar(100))
INSERT INTO #temp
. . .
```

You would write the following instead:

```
DECLARE @temp TABLE(Id INT, Name nvarchar(100))
INSERT INTO @temp
. . .
```

Table variables have these advantages over temporary tables:

- SQL Server is more likely to store them in memory rather than `tempdb`. That means less traffic and locking in `tempdb`.

- No transaction log overhead.

- Fewer stored procedure recompilations.

However, there are disadvantages as well:

- You can't add indexes or constraints to a table variable after it has been created. If you need an index, it needs to be created as part of the `DECLARE` statement:

  ```
  DECLARE @temp TABLE(Id INT primary key, Name nvarchar(100))
  ```

- They are less efficient than temporary tables when they have more than about 100 rows, because no statistics are created for a table variable. This makes it more difficult for the query optimizer to come up with an optimal execution plan.

Using full-text search instead of LIKE

You may be using `LIKE` to search for substrings in text columns, as shown:

```
SELECT Title, Author FROM dbo.Book WHERE Title LIKE '%Quixote'
```

However, unless the wildcard starts with constant text, SQL Server will not be able to use any index on the column, and so will do a full-table scan instead. Not good.

To improve this situation, consider using SQL Server's Full Text Search feature. This automatically creates an index for all words in the text column, leading to much faster searches. To see how to use Full Text Search, visit:

- Getting Started with Full-Text Search
  http://msdn.microsoft.com/en-us/library/ms142497.aspx

Replacing cursors with set-based code

If you use cursors, consider replacing them with set-based code. Performance improvements of a 1000 times are not uncommon. Set-based code uses internal algorithms that are much better optimized than you could ever hope to achieve with a cursor.

For more information about converting cursors to set based code, visit:

- How Developers Can Avoid Transact-SQL Cursors

  `http://www.code-magazine.com/Article.aspx?quickid=060113`
- Increase your SQL Server performance by replacing cursors with set operations

  `http://blogs.msdn.com/b/sqlprogrammability/archive/2008/03/18/`
  `increase-your-sql-server-performance-by-replacing-cursors-with-`
  `set-operations.aspx`
- Cursors for T-SQL Beginners

  `http://www.sqlservercentral.com/articles/cursors/65136/`

Minimizing traffic from SQL server to web server

Do not use SELECT *. This will return all columns. Instead, only list the specific columns you actually need.

If the website needs only part of a long text value, only send that part, not the entire value. For example:

```
SELECT LEFT(longtext, 100) AS excerpt FROM Articles WHERE ...
```

Object naming

Do not start stored procedure names with sp_. SQL Server assumes stored procedure names starting with sp_ belong to system-stored procedures, and always looks in the master database first to find them even when you prefix the name with your database name.

Prefix object names with the schema owner. This saves SQL Server time identifying objects, and improves execution plan reusability. For example, use the following:

```
SELECT Title, Author FROM dbo.Book
```

Instead of the following:

```
SELECT Title, Author FROM Book
```

Using SET NOCOUNT ON

Always include the command SET NOCOUNT ON at the start of stored procedures and triggers. This prevents SQL Server from sending the number of rows affected after execution of every SQL statement.

Using FILESTREAM for values over 1 MB

Store BLOBs over 1 MB in size in a FILESTREAM column. This stores the objects directly on the NTFS file system instead of in the database data file. To see how to make this work, visit:

- FILESTREAM Overview
  http://msdn.microsoft.com/en-us/library/bb933993.aspx

Avoiding functions on columns in WHERE clauses

Using a function on a column in a WHERE clause prevents SQL Server from using an index on that column.

Take for example the following query:

```
SELECT Title, Author FROM dbo.Book WHERE LEFT(Title, 1)='D'
```

SQL Server doesn't know what values the LEFT function returns, so has no choice but to scan the entire table, executing LEFT for each column value.

However, it does know how to interpret LIKE. Rewrite the query to:

```
SELECT Title, Author FROM dbo.Book WHERE Title LIKE 'D%'
```

SQL Server can now use an index on Title, because the LIKE string starts with constant text.

Using UNION ALL instead of UNION

The UNION clause combines the results of two SELECT statements, removing duplicates from the final result. This is expensive; it uses a work table and executes a DISTINCT select to provide this functionality.

If you don't mind duplicates, or if you know there will be no duplicates, use UNION ALL instead. This simply concatenates the SELECT results together.

If the optimizer determines there will be no duplicates, it chooses UNION ALL even if you write UNION. For example, the select statements in the following query will never return overlapping records, and so the optimizer will replace the UNION clause with UNION ALL:

```
SELECT BookId, Title, Author FROM dbo.Book WHERE Author LIKE 'J%'
UNION
SELECT BookId, Title, Author FROM dbo.Book WHERE Author LIKE 'M%'
```

Using EXISTS instead of COUNT to find existence of records

If you need to establish whether there are records in a result set, don't use COUNT:

```
DECLARE @n int
SELECT @n = COUNT(*) FROM dbo.Book
IF @n > 0
  print 'Records found'
```

This reads the entire table to find the number of records. Instead, use EXISTS:

```
IF EXISTS(SELECT * FROM dbo.Book)
  print 'Records found'
```

This allows SQL Server to stop reading the moment it finds a record.

Combining SELECT and UPDATE

Sometimes, you need to SELECT and UPDATE the same record. For example, you may need to update a "LastAccessed" column whenever you retrieve a record. You can do this with a SELECT and an UPDATE:

```
UPDATE dbo.Book
SET LastAccess = GETDATE()
WHERE BookId=@BookId

SELECT Title, Author
FROM dbo.Book
WHERE BookId=@BookId
```

However, you can combine the SELECT into the UPDATE, as follows:

```
DECLARE @title nvarchar(50)
DECLARE @author nvarchar(50)

UPDATE dbo.Book
SET LastAccess = GETDATE(),
    @title = Title,
    @author = Author
WHERE BookId=@BookId

SELECT @title, @author
```

That saves you some elapsed time, and it reduces the time locks held on the record.

Locking

In this section, you'll see how to determine which queries are involved in excessive locking delays, and how to prevent those delays from happening.

Gathering detailed locking information

You can find out which queries are involved in excessive locking delays by tracing the event "Blocked process report" in SQL Server Profiler.

This event fires when the lock wait time for a query exceeds the "blocked process threshold". To set this threshold to, for example, 30 seconds, run the following lines in a query window in SSMS (locking.sql in the downloaded code bundle):

```
EXEC sp_configure 'show advanced options', 1
RECONFIGURE
EXEC sp_configure 'blocked process threshold', 30
RECONFIGURE
```

Then, start the trace in Profiler:

1. Start SQL Profiler. Click on **Start | Programs | Microsoft SQL Server 2008 | Performance Tools | SQL Server Profiler**.

2. In SQL Profiler, click on **File | New Trace**.

3. Click on the **Events Selection** tab.

4. Select **Show all events checkbox** to see all events. Also select **Show all columns** to see all the data columns.

5. In the main window, expand **Errors and Warnings** and select the **Blocked process report** event. Make sure the checkbox in the **TextData** column is checked—scroll horizontally if needed to find it.

6. If you need to investigate deadlocks, also expand **Locks** and select the **Deadlock graph** event. To get additional information about deadlocks, have SQL Server write information about each deadlock event to its error log, by executing the following from an SSMS query window:

   ```
   DBCC TRACEON(1222,-1)
   ```

7. Uncheck all the other events, unless you are interested in them.

8. Click on **Run** to start the trace.

9. Save the template, so that you don't have to recreate it the next time. Click on **File | Save As | Trace Template**. Fill in a descriptive name and click on **OK**. Next time you create a new trace by clicking on **File | New Trace**, you can retrieve the template from the **Use the template** drop-down.

10. Once you have captured a representative sample, click **File | Save** to save the trace to a trace file for later analysis. You can load a trace file by clicking on **File | Open**.

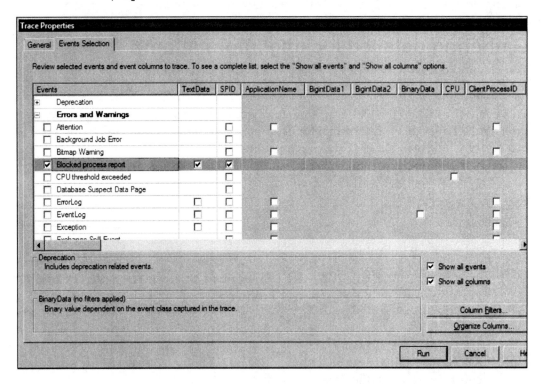

When you click a **Blocked process report** event in Profiler, you'll find information about the event in the lower pane, including the blocking query and the blocked query. You can get details about Deadlock graph events the same way.

To check the SQL Server error log for deadlock events:

1. In SSMS expand the database server, expand **Management** and expand **SQL Server Logs**. Then double-click on a log.

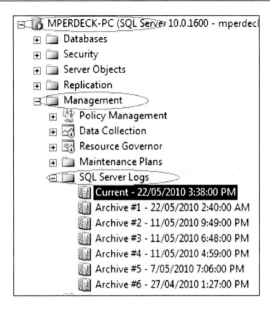

2. In the Log File Viewer, click on **Search** near the top of the window and search for "deadlock-list". In the lines that chronologically come after the deadlock-list event, you'll find much more information about the queries involved in the deadlock.

Reducing blocking

Now that you identified the queries involved in locking delays, it's time to reduce those delays. The most effective way to do this is to reduce the length of time locks are held as follows:

- Optimize queries. The lesser time your queries take, the lesser time they hold locks. See the *Missing indexes and expensive queries* section.

- Use stored procedures rather than ad hoc queries. This reduces time spent compiling execution plans and time spent sending individual queries over the network. The *Execution plan reuse* section shows how to introduce stored procedures.

- If you really have to use cursors, commit updates frequently. Cursor processing is much slower than set-based processing.

- Do not process lengthy operations while locks are held, such as sending e-mails. Do not wait for user input while keeping a transaction open. Instead, use optimistic locking, as described in:

  - Optimistic Locking in SQL Server using the ROWVERSION Data Type
    `http://www.mssqltips.com/tip.asp?tip=1501`

A second way to reduce lock wait times is to reduce the number of resources being locked:

- Do not put a clustered index on frequently updated columns. This requires a lock on both the clustered index and all non-clustered indexes, because their row locator contains the value you are updating.

- Consider including a column in a non-clustered index. This would prevent a query from having to read the table record, so it won't block another query that needs to update an unrelated column in the same record.

- Consider row versioning. This SQL Server feature prevents queries that read a table row from blocking queries that update the same row and vice versa. Queries that need to update the same row still block each other.

  Read versioning works by storing rows in a temporary area (in `tempdb`) before they are updated, so that reading queries can access the stored version while the update is taking place. This does create an overhead in maintaining the row versions—test this solution before taking it live. Also, in case you set the isolation level of transactions, row versioning only works with the Read Committed isolation mode, which is the default isolation mode.

  To implement row versioning, set the `READ_COMMITTED_SNAPSHOT` option as shown in the following code (`locking.sql` in the downloaded code bundle). When doing this, you can have only one connection open—the one used to set the option. You can make that happen by switching the database to single user mode; warn your users first. Be careful when applying this to a production database, because your website won't be able to connect to the database while you are carrying out this operation.

```
ALTER DATABASE mydatabase SET SINGLE_USER WITH ROLLBACK
    IMMEDIATE;
ALTER DATABASE mydatabase SET READ_COMMITTED_SNAPSHOT ON;
ALTER DATABASE mydatabase SET MULTI_USER;
```

  To check whether row versioning is in use for a database, run:

```
select is_read_committed_snapshot_on
from sys.databases
where name='mydatabase'
```

Finally, you can set a lock timeout. For example, to abort statements that have been waiting for over five seconds (or 5000 milliseconds), issue the following command:

```
SET LOCK_TIMEOUT 5000
```

Use 1 to wait indefinitely. Use 0 to not wait at all.

Reducing deadlocks

Deadlock is a situation where two transactions are waiting for each other to release a lock. In a typical case, transaction 1 has a lock on resource A and is trying to get a lock on resource B, while transaction 2 has a lock on resource B and is trying to get a lock on resource A. Neither transaction can now move forward, as shown below:

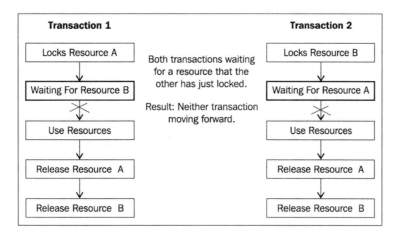

One way to reduce deadlocks is to reduce lock delays in general, as shown in the last section. That reduces the time window in which deadlocks can occur.

A second way is suggested by the diagram—always lock resources in the same order. If, as shown in the diagram, you get transaction 2 to lock the resources in the same order as transaction 1 (first A, then B), then transaction 2 won't lock resource B before it starts waiting for resource A. Hence, it doesn't block transaction 1.

Finally, watch out for deadlocks caused by the use of HOLDLOCK or Repeatable Read or Serializable Read isolation levels. Take for example the following code:

```
SET TRANSACTION ISOLATION LEVEL REPEATABLE READ
BEGIN TRAN
   SELECT Title FROM dbo.Book
   UPDATE dbo.Book SET Author='Charles Dickens'
   WHERE Title='Oliver Twist'
COMMIT
```

Imagine two transactions running this code at the same time. Both acquire a Select lock on the rows in the Book table when they execute the SELECT. They hold onto the lock because of the Repeatable Read isolation level. Now, both try to acquire an Update lock on a row in the Book table to execute the UPDATE. Each transaction is now blocked by the Select lock the other transaction is still holding.

To prevent this from happening, use the UPDLOCK hint on the SELECT statement. This causes the SELECT to acquire an Update lock, so that only one transaction can execute the SELECT. The transaction that did get the lock can then execute its UPDATE and free the locks, after which the other transaction comes through. The code is as follows:

```
SET TRANSACTION ISOLATION LEVEL REPEATABLE READ
BEGIN TRAN
   SELECT Title FROM dbo.Book WITH(UPDLOCK)
   UPDATE dbo.Book SET Author='Charles Dickens'
   WHERE Title='Oliver Twist'
COMMIT
```

Execution plan reuse

You can boost execution plan reuse in your site by making it easier for SQL Server to work out which bits of a query's execution plan can be reused by a similar query.

Ad hoc queries

Take this simple ad hoc query:

```
SELECT b.Title, a.AuthorName
FROM dbo.Book b JOIN dbo.Author a ON b.LeadAuthorId=a.Authorid
WHERE BookId=5
```

When SQL Server receives this query for the very first time, it will compile an execution plan, store the plan in the plan cache, and execute the plan.

If SQL Server then receives this query again, it will reuse the execution plan if it is still in the plan cache, provided that:

- All object references in the query are qualified with at least the schema name. Use dbo.Book instead of Book. Adding the database would be even better.

- There is an exact match between the texts of the queries. This is case-sensitive, and any white space differences also prevent an exact match.

As a result of the second rule, if you use the same query as above but with a different `BookId`, there will be no match:

```
SELECT b.Title, a.AuthorName
FROM dbo.Book b JOIN dbo.Author a ON b.LeadAuthorId=a.Authorid
WHERE BookId=9 -- Doesn't match query above, uses 9 instead of 5
```

Obviously, this is not a recipe for great execution plan reuse.

Simple parameterization

To make it easier for ad hoc queries to reuse a cached plan, SQL Server supports simple parameterization. This automatically figures out the variable bit of a query. Because this is difficult to get right and easy to get wrong, SQL Server attempts this only with very simple queries with one table, for example:

```
SELECT Title, Author FROM dbo.Book WHERE BookId=5
```

It can reuse the execution plan generated for:

```
SELECT Title, Author FROM dbo.Book WHERE BookId=9
```

sp_executesql

Instead of getting SQL Server to guess which bits of a query can be turned into parameters, you can use the system-stored procedure `sp_executesql` to simply tell it yourself. Calling `sp_executesql` takes the following form:

```
sp_executesql @query, @parameter_definitions, @parameter1,
  @parameter2, ...
```

For example:

```
EXEC sp_executesql
  N'SELECT b.Title, a.AuthorName
  FROM dbo.Book b JOIN dbo.Author a ON b.LeadAuthorId=a.Authorid
  WHERE BookId=@BookId',
  N'@BookId int',
  @BookId=5
```

Note that `sp_executesql` expects `nvarchar` values for its first two parameters, so you need to prefix the strings with `N`.

Stored procedures

Instead of sending individual queries to the database, you can package them in a stored procedure that is permanently stored in the database. That gives you the following advantages:

- Just as with `sp_executesql`, stored procedures allow you to define parameters explicitly to make it easier for SQL Server to reuse execution plans.

- Stored procedures can contain a series of queries and T-SQL control statements such as `IF...THEN`. This allows you to simply send the stored procedure name and parameters to the database server, instead of sending individual queries, saving networking overhead.

- Stored procedures make it easier to isolate database details from your website code. When a table definition changes, you may only need to update one or more stored procedures, without touching the website.

- You can implement better security, by only allowing access to the database via stored procedures. That way, you can allow the users to access the information they need through stored procedures, while preventing them from taking unplanned actions.

To create a stored procedure in SQL Server Management Studio, expand your database, expand **Programmability**, and then expand **Stored Procedures**. Right-click on **Stored Procedures** and choose **New Stored Procedure**. A new query window opens where you can define your new stored procedure:

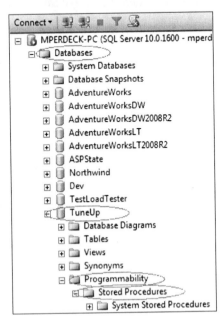

A stored procedure to execute the query you saw in the previous section would look like this (`storedprocedure.sql` in the downloaded code bundle):

```
CREATE PROCEDURE GetBook
  @BookId int
AS
BEGIN
  SET NOCOUNT ON;

  SELECT Title, Author FROM dbo.Book WHERE BookId=@BookId
END
GO
```

This creates a stored procedure with name `GetBook`, and a parameter list with one parameter `@BookId` of type `int`. When SQL Server executes the stored procedure, occurrences of that parameter in the body of the stored procedure get replaced by the parameter value that you pass in.

Setting `NOCOUNT` to `ON` improves performance by preventing SQL Server from sending a message with the number of rows affected by the stored procedure.

To add the stored procedure to the database, press *F5* to execute the `CREATE PROCEDURE` statement.

To verify that the stored procedure has been created, right-click on **Stored Procedures** and choose **Refresh**. Your new stored procedure should now appear in the list of stored procedures. To modify the stored procedure, right-click on **Stored Procedures** and choose **Modify**.

To execute the stored procedure in a query window, use the following:

```
EXEC dbo.GetBook @BookId=5
```

You could also simply use the following:

```
EXEC dbo.GetBook 5
```

Using a stored procedure from your C# code is similar to using an ad hoc query, as shown below (working sample in folder `AccessStoredProcedure` in the downloaded code bundle):

```
string connectionString = "...";
using (SqlConnection connection =
    new SqlConnection(connectionString))
{
    string sql = "dbo.GetBook";
    using (SqlCommand cmd = new SqlCommand(sql, connection))
```

```
        {
                cmd.CommandType = CommandType.StoredProcedure;
                cmd.Parameters.Add(new SqlParameter("@BookId", bookId));
                connection.Open();

                // Execute database command ...
        }
    }
```

Make sure that the command text has the name of the stored procedure, instead of the text of a query. Set the `CommandType` property of the `SqlCommand` object to `CommandType.StoredProcedure`, so that SQL Server knows you're calling a stored procedure. Finally, add parameters to the command that match the parameters you used when you created the stored procedure.

To find out more about stored procedures, visit the site at `http://msdn.microsoft.com/en-us/library/ms190669.aspx`.

Now that you've seen how to improve reuse of execution plans, let's see how to prevent plan reuse, and why you would want to do that.

Preventing reuse

You may not always want to reuse an execution plan. When the execution plan of a stored procedure is compiled, that plan is based on the parameters used at the time. When the plan is reused with different parameters, the plan generated for the first set of parameters is now reused with the second set of parameters. However, this is not always desirable.

Take for example the following query:

```
SELECT SupplierName FROM dbo.Supplier WHERE City=@City
```

Assume that the Supplier table has an index on City. Now assume half the records in Supplier have City "New York". The optimal execution plan for "New York" will then be to use a table scan, rather incurring the overhead of going through the index. If however "San Diego" has only a few records, the optimal plan for "San Diego" would be to use the index. A good plan for one parameter value may be a bad plan for another parameter value. If the cost of using a sub-optimal query plan is high compared to the cost of recompiling the query, you would be better off to tell SQL Server to generate a new plan for each execution.

When creating a stored procedure, you can tell SQL Server not to cache its execution plan with the WITH RECOMPILE option:

```
CREATE PROCEDURE dbo.GetSupplierByCity
  @City nvarchar(100)
  WITH RECOMPILE
AS
BEGIN
...
END
```

Also, you can have a new plan generated for a specific execution:

```
EXEC dbo.GetSupplierByCity 'New York' WITH RECOMPILE
```

Finally you can cause a stored procedure to be recompiled the next time it is called with the system stored procedure sp_recompile:

```
EXEC sp_recompile 'dbo.GetSupplierByCity'
```

To have all stored procedures that use a particular table recompiled the next time they are called, call sp_recompile with that table:

```
EXEC sp_recompile 'dbo.Book'
```

Fragmentation

SQL Server provides two options to defragment tables and indexes, rebuild and reorganize. In this section, we'll examine their advantages and disadvantages.

Index rebuild

Rebuilding an index is the most effective way to defragment an index or table. To do a rebuild, use the following command:

```
ALTER INDEX myindex ON mytable REBUILD
```

This rebuilds the index physically using fresh pages to reduce fragmentation to a minimum.

If you rebuild a clustered index, that has the effect of rebuilding the underlying table because the table is effectively part of the clustered index.

To rebuild all indexes on a table, use the following command:

```
ALTER INDEX ALL ON mytable REBUILD
```

Index rebuilding has the disadvantage that it blocks all queries trying to access the table and its indexes. It can also be blocked by queries that already have access. You can reduce this with the ONLINE option:

```
ALTER INDEX myindex ON mytable REBUILD WITH (ONLINE=ON)
```

However, this will cause the rebuild to take longer.

Another issue is that rebuilding is an atomic operation. If it is stopped before completion, all defragmentation work done so far is lost.

Index reorganize

Unlike index rebuilding, index reorganizing doesn't block the table and its indexes and if it is stopped before completion, the work done so far isn't lost. However, this comes at the price of reduced effectiveness. If an index is between 20 percent and 40 percent fragmented, reorganizing the index should suffice.

To reorganize an index, use the command:

```
ALTER INDEX myindex ON mytable REORGANIZE
```

Use the LOB_COMPACTION option to consolidate columns with **Large Object (LOB)** data, such as image, text, ntext, varchar(max), nvarchar(max), varbinary(max) and xml:

```
ALTER INDEX myindex ON mytable REORGANIZE WITH (LOB_COMPACTION=ON)
```

Index reorganizing is much more geared towards being performed in a busy system than index rebuilding. It is non-atomic, and so if it fails, not all defragmentation work is lost. It requests a small numbers of locks for short periods while it executes, rather than blocking entire tables and their indexes. If it finds that a page is being used, it simply skips that page without trying again.

The disadvantage of index reorganization is that it is less effective, because of the skipped pages, and because it won't create new pages to arrive at a better physical organization of the table or index.

Heap table defragmentation

A heap table is a table without a clustered index. Because it doesn't have a clustered index, it cannot be defragmented with ALTER INDEX REBUILD or ALTER INDEX REORGANIZE.

Fragmentation in heap tables tends to be less of a problem, because records in the table are not ordered. When inserting a record, SQL Server checks whether there is space within the table, and if so, inserts the record there. If you always insert records, and not update or delete records, all records are written at the end of the table. If you update or delete records, you may still wind up with gaps in the heap table.

Since heap table defragmentation is not normally an issue, it is not discussed in this book. Here are a few options though:

- Create a clustered index and then drop it
- Insert data from the heap table into a new table
- Export the data, truncate the table, and import the data back into the table

Memory

These are the most common ways to relieve memory stress:

- Add more physical memory.
- Increase the amount of memory allocated to SQL Server. To see how much is currently allocated, run:

```
EXEC sp_configure 'show advanced option', '1'
RECONFIGURE
EXEC sp_configure 'max server memory (MB)'
```

  If more physical memory is available on the server, increase the allocation. For example, to increase the allocation to 3000 MB, run:

```
EXEC sp_configure 'show advanced option', '1'
RECONFIGURE
EXEC sp_configure 'max server memory (MB)', 3000
RECONFIGURE WITH OVERRIDE
```

  Do not allocate all physical memory. Leave a few hundred MB free for the operating system and other software.

- Reduce the amount of data read from disk. Each page read from disk needs to be stored and processed in memory. Table scans, aggregate queries, and joins can read large amounts of data. Refer to the *Missing indexes and expensive queries* subsection in the *Pinpointing bottlenecks* section to see how to reduce the amount of data read from disk.

- Promote reuse of execution plans, to reduce memory needed for the plan cache. See the *Pinpointing bottlenecks* section, *Execution plan reuse* subsection.

Disk usage

Here are the most common methods to reduce stress on the disk system:

- Optimizing query processing
- Moving the logfile to a dedicated physical disk
- Reducing fragmentation of the NTFS file system
- Moving the `tempdb` database to its own disk
- Split the data over two or more disks to spread the load
- Alternatively, move heavily used database objects to another disk
- Use the optimal RAID configuration

Let's go through these options one-by-one.

Optimizing query processing

Make sure you have the correct indexes in place and optimize the most expensive queries. Refer to the *Missing indexes and expensive queries* subsection in the *Pinpointing bottlenecks* section.

Moving the logfile to a dedicated physical disk

Moving the read/write head of a disk is a relatively slow process. The logfile is written sequentially, which by itself requires little head movement. This doesn't help you though if the logfile and data file are on the same disk, because then the head has to move between logfile and data file.

However, if you put the logfile on its own disk, head movement on that disk is minimized, leading to faster access to the log file. That in turn leads to quicker modification operations, such as UPDATES, INSERTS, and DELETES.

To move the logfile to another disk for an existing database, first detach the database. Move the logfile to the dedicated disk. Then reattach the database, specifying the new location of the logfile.

Reducing fragmentation of the NTFS filesystem

When the actual NTFS database files become fragmented, the disk head has to hunt around the disk for the fragments when reading a file. To reduce fragmentation, set a large initial file size (for your database and logfiles) and a large increment size. Better still, set it large enough so that neither file ever has to grow; the objective is to prevent growing and shrinking the files.

If you do need to grow and shrink the database or log files, consider using a 64-KB NTFS cluster size to match SQL Server reading patterns.

Considering moving the tempdb database to its own disk

tempdb is used for sorting, sub-queries, temporary tables, aggregation, cursors, and so on. It can be very busy. That means that it may be a good idea to move the tempdb database to its own disk, or to a disk that is less busy.

To check the level of activity of the database and logfiles of tempdb and the other databases on the server, use the dm_io_virtual_file_stats DMV (diskusage.sql in the downloaded code bundle):

```
SELECT d.name, mf.physical_name, mf.type_desc, vfs.*
FROM sys.dm_io_virtual_file_stats(NULL,NULL) vfs
JOIN sys.databases d ON vfs.database_id = d.database_id
JOIN sys.master_files mf ON mf.database_id=vfs.database_id AND
mf.file_id=vfs.file_id
```

To move the tempdb data and logfiles to for example the G: disk, setting their sizes to 10 MB and 1 MB, run this code (diskusage.sql in downloaded code bundle). Then restart the server:

```
ALTER DATABASE tempdb MODIFY FILE (NAME = tempdev, FILENAME = 'G:\
tempdb.mdf', SIZE = 10MB)
GO
ALTER DATABASE tempdb MODIFY FILE (NAME = templog, FILENAME = 'G:\
templog.ldf', SIZE = 1MB)
GO
```

To reduce fragmentation, prevent growing and shrinking of the tempdb data and logfiles by giving them as much space as they are likely to ever need.

Splitting the database data over two or more disks

By splitting the database's data file over two or more disks, you spread the load. And because you wind up with more but smaller files, this also makes backup and moving the database easier.

To make this happen, add a file to the PRIMARY filegroup of the database. SQL Server then spreads the data over the existing file(s) and the new file. Put the new file on a new disk or a disk that isn't heavily used. If you can, make its initial size big enough so it doesn't have to grow further, thereby reducing fragmentation.

For example, to add a file to database `TuneUp` on the `G:` disk with an initial size of 20 GB, run the following command (`diskusage.sql` in the downloaded code bundle):

```
ALTER DATABASE TuneUp
ADD FILE (NAME = TuneUp_2, FILENAME = N'G:\TuneUp_2.ndf', SIZE = 20GB)
```

Note that the file has extension `.ndf`, the recommended extension for secondary files.

Moving heavily-used database objects to another disk

You could move heavily used database objects such as indexes, to a new disk, or to less busy disks. In the *Pinpointing bottlenecks* section, subsection *Missing indexes and expensive queries*, you saw how to use the DMV `dm_db_index_usage_stats` to determine the number of reads and writes executed on each index. There it was used to find unused indexes, but you can also use it to find the busiest indexes.

And if your server has multiple disks, in the *Pinpointing bottlenecks* section, *Disk usage* subsection you saw how to measure the usage of your disks. Use this information to decide which objects to move to which disk.

To move an index to another disk, first create a new user-defined file group. For example, this statement creates a file group `FG2` (`diskusage.sql` in downloaded code bundle):

```
ALTER DATABASE TuneUp ADD FILEGROUP FG2
```

Then add a file to the file group:

```
ALTER DATABASE TuneUp
ADD FILE (NAME = TuneUp_Fg2, FILENAME = N'G:\TuneUp_Fg2.ndf', SIZE =
200MB)
TO FILEGROUP FG2
```

Finally move the object to the file group. For example, here is how to move a non-clustered index `IX_Title` on column `Title` in table `Book` to file group `FG2`:

```
CREATE NONCLUSTERED INDEX [IX_Title] ON [dbo].[Book]([Title] ASC)
WITH DROP_EXISTING ON FG2
```

You can assign multiple objects to a file group. And you can add multiple files to a file group, allowing you to spread for example a very busy table or index over multiple disks.

Have tables and their non-clustered indexes on separate disks, so one task can read the index itself and another task can do key lookups in the table.

Using the optimal RAID configuration

To improve performance and/or fault tolerance, many database servers use Redundant Array of Inexpensive Disks (RAID) subsystems instead of individual drives. RAID subsystems come in different configurations. Choosing the right configuration for your data files, logfiles, and `tempdb` files can greatly affect performance.

The most commonly used RAID configurations are:

RAID Configuration	Description
RAID 0	Each file is spread ("striped") over each disk in the array. When reading or writing a file, all disks are accessed in parallel, leading to high transfer rates.
RAID 5	Each file is striped over all disks. Parity information for each disk is stored on the other disks, providing fault tolerance. File writes are slow — a single file write requires 1 data read + 1 parity read + 1 data write + 1 parity write = 4 accesses.
RAID 10	Each file is striped over half the disks. Those disks are mirrored by the other half, providing excellent fault tolerance. A file write requires 1 data write to a main disk + 1 data write to a mirror disk.
RAID 1	This is RAID 10 but with just 2 disks, a main disk and a mirror disk. That gives you fault tolerance but no striping.

This translates to the following performance characteristics compared with an individual disk. N is the number of disks in the array.

	Read Speed	Write Speed	Fault Tolerant
Individual Disk	1	1	no
RAID 0	N	N	no
RAID 5	N	N/4	yes
RAID 10	N	N/2	yes
RAID 1	2	1	yes

So, if you have a RAID 10 with 4 disks (2 main + 2 mirror) and N = 4, read performance will be four times better than an individual disk, while write performance will be 4/2 = 2 times better. This is assuming that the individual disk has the same speed as the disks in the RAID 10.

From this follows the optimal RAID configuration to use for your `tempdb`, data, and logfiles:

Files	Performance related attributes	Recommended RAID configuration
tempdb	Requires good read and write performance for random access. Relatively small. Losing temporary data may be acceptable.	RAID 0, RAID 1, RAID 10
log	Requires very good write performance, and fault tolerance. Uses sequential access, so striping is no benefit.	RAID 1, RAID 10
data (writes make up less than 10 percent of accesses)	Requires fault tolerance. Random access means striping is beneficial. Large data volume.	RAID 5, RAID 10
data (writes make up over 10 percent of accesses)	Same as above, plus good write performance.	RAID 10

Having a battery-backed caching RAID controller greatly improves write performance, because this allows SQL Server to hand over write requests to the cache without having to wait for the physical disk access to complete. The controller then executes the cached write requests in the background.

CPU

Common ways to resolve processor bottlenecks include:

- Optimize CPU-intensive queries. In the *Pinpointing bottlenecks* section, *Missing indexes and expensive queries* subsection, you saw how to identify the most expensive queries. The DMVs listed there give you the CPU usage of each query. See the *Missing indexes* and *Expensive queries* sections on how to optimize these queries.

- Building execution plans is highly CPU-intensive. Refer to *Pinpointing bottlenecks* section, *Execution plan reuse* subsection to improve reuse of execution plans.

- Install more or faster processors, L2/L3 cache, or more efficient drivers.

Find out more

Here are more online resources:

- **General Index Design Guidelines**
  `http://msdn.microsoft.com/en-us/library/ms191195.aspx`

- **About the Missing Indexes Feature**
  `http://msdn.microsoft.com/en-au/library/ms345524.aspx`

- **SQLdiag Utility**
  `http://msdn.microsoft.com/en-us/library/ms162833.aspx`

- **SQL SERVER – 2005 – Forced Parameterization and Simple Parameterization – T-SQL and SSMS**
  `http://blog.sqlauthority.com/2007/10/25/sql-server-2005-forced-parameterization-and-simple-parameterization-t-sql-and-ssms/`

- **Parameterized Queries**
  `http://www.databasejournal.com/features/mssql/article.php/3834501/Parameterized-Queries.htm`

- **The Curse and Blessings of Dynamic SQL**
  `http://www.sommarskog.se/dynamic_sql.html`

- **How to specify output parameters when you use the** `sp_executesql` **stored procedure in SQL Server**
  `http://support.microsoft.com/kb/262499`

- **Creating Stored Procedures (Database Engine)**
  `http://msdn.microsoft.com/en-us/library/ms190669.aspx`

- **Activity Monitor**
  `http://msdn.microsoft.com/en-us/library/cc879320.aspx`

- **Batch Compilation, Recompilation, and Plan Caching Issues in SQL Server 2005**
  `http://technet.microsoft.com/en-us/library/cc966425.aspx`

- **Temporary Tables versus Table Variables and Their Effect on SQL Server Performance**
  `http://www.sql-server-performance.com/articles/per/temp_tables_vs_variables_p1.aspx`

- **Understanding Row Versioning-Based Isolation Levels**
  `http://msdn.microsoft.com/en-us/library/ms189050.aspx`

- **Getting Started with Full-Text Search**
  `http://msdn.microsoft.com/en-us/library/ms142497.aspx`

- **Minding Memory**
  `http://www.windowsitpro.com/article/internals-and-architecture/minding-memory.aspx`

- SQL Server 2005 Waits and Queues
  `http://technet.microsoft.com/en-us/library/cc966413.aspx`

- Server Memory Options
  `http://msdn.microsoft.com/en-us/library/aa196734(SQL.80).aspx`

- Configuring SQL Server memory settings
  `http://searchsqlserver.techtarget.com/tip/Configuring-SQL-Server-memory-settings`

- Move SQL Server transaction log files to a different location via T-SQL and SSMS
  `http://www.mssqltips.com/tip.asp?tip=1774`

Summary

In this chapter, we looked at improving the performance of your SQL Server database.

First, we saw how to pinpoint performance bottlenecks associated with the database such as missing indexes, expensive queries, and locking. We also looked at execution plan reuse and fragmentation. In addition to this, the possible hardware-related bottlenecks, including the database server's CPU, memory, and disk usage were discussed.

We then dug deeply into fixing the bottlenecks which we found. The two types of indexes: clustered and non-clustered, how they work, and when to use them were discussed. We saw the advantages and disadvantages of reducing the size of table records and discussed other ways to speed up queries such as caching aggregation queries. Then, we learned how to gather detailed information about locking-related bottlenecks, and how to reduce blocking and deadlocks.

We also discussed how to improve execution plan reuse dramatically, through the use of stored procedures and `sp_executesql`. Also, we saw the two types of index defragmentation: index rebuilding and index reorganizing.

Finally, ways to make more optimal use of the available disks were detailed, including moving the logfile to its own separate disk. This was followed by significant ways to reduce memory usage and CPU usage on the database server.

In the previous few chapters, we've been looking at speeding up a generation of the main `.aspx` file on the server. In the next chapter, we'll turn to another major area of slowdowns — the time it takes to move the file from the server to the browser.

Reducing Time to Last Byte

The "time to last byte" is the time it takes to generate the `.aspx` file and move it across the Internet to the browser. While chapters 2 to 8 are concerned with speeding up the generation of the file, this chapter along with chapter 10 and chapter 11 deal with reducing the time required to move the `.aspx` file to the browser. Because Internet is relatively slow, it makes sense to speed up moving the page by reducing the number of bytes traveling over the wire. An additional benefit is that you pay less for bandwidth.

This chapter consists of three major sections:

- The *Pinpointing bottlenecks* section shows how to pinpoint a number of common bottlenecks that make your `.aspx` file bigger than it could be, including lack of compression of files being sent by the server, bloated ViewState, and excessive white space. This helps you find out which bottlenecks to fix and their priority, so that you can spend your time where it counts the most.

- The *Fixing bottlenecks* section then shows how to actually fix each of the bottlenecks you prioritized in the first section. Two of the issues we look at in in the *Pinpointing bottlenecks* section are dealt with in their own chapters— *Chapter 10, Compression* and *Chapter 11, Optimizing Forms*.

- Finally, the *Additional measures* section shows some additional measures you can take, such as removing event validation, reducing space taken by ASP. NET IDs and preventing HTML comments from going to the browser.

Pinpointing bottlenecks

Before diving in and making changes to your website, it makes sense to first look at a few common bottlenecks and the extent in which they affect your site. That helps you prioritize areas with high expected payoff.

Each potential bottleneck has a subsection that helps you find out whether it applies to you. After you identify the bottlenecks that need fixing, turn to the corresponding subsections in the *Fixing bottlenecks* section to fix them.

Compression

Compression is so effective, that it alone may be enough to make the time to last byte acceptable for your site.

Your main .aspx file and the CSS and JavaScript files it uses are all text files. Because they contain a lot of white space and many repeating keywords, they are highly compressible by algorithms such as **GZIP**. Compressing an HTML file to one-third its size or less is common.

Because of this, IIS from version 5 onwards has supported compression of outgoing text files, using either the deflate or GZIP compression algorithms depending on browser capability. However by default, IIS 5 and IIS 6 don't enable compression, and IIS 7 by default only compresses static files such as CSS and JavaScript, but not .aspx files.

Before going any further, check to see if your site already uses compression. If it does, you can skip this section.

Enter your site address at any of these websites for a quick answer:

- http://www.whatsmyip.org/http_compression/
- http://www.port80software.com/

To further pinpoint which files making up your page get compressed and by how much, get the **Web Developer** add-on for Firefox. This gives you a lot of information about a web page, including the compressed and uncompressed sizes of the files making up the page:

1. Using Firefox, visit http://chrispederick.com/work/web-developer/ to download and install the Web Developer add-on.

2. After you have installed Web Developer, load the page you are interested in, using Firefox.

3. Click on **Tools | Web Developer | Information | View Document Size**. A new window appears showing the groups of files making up the page.

4. Expand the **Documents** group to see the main HTML file. You will see its size. If it was compressed while travelling over the Internet, you will also see its compressed size.

5. For more information, expand the **Scripts** and **Style Sheets** groups as well.

If you find that your site does not use compression, refer to chapter 10 to see how to enable compression.

ViewState

The ASP.NET ViewState feature has the potential to make your `.aspx` file much bigger than it needs to be. Here is how to measure your ViewState, and why you want to reduce it.

What is ViewState?

The ASP.NET programming model creates the illusion that you are programming an application on the local computer. Each control on the page is represented as an object that seems to keep its state in memory and receives events from the user interface.

In reality, the objects representing controls exist only while the server handles a request from the page. When the request is received, ASP.NET creates the objects based on the HTML on your page and data POSTed from the server. Your code then manipulates those objects, after which ASP.NET translates them to HTML. This HTML is sent to the browser, along with the literal HTML on your page. The objects are then destroyed. As a result, the state of each control needs to be stored somehow in between requests.

HTTP doesn't store state natively; so, ASP.NET stores the state of each control on the page itself, in a hidden form field called __VIEWSTATE. When a postback occurs, the ViewState is posted back to the server along with the values of the other form fields, allowing ASP.NET to rebuild the state of the objects representing the controls on the page.

The ViewState feature is enabled by default for all controls on the page, even for those that don't need it.

Some controls need some ViewState to function correctly. This is called **controlstate**, and is stored in the same hidden form field __VIEWSTATE. You can't switch this off. This means you may be left with some ViewState even if you disable ViewState for all controls.

You'll find much more about the ViewState feature at `http://msdn.microsoft.com/en-us/library/ms972976.aspx`.

Why reduce ViewState?

It makes sense to reduce the amount of ViewState on the page even if dynamic file compression is enabled on the server, because of the following:

- ViewState not only travels from the server to the browser, but also as part of requests from the browser to the server. Keep in mind that requests are never compressed and that for many visitors, the uplink is slower than the downlink.
- ViewState doesn't compress as well as normal HTML.
- Serializing and deserializing object states to and from ViewState increases CPU usage.

Measuring your ViewState

Is it worthwhile to reduce ViewState? To find out, measure its size.

Quickly finding where ViewState is an issue

The simplest way to find the size of the ViewState on a page is to view its source, copy the contents of hidden field __VIEWSTATE to a new text file, and check the size of the file.

A quicker and easier way is to use the free tool **ASP.NET ViewState Helper**. For each page you visit, this shows the overall size of the .aspx file, the size of the ViewState within the .aspx file, and what percentage of the .aspx file size is taken by ViewState.

It can decode the ViewState, but this doesn't provide much information. It only works with Firefox and Internet Explorer. Download this free tool at http://www.binaryfortress.com/aspnet-viewstate-helper/.

Measuring compressed ViewState

The numbers that ASP.NET ViewState Helper gives you relate to the uncompressed file size, and therefore the uncompressed ViewState size. However, if the server has dynamic file compression enabled, then you want to know the compressed file size and ViewState size as well.

One way to achieve this is to find the compressed size of the file with ViewState enabled, and then the compressed size of the file with ViewState disabled. The difference between the two is the compressed size of the ViewState.

To do this in your development environment, switch on dynamic file compression in IIS on your development machine and make sure Visual Studio uses IIS, not Cassini, the web server built into Visual Studio (as described in *Chapter 10, Compression*). To measure the file sizes, you could use the Web Developer add-on for Firefox that you saw earlier.

To disable ViewState in your entire site, modify the `<pages>` element under `<system.web>` in the `web.config` file as follows:

```
<pages enableViewState="false">
```

Make sure that ViewState is not turned on for individual pages.

Having ViewState size on status bar

You may find it handy to have the ViewState size of a page on the browser toolbar, so you can easily keep an eye on it. The Viewstate Size add-on for Firefox makes that happen. Download it at `https://addons.mozilla.org/en-US/firefox/addon/5956/?src=api`.

Optimizing forms

In a classic ASP.NET website, form submissions are more expensive than needed because of the need to store ViewState, and the fact that each submission involves a complete refresh of the page.

If form submissions make up a fair proportion of your traffic or if there is a business case for focusing on a specific form, refer to chapter 11.

White space

White space can make your `.aspx` files a lot bigger than they need to be.

To get a rough and slightly optimistic idea of how much you could save if you reduced white space, save the HTML to a file. Find the length of the file in bytes. Then, open the file in a text editor and replace all the double spaces (two spaces in a row) with a single space, repeating the process until no more double spaces are left in the file. Leave the line breaks in place. Save the file and check the length again.

If you use dynamic file compression, zip both versions of the file and check the compressed sizes. You'll probably find that after compression, the difference made by reducing white space is simply not worth the effort. White space reduction is typically something you do if you can't use compression.

Fixing bottlenecks

Now that you have pinpointed the bottlenecks to prioritize, skip to the appropriate subsection to find out how to fix those bottlenecks.

ViewState

ViewState is such an integral part of the ASP.NET environment that it is very easy to get to a situation where your pages are carrying more ViewState than they need to.

This section first shows how to find out which controls are responsible for most of the ViewState on a page. You then see how to disable ViewState. After that, we get to solutions for actually reducing ViewState.

Preserving state by preventing refreshes

Remember that ViewState is a way to remember the state of controls on the page across page refreshes. This means that you can get rid of ViewState completely if you simply do not refresh the page and instead, always use AJAX-style asynchronous requests.

To explore this further, refer to chapter 11.

Seeing ViewState generated by each control

In the *Pinpointing bottlenecks* section, we learnt how to find the total amount of ViewState on a page. To break that down to ViewState used per control, use a page trace.

To get a trace, add this line to the `<system.web>` section in the `web.config` file in your development environment:

```
<trace enabled="true" />
```

Visit the pages you are interested in. Then, open the trace at the pseudo page `trace.axd`. If, for example, your site has address `http://localhost:1080`, then open `http://localhost:1080/trace.axd`.

In the trace, click on the **View Details** link and scroll down to the **Control Tree** section. There you will find the ViewState size and ControlState size for each control.

Disabling Viewstate

ViewState is enabled by default for all controls. You can enable or disable ViewState on a site, page, or control level.

Enable or disable ViewState for the entire site by modifying the `<pages>` element under `<system.web>` in the `web.config` file, as shown:

```
<pages enableViewState="false">
```

You can override this per page in the `Page` directive:

```
<%@ Page Language="C#" EnableViewState="true" ... %>
```

If ViewState is enabled for a page, you can then disable it per control:

```
<asp:Literal ID="Literal1" runat="server"
  EnableViewState="false" />
```

Until ASP.NET 3.5, you couldn't disable ViewState for a page and then enable it per control. This meant that if you needed ViewState for a single control on a page, you had to enable ViewState for the entire page, and then disable ViewState for all controls except the one that needed it.

ASP.NET 4 fixes this by introducing a new attribute that can be applied to both pages and controls—`ViewStateMode`. This can take the values `Enabled`, `Disabled`, and `Inherit`. `Inherit` is the default for controls, and causes them to inherit their view state mode from the page's view state mode. The default for pages is `Enabled`. As a result, in ASP.NET 4, you can disable ViewState for an entire page, and then enable it per control as shown in the following code:

```
<%@ Page Language="C#" ViewStateMode="Disabled" ... %>
<asp:Literal ID="Literal1" runat="server"
  ViewStateMode="Enabled" />
```

Now that we know how to switch off ViewState, let's see how to identify those controls where we can safely do that.

Identifying controls that do not need ViewState

To see for which controls ViewState is really needed and for which ones it isn't, let's first have a deeper look at what it does. As you saw in the *What is Viewstate?* subsection in the *Pinpointing bottlenecks* section, controls are represented by objects while your page code runs. However, after the objects have been translated to HTML, they are destroyed.

This means that if you set for example, the Text property of a Literal control to "abc", that property value will be translated to HTML. However, it will then be lost when the Literal object is destroyed. Also, because HTML is not posted back to the server, there will be no way for ASP.NET to restore the Text property value when it recreates the Literal object during the next postback, unless it stores the property value in the __VIEWSTATE hidden field (which *does* get posted back). Note that some property values do get posted back, for example, the value of the Text property of a TextBox, because a TextBox translates to an HTML input control:

```
<input name="TextBox1" type="text" value="abc" />
```

Based on this discussion, you can disable ViewState for the following controls:

- Controls on pages that never do a postback, such as pages with only text and images. If a page doesn't postback, it will never postback its own ViewState.

- Controls where you do not set properties that are not posted back. For example, if the only property you set on a TextBox is its Text property, you can disable ViewState for that TextBox, because the Text property will be posted back anyway, as we saw during the discussion.

- Controls whose properties are set on each page load. During the discussion, we saw that the Text property of a Literal control will be lost unless it is stored in ViewState. But if you assign a new value to the Text property during every single request, there is no reason to store the old value in ViewState.

- Controls whose properties do not need to be saved. For example, if you use a Literal to show a temporary message that needs to be removed at the next postback, there is no need to save the message first in ViewState, only to remove it in code.

Reloading from database cache

People often enable ViewState on a control so that it doesn't need to be reloaded from the database. This only makes sense if the database overhead is big and the ViewState overhead small. If it's the other way round — ViewState is big and the database overhead small, it makes sense to not use ViewState and always reload the control. As shown below, this is especially true if you use database caching.

Take a drop-down menu where the drop-down values are loaded from the database, such as a drop-down with country names:

```
<asp:DropDownList ID="ddlCountries" runat="server"
  DataTextField="name" DataValueField="id">
</asp:DropDownList>
```

The classic way to create a drop-down list with the countries would be to load them from a database when the page first loads (page `DropdownWithViewState.aspx` in the `ViewState` folder in the downloaded code bundle):

```
protected void Page_Load(object sender, EventArgs e)
{
  if (!Page.IsPostBack)
  {
    ddlCountries.DataSource = DataAccess.Country.GetAll();
    ddlCountries.DataBind();
  }
}
```

The `DataAccess.Country.GetAll` method retrieves the names and IDs of all the countries from the data access layer.

Because ViewState has not been disabled in the `DropDownList` control, the list effectively is cached in ViewState. That allows you to access the database only when the page initially loads, that is, when `Page.IsPostBack` is false.

However, the list of countries will be used every single time the page is accessed by any visitor. The data access layer should already cache this information (to learn more about caching, see *Chapter 5, Caching*).

That means that each time you access the list of countries, it probably comes from the cache rather than the database. That makes it cheaper to reload the drop-down list each time the page loads than to store the list in ViewState. Remember that the entire ViewState is included not only in the `.aspx` file sent by the browser, but also in postbacks from the browser.

To implement this, reload the drop-down in `Page_Init` rather than `Page_Load`, otherwise the control loses the current selection (page `DropdownNoViewState.aspx` in folder `ViewState` in the downloaded code bundle):

```
protected void Page_Init(object sender, EventArgs e)
{
  // GetAll caches the country list,
  // instead of accessing the database on each call.
  ddlCountries.DataSource = DataAccess.Country.GetAll();
  ddlCountries.DataBind();
}
```

If instead of a data access layer you use a data source control such as `SqlDataSource`, set its `EnableCaching` property to `true` to enable caching.

Now, you can disable ViewState on the drop-down control:

```
<asp:DropDownList ID="ddlCountries" runat="server" DataTextField
  ="name" DataValueField="id" EnableViewState="false">
</asp:DropDownList>
```

In the sample code where the drop-down shows a full list of countries, this solution reduces ViewState by 5 KB or 3 KB after compression. On a postback, that means 10 KB less going over the wire (5 KB in the request + 5 KB in the response), or 8 KB if you use compression (5 KB in the request + but 3 KB in the response).

Storing a shorter version of the property value

Sometimes, a long property value has a one-to one relationship with a shorter value. In that case, you can reduce ViewState overhead by storing the shorter value. Let's have a look at an example of this.

Many websites need to be able to show messages in different languages. To make translation easier, they can store all messages in an array. Each message is now identified by an index. As a result, when you assign a message to a control, you wind up with code such as the following one (page `ViewStateMessage` in `ViewState` folder in the downloaded code bundle):

```
int messageId = ...;
lblMessage.Text = Messages[messageId];
```

However, because `messageId` is an integer, it probably takes much less room in ViewState than the message itself. Seeing that there is a one-to-one relationship between `messageId` and the message itself, we can save space by storing `messageId` in ViewState instead of the message itself.

Firstly, when assigning the message to the control, store `messageId` in ViewState (page `ViewStateShortended` in `ViewState` folder in the downloaded code bundle):

```
int messageId = ...;
ViewState["messageId"] = messageId;
lblMessage.Text = Messages[messageId];
```

Secondly, during Page Load when processing a postback, retrieve `messageId` from ViewState, and then restore the control's `Text` property based on `messageId`:

```
protected void Page_Load(object sender, EventArgs e)
{
  if (Page.IsPostBack)
  {
    // Retrieve messageId from ViewState
    int messageId = 0;
```

```
      Int32.TryParse(ViewState["messageId"].ToString(),
        out messageId);
      // Restore Text property
      lblMessage.Text = Messages[messageId];
    }
  }
```

Finally, assuming that the `Text` property is the only `lblMessage` property you use, you can disable ViewState for `lblMessage`:

```
<asp:Label ID="lblMessage" EnableViewState="false"
  runat="server">
</asp:Label>
```

WARNING

Do not store enums in ViewState. They take much more space than the underlying integer, because ASP.NET stores additional information, including the type name and assembly name. Instead, cast the enum to an integer and then store the integer.

Storing ViewState on the server

If after the preceding optimizations your ViewState is still too big, you could consider storing the ViewState on the server instead of on the page. Before you do that though, consider the following options and their issues:

- **Storing the ViewState in cache or the session object**: Seeing that the ViewState is pretty big, this will take up quite a bit of memory for the duration of the session. Multiply that by the maximum number of concurrent sessions to see how much memory this will take. Also, if the cache manager decides to free up the cache item, or if the session expires, or the application pool or web server is restarted, you lose the ViewState.

- **Storing in session**: Storing in cache wouldn't work well with a server farm, because the next postback may go to a different server. Storing in session would work if you store the session in the database or a state server.

- **Storing the ViewState in Application State or Application Static Variables**: This has the same issues as using cache or session, except that application state and application static variables do not expire. They will still go away though, if the application pool or web server is restarted. Also, you need to implement code to purge stale ViewStates.

- **Storing the ViewState in the database**: This way, the ViewState won't suddenly disappear, and it will work well with a server farm. However, you'll generate a lot of database updates and inserts, and you will need to implement code to purge stale ViewStates.

Still want to store ViewState on the server? Ok, here is how to do it.

ViewState is saved and loaded by two methods of the Page class, `SavePageStateToPersistenceMedium` and `LoadPageStateFromPersistenceMedium`. To change the way ViewState is handled, you derive a new class from `Page` and override these two methods. Then, modify the code behind of the pages for which you want to save ViewState on the server, and derive their page classes from your new page class, rather than directly from `Page`.

Creating your new page class would go like this (folder `ViewState` in the downloaded code bundle):

1. First, create a new class and derive it from `Page`:

   ```
   public class ViewStateInCachePage : System.Web.UI.Page
   {
   ```

2. Whether you store the ViewState in cache, session, the database, or wherever else, you need to give it a unique key to identify the ViewState for a particular page. Remember that your server handles different pages for multiple visitors concurrently. Also, a visitor may have the same page open in two browser windows.

3. To provide a direct link between the page and its ViewState, the key needs to be stored on the page itself in a hidden form field.

   To implement this, first create a constant with the name of the hidden form field where you'll store the key:

   ```
   private const string viewStateKeyId = "__vsk";
   ```

4. Now, override the `SavePageStateToPersistenceMedium` method. The default implementation of this method takes an object, serializes it, and puts it on the page in the `__VIEWSTATE` hidden form field. Our overridden version will store it in cache instead. If you want to store your ViewState somewhere else, modify this solution:

   ```
   protected override void SavePageStateToPersistenceMedium
      (object viewState)
   {
   ```

5. Generate a new unique key:

   ```
   string viewStateKey = Guid.NewGuid().ToString();
   ```

6. Store the object in cache. To save memory, we need to expire the object from cache — there is no point in keeping it long after the visitor is gone. It makes sense to do that at the same time the session expires. To implement this, the code finds how long the session will be active from `Session.Timeout`, and sets the cache item to expire those many minutes from now:

```
Cache.Add(viewStateKey, viewState, null,
  DateTime.Now.AddMinutes(Session.Timeout),
  TimeSpan.Zero, CacheItemPriority.Default, null);
```

7. Store the key on the page in a hidden form field:

```
ClientScript.RegisterHiddenField(viewStateKeyId, viewStateKey);
}
```

8. Using `ClientScript.RegisterHiddenField` can create issues if you use ASP.NET AJAX UpdatePanels. In that case, try replacing it with `ScriptManager.RegisterHiddenField`.

9. Now that `SavePageStateToPersistenceMedium` is done, override `LoadPageStateFromPersistenceMedium`. The default implementation gets the ViewState from the hidden form field `__VIEWSTATE`, deserializes it, and returns the resulting object. Our version will simply read the object from cache:

```
protected override object LoadPageStateFromPersistenceMedium()
{
```

10. In `SavePageStateToPersistenceMedium`, we stored the key in a hidden form field on the page. Now, retrieve the key from that hidden form field:

```
string viewStateKey = Request.Form[viewStateKeyId];
```

11. You will also want to do validation on the key, because it could have been tampered with by the visitor:

```
if (viewStateKey == null)
  throw new InvalidOperationException("Invalid viewstate key:"
    + viewStateKey);
```

12. Get the ViewState object from cache:

```
object viewState = Cache[viewStateKey];
```

13. The key may not identify any object in cache, either because it was tampered with, or because it expired from cache:

```
if (viewState == null)
  throw new InvalidOperationException
    ("ViewState not in cache");
```

14. Return the ViewState object and you're done!

```
    return viewState;
  }
}
```

Finally to get a page to use this new functionality, derive it from your new page class instead of from `Page`. Use the following:

```
public partial class ViewStateInCache : ViewStateInCachePage
```

Instead of the following:

```
public partial class ViewStateInCache : System.Web.UI.Page
```

There are some obvious ways this code could be improved. You could make it more tamperproof by encrypting the ViewState key. If memory is scarce but you have enough CPU resources, compress the object before caching it using GZipStream. If you use a server farm, store the ViewState in the session object or the database rather than cache.

Instead of using a page base class, you could use a page adapter. This would modify the functionality of all pages without having to change their base classes. That's great if you want to store ViewState on the server for all pages, but not so great if you want to store ViewState only for pages where the ViewState is very large. To find out how to store ViewState for all pages using the GetStatePersister method of the PageAdapter class, visit:

- PageStatePersister Class
  http://msdn.microsoft.com/en-us/library/system.web.
  ui.pagestatepersister.aspx
- PageAdapter Class
  http://msdn.microsoft.com/en-us/library/system.web.ui.adapters.
  pageadapter.aspx

Compressing Viewstate

Instead of storing ViewState on the server, you could still store it on the page but in compressed form.

Because this solution stores the ViewState on the page, it doesn't cause increased memory use or database accesses. However, if you use server compression, compressing the ViewState is not going to reduce your `.aspx` file size as it goes over the wire from server to browser. On the other hand, because ViewState is stored in the __VIEWSTATE hidden field, it is included in every request from the browser to the server, and requests are never compressed; so you'll get a saving there.

Keep in mind that this solution is very CPU-intensive. Also, it only works if your ViewState is large. If it isn't, the compression algorithm may actually increase the ViewState.

Implementing compression

To implement ViewState compression, we'll need to take care of three things:

- **Tying in with the ASP.NET framework**: This goes along the same lines as storing ViewState on the server. We'll derive a class from `Page` and override the `LoadPageStateFromPersistenceMedium` and `SavePageStateToPersistenceMedium` methods.

- **Serializing/deserializing the object to be stored**: We'll use the same `LosFormatter` object (namespace `System.Web.UI`) as used by the default implementations of `LoadPageStateFromPersistenceMedium` and `SavePageStateToPersistenceMedium`.

- **Compression**: This will be done by the `GZipStream` object in the `System.IO.Compression` namespace.

Getting the `LosFormatter` and `GZipStream` objects to work together requires an odd little dance. The basic idea when saving an object to ViewState is to first serialize the object using `LosFormatter`, and then compress the result using `GZipStream`. `GZipStream` produces a `Stream` of bytes, which need to be encoded to base 64 characters before they can be placed in the `__VIEWSTATE` hidden form field. Interestingly, when `LosFormatter` serializes an object, it produces a `Stream` of base 64 characters, which the default implementation of `SavePageStateToPersistenceMedium` stores directly in `__VIEWSTATE`. We could pass the base 64 characters produced by the `LosFormatter` directly to the `GZipStream` object, but that results in a longer ViewState than necessary. This is because each base 64 character takes an 8-bit byte, while it represents only 6 bits of information. So we'll decode the base 64 characters produced by `LosFormatter` to a byte `Stream` which we then compress using `GZipStream`. This results in the following flow chart:

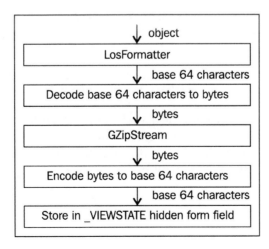

Let's convert this general approach to code. First derive your new page class from
`Page`, and put the name of the hidden form field where you'll store the compressed
ViewState in a constant (folder `ViewState` in the downloaded code bundle):

```
public class CompressedViewStatePage : System.Web.UI.Page
{
  private const string viewStateFormId = "__vsk";
```

Override the `SavePageStateToPersistenceMedium` method; it will compress the
ViewState and then put it in the hidden form field:

```
protected override void SavePageStateToPersistenceMedium
  (object viewState)
{
```

Use a `LosFormatter` to serialize the object to be stored (passed in via parameter
`viewState`). Store the resulting base 64 characters in a string:

```
LosFormatter losFormatter = new LosFormatter();
StringWriter stringWriter = new StringWriter();
losFormatter.Serialize(stringWriter, viewState);
string uncompressedViewStateString = stringWriter.ToString();
```

Compress the ViewState with a utility method that compresses base 64 strings. We'll
get to that method in a moment.

```
string compressedViewStateString =
  CompressBase64(uncompressedViewStateString);
```

Put the resulting string in the hidden form field. The name of that hidden form field
is in the constant `viewStateFormId`:

```
ClientScript.RegisterHiddenField(viewStateFormId,
  compressedViewStateString);
}
```

That concludes the `SavePageStateToPersistenceMedium` method. Now, it's time to
implement the `CompressBase64` method that we just used.

The `GZipStream` object that will do the actual compression reads from a `Stream`
and outputs to another `Stream`. So we'll have to take the base 64 string that was
generated by the `LosFormatter`, convert it to a `Stream`, compress the `Stream` with
GZipStream, and then convert the result back to a base 64 string for use in the hidden
form field:

```
private static string CompressBase64(string uncompressedBase64)
{
```

Instantiate a GZipStream object that will write compressed data to compressedStream:

```
MemoryStream compressedStream = new MemoryStream();
GZipStream gzipStream = new GZipStream(compressedStream,
  CompressionMode.Compress, true);
```

Convert the uncompressed base 64 string to a byte array, so that it can be written to the GZipStream object.

```
byte[] uncompressedData =
  Convert.FromBase64String(uncompressedBase64);
```

Write the byte array to the GZipStream object. The GZipStream object then compresses the array on the fly and writes the compressed output to compressedStream:

```
gzipStream.Write(uncompressedData, 0, uncompressedData.Length);
gzipStream.Close();
```

Turn compressedStream into a byte array, and convert the byte array to a base 64 string. Finally, return the base 64 string:

```
byte[] compressedData = compressedStream.ToArray();
string compressedBase64 =
  Convert.ToBase64String(compressedData);
return compressedBase64;
}
```

Implementing decompression

Decompression follows the same path as compression, but in reverse. We'll do this by overriding the LoadPageStateFromPersistenceMedium method. We'll get the compressed ViewState from the hidden form field, decompress it, and then deserialize it (folder ViewState in the downloaded code bundle):

```
protected override object LoadPageStateFromPersistenceMedium()
{
```

Get the compressed ViewState from the hidden form field:

```
string compressedViewState = Request.Form[viewStateFormId];
```

This compressed ViewState is in the form of a base 64 string. Decompress it with the utility method `DecompressBase64`. That will produce the decompressed ViewState as a base 64 string that the `losFormatter` can deserialize (we'll get to `DecompressBase64` in a moment):

```
string decompressedViewState =
    DecompressBase64(compressedViewState);
```

Deserialize the decompressed ViewState and return the resulting object:

```
LosFormatter losFormatter = new LosFormatter();
return losFormatter.Deserialize(decompressedViewState);
}
```

That completes the `LoadPageStateFromPersistenceMedium` method. Now, it's time to do `DecompressBase64`. Similar to `CompressBase64`, `DecompressBase64` converts a base 64 string to a `Stream` of bytes, uses `GZipStream` to decompress that `Stream`, and converts the result back to a base 64 string:

```
private static string DecompressBase64(string compressedBase64)
{
```

First, convert the compressed base 64 string to a byte array:

```
byte[] compressedData =
    Convert.FromBase64String(compressedBase64);
```

Write the byte array into a `MemoryStream` so that it can be processed by `GZipStream`:

```
MemoryStream compressedStream = new MemoryStream();
compressedStream.Write(compressedData, 0, compressedData.Length);
compressedStream.Position = 0;
```

Instantiate a `GZipStream` object that will read from the `MemoryStream` you just created:

```
GZipStream gzipStream = new GZipStream
    (compressedStream, CompressionMode.Decompress, true);
```

Copy the decompressed output stream from the `GZipStream` object to a new `MemoryStream`. .NET 4 introduced the `CopyTo` method that copies one stream to another. However, because that feature is not supported by .NET 3.5 or earlier, this code uses a trivial utility method `CopyStream`. You'll find its source in the download.

```
MemoryStream uncompressedStream = new MemoryStream();
CopyStream(gzipStream, uncompressedStream);
gzipStream.Close();
```

Convert this `MemoryStream` to a byte array and then to a base 64 string. Return the result:

```
    return Convert.ToBase64String(uncompressedStream.ToArray());
}
```

Using ViewState compression on a page

As was the case with storing ViewState on the server, derive those pages for which you want to use compressed ViewState from `CompressedViewStatePage`, rather than `Page`:

```
    public partial class ViewStateCompressed : CompressedViewStatePage
```

To experiment with this, you can use two pages in folder `ViewState` in the downloaded code bundle that generate a very long, but very compressible ViewState: `ViewStateRepeatedMessage.aspx` which does not compress ViewState, and `ViewStateCompressed.aspx` which does.

There are some obvious ways this code could be improved. You could have it check whether the compressed ViewState is actually smaller than the original, and if not, use the original. If you do this, you will need to store a flag with the ViewState indicating whether it is compressed or not. Another possible improvement would be to check the `Accept-Encoding` request header, and only compress if the server is not going to use compression on the outgoing `.aspx` file.

Reducing white space

If you have a look at the source of an average web page, you'll find it often has an amazing amount of white space. If your server uses dynamic file compression, there is no need to worry about this too much, because the compression algorithm greatly reduces white space. Otherwise, you will want to try to get rid of as much white space as you can.

One way to do this would be to remove white space from the HTML in your page definitions. But that would make them hard to read.

Another solution is to make use of the fact that after ASP.NET has generated the HTML of the page which will be sent to the browser, it sends that HTML through an output stream and it allows you to place a filter in that stream. That filter can then remove the white space.

To make this work, we'll need to take three steps:

1. Create the filter itself.

2. Write an HTTP Module that installs the filter. An HTTP Module is a class that can be plugged into the ASP.NET page-processing pipeline. In it, you can insert handlers for events that are fired while a page is processed.

3. Plug the HTTP Module into the page-processing pipeline by updating `web.config`.

> **More about HTTP Modules**
>
> To find out more about HTTP Modules and the events they handle, visit the following addresses:
>
> `http://www.15seconds.com/Issue/020417.htm`
>
> `http://msdn.microsoft.com/en-us/library/zec9k340(v=VS.71).aspx`
>
> `http://support.microsoft.com/kb/307996`

A great advantage of this approach is that it doesn't require changing your code. All you need to do is add the filter and HTTP Module to your project, and update your `web.config`.

One limitation of this solution is that if you use dynamic file compression and you have enabled `dynamicCompressionBeforeCache` as discussed in the *Configuring compression in IIS 7* section in *Chapter 10, Compression*, compression will happen before the filter is invoked. This means that the filter won't work. In that case, it is easier not to reduce white space and let the compression algorithm deal with it.

Creating the filter

The white space filter is a class derived from Stream. You will want to store the class in its own project, together with the HTTP Module, which we'll get to next.

This code collapses rows of white space into a single space. In order to not break inline JavaScript, if the row contains a line break, the row is collapsed into a line break instead. To keep it simple, it doesn't deal with the `<pre>` tag, because that tag is rarely used (project `WhiteSpaceFilter` in folder `WhiteSpaceFilter` in the downloaded code bundle):

```
using System;
using System.IO;
namespace WhiteSpaceFilter
{
    class WhiteSpaceFilterStream : Stream
    {
```

The constructor takes a Stream parameter. The class needs to write its white space reduced output to that stream, so store it in a private variable:

```
private Stream outputStream = null;
public WhiteSpaceFilterStream(Stream outputStream)
{
    this.outputStream = outputStream;
}
```

Instead of using the `Replace` method and regular expressions, this method copies the bytes from the given buffer to the output stream one-by-one, keeping track of whether it is in a row of white space characters and if so, whether there is a line break in that row. Because a row of white space characters can straddle calls to the Write method, we need class-level variables to keep track of the current state, rather than variables that are local to the method:

```
private bool inWhiteSpaceRun = false;
private bool whiteSpaceRunContainsLineBreak = false;
```

Now, override the `Write` method. This is where we actually get to filter out white space. It takes a buffer with bytes and copies it to the output stream. The offset parameter indicates where in the buffer the actual data begins. The count parameter shows how many bytes to process.

```
public override void Write(byte[] buffer, int offset, int count)
{
```

Visit each character in the buffer:

```
int dataLimit = offset + count;
for (int i = offset; i < dataLimit; i++)
{
    char c = (char)buffer[i];
```

Note that this code treats bytes as characters. This is normally not recommended because the buffer contains UTF-8 encoded characters, which take one to four bytes. So, there is no one-to-one correspondence between bytes and characters. However, we're interested only in white space characters here, which all sit in the ASCII range and therefore, fit in a single byte. Moreover, the UTF-8 encoding standard says that none of the bytes in a multi-byte character ever matches an ASCII character. So in this special case, we can get away with treating bytes as characters, making things a lot simpler. More information on UTF-8 is at http://www.utf8.com.

If we're currently at a white space character, record the fact that we're in a row of white space characters. Also check whether it is a line break; do not copy the character to the output stream yet:

```
if (Char.IsWhiteSpace(c))
{
  inWhiteSpaceRun = true;

  if ((c == '\r') || (c == '\n'))
  {
    whiteSpaceRunContainsLineBreak = true;
  }
}
```

If we're currently not at a white space character, check whether the current character has just terminated a row of white space characters. If that is the case, write a space to the output stream. However, if there was a line break in the row of white space characters, write a line break instead:

```
else
{
  if (inWhiteSpaceRun)
  {
    if (whiteSpaceRunContainsLineBreak)
    {
      outputStream.WriteByte((byte)'\r');
      outputStream.WriteByte((byte)'\n');
    }
    else
    {
      outputStream.WriteByte((byte)' ');
    }
  }
```

Write the non-white space character itself. This could actually be just one byte of a multi-byte character, but seeing that we're simply copying bytes here, it doesn't matter:

```
outputStream.WriteByte((byte)c);
```

Record the fact that we're not in a row of white space characters:

```
  inWhiteSpaceRun = false;
  whiteSpaceRunContainsLineBreak = false;
}
```

This is the end of the `for` loop.

```
    }
  }
```

That's the end of the `Write` method. All that's left now is the implementation of boilerplate methods and properties. Because this boilerplate doesn't add to the discussion, it has been left out. You will find it though in the sample code:

```
    // boilerplate implementation of other Stream methods and
      properties.
  }
}
```

Now that the filter has been done, let's turn to the HTTP Module that will insert it into the output stream.

Creating the HTTP Module

An HTTP Module is a class that implements `IHttpModule`. In that class, you can include handlers for events that are fired during the page life cycle. One of these is `PostRequestHandlerExecute`, which fires when the page has been generated and is ready to go to the browser. Because that is the moment that the white space filter needs to be installed, our HTTP Module implements a handler for that event which install the white space filter (project `WhiteSpaceFilter` in folder `WhiteSpaceFilter` in the downloaded code bundle):

```
using System;
using System.Web;
namespace WhiteSpaceFilter
{
  public class Module: IHttpModule
  {

    private void OnPostRequestHandlerExecute(Object sender,
      EventArgs e)
    {
      HttpApplication httpApplication = (HttpApplication)sender;
      HttpResponse httpResponse =
        httpApplication.Context.Response;
```

You only want to filter white space on HTML content, because the filter is optimized for HTML files. There are better optimizers for CSS and JavaScript, and you can't strip white space from graphics files.

```
    if (httpResponse.ContentType == "text/html")
    {
```

Both the new white space filter and `httpResponse.Filter` are Streams. Pass the current filter into the constructor when instantiating the new filter, so that the new filter writes to that Stream. Then assign the new filter to `httpResponse.Filter`. This allows multiple HTTP Modules to daisy chain a series of filters.

```
httpResponse.Filter = new WhiteSpaceFilterStream
    (httpResponse.Filter);
    }
}
```

Now that the `PostRequestHandlerExecute` event handler has been written, make sure it is executed when the event fires. We'll do this within the `Init` method, which is called when ASP.NET initializes the HTTP Module:

```
public void Init(HttpApplication httpApplication)
{
  httpApplication.PostRequestHandlerExecute +=new EventHandler
    (OnPostRequestHandlerExecute);
}
```

Finally, every class that implements `IHttpModule` has to implement a `Dispose` method, even if it doesn't do anything.

```
        public void Dispose()
        }
      }
    }
}
```

Finally, we'll see how to plug the new HTTP Module into the request pipeline.

Adding the HTTP Module to web.config

After you have compiled the completed HTTP Module to a DLL, create a reference to that DLL in the website where you want to use white space filtering. Then, add it to the `<httpModules>` section of the `web.config` of the site as shown:

```
<system.web>
...
  <httpModules>
    <add name="WhiteSpaceFilter"
      type="WhiteSpaceFilter.Module, WhiteSpaceFilter" />
  </httpModules>
...
</system.web>
```

Done! Run the site and see how many bytes you saved by reducing white space.

Additional measures

The measures in this section won't have a dramatic effect, especially if you use dynamic file compression. However, they don't take much time, so may still be worthwhile.

Event validation

If you take a page with input elements and look at its page source, you will probably come across a hidden form field called __EVENTVALIDATION.

This is part of a security feature that was introduced in ASP.NET 2.0. It records all input elements in that hidden form field. This way, after a postback, the page can check whether all incoming data was generated by known input elements. That makes it a bit harder for malicious users to confuse your application with bogus data.

 For more information, visit http://www.gdssecurity.com/ l/b/2009/03/19/when-aspnet-eventvalidation-doesnt-work/.

One issue with event validation is that it stops you from generating new input elements on the client using JavaScript. Another issue is that it can take a lot of space on the page, especially if you have long drop-downs, such as a countries drop-down.

If you decide that clawing back the space taken by event validation is more important than the security provided by this feature, you can disable event validation per page as follows:

```
<%@ Page Language="C#" EnableEventValidation="false" ... %>
```

To disable it for the entire website, edit the `<pages>` element in `web.config`:

```
<configuration>
  <system.web>
    <pages enableEventValidation="false">
  </system.web>
</configuration>
```

Whatever you do, be sure to always check all data sent from the browser, including POST data and cookies.

Inline JavaScript and CSS

If you have substantial inline JavaScript or CSS in your pages that is shared with other pages, move it to an external file. That way, it can be cached by the browser. As a result, when the visitor opens another page, the JavaScript or CSS file is already in cache and so, doesn't need to be loaded as a part of the page. And when the file is not in cache, the browser can often load it in parallel with other elements of the `.aspx` file.

To move shared inline JavaScript to an external file, follow these steps:

1. In Visual Studio, right-click on the website and choose **Add New Item**. From the available file types, click **JScript File**. Enter a filename and click on **Add**.

2. Move your shared inline JavaScript to the new JavaScript file. Do not put `<script>` tags in the JavaScript file.

3. Finally, add an HTML link tag to the head of your page to load the external JavaScript:

```
<head runat="server">
  <script type="text/javascript" language="javascript"
    src="myscriptfile.js"></script>
</head>
```

To move shared inline CSS to an external file, follow these steps:

1. In Visual Studio, right-click on the website and choose **Add New Item**. From the available file types, click on **Style Sheet**. Enter a filename and click on **Add**.

2. Move your shared inline CSS to the new style sheet file. Do not put `<style>` tags in the style sheet file.

3. Finally, add an HTML link tag to the head of your page to load the external style sheet in your page:

```
<head runat="server">
  <link href="mystylesheet.css" type="text/css"
    rel="Stylesheet" />
</head>
```

See *Chapter 13, Improving JavaScript Loading* for more information on reducing JavaScript and CSS load times.

Avoiding inline styling

Instead of using HTML as follows:

```
<span style="color: Red; font-weight: bold;">Error Message</span>
```

Create a class in your CSS file:

```
.errormsg
{
  color: Red;
  font-weight: bold;
}
```

Then, use the class in your HTML:

```
<span class="errormsg">Error Message</span>
```

That is a lot easier to maintain, and you get to save a few bytes. Yes, your CSS file will be bigger. However, the browser normally loads CSS files in parallel with your main page. And when your visitors move to subsequent pages on your site, the CSS file will still be in cache.

> **Image and Hyperlink controls**
>
> Two major sources of inline CSS in ASP.NET 3.5 and before are the Image and Hyperlink controls. Both insert inline styling to remove any border around images. Refer to the *Image control adapter* section in *Chapter 12, Reducing Image Load Times* to see how to get rid of this behavior.

Reducing space taken by ASP.NET IDs

When ASP.NET renders server controls such as Images and Labels, it also renders their ASP.NET IDs. These IDs can be quite lengthy. They are also not really necessary if the control is not used to post information back to the browser.

Take a look at this simple page (folder RemoveId in the downloaded code bundle):

```
<asp:Repeater ID="Repeater1" runat="server">
  <ItemTemplate>
  <p>
    <asp:Label ID="Label1" runat="server">Simple label</asp:Label>
  </p>
  </ItemTemplate>
</asp:Repeater>
```

The body of this page consists of a simple Repeater control with a Label child control. If the code behind of this page generates four iterations of the Repeater, the Repeater produces the following HTML:

```
<p><span id="Repeater1_ctl00_Label1">Simple label</span></p>
<p><span id="Repeater1_ctl01_Label1">Simple label</span></p>
<p><span id="Repeater1_ctl02_Label1">Simple label</span></p>
<p><span id="Repeater1_ctl03_Label1">Simple label</span></p>
```

Because each Label is a child control of the Repeater, the ID of the Repeater itself is prepended to the ID of the Label itself, together with its index in the Repeater. This uniquely identifies each individual Label, but it also makes for very long IDs.

Opting out of IDs

If you don't need to refer to a control from JavaScript or code behind, simply don't give it an ID and there will be no ID in the generated HTML.

If you do need IDs but only use them in the code behind, you can remove the IDs programmatically after you're done with them by setting them to null:

```
Label2.Text = "abc";
Label2.ID = null;
```

If you need to remove the IDs of a control with child controls such as the Repeater, you can use a simple recurrent method:

```
private void RemoveIDs(Control c)
{
  c.ID = null;
  foreach (Control cc in c.Controls)
  {
    RemoveIDs(cc);
  }
}
```

Now, you can get rid of all the IDs within the Repeater in one step:

```
RemoveIDs(Repeater1);
```

You could also remove all IDs from all controls on the page in the PreRender event handler:

```
protected void Page_PreRender(object sender, EventArgs e)
{
  RemoveIDs(this);
}
```

Keep in mind though that you can't remove IDs from controls that are involved in postbacks. This technique is only for read-only controls, not for forms.

Keeping IDs short

If you can't get rid of IDs completely, you can always try to keep them short. Don't overdo this; make sure that the savings in page weight outweigh any loss in maintainability.

Focus on the IDs of container controls, because they get prepended to the IDs of each of their child controls.

If you use master pages, then the ultimate container control here is the ContentPlaceHolder control in the master page. Its ID is added to the ID of every control in the content pages.

The ID of a ContentPlaceHolder control by default is ContentPlaceHolder1. This means that ContentPlaceHolder1 shows up in the IDs of all controls on content pages using this master page. If a control has a name attribute, it will show up there as well, resulting in HTML such as the following:

```
<input type="submit" name="ctl00$ContentPlaceHolder1$btn0"
  value="" id="ctl00_ContentPlaceHolder1_btn0" />
```

As a result of this, you will want to consider giving the ContentPlaceHolder a short ID, such as in the following code:

```
<asp:ContentPlaceHolder id="C" runat="server">
</asp:ContentPlaceHolder>
```

If you have multiple content place holders, make sure they all have a unique ID.

Using ASP.NET comments instead of HTML comments

If you use comments in your .aspx files, do not use normal HTML comments because they will be sent to the browser:

```
<!--normal html comments get sent to the browser-->
```

Instead, use ASP.NET comments. They are just as informative in your .aspx file, but they do not get sent to the browser:

```
<%--ASP.NET comments do not get sent to the browser--%>
```

Using Literal control instead of Label control

If you use a lot of Label controls, consider replacing them with Literal controls.

The Label control wraps its contents in a `<span>` tag, while the Literal control renders its contents without additions.

Avoiding repetition

If you do not use dynamic file compression on the server, then it makes sense to go through the page source code and identify repeating HTML. If you do use compression, this makes less sense because the compression algorithm factors out repeating code efficiently.

Take for example a repeating CSS class like this:

```
<ul>
  <li class="country">Gabon</li>
  <li class="country">Gambia</li>
  <li class="country">Georgia</li>
</ul>
```

You could shorten this by factoring out the repeating class, using a CSS contextual selector:

```
<ul class="countrylist">
  <li>Gabon</li>
  <li>Gambia</li>
  <li>Georgia</li>
</ul>
```

The `countrylist` selector would look like this in your style sheet:

```
ul.countrylist li  { ... }
```

This selects all the `<li>` tags contained within the element with the `countrylist` class. This way, there is no need to add the class "country" to each individual `<li>` tag.

CSS selectors can be very powerful, providing you with more scope to reduce repeated content. Read more about selectors at `http://reference.sitepoint.com/css/selectorref`.

Be warned though that the various versions of Internet Explorer have had issues with CSS compatibility. More details are available at `http://msdn.microsoft.com/en-us/library/cc351024(VS.85).aspx?ppud=4`.

Using shorter URLs

Long URLs not only take more space on the page, they also take more space in the request message going to the server.

You can shorten URLs by making them relative. Not only can you leave out your own domain, you can also leave out folders and even the protocol.

If the current page is `http://www.myserver.com/folder/mypage.aspx`, then here are some relative URLs you can use:

Full URL	Relative URL	Comment
`http://otherserver.com`	`//otherserver.com`	same protocol
`http://www.myserver.com/` `default.aspx`	`/default.aspx`	same server, different folder
`http://www.myserver.com/folder/` `mypage2.aspx`	`mypage2.aspx`	same server, same folder
`http://www.myserver.com/folder/` `mypage.aspx?id=5`	`?id=5`	same page, different query string

More information about relative URLs is available at `http://www.w3.org/Addressing/rfc1808.txt`.

Although relative URLs are shorter, absolute URLs do have a few advantages:

- **SEO**: If your domain is keyword-rich, having the domain duplicated throughout your HTML via the use of absolute URLs may influence your search engine page ranking. It also makes it easier for search engines to follow your links.

- **Protection against theft**: If your site contains generally useful information, people may copy your HTML and put it on their own sites, to attract traffic and make money from ads. Many of these people, however, don't bother to update the links in the content they steal. So if you use absolute links, they will still point to your site. This makes it easier for you to show the content is stolen from you, and you'll get some traffic from the links.

In general, try to keep your URLs as short as possible. Avoid long folder names and deep folder hierarchies.

If you are stuck with long folder names or hierarchies on the server, you can use virtual directories on the server to shorten your URLs. In IIS Manager, right-click on your site and add a virtual directory. In the **Alias** field, specify the short name you'll use in your URLs. Also specify the path on the server to the physical folder:

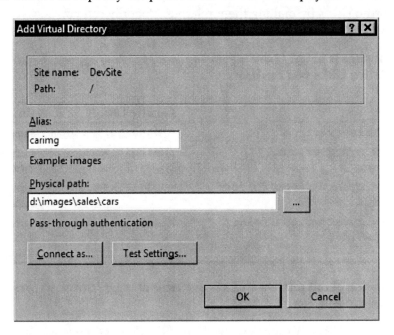

Find out more

Here are more online resources:

- W3compiler
  `http://www.w3compiler.com/`

- Gzip algorithm
  `http://www.gzip.org/algorithm.txt`

- Using Visual Studio 2008 with IIS 7
  `http://learn.iis.net/page.aspx/387/using-visual-studio-2008-with-iis-7/`

- Using Visual Studio 2005 with IIS 7.0
  `http://learn.iis.net/page.aspx/431/using-visual-studio-2005-with-iis-70/`

- Understanding ASP.NET View State
  `http://msdn.microsoft.com/en-us/library/ms972976.aspx`

- ViewState Provider - an implementation using Provider Model Design Pattern
  `http://www.codeproject.com/KB/viewstate/ViewStateProvider.aspx`

Summary

In this chapter, we first saw how to pinpoint a number of bottlenecks related to the size of the `.aspx` page as it goes over the wire. These included IIS-based file compression, ViewState, and white space overhead.

This was followed by a discussion of how to reduce ViewState and/or store it on the server rather than sending it back and forth between server and browser in a hidden field. In addition to this, a method to reduce white space was described. Compression is discussed in *Chapter 10, Compression*, and *Chapter 11, Optimizing Forms* deals with forms-related optimizations.

Finally, we saw a number of additional measures to reduce the size of `.aspx` pages, including disabling event validation, reducing space taken by ASP.NET IDs and using ASP.NET comments instead of HTML comments.

The next chapter is about compression, an extremely effective way to reduce load times. It has detailed discussions on how to enable compression in IIS 7 and IIS 6, including compression levels and caching compressed files.

10
Compression

Using compression is the single most important way to reduce load times. The .aspx files sent by the server to the browser consist of HTML. HTML is highly compressible by algorithms such as GZIP. Because of this, modern web servers, including IIS 5 and later, have the ability to compress outgoing files, and modern browsers have the ability to decompress incoming files.

A disadvantage of compression is that it is CPU-intensive. Because of this, IIS 7 by default compresses only static files, because their compressed versions are cached. Dynamic files, however, may be different for each request and therefore cannot be cached easily by IIS. So, they are not compressed by default.

In this chapter, we'll go through the following:

- How server and browser agree on compression
- How to switch compression on or off for dynamic and static files for both IIS 6 and IIS 7
- Setting the compression level, allowing you to trade off more CPU usage for higher compression
- Disabling compression when CPU usage goes over a preset limit
- Caching compressed dynamic files, so they don't have to be compressed for each request
- Switching on compression in your development environment, so you can keep track of the sizes of your pages as they'll go over the wire
- How to measure the difference between uncompressed and compressed files
- How to improve the compressibility of a file

Let's start off by seeing how server and browser agree on compression.

Agreeing on compression

How does the server know that the browser can accept compressed content? And how does the browser know that the content it received is compressed?

When a browser that supports compression sends a request to the server, it includes the request header `Accept-Encoding`, telling the server which compression algorithms it supports. For example:

```
Accept-Encoding: gzip,deflate
```

If the server then uses compression for its response, it includes the response header `Content-Encoding` in the (uncompressed) file header to say how the file has been compressed, as shown:

```
Content-Encoding: gzip
```

This keeps the browser and server in sync compression-wise. However, as described in *Chapter 5, Caching*, the *Proxy caching* section, it isn't only browsers and servers that send and receive requests and responses, but proxies as well. And, proxies can cache responses and serve subsequent requests from their cache. When a proxy caches a compressed file, how do we make sure that the proxy doesn't send that compressed file to a browser that can't process compressed files?

The solution adopted by IIS 6 and IIS 7 is to tell the proxy to only serve a request from its cache if the request has the same `Accept-Encoding` request header as the original request. IIS 6 and 7 make this happen by sending a `Vary` header in the response from the server when compression is enabled as shown:

```
Vary: Accept-Encoding
```

IIS 6 also lets you override the `Cache-Control` and `Expires` headers for compressed files via properties in its metabase. This allows you to suppress proxy caching for compressed files. The IIS 6 metabase is described in the *Configuring compression in IIS 6* section, *Updating the metabase* subsection, while the metabase properties that override the `Cache-Control` and `Expires` headers can be found at:

- HcCacheControlHeader
  http://msdn.microsoft.com/en-us/library/ms525179(VS.90).aspx

Configuring compression in IIS 7

In this section, we'll see how to use compression in IIS 7. If you use IIS 6, skip to the *Configuring compression in IIS 6* section.

Switching on compression in IIS 7 by itself is fairly easy. However, the moment you try to use some of the more advanced features, you find yourself using the command prompt or modifying a configuration file.

Here, we'll first switch on compression, and then get into those more advanced features.

Installing the dynamic content compression module

If you want to use compression for dynamic files, first install the dynamic content compression module. The steps to do this are different depending on whether you use Vista/Windows 7 or Windows Server 2008.

On Windows Server 2008:

1. Click **Start | Administrative Tools | Server Manager**.

2. On the left-hand side, expand **Roles** and then click on **Web Server (IIS)**.

3. Scroll down to the **Role Services** section and then click on **Add Role Services**. The **Add Role Services** wizard opens:

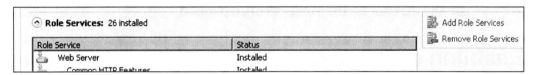

4. On the **Select Role Services** page, scroll down to the **Performance** section, and select **Dynamic Content Compression**. Click on **Next**.

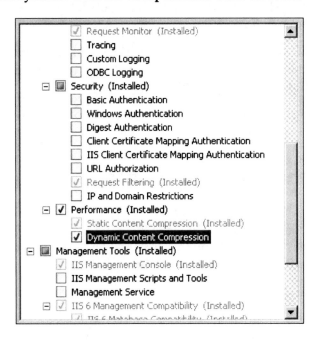

5. Read the message and click on **Install**.

6. Once the installation is done, close the wizard.

On Vista or Windows 7:

1. Click on **Start | Control Panel | Programs | Turn Windows features on or off**. The **Windows Features** dialog opens.

2. Expand **Internet Information Services**, expand **World Wide Web Services**, and expand **Performance Features**. Select **Http Compression Dynamic**.

3. Click on **OK**. Wait for the feature to be configured.

Enabling compression

Now enable compression in the IIS manager:

1. Open IIS manager. Click on **Start | Control Panel**. Type "admin" in the search box. Click on **Administrative Tools**. Double-click on **Internet Information Services (IIS) Manager**.

2. Click on your machine. Then, double-click on the **Compression** icon on the right-hand side.

3. The compression window opens. Here, you can enable compression for dynamic content and static content. The window shows the following items:

   ° **Enable dynamic content compression**: Unless your server already uses a lot of CPU, you will want to enable dynamic content compression.

   ° **Enable static content compression**: You can safely enable static content compression because compressed static content gets cached. So, only the initial compression takes CPU cycles.

   ° **Only compress files larger than (in bytes)**: It makes sense to not compress small files. Because compression produces some overhead in the file, compressing a small file may actually make it bigger rather than smaller.

   ° **Cache directory**: This is where compressed static files are stored. If you are short on disk space on the system drive, consider putting this on another drive. Make sure that the drive is a local drive or NTFS partition, and that it isn't compressed or shared.

   ° **Per application pool disk space limit (in MB)**: If you have lots of application pools and limited disk space, you may want to adjust this. If you have 100 application pools and you leave this at 100 MB, 100 x 100 MB = 10 GB may be used to cache static compressed files.

4. On the right-hand side of the window, click on **Apply**. Compression is now enabled.

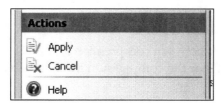

Setting compression by site, folder, or file

In addition to enabling or disabling compression for all sites on the server, you can enable or disable compression at a site level, or even a folder or file level.

To make this work:

1. Open the IIS Manager and on the left-hand side, click on the site, folder, or file whose compression status you want to change.

2. Make sure that the middle pane is switched to **Features View**, and double-click on the **Compression** icon.

3. This will open a window where you can enable or disable compression for dynamic or static files:

Compression level

You can tweak the tradeoff between compression and CPU usage by setting the compression level. The higher the compression level, the greater is the compression and CPU usage.

The compression level can be set separately for static and dynamic files. For static files, use 9, the highest level. For dynamic files, compression level 4 seems to be the sweet spot, as shown in this study:

- IIS 7 Compression. Good? Bad? How much?
  http://weblogs.asp.net/owscott/archive/2009/02/22/iis-7-compression-good-bad-how-much.aspx

However, the optimal compression level for your website may be different, depending on how much spare CPU capacity you have, the compressibility of your pages, and your bandwidth costs. Experiment with different levels to see which one works the best for you.

To set the compression level:

1. Execute this from the command prompt:

```
C:\Windows\System32\Inetsrv\Appcmd.exe
  set config -section:httpCompression
  -[name='gzip'].staticCompressionLevel:9
  -[name='gzip'].dynamicCompressionLevel:4
```

   (This sets compression level 9 for static files and compression level 4 for dynamic files).

2. Reset the IIS server to make the new compression level take effect. In IIS Manager, click on the server at the top of the tree, and then click on **Restart** on the right-hand side.

Disabling compression based on CPU usage

To make sure that compression doesn't overload the CPU, IIS 7 calculates average CPU usage every 30 seconds. It automatically switches off compression when CPU usage exceeds a given limit. Then when CPU usage drops below a second limit, it switches on compression again.

The default values for these limits are:

	Switch compression off at (CPU usage)	Switch back on at (CPU usage)
Dynamic files	90 percent	50 percent
Static files	100 percent	50 percent

Note that this means that if CPU usage on your server is consistently over 50 percent, and when it spikes over 90 percent, compression for dynamic files will be switched off, but will never be switched back on again.

You can change these limits by modifying the applicationHost.config file, which is normally in folder C:\Windows\System32\inetsrv\config:

1. Make a backup copy of applicationHost.config.

2. Open applicationHost.config with a text editor.

3. Find the <httpCompression> section.

4. To change the CPU usage at which compression for dynamic files is switched back on to 70 percent, add the dynamicCompressionEnableCpuUsage attribute to the httpCompression element, as shown:

```
<httpCompression dynamicCompressionEnableCpuUsage="70" .... >
```

Note that you provide a number to the attribute, not a percentage, so don't write a percentage sign when setting the attribute. The value 70 shown here is simply an example, not a recommendation. You need to determine the optimal value for your own site.

5. Save the applicationHost.config file.

6. Reset the IIS server to make the new compression level take effect. Start IIS Manager, click on the server at the top of the tree, and then click on **Restart** on the right-hand side.

In case you want to change any of the other limits, here are the matching attributes:

	Switch compression off at (CPU usage)	Switch back on at (CPU usage)
Dynamic files	dynamicCompression DisableCpuUsage	dynamicCompression EnableCpuUsage
Static files	staticCompression DisableCpuUsage	staticCompression EnableCpuUsage

If you want to stop IIS from ever switching off compression based on CPU usage, set all these attributes to 100.

You will find all the elements and attributes that can be used with httpCompression at:

- HTTP Compression <httpCompression>
  http://www.iis.net/ConfigReference/system.webServer/
  httpCompression

Setting the request frequency threshold for static compression

As you saw earlier, IIS 7 caches the compressed versions of static files. So, if a request arrives for a static file whose compressed version is already in the cache, it doesn't need to be compressed again.

But what if there is no compressed version in the cache? Will IIS 7 then compress the file right away and put it in the cache? The answer is yes, but only if the file is being requested frequently. By not compressing files that are only requested infrequently, IIS 7 saves CPU usage and cache space.

By default, a file is considered to be requested frequently if it is requested twice or more times per 10 seconds. This is determined by two attributes in the `serverRuntime` Element in `web.config`:

serverRuntime attribute	Description
frequentHitThreshold	Number of times a URL must be requested within the time span specified in the `frequentHitTimePeriod` attribute to be considered frequently hit. Must be between 1 and 2147483647. Default is 2.
frequentHitTimePeriod	Time interval in which a URL must be requested the number of times specified in the `frequentHitThreshold` attribute before it is considered to be frequently hit. Default is 10 seconds.

This means that when a static file is requested for the very first time, it won't be compressed.

For example, to specify that static files needs to be hit seven times per 15 seconds before they will be compressed, use:

```
<configuration>
. . .
  <system.webServer>
    <serverRuntime frequentHitThreshold="7"
      frequentHitTimePeriod="00:00:15" />
  </system.webServer>
. . .
</configuration>
```

Caching compressed dynamic files

You've seen that IIS 7 caches only the compressed version of static files, and that dynamic files are compressed for each request (provided that dynamic file compression is enabled). This means that compressing dynamic files takes much more CPU than static files.

That makes sense if the dynamic files are different for each visitor, for example if each page contains personal information. However, if the dynamic pages are fairly static and the same for all visitors, it makes sense to cache their compressed versions too.

You may already use the ASP.NET `OutputCache` directive for exactly this situation. The issue is that by default, IIS stores the uncompressed version of the file in the output cache. For each request, IIS then has to compress the contents of the cache before sending it to the browser. This is not very efficient.

Storing compressed files in the output cache

Here is how to get IIS to cache the compressed version of the file, rather than the uncompressed version. That way, it doesn't have to compress the file for each request, reducing CPU usage.

Because this uses ASP.NET output caching, you need to use the `OutputCache` directive in your pages, as shown:

```
<%@ OutputCache Duration="300" VaryByParam="none" %>
```

This caches the page for 300 seconds. More information about caching is in *Chapter 5, Caching*.

Now, to get IIS to cache the compressed version rather than the uncompressed version, modify the `applicationHost.config` file. You'll normally find this file in folder `C:\Windows\System32\inetsrv\config`:

1. Make a backup copy of `applicationHost.config`.
2. Open `applicationHost.config` with a text editor.
3. Find the `<urlCompression>` section.
4. Add the `dynamicCompressionBeforeCache="true"` attribute to the `urlCompression` element, as shown:

   ```
   <urlCompression dynamicCompressionBeforeCache="true" ...  />
   ```
5. Save the `applicationHost.config` file.
6. Reset the IIS server to make the new attribute take effect.
7. Start IIS Manager, click the server at the top of the tree, and then click on **Restart** on the right-hand side.

What if a client doesn't accept compressed content?

Now that we're caching compressed content, what happens if someone visits your site with a browser that doesn't accept compressed content?

To simulate this eventuality, we'll send a request to the server that doesn't have the `Accept-Encoding` request header. This should force the server to send uncompressed content.

To do this, we'll use Fiddler, a free proxy which allows you to "fiddle" with requests and responses while they are travelling between browser and server:

1. Download Fiddler at `http://www.fiddler2.com/fiddler2/`.

2. Install Fiddler and start it.

3. Start the Firefox browser. On the Firefox status bar, switch on forcing traffic to Fiddler:

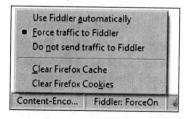

4. At this stage, when you visit a page with Firefox, the server should still use compression (assuming the request has an `Accept-Encoding` request header allowing GZIP compression). You saw how to verify this with Web Developer in the *Pinpointing bottlenecks* section.

5. Now get Fiddler to strip off the `Accept-Encoding` request header from the request going from Firefox to the web server. In the Fiddler window on the right-hand side, click on the **Filters** tab, select **Use Filters**, select **Delete request header**, and fill in "Accept-Encoding".

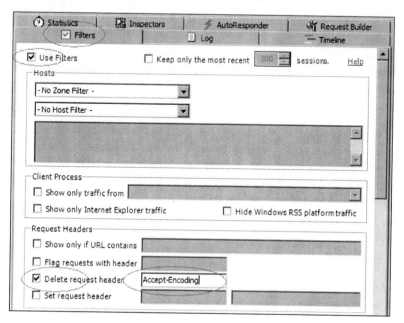

6. Refresh the page in Firefox. Check the file size again with Web Developer. You should find that no compression was used with this request. That will make browsers that do not support compression happy. So far, so good.

7. In Fiddler, uncheck the **Delete request header** checkbox. As a result, the Accept-Encoding request header now makes it to the web server again.

8. Refresh the page. The server should now compress the file again. But if you check with Web Developer, you'll find that it is still sending files uncompressed!

    This is because when IIS received the request for uncompressed content, it threw away the compressed contents in the cache, regenerated the content and stored it uncompressed in the cache. It then keeps serving this uncompressed content until the cache expires, even to clients that accept compressed content.

9. You can prevent this from happening by caching both compressed and uncompressed content. You do that by including VaryByContentEncoding in the OutputCache directive, as shown in the following code:

```
<%@ OutputCache Duration="300" VaryByParam="none"
   VaryByContentEncoding="gzip;deflate" %>
```

10. If you now delete the Accept-Encoding header and then let it go through again, you'll see that the server always sends compressed content to clients that accept it, even if another client didn't accept it.

11. Before you end this experiment and close Fiddler, go back to the Firefox status bar and stop sending traffic to Fiddler. Otherwise, Firefox will complain about the missing proxy when you close Fiddler.

A drawback of using VaryByContentEncoding in the OutputCache directive is that it disables kernel caching for this file. Kernel caching was discussed in *Chapter 5, Caching*.

So, should you use VaryByContentEncoding in the OutputCache directive? Seeing that you are reading this chapter, the gain in compression by using VaryByContentEncoding may well outweigh the loss of kernel caching, especially seeing that you already use output caching. Your best bet would be to try both scenarios in production for a while, and compare CPU usage, response times, and bandwidth used per request for each scenario.

Configuring compression in IIS 6

Configuring compression on IIS 6 is far from straightforward. It involves four steps:

1. Switching on compression in the IIS Manager.
2. Setting permissions on the folder where compressed static files are cached.
3. Updating the metabase.
4. Resetting the IIS server.

Let's go through each step.

Switching on compression in the IIS Manager

Switching on compression in the IIS Manager consists of these steps:

1. Start IIS manager: Click on **Start | Administrative Tools | Internet Information Services (IIS) Manager**.

2. Backup the metabase: Right-click on your server, and then click on **All Tasks | Backup/Restore Configuration**. Click on the **Create Backup** button, enter a name for your backup, such as today's date, and click on **OK**. Finally, click on **Close** to get back to the IIS manager.

3. Expand your server. Then, right-click on the **Web Sites** node and click on **Properties | Service**.

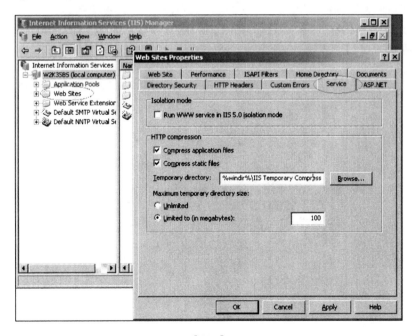

4. If your server has enough spare CPU capacity, select **Compress application files**. Because there is no caching for dynamic files of compressed content, this will cause IIS to compress dynamic files on the fly for every request. As a result, dynamic file compression takes more CPU than compressing static files.

5. Select **Compress static files**.

6. The temporary directory is where compressed static files are cached. Leave the default for **Temporary directory**, or enter a different directory. If you enter a different directory, make sure it sits on an uncompressed and unshared local NTFS volume.

7. Set a maximum size for the temporary directory.

8. Click on **OK**.

Setting permissions on the folder where compressed static files are cached

For static compression to work, the IIS_WPG group or the identity of the application pool must have Full Control access to the folder where the compressed files are stored.

Unless you changed the folder in the previous step (in the **Temporary directory** field), it will be at C:\WINDOWS\IIS Temporary Compressed Files.

1. Right-click on the folder and click on **Properties | Security**.

2. Click on the **Add** button and add the **IIS_WPG** group, or the identity of the application pool.

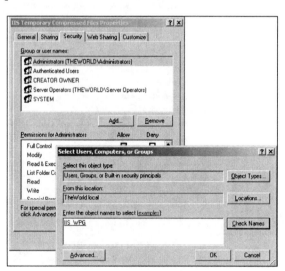

3. Allow **Full Control** to the identity you just added and click on **OK**.

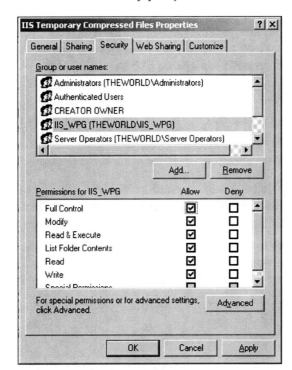

IIS_WPG or IUSR_{machinename}?

There is conflicting advice on various websites as to whether you should give the IIS_WPG group or the IUSR_{machinename} account access to the folder where the compressed files are stored. However, testing for this book with a clean install of Windows Server 2003 and IIS 6 has shown that IIS 6 will only compress static files if the IIS_WPG group has Full Control access to that folder, irrespective of the level of access by IUSR_{machinename}.

Updating the metabase

Next, modify the metabase:

1. Get IIS to allow you to edit the metabase. In IIS manager, right-click on your IIS server near the top of the tree on the left-hand side. Click on **Properties**, check **Enable Direct Metabase Edit**, and click on **OK**.

2. You'll normally find the metabase in directory `C:\Windows\system32\inetsrv`, in file the `metabase.xml`. Open that file with a text editor.

3. Find the IIsCompressionScheme elements. There should be two of these: one for the deflate compression algorithm and one for GZIP.

4. In both the elements, extend the HcFileExtensions property with the extensions you need for static files used in your pages, such as .css and .js. You will wind up with something like the following:

```
HcFileExtensions="htm
  html
  css
  js
  xml
  txt"
```

Keep in mind that there is no point in including image files here, such as .gif, .jpg, and .png. These files are already compressed because of their native format.

5. Also in both elements, extend the HcScriptFileExtensions property with the extensions you need for dynamic files, such as .aspx. You will wind up with something like the following:

```
HcScriptFileExtensions="asp
  dll
  exe
  aspx
  asmx
  ashx"
```

6. The compression level for dynamic files is set by the HcDynamicCompressionLevel property in both IIsCompressionScheme elements. By default, this is set to zero, which is too low. The higher you set this, the better the compression but the greater the CPU usage. You might want to test different compression levels to see which one gives you the best tradeoff between CPU usage and file size. Start testing at a low compression level, and then increase this until CPU usage gets too high. The highest possible compression level is 10:

```
HcDynamicCompressionLevel="1"
```

7. The compression level for static files is set by the HcOnDemandCompLevel property in both IIsCompressionScheme elements. By default, this is set to 10, meaning maximum compression. Because compressed static files are cached (so that static files are not compressed for each request), this causes little CPU usage. As a result, you will want to stick with the default.

8. Save the file.

9. Disallow editing of the metabase. Right-click on your IIS server, click on **Properties**, uncheck **Enable Direct Metabase Edit**, and click on **OK**.

You'll find a full list of the available metabase properties at:

Metabase Property Reference (IIS 6.0)
```
http://www.microsoft.com/technet/prodtechnol/
WindowsServer2003/Library/IIS/c63788cc-70b4-4a44-a9a3-
329fa8fb3afb.mspx?mfr=true
```

Instead of editing the metabase directly, you can run the adsutil.vbs utility from the command line to change the metabase. This allows you to write a script so you can quickly update a number of servers. For example, setting HcDoStaticCompression to true will enable static compression. This is done as follows:

1. Open command prompt and change the directory to C:\Inetpub\ AdminScripts

2. Run the following command:

```
cscript adsutil.vbs set w3svc/filters/compression/parameters/
HcDoStaticCompression true
```

For more information about adsutil.vbs, visit:

- Using the Adsutil.vbs Administration Script (IIS 6.0)
  ```
  http://www.microsoft.com/technet/prodtechnol/WindowsServer2003/
  Library/IIS/d3df4bc9-0954-459a-b5e6-7a8bc462960c.mspx?mfr=true
  ```

Resetting the IIS server

Finally, reset the server, so that it picks up your changes. Right-click on your IIS server and then click on **All Tasks | Restart IIS**.

Alternatively, the open command prompt and run:

```
iisreset
```

Static files are not always served compressed

If a static file is requested and there is no compressed version of the file in the temporary directory where compressed static files are cached, IIS 6 will send the uncompressed version of the file. It then compresses the file and stores the compressed version in the temporary directory, ready to be served in response to a subsequent request for the file.

Configuring compression in IIS 5

IIS 5 is beyond the scope of this book. If you still use IIS 5, see how to use compression at `http://technet.microsoft.com/en-au/library/bb742379.aspx`.

Using compression in your development environment

When you make changes to your site in Visual Studio, you want to know the effect those changes have on file sizes, both before and after compression. Unfortunately, the Cassini development server included with Visual Studio doesn't support compression. So, you'll need to use IIS instead of Cassini during development.

Making this happen involves a simple four-step process:

1. Installing IIS 7.
2. Enabling compression.
3. Creating a development site in IIS.
4. Modifying your project so it uses the development site.

To use Visual Studio with IIS, you need to run Visual Studio in administrator mode. If you are not normally logged in as administrator, right-click on the Visual Studio executable file and choose **Run as administrator**. To make things easier, you could also create a shortcut to Visual Studio and on the **Compatibility** tab of the **Shortcut Properties**, select **Run this program as an administrator**.

Installing IIS 7

Follow these steps to install IIS on Vista or Windows 7:

1. Click on **Start | Control Panel | Programs | Turn windows features on or off**.
2. Check **Internet Information Services**.
3. Expand the **Internet Information Services** node, expand **Web Management Tools**, and make sure **IIS Management Console** is checked. This will allow you to run the IIS Manager.
4. Expand **IIS 6 Management Compatibility** and make sure **IIS Metabase and IIS 6 configuration compatibility** is checked. You need this to be able to use IIS from Visual Studio.

5. Expand the **World Wide Web Services** node and then the **Application Development Features** node. Make sure that **ASP.NET** is checked so that the server can run ASP.NET applications.

6. Still under **World Wide Web Services**, expand **Performance Features**, and make sure **Http Compression Dynamic** is selected. This enables the server to compress `.aspx` files.

7. Also under **World Wide Web Services**, expand **Security** and make sure **Windows Authentication** is selected. You need this to be able to use IIS from Visual Studio.

8. Click on **OK**. Windows will take a while to implement the changes.

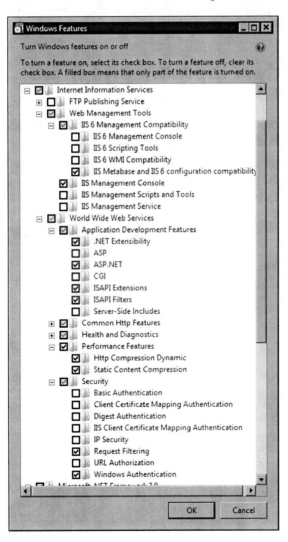

Enabling compression

You've seen how to do this earlier on, in the *Configuring compression in IIS 7* section. Here is a recap:

1. Open IIS manager. Click on **Start | Control Panel**. Type "admin" in the search box. Click on **Administrative Tools** and double-click on **Internet Information Services (IIS) Manager**.

2. Click on your machine. Then double-click on the Compression icon on the right-hand side. The compression window opens.

3. Enable compression for dynamic content and/or static content; the same settings you apply in your production environment. Click on **Apply** to enable compression.

Creating a development site in IIS

Create a site in IIS to use from Visual Studio:

1. While still in IIS Manager, expand your server. Right-click on **Sites** and choose **Add Web Site**. The **Add Web Site** dialog opens.

2. Make up a site name. As the physical path, enter the root folder of your source files, that is, the one with `default.aspx` and `web.config`. Enter a port that isn't already in use, for example 1080, and click on **OK**.

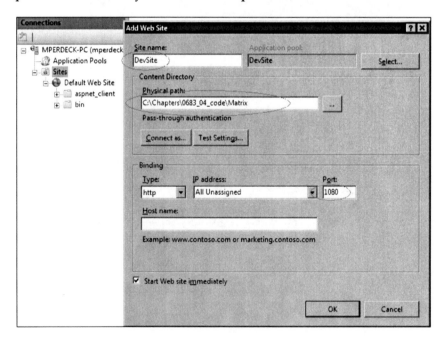

3. Enable **Windows Authentication**. Double-click on your new site, double-click on **Authentication**, right-click on **Windows Authentication**, and choose **Enable**.

Modifying your project so it uses the development site

Finally, swap Cassini for IIS in your project. How to do this depends on whether you use a website or a web application.

If you use a website:

1. Run Visual Studio as administrator. Right-click on the website and choose **Start Options**. The **Property Pages** window opens, with the **Start Options** tab selected.

2. In the **Server** section, select **Use custom server**. In the **Base Url** field, enter the localhost address with the port you entered when you created the development site in IIS manager:

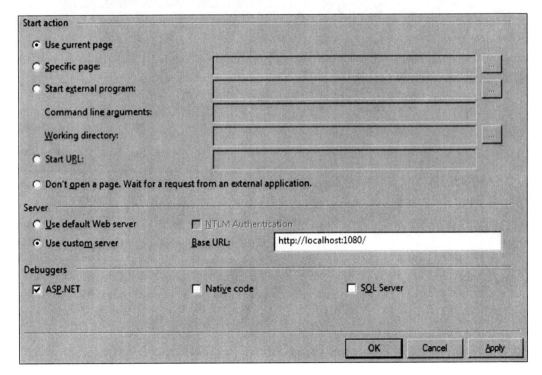

3. Click on **OK**.

If you use a web application:

1. In Visual Studio, right-click on the web application and choose **Properties**. The **Properties** window opens.

2. Click on the **Web** tab.

3. Scroll down to the **Servers** section and select **Use Local IIS Web server**. In the **Project Url** field, enter the localhost address with the port you entered when you created the development site in IIS manager.

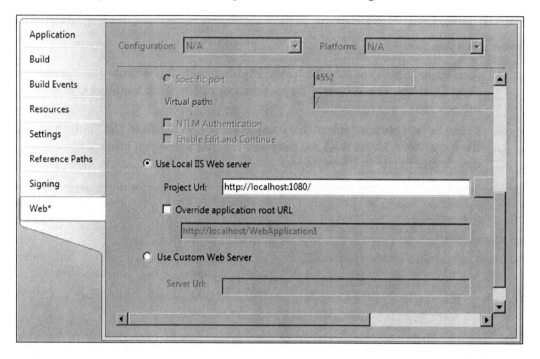

4. **Save** the properties.

To see more options such as using Visual Studio with a remote IIS 7 Server, visit:

- `http://learn.iis.net/page.aspx/387/using-visual-studio-2008-with-iis-7/` (for Visual Studio 2008)

- `http://learn.iis.net/page.aspx/431/using-visual-studio-2005-with-iis-70/` (for Visual Studio 2005)

Be aware that if you use output caching, when you refresh a page, the server will get the page from cache and your breakpoints won't be hit. Refer to *Chapter 5, Caching* for a solution for this.

Measuring the difference compression makes

As you saw, enabling compression means giving up CPU capacity to achieve reduced file sizes. Now that you have enabled compression, you will want to evaluate whether it works for you.

To see the difference in file size, use the Web Developer add-on for Firefox. We saw how to use this earlier on in the *Pinpointing bottlenecks* section.

To see the difference in CPU usage, stress test your site with compression switched off and then switched on (*Chapter 14, Load Testing* shows how to do a load test):

1. With compression switched on, start a load generator that puts a heavy load on your test site. This test isn't meant to simulate the real world, so do not use think times. Make sure that the request headers that are sent by the load generator contain `Accept-Encoding: gzip,deflate`, forcing the web server to provide compressed responses.

2. Run `perfmon` from the command prompt. Expand the **CPU** bar. You should find that the **IIS Worker Process** is the heaviest user of CPU cycles. Write down the **Average CPU** for that process.

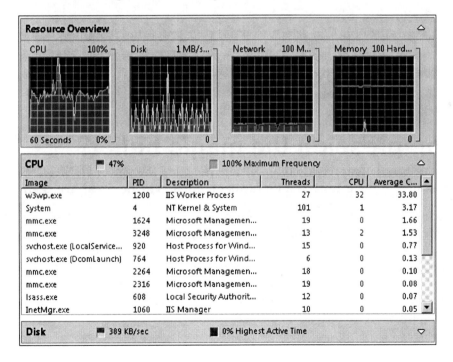

3. Now, do the same with compression switched off.

4. Compare the average CPU usage of both scenarios. Average CPU usage with compression enabled should be higher, unless you use IIS 7 and cache the compressed versions of dynamic files.

Improving the compressibility of your pages

If your server uses compression, then it makes sense to optimize compressibility of your text files. Compression algorithms like repeating content, which puts a premium on consistency:

- Always specify HTML attributes in the same order. One way to achieve this is to have all your HTML generated by high-level web controls and custom server controls, instead of low-level HTML server controls. This will slightly increase CPU usage, but will give you assured consistency. For example, write the following:

  ```
  <asp:Hyperlink runat="server"......>
  ```

  Instead of the following:

  ```
  <a runat="server" .... >
  ```

- Likewise, within CSS selectors, write your properties in alphabetical order.
- Use consistent casing. Use all lowercase for HTML tags and attributes, and you'll be XHTML-compliant as well.
- Use consistent quoting: Don't mix " . . . . " and ' . . . . '.

Is compression the magic bullet?

With server-based compression dramatically reducing the size of HTML, CSS, and JavaScript files, is there any room for further reduction in file sizes? Yes, there is.

Introducing AJAX-style asynchronous form submission and AJAX-style grids and other user interface elements will still make a big difference, even with compression enabled. And if you can do so without too much effort, it is worthwhile to reduce ViewState. On the other hand, removing repetitive content such as white space will make less sense, because compression algorithms are very good at compressing such content. Reducing ViewState is described in *Chapter 9, Reducing Time to Last Byte*, optimizing forms in *Chapter 11, Optimizing Forms*.

Also, even with compression enabled for dynamic files in your server and most browsers supporting compression, your server will still be sending uncompressed content to some of your visitors:

- Some anti-virus packages and web proxies strip off or mangle the `Accept-Encoding` request header going from the browser to the server. That way, the server sends back uncompressed content, which is easier to process for those anti-virus packages and web proxies.

- In the *Configuring compression in IIS 7* section, you saw that if you cache the compressed versions of dynamic files without using `VaryByContentEncoding`, a request for uncompressed content will cause the server to send uncompressed content to all clients, until the files expire from cache.

- In that same section, you saw how a spike in CPU load can stop compression until the load drops far enough to re-enable compression.

To optimize download times in these cases, you will need to reduce the size of your HTML, as discussed in *Chapter 9, Reducing Time to Last Byte*, for example by reducing ViewState, removing inline JavaScript, and reducing white space.

Find out more

Here are more online resources:

- 10 Tips for Writing High-Performance Web Applications
  `http://msdn.microsoft.com/en-us/magazine/cc163854.aspx`

- Configuring HTTP Compression in IIS 7
  `http://technet.microsoft.com/en-us/library/cc771003(WS.10).aspx`

- IIS 6.0 Technical Reference
  `http://technet.microsoft.com/en-us/library/cc775635(WS.10).aspx`

- IIS Compression in IIS6.0
  `http://weblogs.asp.net/owscott/archive/2004/01/12/57916.aspx`

- Everything you ever wanted to know about compression, but were afraid to ask
  `http://geekswithblogs.net/JamesFleming/archive/2010/02/04/everything-you-ever-wanted-to-know-about-compression-but-were.aspx`

- Measuring the Performance Effects of Dynamic Compression in IIS 7.0
  `http://www.webperformanceinc.com/library/reports/iis7_compression/`

- Let's make the web faster
  `http://code.google.com/speed/articles/use-compression.html`
- Page Speed tool
  `http://code.google.com/speed/page-speed/download.html`

Summary

In this chapter, we had a detailed look at server-based compression, the most effective way to reduce the sizes of files as they go over the wire from your server to the browser.

We started off by looking at how server and browser agree on compression, including the HTTP headers involved. This was followed by detailed instructions on enabling compression in IIS 7 and IIS 6. This included specifying which types of files will be compressed, setting a compression level to fine-tune the tradeoff between CPU usage and file size, and setting a CPU usage limit above which compression is automatically disabled.

We also looked at how to enable compression in your development environment, so you can keep track of the size of the files your site is going to produce. This was followed by quick discussions on how to measure the impact of compression, both on file sizes and CPU usage, and on how to improve the compressibility of a file.

In the next chapter, we'll find out how to dramatically reduce the number of bytes sent over the wire by pages with forms.

11
Optimizing Forms

In a classic ASP.NET website, when you send user input to the server via a form, the existing page in the browser is replaced ("refreshed") by a new page sent by the browser. However, that new page is often almost the same as the existing page. This means, there is scope to cut down the number of bytes sent to the browser to only that content which is new. Also, when the existing page is replaced by the new page, the state of the controls on the existing page is lost, necessitating the introduction of ViewState. This is a problem, especially with `GridView` controls, which can generate a lot of ViewState overhead.

You can dramatically improve form responsiveness by:

- Reducing the number of trips to the server
- Speeding up those trips that are unavoidable by reducing the number of bytes going over the wire

This chapter takes you through three ways to do that:

- **Client-side validation**: We'll look at two options: ASP.NET validation controls and a JavaScript library called Validate

- **Asynchronous form submission**: We'll touch five technologies that let you interact with the server without refreshing the whole page: the `UpdatePanel` control, page methods, web services, using a generic handler, and WCF Data Services and the Entity Framework combined with live data-binding, as supported by ASP.NET AJAX 4

- **AJAX-type grids**: Because grids are especially expensive in ASP.NET, we'll have a quick look at options to implement AJAX-type grids

Ultimately, what it comes down to is that you shift functionality from the server to the browser, meaning more client-side development. JavaScript, AJAX, and JavaScript libraries such as jQuery and Microsoft's ASP.NET AJAX are big subjects in themselves. As a result, we'll only briefly touch each of the available technologies here, so that you can select which ones you want to study further.

Let's start with client-side validation.

Client-side validation

If you use input forms on your site, you probably use input validation—required fields, correct e-mail format, and so on. If you currently do all your validation on the server, you can greatly decrease traffic between browser and server by adding client-side validation.

This means that a bit of JavaScript on the page validates the form before it is sent to the server, and shows an error message if something is wrong. This way, the visitor doesn't have to wait for a postback before finding out that they made a mistake, and you get to save bandwidth. Client-side validation doesn't replace server-side validation—a malicious user can easily circumvent it and send invalid data.

Introducing client-side validation is pretty easy, and doesn't require a lot of JavaScript coding. We'll have a look at two popular ways to implement client-side validation: ASP.NET validation controls, and the Validate JavaScript library.

ASP.NET validation controls

ASP.NET comes with five validation controls that will satisfy most of your validation needs.

This section gives only a high-level overview of ASP.NET validation controls. For all the details, visit:

- Validating ASP.NET Server Controls

  `http://msdn.microsoft.com/en-us/library/aa479013.aspx`

- ASP.NET Validation in Depth

  `http://msdn.microsoft.com/en-us/library/aa479045.aspx`

Quick example

The code for this example is in the page `AspNetValidation.aspx` in the `ClientSideValidation` folder in the downloaded code bundle.

Imagine you have a textbox on your form asking for a name:

```
<asp:TextBox ID="txtName" runat="server"></asp:TextBox>
```

To make that field required, so that the visitor is forced to enter something in that field, add one of the ASP.NET validation controls, `RequiredFieldValidator`:

```
<asp:TextBox ID="txtName" runat="server"></asp:TextBox>
<asp:RequiredFieldValidator ID="RequiredFieldValidator1"
  runat="server"
ControlToValidate="txtName">*</asp:RequiredFieldValidator>
```

As you see, it requires the name of the control to validate. It also takes some HTML, which is an asterisk in this case.

The validator control generates JavaScript that validates the control when the visitor tries to submit the form. If the validation fails, it aborts the submission and shows the HTML.

Validator controls not only provide client-side validation, but also provide the corresponding server-side validation. If any of the validations on a page has failed, the `IsValid` property of the `Page` object evaluates to `false`. So instead of writing validation logic in your code behind, you place a simple test in the click event handler of the submission button:

```
protected void btnSave_Click(object sender, EventArgs e)
{
  if (!Page.IsValid)
  {
    return;
  }

  //Process Page
  ...
}
```

Available validator controls

Here is a short description of each of the five ASP.NET validator controls. For more details, search MSDN (`http://msdn.microsoft.com/`) for more information on each control.

Validator	Description
RequiredFieldValidator	Ensures that the control is not empty.
RangeValidator	Ensures that the control value falls within a specified range.
CompareValidator	Compares the value in one control with the value in another control, or with a fixed value.
RegularExpressionValidator	Matches the control value against a regular expression. You would use this to validate e-mail addresses, phone numbers, and so on.
CustomValidator	Allows you to write your own client-side and server-side validation code.

You can use multiple validator controls for the one-input control. Each validator control will validate the control value, and show its HTML if the validation fails.

Validation summary

To show a summary of all failed validations, insert a `ValidationSummary` control at the spot where you want the summary:

```
<asp:ValidationSummary ID="ValidationSummary1" runat="server" />
```

To set the messages that are shown in the summary, use the `ErrorMessage` attribute on each validator control, for example:

```
<asp:TextBox ID="txtName" runat="server"></asp:TextBox>
<asp:RequiredFieldValidator ID="RequiredFieldValidator1"
    runat="server" ControlToValidate="txtName"
    ErrorMessage="Enter your name">*</asp:RequiredFieldValidator>
```

If this validation fails, the asterisk is shown next to the field, and the string `Enter your name` is shown in the validation summary.

Disabling validation

You may have buttons on your page that cause a postback, but are not related to the form. When a visitor clicks one of those buttons, you don't want the postback to be blocked when the form validation fails.

To solve this, set the `CausesValidation` attribute to `false` on the controls that shouldn't cause a validation, as shown:

```
<asp:Button ID="btnSave" runat="server"
  CausesValidation="false" Text="Save" OnClick="btnSave_Click" />
```

Alternatively, you could have a page with multiple forms, such as a search box and an input form. When you submit one of the forms, you want only that form to be validated and not any other form.

You deal with this by putting each form in its own validation group. Simply make up a name for each group, and set the `ValidationGroup` attribute of the validator controls and submit buttons of each form to that name. Consider the two forms in the following code, one using validation group `search`, and the other using validation group `input`:

```
<div id="searchform">
  <asp:TextBox ID="txtSearch" runat="server"></asp:TextBox>
  <asp:RequiredFieldValidator ID="rfvSearch"
    runat="server" ValidationGroup="search"
    ControlToValidate="txtSearch">*</asp:RequiredFieldValidator>

  <asp:Button ID="Button1" runat="server" ValidationGroup="search"
    Text="Search" OnClick="btnSearch_Click" />
</div>

<div id="inputform">
  <asp:TextBox ID="txtName" runat="server"></asp:TextBox>
  <asp:RequiredFieldValidator ID="rfvName"
    runat="server" ValidationGroup="input"
    ControlToValidate="txtName">*</asp:RequiredFieldValidator>

  <asp:Button ID="btnSave" runat="server" ValidationGroup="input"
    Text="Save" OnClick="btnSave_Click" />
</div>
```

Finally, you can switch off a validator control in code, via its `Enabled` property:

```
rfvName.Enabled = false;
```

Overhead

ASP.NET validator controls are useful, but they come at a cost. Using them causes ASP.NET to add a lot of inline JavaScript code on the `.aspx` page—about 5 KB or 1 KB compressed, for a simple form with four text boxes.

It also causes ASP.NET to download two JavaScript files from your server, totaling 41 KB (11 KB compressed). However, because these files are cached on the browser, they wouldn't be loaded again if someone visits a second form on your page.

Use the Web Developer add-on for Firefox to determine the overhead for your particular forms.

Read on to find out about a more efficient solution, the Validate JavaScript library.

Validate JavaScript library

Validate is a popular JavaScript library that lets you specify validation methods by adding CSS classes. For example, to make a control required, you add the `required` class:

```
<asp:TextBox ID="txtName" runat="server"
  CssClass="required"></asp:TextBox>
```

Unlike the ASP.NET validator controls, the Validate library doesn't add inline JavaScript. So, the increase in size of your `.aspx` file is trivial. On the other hand, it only caters to client-side validation; so, you still have to do your own server-side validation.

The home page of the Validate library is at `http://bassistance.de/jquery-plugins/jquery-plugin-validation/`.

When you download the library, you'll receive a `ZIP` file with several files. The file you want to load in your page via the script tag is `jquery.validate.min.js`.

The Validate library is an extension or "plugin" of the jQuery library. This means that you need to load jQuery in your page as well. Its home page is at `http://jquery.com/`.

There are a few different versions of the jQuery library. You'll want the production version, which has been compressed to minimize download size. Its name ends in `.min.js`. At the time of writing this book, the latest version was `jquery-1.4.2.min.js`.

Initialization

After you have loaded the jQuery and Validate libraries, the Validate library needs to be initialized for the form where it will find the controls to validate. If the form has ID form1 (as is the default on an ASP.NET page without a master page), the code will look similar to the following (page jQueryValidation.aspx in the folder ClientSideValidation in the downloaded code bundle):

```
<script type="text/javascript" language="javascript">
  $(document).ready(function() {
    $("#form1").validate()
  });
</script>
```

 Note that on an ASP.NET page with a master page, the ID of the form by default is aspnetForm.

The initialization code may look a bit strange if you're not familiar with jQuery. The ready function registers an unnamed function that is called when the DOM has been loaded. The unnamed function gets the form with id form1 and calls validate() to initialize the Validate library.

Built-in validation methods

Earlier on, we saw how you specify validation methods by adding CSS classes, as in the following code:

```
<asp:TextBox ID="txtName" runat="server"
  CssClass="required"></asp:TextBox>
```

Let's have a closer look at those validation methods.

Validate recognizes a number of CSS classes that specify the format of the input, such as email, number, and date. For example, to ensure that the visitor enters a valid e-mail address, use:

```
<asp:TextBox ID="txtEmail" runat="server"
  CssClass="email"></asp:TextBox>
```

To make this e-mail field required, combine the email and required classes:

```
<asp:TextBox ID="txtEmail" runat="server" CssClass="required
  email"></asp:TextBox>
```

Validate also supports validation methods that include a parameter, for example, `minlength` (requires input with a minimum length) and `max` (specifies a maximum numeric value).

Because these methods use a parameter, they don't use a CSS class. Instead, if you use a web control such as TextBox, you would give the control an attribute in the code behind, as shown:

```
txtCity.Attributes.Add("minlength", "4");
```

If you use an HTML server control, it would look similar to the following code:

```
<input type="text" runat="server" minlength="4" id="txtCity" />
```

At the time of writing, the Validate library supported 15 validation methods, including `remote`, which allows you to run a method on the server and `equalTo`, which compares a control with another control. The full documentation is available at:

- Plugins/Validation - jQuery JavaScript Library

  http://docs.jquery.com/Plugins/Validation

Adding validation methods

If the built-in validation methods do not give you what you need, you can add it on your own. For example, to add a validator that checks for a valid zip code as used in the United States, run the following code (`jQueryValidationZip.aspx` in the `ClientSideValidation` folder in the downloaded code bundle):

```
jQuery.validator.addMethod(
  "zip",
  function(value, element) {
    return this.optional(element) ||
      /^\d{5}((-|\s)?\d{4})?$/.test(value);
  },
  "Please specify a correct zip code");
```

The `addMethod` function takes the name of the new validation method `zip`, a function that returns `true` if the value passes the validation, and the error message that is shown if it doesn't pass the validation.

The function takes two arguments: the value to be validated, and the input element. It returns `true` if the value either matches the given regular expression, or if the value is empty and the element is not required. That way, visitors can choose not to enter their zip code without getting an error message.

You can use the new validation method in the same way as the built-in validation methods. Because this method doesn't take parameters, you have to use a class:

```
<asp:TextBox ID="txtZip" runat="server"
  CssClass="zip"></asp:TextBox>
```

You'll find out more about `addMethod` at `http://docs.jquery.com/Plugins/Validation/Validator/addMethod`.

Formatting error messages

When a form field fails validation, the validator code does two things:

- It adds the error class to the form field itself.
- It adds a label tag after the form field containing the error message. This label tag, too, has the error class.

As a result, the DOM winds up as shown:

```
<input name="txtZip" type="text" id="txtZip" class="zip error">
<label for="txtZip" generated="true" class="error">
  Please specify a correct zip code
</label>
```

One way to see the current state of the DOM is to load the page in Google Chrome, enter an invalid value, right-click on the page, and choose **Inspect element**.

This means that you can easily style the error message in your stylesheet, along the following lines:

```
label.error
{
{
  display: block;
  color: Red; font-size: small;
}
}
```

This moves the error message below the form field by making it a block element instead of an inline element. It sets the color of the message to red, and uses a smaller font.

Styling the offending input form field goes along the same lines. To make its background light red so that it stands out better, use the following code:

```
input.error
{
  background-color: #FF6565;
}
```

Content Delivery Network (CDN)

The Validate and jQuery libraries are hosted on Microsoft's free **Content Delivery Network (CDN)**. A CDN is a worldwide network of servers with a single domain. When a visitor requests files from the CDN, the requests are automatically sent to the nearest server in the network, resulting in reduced response times. Also, you save on bandwidth because the files are no longer served from your server.

A list of files hosted on the Microsoft CDN is available at:

- Microsoft Ajax Content Delivery Network

  `http://www.asp.net/ajaxlibrary/cdn.ashx`

You can load the libraries from the Microsoft CDN with normal script tags, as in the following code (check the Microsoft CDN website for latest versions of the JavaScript files):

```
<script type="text/javascript"
  src="http://ajax.microsoft.com/ajax/jquery/jquery-1.4.2.min.js">
</script>
<script type="text/javascript"
  src="http://ajax.microsoft.com/ajax/jquery.validate/
  1.7/jquery.validate.min.js">
</script>
```

Google, too, has a free CDN. It hosts jQuery, but not Validate. A list of files hosted on the Google CDN is available at:

- Google Libraries API - Developer's Guide

  `http://code.google.com/apis/libraries/devguide.html#jquery`

What happens if the Microsoft CDN is down? That would break your page. The solution is to find a symbol defined in the jQuery library, and then test whether that symbol has been defined after the `script` tag. If it hasn't, the Microsoft CDN is down and it's time to try the Google CDN. In the unlikely event that that's also down, fall back to your own server. A good symbol to test for is `jQuery`, resulting in the following code (page `jQueryValidation.aspx` in folder `ClientSideValidation` in the downloaded code bundle):

```
<script type="text/javascript"
  src="http://ajax.microsoft.com/ajax/jquery/
    jquery-1.4.2.min.js">
</script>
<script type="text/javascript">
  if (typeof jQuery == 'undefined') {
```

```
    document.write(unescape("%3Cscript
      src='http://ajax.googleapis.com/ajax/libs/jquery/1.4.2/
      jquery.min.js' type='text/javascript'%3E%3C/script%3E"));
  }
  if (typeof jQuery == 'undefined') {
    document.write(unescape("%3Cscript src='js/
      jquery-1.4.2.min.js'
      type='text/javascript'%3E%3C/script%3E"));
  }
</script>
```

You will want to do the same thing with the Validate library. A good symbol to test here is jQuery.validator. Because the Google CDN doesn't host the Validate library, we'll fall back to our own server if the Microsoft CDN fails:

```
<script type="text/javascript"
  src="http://ajax.microsoft.com/ajax/
  jquery.validate/1.7/jquery.validate.min.js">
</script>
<script type="text/javascript">
  if (typeof jQuery.validator == 'undefined') {
    document.write(unescape("%3Cscript
      src='js/jquery.validate.min.js'
      type='text/javascript'%3E%3C/script%3E"));
  }
</script>
```

Overhead

Unlike ASP.NET validator controls, using the Validator script adds minimal amount of code to the page.

However, the browser still has to load the jQuery library at some stage—version 1.4.2 clocks in at 71 KB, or 30 KB compressed. The Validate library comes in at 25 KB, or 9 KB compressed. Remember that both JavaScript files will be cached by the browser.

Purely from the point of view of reducing download sizes, using the jQuery/Validator combination probably has the edge if you decide to use the jQuery library for other things except validation. If you do not use dynamic file compression on the server, then the overheads introduced by ASP.NET to support the validator controls will really tip the balance.

Submitting forms asynchronously

On a classic ASP.NET page, when the browser POSTs form values, the server processes the values, regenerates the entire web page with a success or failure status message tacked on, and then sends the entire page back to the browser. The browser then replaces the existing page with the new page from the server.

To add to the overhead, the current state of the controls needs to be stored in ViewState because the entire page is replaced. The current state is sent in both, the request from the browser carrying the form data, and in the response from the server carrying the new page with the status message. ViewState is discussed in *Chapter 9, Reducing Time to Last Byte* in the *ViewState* section. An example of this type of form is in the downloaded code bundle in folder AsynchFormSubmission, page SynchSubmission.aspx. Obviously, it would be much more efficient to send the form values asynchronously in AJAX-style, so that the server has to send only the status message. This saves time and bandwidth. And because the existing page stays in the browser, there is no need to use ViewState to save state.

To implement this, we have a number of options provided by the ASP.NET AJAX and jQuery libraries. There are more libraries, but ASP.NET AJAX and jQuery are directly supported by Visual Studio, so we'll focus on them here. We'll look at the following options (the classic ASP.NET case has been included for comparison):

Method	Overhead	Description
Classic ASP.NET	Very High	Very easy to use. Causes full-page refresh, requiring ViewState to maintain state of each control.
UpdatePanel control	High	Very easy and quick to use. No need to write JavaScript.
Page Methods	High	Lets you call C#/VB code behind methods with a single line of JavaScript.
Web Service	Medium	Lets you call web services with a single line of JavaScript.
Generic Handler	Low	The JavaScript to call an ASP.NET Generic Handler is a bit more involved. Provides most scope for performance improvements.
WCF Data Services and the Entity Framework	Medium	Allows you to generate the server-side data access code using Visual Studio.

Ultimately, all these options use the XMLHttpRequest object built into JavaScript. Therefore, an additional option would be to use that object directly, rather than via a library. However, that would mean dealing with cross-browser issues that would take us outside the scope of this book.

Let's go through each of the options. The downloaded code bundle contains a website in folder AsynchFormSubmission that has working sample pages demonstrating each option.

UpdatePanel control

UpdatePanel controls let you carry out a partial refresh of the page, instead of a full refresh. Apart from that, forms using UpdatePanel behave essentially like classic ASP.NET forms.

To use UpdatePanel controls on your page, first add the ScriptManager control to the start of the page body. This loads the required JavaScript and adds inline JavaScript to the page required by the UpdatePanel controls (page UpdatePanel.aspx in folder AsynchFormSubmission in the downloaded code bundle):

```
<body>
  <form id="form1" runat="server">
  <asp:ScriptManager ID="scriptManager" runat="server" />
```

If you use ASP.NET 4, you can have the required JavaScript loaded from Microsoft's CDN by setting EnableCdn to true:

```
<asp:ScriptManager ID="scriptManager" EnableCdn="True"
  runat="server" />
```

Then, place your form inside an UpdatePanel:

```
<asp:UpdatePanel ID="updatePanel" runat="server" >
  <ContentTemplate>
    <p><asp:Label ID="lblMessage" runat="server"></asp:Label></p>
    <p>Title: <asp:TextBox ID="txtTitle" runat="server">
      </asp:TextBox></p>
    <p>Author: <asp:TextBox ID="txtAuthor" runat="server">
      </asp:TextBox></p>
    <p>Price: <asp:TextBox ID="txtPrice" runat="server">
      </asp:TextBox></p>
    <p><asp:Button ID="btnSave" runat="server"
                Text="Save" OnClick="btnSave_Click" />
    </p>
  </ContentTemplate>
</asp:UpdatePanel>
```

Now, when a visitor clicks on the **Save** button:

1. The content of the form fields is POSTed to the server.

2. The page goes through its complete life cycle, firing the Page Load event handler, button-click handlers, and so on. As a result, all HTML to completely regenerate the page is generated.

3. The response is sent back to the browser, containing only the HTML needed to refresh the area within the UpdatePanel control.

4. The browser refreshes the area within the UpdatePanel control.

As a result, using an UpdatePanel gives you the same situation as the classic ASP. NET form, except that only the area within the UpdatePanel is refreshed, instead of the entire page.

To show the visitor that the form is being processed, simply add an UpdateProgress control. Any HTML contained within this control is shown only while the associated UpdatePanel is waiting for the server:

```
<asp:UpdateProgress runat="server" id="updateProgress"
  AssociatedUpdatePanelID="updatePanel">
  <ProgressTemplate>
    <img src="images/progress.gif" height="16" width="16"
      alt="Form being processed"/>
  </ProgressTemplate>
</asp:UpdateProgress>
```

The advantage of using UpdatePanel compared to the other options is that it is extremely easy. The disadvantage is that the POST requests and their responses contain a lot of overhead:

- Because the area within the UpdatePanel is completely refreshed, the response from the server needs to contain the HTML for that area. That makes it far bigger than if it had contained only the status message, as is the case with the other methods.

- You may still need to use ViewState for the controls inside the UpdatePanel.

To make the UpdatePanel controls work, the ScriptManager control also adds inline JavaScript to the page (about 1.8 KB for the sample page) and loads JavaScript libraries (about 90 KB). The other options also incur this type of overhead.

You will find more information about the `UpdatePanel` control at:

- UpdatePanel Control Overview

  `http://msdn.microsoft.com/en-us/library/bb386454.aspx`

- UpdatePanel Tips and Tricks

  `http://msdn.microsoft.com/en-us/magazine/cc163413.aspx`

Page Methods

Page Methods is a mechanism to call C# or VB methods that live in the code behind of your page from JavaScript.

To make this work, first add a `ScriptManager` control to the top of the page body. This generates a JavaScript proxy object in your page that your JavaScript can use to call a method in the code behind. The `ScriptManager` control needs to have the `EnablePageMethods` attribute set to `true`, as shown in the following code (page `PageMethod.aspx` in the folder `AsynchFormSubmission` in the downloaded code bundle):

```
<body>
  <form id="form1" runat="server">
  <asp:ScriptManager ID="ScriptManager1" runat="server"
    EnablePageMethods="True" />
```

Secondly, decorate the methods you want to call from JavaScript with the `WebMethod` attribute. Because of that attribute, these methods are called "web methods". These methods need to be static and public, and they can optionally return a value which will be sent back to the JavaScript code, for example:

```
[System.Web.Services.WebMethod]
public static string SaveForm(string title, string author,
  string price)
{
  . . .
}
```

The web method has access to the request context, so that you can write, for example:

```
string userAgent = HttpContext.Current.Request.UserAgent;
```

Now that you have a web method, you can call it from JavaScript, as shown:

```
PageMethods.SaveForm(title, author, price, onSuccess, onError);
...
function onSuccess(result) {
...
}
function onError(result) {
...
}
```

When calling a web method from JavaScript, you pass in the parameters expected by the method. You can also pass in a JavaScript callback function that will be called when the asynchronous request succeeds, and a second callback for when there was an error.

The `result` parameter contains the value returned by the web method.

As far as overhead is concerned, the proxy code inserted in the page is bulky—4.7 KB for a sample page that accesses a single web method. Also, 86 KB worth of JavaScript files is loaded.

If you are familiar with jQuery, you can replace the proxies and the loaded JavaScript files with a bit of jQuery code, as demonstrated by page `PageMethod_jQuery.aspx` in the folder `AsynchFormSubmission` in the downloaded code bundle. In this case, you would need to load other libraries including jQuery, but this would amount to only 33 KB.

This was a very short overview of some of the features offered by `Page Methods`. You will find more information on this at:

- PageMethods In ASP.NET AJAX

  http://aspalliance.com/1922_PageMethods_In_ASPNET_AJAX.all

Web service

A web service is an object whose methods are accessible via the Internet. Traditionally, web services have been accessed using the heavy weight SOAP protocol, but the web services you build with Visual Studio can now communicate using the light-weight JSON protocol as well. This means that requests to web services and their responses are no bigger than their counterparts for `Page Methods`, which use JSON as well. JSON is described at:

- An Introduction to JavaScript Object Notation (JSON) in JavaScript and .NET

  http://msdn.microsoft.com/en-us/library/bb299886.aspx#intro_to_json_topic2

Unlike `Page Methods`, using a web service involves moving your web methods from the code behind of a page to one or more separate web services. You would do this if you decide that this is a better way to organize your web methods. Using a web service incurs slightly less overhead than using `Page Methods`.

To go down this route, first create the web service (file `FormService.cs` in the folder `AsynchFormSubmission` in the downloaded code bundle):

1. Right-click on your website. Choose **Add New Item**, click on the **Web Service** icon, and give your new web service a name, such as `FormService.asmx`. A new editor window will open with the code of the web service.

2. Uncomment the `ScriptService` attribute, so that the methods in the web service can be invoked from JavaScript.

3. Add one or more methods. Decorate them with the `WebMethod` attribute, so that they can be called from JavaScript:

```
[WebMethod]
public string SaveForm(string title, string author,
  string price)
{
  ...
}
```

   Similar to web methods used with `Page Methods`, these web methods can access the `Request` context:

```
string userAgent = HttpContext.Current.Request.UserAgent;
```

4. Next, add a `ScriptManager` control to the top of the body of the page where you are calling the web service. Give it a `ServiceReference` with the name of your web service. This will generate a JavaScript proxy for the web service (page `WebService.aspx` in folder `AsynchFormSubmission` in the downloaded code bundle):

```
<body>
  <form id="form1" runat="server">
    <asp:ScriptManager ID="ScriptManager1" runat="server" >
      <Services>
        <asp:ServiceReference Path="FormService.asmx" />
      </Services>
    </asp:ScriptManager>
```

5. Finally, here is how you call a web method exposed by the web service from JavaScript:

```
FormService.SaveForm(title, author, price, onSuccess, onError,
  onTimeout);
  ...
```

```
function onSuccess(result) {
}
function onError(result) {
}
function onTimeout(result) {
}
```

This works in the same way as with `Page Methods`, except that you can define an additional callback for timeouts.

Regarding overhead, the `ScriptManager` control inserts 1.6 KB of inline JavaScript in the sample page to create the proxy, and loads 90 KB worth of JavaScript files. If you are familiar with jQuery, you can replace the proxy by a bit of jQuery code; see page `WebService_jQuery.aspx` in the folder `AsynchFormSubmission` in the downloaded code bundle.

Here is more information about calling web services from JavaScript code:

*   ASP.NET AJAX and Web Services

    `http://msdn.microsoft.com/en-us/library/bb398785.aspx`

Generic handler

Instead of a web service, you can use a generic handler. A generic handler has very little overhead, and it allows you to access the database asynchronously to make better use of the available IIS worker threads, as described in *Chapter 6, Thread Usage* in the *Asynchronous generic handlers* section. This makes it the best choice if you are prioritizing performance over ease of implementation. Unlike web services, generic handlers expose only one method, and use extension `.ashx` instead of `.asmx`.

Let's start with building the generic handler, and then see how to access it using jQuery code.

Building the generic handler

To generate a generic handler, right-click on your website, choose **Add New Item**, and then pick **Generic Handler**. Give your new handler a name, such as `FormHandler.ashx` and click on **Add**. A new editor window will open with the code of your new generic handler.

When a request is received by a generic handler, it calls the method `ProcessRequest` to process the request and send a response. It receives the request context as a parameter (file `FormHandler.ashx` in folder `AsynchFormSubmission` in the downloaded code bundle):

```
public void ProcessRequest (HttpContext context)
{
```

To prevent cross site request forgery attacks (explained in the next section), make sure that the HTTP method of the request is POST and its content type is `application/json; charset=utf-8`:

```
if ((context.Request.HttpMethod != "POST") ||
    (context.Request.ContentType != "application/json;
    charset=utf-8"))
{
    context.Response.ContentType = "text/plain";
    context.Response.Write("Access Denied");
    return;
}
```

In keeping with the `application/json` content type, the JavaScript will send the form field values as a JSON object in the body of the POST request. Retrieve the string with that JSON object from the request body using the utility method `RequestBody` (source included in the sample code):

```
string json = RequestBody(context.Request);
```

Then, deserialize the JSON object into a `FormData` object (definition shown in a moment) using the `JavaScriptSerializer` class (included in .NET 3.5 and later):

```
JavaScriptSerializer js = new JavaScriptSerializer();
FormData formData = js.Deserialize<FormData>(json);
```

Now that we have the field values, call a method to process them:

```
string message = Business.ProcessForm(formData.title,
    formData.author, formData.price);
```

Finally, send a string with the message back to the JavaScript:

```
context.Response.ContentType = "text/plain";
context.Response.Write(message);
}
```

The `FormData` class simply has a public field for each property of the JSON object sent by the JavaScript:

```
private class FormData
{
  public string title = null;
  public string author = null;
  public string price = null;
}
```

Cross Site Request Forgery (CSRF) attacks

Why does disallowing GET requests and requiring the content type `application/json; charset=utf-8` block **Cross Site Request Forgery (CSRF)** attacks? And what are these attacks anyway?

In a CSRF attack, a visitor is tricked into executing a bit of HTML that sends an unwanted request to a site where the visitor is logged in. For example, take a visitor who just logged into their account at `bank.com`. The login will have caused `bank.com` to place a cookie on the visitor's computer, to remember that the visitor is logged in. If the visitor is then lured into visiting a page at `evil.com`, that page may contain an unwanted request to `bank.com` along these lines:

```
<img src="http://bank.com?withdraw=1000;sendto=evil" />
```

The visitor's browser will send a GET request to `bank.com` in order to load the image. That request will include the cookie saying that the visitor is logged in. So now, `evil.com` has sent a request to `bank.com` on behalf of the visitor.

To thwart this attack, you can disallow GET requests. `evil.com` could counter this by having a form on its page that sends POST requests. It could then submit the form using some JavaScript code, or lure the visitor into submitting the form. One way to defend against this is to only allow requests with a content type that is not used by forms, such as `application/json; charset=utf-8`.

Calling the generic handler

To reduce overhead to a minimum, instead of using a proxy, this time we'll call the generic handler using a method defined in the jQuery library (page `Handler_jQuery.aspx`, folder `AsynchFormSubmission`, in the downloaded code bundle):

1. Load the jQuery library. To see how, refer to the *Content Delivery Network (CDN)* subsection in the *Validate JavaScript library* section.

2. Load the JSON plugin. This defines the toJSON function, which we'll need in a moment. The library can be found at http://code.google.com/p/jquery-json/.

```
<script type="text/javascript" src="js/jquery.json-2.2.min.js">
</script>
```

3. Create a JSON object with the form data:

```
var formdata = {
    'title': ...,
    'author': ...,
    'price': ...
};
```

4. Finally, send the JSON object in an asynchronous request to the generic handler we earlier built. We can do this by calling jQuery function ajax:

```
$.ajax({
  type: "POST",
  url: "FormHandler.ashx",
  data: $.toJSON(formdata),
  contentType: "application/json; charset=utf-8",
  dataType: "text/plain",
  success: onSuccess,
  error: onError
});
...
function onSuccess(result) {
}
function onError(result) {
}
```

Note that the JSON object is converted to a string before it is passed to the ajax function using the toJson function, which is defined in the JSON plugin. If you don't, the ajax function will translate each object property into an individual request header, which is not the intention.

If you want to send a request without passing in any data, set data to the empty object "{}". If you leave data completely empty, function ajax won't set the content-length header in the request, which may cause IIS to block the request.

After the response from the generic handler has been received, the result parameter of the callback function contains the return value sent by the generic handler.

WCF Data Services and the Entity Framework

This solution is based on three Microsoft technologies: the ADO.NET Entity Framework, WCF Data Services (formerly known as ADO.NET Data Services), and a number of advanced features in version 4 of ASP.NET AJAX:

- The ADO.NET Entity Framework (EF) is Microsoft's preferred Object to Relational Mapping (ORM) tool. It lets you automatically generate an object-oriented data layer called an Entity Data Model from your database schema. This means that instead of having to write code to access a Book table, you now work with a collection of Book objects. Version 4 also lets you create an Entity Data Model first, and then generate a database schema from the model.

   The use of ORM tools such as EF is controversial. On the one hand, it makes it easier to access the database, improves reliability if there is less code to write, and if the database schema changes, you may only need to change the mapping between the database and the Entity Data Model. On the other hand, translating operations against objects into operations against a relational database can lead to seriously inefficient database accesses.

- WCF Data Services allows you to generate a RESTful data access service on top of an Entity Data Model. This means that your JavaScript code can retrieve, insert, update, and delete objects in the Entity Data Model, and therefore the database, by sending simple HTTP requests. You can send and receive data in either JSON or the AtomPub format to create a web feed with, for example, news stories.

   In effect, WCF Data Services takes care of all the server-side data access code, leaving you to focus on the client-side JavaScript.

- ASP.NET AJAX 4 supports a style of programming closer to ASP.NET or WPF rather than "traditional" JavaScript. It includes the `AdoNetDataContext` class (which takes care of all communication with a WCF Data Service), the `DataView` class (which generates forms and grids based on an HTML template), and live data binding (which allows you to set and get form field values without writing code). Although ASP.NET AJAX 4 is included with ASP.NET 4, you can also use it from ASP.NET 3.5 websites, as you'll see later on.

These are complex and powerful technologies in their own right. Here we'll only scratch the surface of what they can do. To learn more, follow the links in the *Find out more* section at the end of this chapter.

Let's first see how to generate an Entity Data Model. Then, we'll build a WCF Data Service on top of that. Finally, we'll use ASP.NET AJAX 4 to access the WCF Data Service from JavaScript.

Creating the entity data model

The easiest way to create an entity data model is to generate it from an existing database. In the downloaded code bundle, you'll find two files with SQL instructions that will generate one for you on a SQL Server database server:

- `tuneup.database.sql`: Creates a database `TuneUp`
- `book.table.sql`: Creates a table `Book` with a list of books.

If you do not have a SQL Server installed, the *Installing a database* section in *Chapter 14, Load Testing* shows how to do so.

Now that you have a database with a table, let's create the Entity Data Model based on that database:

1. Right-click on your website, choose **Add New Item**, and then pick **ADO.NET Entity Data Model**. Give your new model a name such as `TuneUpModel.edmx` and click on **Add**.

2. Agree to put the model in the `App_Code` folder.

3. A wizard starts to identify the source of your new model. Choose to generate the model from a database and click on **Next**.

4. Create a connection to the `TuneUp` database on your database server and click on **Next**.

5. Include the **Book** table in your model and click on **Finish**.

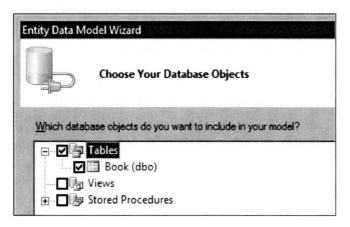

Creating the WCF Data Service

With the Entity Data Model done, it is time to build the WCF Data Service on top of it:

1. Right-click on your website, choose **Add New Item**, and then pick **WCF Data Service (ADO.NET Data Service** in Visual Studio 2008). Give your new service a name such as `TuneUpService.svc` and click on **Add**.

2. A new editor window will open with `TuneUpService.cs`, which holds the definition of your new service. It has two TODO functions.

3. At the first TODO, enter the class defining the Entity Data Model you created earlier. You'll find this information in file `App_Code/TuneUpModel.Designer.cs` in the downloaded code bundle:

```
public class TuneUpService :
    DataService<TuneUpModel.TuneUpEntities>
```

4. At the second TODO, give full access to the Book collection. In a production environment, you might be more selective; but for this demonstration, we can live dangerously:

```
config.SetEntitySetAccessRule("Book", EntitySetRights.All);
```

A sample site with a working WCF Data Service is in folder `AsynchFormSubmission` in the downloaded code bundle. To make it work:

1. Edit `web.config` and replace `MPERDECK-PC` with the name of your own database server.

2. Run the website in Visual Studio.

3. On the home page, click on the link **List all books via WCF Data Service**.

If you try to retrieve data from a WCF Data Service in IE 8, you'll find that it doesn't show all the data. This is because it tries to present the data as an RSS feed because the data is in AtomPub format. To see the data as raw XML, follow these steps in IE 8:

1. Click on **Tools | Internet Options | Content** tab.

2. Click the **Settings** button in the **Feeds and Web Slices** section.

3. Uncheck **Turn on feed reading view**.

4. Click twice on **OK** to close the dialogs.

5. To make sure that the change is picked up, close all instances of Internet Explorer and then restart Internet Explorer.

What happens if a request is sent to insert or update an object with invalid data? If the request has a value that can't be stored in the database such as a non-number in a numeric column, an exception will result, which the WCF Data Service translates into an error response to the request.

To impose additional validations, you can add `ChangeInterceptor` methods to `TuneUpModel.Designer.cs`, as in the following code (file `TuneUpModel.Designer.cs` in the folder `AsynchFormSubmission` in the downloaded code bundle):

```
[ChangeInterceptor("Book")]
public void OnChangeBook(TuneUpModel.Book book,
  UpdateOperations operations)
{
  if (book.Price < 0.0M)
  {
    throw new DataServiceException("Price cannot be
      lower than 0");
  }
}
```

The string passed into the `DataServiceException` constructor will now be sent in the response back to the browser.

Calling the WCF Data Service from JavaScript

The solution we'll look at here has these elements:

- After the page is loaded, we'll create an `AdoNetDataContext` object. This object keeps track of all changes made in the form. When a visitor clicks on the **Save** button, we'll call the `saveChanges` method exposed by `AdoNetDataContext` to send all changes to the WCF Data Service.

- We'll create a `DataView` object that will generate the actual update form. This object will also pass on changes from the form to the `AdoNetDataContext` object.

- Finally, the `DataView` object needs an HTML template to generate the form.

A working implementation with all the source code is in the downloaded code bundle in the folder `AsynchFormSubmission`, page `DataService.aspx`. You'll find a jQuery version with more conventional coding in page `DataService_jQuery.aspx`.

We'll start with loading a small library that will load all the required classes on demand. At the time of writing, this functionality was still in beta:

```
<script type="text/javascript"
  src="http://AJAX.microsoft.com/AJAX/beta/0911/Start.js">
</script>
```

As described in the *Content Delivery Network (CDN)* section earlier, you could add JavaScript code here that loads the library from your server if the Microsoft CDN fails.

Now, it's time to do the actual code. First, create a variable that will refer to the `AdoNetDataContext` object that handles all communication with the WCF Data Service:

```
<script type="text/javascript">
var tuneupService;
```

Use function `Sys.onReady` to register an anonymous function that will be called after the page has loaded:

```
Sys.onReady(function() {
```

The first step in this anonymous function is to call `Sys.require` to load the `DataView` and `AdoNetDataContext` components. Its second parameter is an anonymous function to be called when those components have been loaded:

```
Sys.require(
  [Sys.components.dataView, Sys.components.adoNetDataContext],
    function() {
```

After the `DataView` and `AdoNetDataContext` components are loaded, create an `AdoNetDataContext` object. This will handle communications with the WCF Data Service. Provide it with the URL of the WCF Data Service, which is `TuneUpService.svc`:

```
tuneupService = Sys.create.adoNetDataContext(
  {
    serviceUri: "TuneUpService.svc"
  });
```

Also, create the `DataView` object that will generate the update form. We need to tell its constructor a few critical bits of information:

- The HTML element that holds the template to use. Here, that's an element with ID `BookDataView` (we'll come to that element in a minute).
- The data provider `AdoNetDataContext` we just created.

- The specific object exposed by the WCF Data Service that the update form will update. Here, we're using the `Book` object whose primary key equals `1`.

- The `autoFetch` status — we're setting that to true here, so that `DataView` gets the `AdoNetDataContext` to load the book object after the page is loaded.

This results in the following code:

```
var bookDataView = Sys.create.dataView("#BookDataView",
    {
      dataProvider: tuneupService,
      fetchOperation: "Book(1)",
      autoFetch: true
    });
  })
});
```

Now that the `AdoNetDataContext` and `DataView` objects have been created, all that's left is the code that saves any changes to the WCF Data Service:

```
function saveform() {
  tuneupService.saveChanges(saveSuccess, saveFail);
}

function saveSuccess() {
  $get('lblMessage').innerHTML = 'Data updated';
}

function saveFail(result) {
  var errormessage = result._message;
  $get('lblMessage').innerHTML = errormessage;
}
</script>
```

Turning to the HTML template for the `DataView` object, the first thing to take care of is defining the `sys` namespace in the body element. We'll need that namespace in a moment:

```
<body xmlns:sys="javascript:Sys">
  <form id="form1">
```

Now, create the actual HTML template. This is a `<div>` tag containing the labels and input elements making up the form. By convention, the template has CSS class `sys-template`.

The code uses bindings such as {binding Title} tell DataView that there is a two-way binding between this input element and the Title property of the Book object that the DataView is bound to. This way, it can set the input element's value when the page is loaded, and when the visitor updates the input element, its value flows back to the DataView object.

Because the bindings only have meaning to the DataView object, the input elements use sys:value.

```
<div id="BookDataView" class="sys-template">
  <p>Title: <input id="title" type="text" sys:value=
    "{binding Title}" /></p>
  <p>Author: <input id="author" type="text" sys:value=
    "{binding Author}" /></p>
  <p>Price: <input id="price" type="text" sys:value=
    "{binding Price}" /></p>
</div>
```

To complete the form, here is the span element used to show the status message, and the Save button. The Save button calls the saveform function we saw earlier in the JavaScript:

```
<p><span id="lblMessage"></span></p>
<p><input type="button" onclick="saveform() "value="Save" />
</p>
</form>
</body>
```

Finally, we don't want to show the template to the visitor. So, define the CSS class sys-template to make it invisible:

```
<style type="text/css">
  .sys-template
  {
    display: none;
  }
</style>
```

Bugs and limitations in WCF Data Services

At the time of writing, WCF Data Services suffered from a number of niggling issues that you should be aware of before going live with this technology.

Allowing the precompiled site to be updatable when publishing your site

When you publish your website using **Build | Publish Web Site**, on the **Publish Web Site** dialog, check **Allow this precompiled site to be updatable**.

Otherwise, when you try to access your data service when running under IIS, the server returns a 404 "The resource cannot be found" error.

Note that this doesn't apply to Visual Studio Express, because this version doesn't include the "Publish Web Site" feature.

Providing database access to [NT AUTHORITY\NETWORK SERVICE]

When you created the database connection for the Entity Data Model back in the *Creating the entity data model* section, you had a choice between using Windows Authentication and SQL Server Authentication. If you chose Windows Authentication, you need to give user NT AUTHORITY\NETWORK SERVICE access to your database so that the application pool can access the database; otherwise, the server will respond with a 500 Internal Server Error when your website tries to access the WCF Data Service while running in IIS.

A simple script to do this is in the downloaded code bundle in the file `create access for wcf data service.sql`.

Disabling batch compilation

In `web.config`, make sure that batch compilation is disabled:

```
<compilation debug="false" batch="false">
```

This prevents intermittent exceptions where the system can't find a generated assembly, as shown:

Could not load file or assembly 'App_Web_ian0nqei, Version=0.0.0.0, Culture=neutral, PublicKeyToken=null' or one of its dependencies. The system cannot find the file specified.

Creating an activity indicator

When you study the sample code in the downloaded code bundle, you'll find that it uses an activity indicator to tell the visitors that the form is being saved. That way, the visitors don't think the page has crashed or is ignoring them.

The indicator could be as simple as a short message:

```
<span id="spActivity">Loading ... </span>
```

For a more sophisticated look, you could use a rotating spinner as used in the sample code:

```
<img src="activity.gif" id="imgActivity"
  alt="Form being processed"/>
```

This is simply an animated GIF image. If you want a different activity indicator than that included with the sample code, you can get one at many places, including:

- `http://ajaxload.info/`
- `http://mentalized.net/activity-indicators/`
- `http://www.ajax.su/`

A good place for the activity indicator would be where the visitor will see it right away, after they have initiated the asynchronous request, for example next to the **Save** button on your form. If you have multiple forms on the same page, put an activity indicator next to each **Save** button, so that the visitor knows which forms are being saved.

AJAX-type grids

A common requirement is to show data in the form of a grid, and to allow the visitor to update the data. ASP.NET provides the GridView control for this purpose. It is reasonably flexible and feature-rich, but doesn't perform well because every update by the visitor leads to a page refresh. It can also generate a lot of ViewState overhead. If you receive a lot of traffic to pages using GridView controls, consider replacing them with AJAX-type grids. Because these submit changes asynchronously, you'll wind up with greater responsiveness and reduced bandwidth usage.

When it comes to implementing an AJAX-type grid, you have a number of options:

- Use a simple readymade, free, and lightweight grid control
- Buy a grid control with lots of features and professional support
- Build your own grid control

Let's go through each of these options.

Free, lightweight grids

These grids have very small download sizes. Some of the good ones include:

- Ingrid (doesn't allow updating of grid values)

  `http://reconstrukt.com/ingrid/`

- Flexigrid (doesn't allow updating of grid values)

  `http://www.flexigrid.info/`

- jqGridView (requires the free jQuery library)

  `http://plugins.jquery.com/project/jqGridView`

  `http://sourceforge.net/projects/jqgridview/`

Paid, heavyweight grids

These enterprise class libraries are far from free, but offer lots of controls besides grids, lots of features, and professional support.

- Telerik

  `http://www.telerik.com/`

- Devexpress

  `http://www.devexpress.com`

- ComponentArt

  `http://www.componentart.com/`

- DHTMLX Suite

  At the time of writing, the standard edition was free under certain conditions.

  `http://dhtmlx.com/`

Building your own grid

Building your own grid allows you to precisely create those features you need, without incurring the overhead of unnecessary features. However, this can be a lot of work.

There are a number of free libraries available that make it easier to build your own grid, including:

- YUI Library

  It is an extensive library offering a powerful, datatable class.

  `http://developer.yahoo.com/yui/`

  `http://developer.yahoo.com/yui/datatable/`

- ASP.NET AJAX

  It is included with ASP.NET 3.5 and higher. The `DataView` object you saw in the *WCF Data Services and the Entity Framework* section can generate not only simple forms, but also grids using an HTML template.

  `http://www.asp.net/ajax`

Working sample code

In the downloaded code bundle, in folder `AsynchFormSubmission`, you'll find working sample code demonstrating the use of the ASP.NET AJAX and DHTMLX libraries. The samples use the following files:

Sample	Files (in folder `AsynchFormSubmission`)
ASP.NET AJAX	`GridWithDataView.aspx`
DHTMLX	`GridWithDHTMLX.aspx`
	`DHTMLXHandler.ashx`
	`DHTMLXcodebase/*`
	`App_Code/TuneUpDataAccess.cs`

This sample code accesses table `Book` in database `TuneUp`. To generate this database, run files `tuneup.database.sql` and `book.table.sql` (both in the downloaded code bundle) in SQL Server Management Studio. Also replace `MPERDECK-PC` in `web.config` with the name of your database server.

To access the database, both samples use the Entity Data Model you saw in the *WCF Data Services and the Entity Framework* section. The ASP.NET AJAX sample also uses the WCF Data Service you saw in that same section.

Find out more

Here are some more online resources.

About the ADO.NET Entity Framework:

- The ADO.NET Entity Framework Overview

  `http://msdn.microsoft.com/en-us/library/aa697427(VS.80).aspx`

- Object-relational mapping

  `http://en.wikipedia.org/wiki/Object-relational_mapping`

About WCF Data Services:

- WCF Data Services

  `http://msdn.microsoft.com/en-us/library/cc668792.aspx`

- Open Data Protocol Documentation

  `http://www.odata.org/developers/protocols`

- Overview: ADO.NET Data Services

  `http://msdn.microsoft.com/en-us/library/cc956153.aspx`

- Using Microsoft ADO.NET Data Services

  `http://msdn.microsoft.com/en-us/library/cc907912.aspx`

- Interceptors (WCF Data Services)

  `http://msdn.microsoft.com/en-us/library/dd744842.aspx`

About ASP.NET AJAX:

- Visit the links in file `ASP.NET-AJAX-resources.htm` in the downloaded code bundle.

Summary

This chapter discussed ways of limiting the number of requests that the browser makes to the server and the size of the requests and their responses. This is to make the visitor feel that the website is more responsive, and reduce the load on the server.

We first looked at introducing client-side validation, which does validation of user input on the browser, rather than only on the server. Here, we looked at ASP.NET validation controls which are easy to implement, but have relatively high overhead. We also saw the Validate plugin for jQuery, which has very low overhead, but is more difficult to use.

This was followed by five ways to send data from the browser to the server without a full-page refresh. These ranged from very easy to implement but high in overhead (UpdatePanel controls) to harder to implement but very efficient (custom-built HTTP handlers). Two solutions in between those extremes were page methods and web services. We also looked at WCF Data Services and the Entity Framework, combined with ASP.NET AJAX 4, a powerful solution with its own complexities.

Finally, we had a brief look at ways to build AJAX-type grids.

In the next chapter, we'll see how to reduce load times of the images on your pages.

12
Reducing Image Load Times

Images often account for most of the load time of a page. Improving the way images are loaded and reducing the number and size of the images can have a dramatic effect on page load times.

In this chapter, we'll see:

- How to make better use of the browser cache, so that images are retained on the browser instead of being loaded repeatedly.

- How to reduce overhead in image requests by serving images from a cookieless domain.

- How to reduce overall image load times by loading more images in parallel. To make it easy to implement these techniques on your site, they have been implemented in an image adapter, which you'll find in the code bundle you download.

- How to reduce the file size of images.

- How to reduce the number of images by combining them or by replacing them with HTML and CSS.

Let's start with storing images in the browser cache.

Caching

You can ask the visitor's browser to cache your images on the visitor's machine. This way, the next time they are needed, they are available immediately. In addition to this, your images may pass through proxy servers on their way from the server to the browser and these proxy servers, too, can cache your images. Although not as effective as caching on the browser itself, this still improves load times because proxy servers tend to be closer to the browser than your server.

Cache-Control response header

IIS tells the browser and proxies whether an image can be cached via the `Cache-Control` response header. Its possible values include:

Cache-Control value	Description
no-cache	Prevents caching in the browser or proxies.
private	Allows caching in the browser, but not in proxies. This is the default value.
public	Allows caching in both the browser and in proxies.

In addition to this, the `Cache-Control: max-age` header specifies the maximum time (in seconds) the browser should use the cached image without asking the server whether there is a newer image available. Note that the image can be evicted earlier due to memory pressures. The HTTP 1.1 specification says that servers should not specify a `max-age` more than one year into the future.

If an image is in cache, and the visitor refreshes the page (*Ctrl* + *F5*), or if the image's `max-age` has expired, the browser sends a conditional request for the image to the server. This has an `If-Modified-Since` request header showing when the cached image was received. If no newer version is available, the server replies with a 304 "Not Modified" response. This response doesn't have the image, because "304" indicates that the browser can use the cached image. If there is a newer version, the server sends a normal 200 response with the new image.

Preventing conditional requests

Any round trip to the server is expensive, even if the response is short, as is the case with a 304 response. It is better to use the maximum `max-age` of one year to prevent conditional requests all together.

What if the image is changed? Would the visitor see the older version of the image for up to a year? To prevent that situation, you can include a version number or the date and time of the last update in the image name, for example `myimage_v2.jpg`. You would need to make sure that your image tags are also updated. That way, when the image changes from `myimage_v2.jpg` to `myimage_v3.jpg`, the browser won't find the new `myimage_v3.jpg` in its cache and request it from the server.

Updating the name of an image and all the image tags that refer to it manually would be a lot of work. Instead, use the adapter you'll come across in the *Image control adapter* section later in the chapter.

Expires header

You may have come across the Expires header. This was used by the predecessor of HTTP 1.1, which is HTTP 1.0. The Cache-Control header always takes precedence over the Expires header. HTTP 1.0 was superseded by HTTP 1.1 in 1997, and there is little reason to use Expires any more.

Configuring Cache-Control in IIS 7

If you use IIS 7, follow these steps to send public Cache-Control response headers with max-age set to 365 days with your images:

1. Open IIS manager. Click on **Start | Control Panel**. Type "admin" in the search box. Click on **Administrative Tools** and double-click on **Internet Information Services (IIS) Manager**.

2. Click on your machine. Then, double-click on the **HTTP Response Headers** icon on the right-hand side.

3. Click on **Add** in the right-most pane. The **Add Custom HTTP Response Header** dialog appears. In the **Name** field, enter **Cache-Control** and in the **Value** field, enter **public**. Click on **OK**.

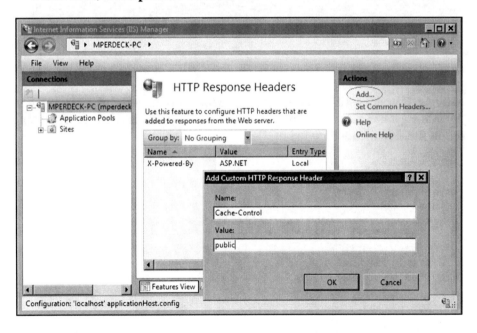

4. While you're at it, remove the **X-Powered-By** header. It is not used by the browser or by proxies, so is simply overhead. Select the header and click on **Remove** in the right-most pane.

5. Click on **Set Common Headers**. The **Set Common HTTP Response Headers** dialog appears.

6. Select **Expire Web Content**. Select **After** and specify **365** days. Click on **OK**.

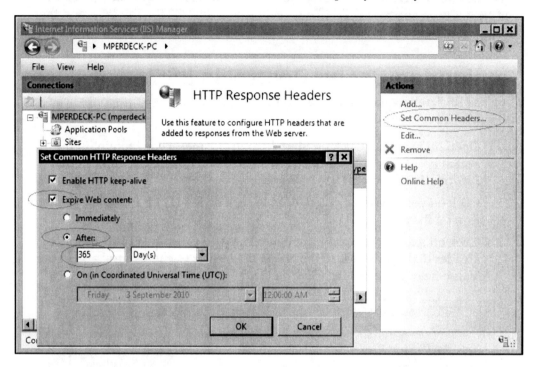

Alternatively, if you use IIS 7 in integrated pipeline mode, you can achieve the same thing by adding a `clientCache` entry in `web.config` (file `web.config` in folder `Adapter` in the downloaded code bundle):

```
<configuration>
...
  <system.webServer>
    <staticContent>
      <clientCache cacheControlCustom="Cache-Control: public"
        cacheControlMode="UseMaxAge"
        cacheControlMaxAge="365.00:00:00"/>
    </staticContent>
  </system.webServer>
...
</configuration>
```

Keep in mind that these settings apply to all static files, including JavaScript and CSS files.

Configuring Cache-Control in IIS 6

If you use IIS 6, follow these steps to send public `Cache-Control` response headers
with `max-age` set to 365 days:

1. Click on **Start | Administration Tools | Internet Information
    Services (IIS) Manager**.

2. Right-click on your website and choose **Properties**. Click on the **HTTP
    Headers** tab.

3. In the **Custom HTTP headers** area, click on the **Add** button. Add a header
    with the name **Cache-Control** and value **max-age=31536000,public**. 31536000
    seconds equals 365 days.

    Leave the **Enable content expiration** checkbox as it is. You could set `max-age`
    by selecting that checkbox, but that wouldn't make **Cache-Control** public.
    And adding the **Cache-Control** header removes the **max-age** you set via the
    Enable content expiration checkbox.

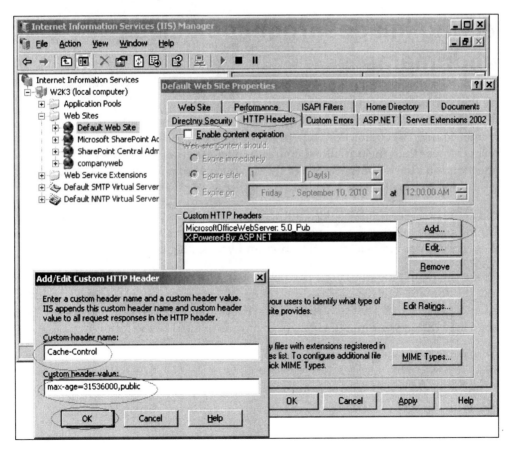

4. While you're at it, remove the **X-Powered-By** and **MicrosoftOfficeWebServer** headers. These are not used by the browser or proxies, so they are simply overhead. Select each header and click on the **Remove** button.

5. Click twice on **OK** to close the dialogs.

Giving identical URLs to identical images

Browsers and proxies cache images and other files by URL. So, it makes sense to always refer to an image with exactly the same URL; otherwise, it will be loaded and cached multiple times. Specifically:

*   Use consistent casing. It's the easiest to write all URLs in lowercase.

*   If you have multiple sites with their own domains using shared images, put the shared images on their own shared domain. Otherwise, the same image will be cached for each individual site domain.

Serving images from cookieless subdomains

When you set a cookie on the browser, all subsequent requests from the browser carry that cookie, including requests for static content, such as images and CSS and JavaScript files. This is magnified by the fact that many visitors will have an asymmetric Internet connection, where the upload connection from browser to server is slower than the download connection from server to browser. If the upload connection is a quarter of the speed of the download connection, a 1000-byte cookie takes as long to transfer as a 4000-byte file.

Because the browser sends cookies only to the domain that actually set it, you can get rid of the cookie overhead by serving static content from a separate subdomain. This makes sense if you serve lots of static files and you set big cookies.

To make this work, log in to your domain registrar account and create an A record for a new subdomain, such as `img.mydomain.com`. Make sure it points to the IP address used by your website. That way, there is no need to move your images. Simply change the URL in your image tags. For example, instead of the following:

```
<img src="/images/picture.jpg" />
```

Write the following:

```
<img src="http://img.mydomain.com/images/picture.jpg" />
```

This does make your HTML slightly longer. However, if you use compression on your .aspx files, there will be hardly any difference in file size. See *Chapter 10, Compression* for more information on compression.

If you serve any content from the base domain—http://mydomain.com instead of http://www.mydomain.com, cookies set on the base domain may be sent by the browser to the subdomains. In that case, register a new domain for your static content instead of using a subdomain.

You shouldn't be in this situation anyway. If you use cookies, be sure to redirect all traffic to your base domain and all traffic to your IP address to your www subdomain. So, if your domain is mydomain.com and your IP address is 125.170.1.75, use permanent 301 redirects from http://mydomain.com and http://125.170.1.75 to http://www.mydomain.com. Otherwise, if a visitor first visits one of these three addresses and then returns to your site via another address, their browser won't send any cookies during the second visit that were set during the first visit.

In the installation instructions for the adapter discussed in the *Image control adapter* section, you'll see how to configure IIS 7 to execute this permanent redirect.

Parallel loading

The browser loads images and CSS and JavaScript files in parallel to reduce the overall page load time. However, the specification of the HTTP 1.1 protocol that governs communication between the browser and the server suggests that browsers download not more than two components in parallel per domain. That made sense back in 1997 when HTTP 1.1 was introduced, and most people still used low bandwidth dial up connections. With broadband connections used by most people these days, you'll want to increase the number of components loaded in parallel.

To visualize this, have a look at this highly simplified Waterfall chart of a web page with eight components, all loaded from the single domain:

In the *Serving images from cookieless domains* section, you saw how you can save bandwidth by serving static components, such as images and CSS and JavaScript files from a separate, cookieless domain.

How about using two separate cookieless domains instead of one? That would double the number of parallel downloads:

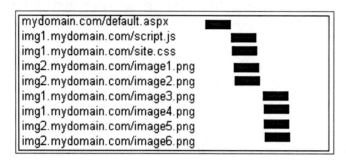

Keep in mind that the browser looks at the hostname and not the IP address. This means that there is no need to move your images to a separate website. Simply point the separate domains to the IP address of your site.

Now, before you start creating lots of separate domains to boost parallel loading, remember that for each domain, the browser needs to do a DNS lookup and create a connection. The latter, especially, can take more time than actually loading the file. Creating an HTTPS connection for a secure page is especially expensive, because it involves browser and server agreeing on the key to encrypt content going over the connection. The cost of creating a connection also goes up with geographical distance. For example, it will be high if your server is in the US and your visitors are in Europe.

There is little point in using multiple domains if your web pages are loading less than say a dozen components from the server. Try different scenarios with different numbers of connections. You'll probably find that the optimum is between one and four. *Chapter 14, Load Testing* shows how to measure the response time of your web pages.

Newer browsers, such as Internet Explorer 8 and Firefox 3 load six components in parallel per domain, instead of two. Consider using only one domain for those browsers.

Make sure that on all pages, the same image always has the same domain. Avoid a situation where on one page you have the following:

```
<img src="http://img1.mydomain.com/picture.jpg" />
```

And on another page, you have the following:

```
<img src="http://img2.mydomain.com/picture.jpg" />
```

Otherwise, the browser will see two different image URLs and cache the image twice.

The solution is to choose the domain based on the image URL, instead of equally spreading images over the domains. For example, if you use two domains, take the hash of the image URL and choose the first domain if the hash is even, and the other domain if the hash is odd. You could also use the length of the filename or the extension, whatever works best for your site.

Image control adapter

To make it easy to implement the recommendations you've seen so far, in the folder `Adapter` in the downloaded code bundle, you'll find a class project `ImageAdapter` that adds the following features to all your Image controls, and all Hyperlink controls that show an image:

- Converts image URL to lowercase.
- Inserts the last modified time of the image in the image URL.
- Optionally replaces the domain of the image URL by a cookieless subdomain you set in `web.config`.
- Optionally uses a second cookieless subdomain to boost parallel downloads. Allows you to exclude modern browsers that already load more than two components in parallel per domain.
- Removes inline style `border-width: 0px;` which is automatically generated by ASP.NET 3.5 and lower (but not by ASP.NET 4 and higher).

Full installation instructions are in the file `Installation.htm`, in the folder `Adapter` in the downloaded code bundle. Those instructions also show how to configure IIS 7 to remove the last modified time from incoming image URLs, so that you don't have to manually insert the last modified time in your actual image filenames.

Image size

Reducing the size of your image files will reduce your bandwidth costs and reduce load times. Unlike caching and parallel loading, this approach is not dependent on the vagaries of browsers and proxies. Later on, we'll see various tools with which you can reduce image file sizes. But first, let's have a look at choosing the optimal image format based on the content of the image.

Using the optimal image format

Most browsers recognize at least the three main image formats: JPEG, GIF and PNG. Each image format stores the image in a compressed form, using its own compression algorithm, and supports different features such as animation:

Format	Compression	Supports Transparency	Supports Animation
JPEG	Lossy: Sacrifices image quality for better compression. Optimized for smooth color transitions, millions of colors. Produces artifacts around sharp transitions of color.	No	No
PNG	Nonlossy: No loss of quality. Compresses better than GIF, except for tiny images.	Yes*	No
GIF	Nonlossy: Allows no more than 256 different colors per image**	Yes***	Yes

*Supports semi-transparency; for example, you can make a pixel 50 percent transparent.

**Each individual color can be chosen from a palette of 16,777,216 colors.

***Only binary transparency is supported; a pixel is either 100 percent transparent or not at all.

The PNG format comes in three different versions:

PNG Version	Description
PNG8	Allows no more than 256 different color/transparency combinations per image. When setting a color/transparency combination, you can choose from 16,777,216 colors and 256 transparency levels (between no transparency at all and full transparency).
	Internet Explorer 6 shows semi-transparent pixels in PNG8 images as fully transparent.
PNG24	Allows 16,777,216 different colors for each pixel, but with no transparency.
PNG32	Allows 16,777,216 different colors, and 256 transparency levels per pixel.
	Internet Explorer 6 gives transparent pixels in PNG32 images a background color.

Note that PNG images almost always have the extension .png, regardless of whether they are PNG8, PNG24 or PNG32. Also, your graphics program may not mention PNG8, PNG24, or PNG32, but only PNG. When you save an image in PNG, it will then pick the right version based on your image's color depth.

Based on the comparisons above, in order to reduce image file sizes, you would use the following formats for these types of images:

Type of image	Preferred format
Photos	JPEG*
Graphics, cartoons, graphs	PNG**
Tiny graphics, such as bullet points	GIF
Animated progress images	GIF

*Choosing JPEG will result in some loss of quality. If that is not acceptable, you could go for PNG24 or PNG32, which preserve quality at the cost of greater image file sizes.

**PNG8 produces a smaller image file size than PNG24 or PNG32. If you have a graphic with 300 different colors, try to reduce it to 256 different colors, so that you can use PNG8.

As you'll see in the *Combining images* section, you should combine small graphics (and even not so small ones) into a single larger image, to reduce the number of requests and the number of bytes going over the wire. PNG is likely to be the best format for the larger combined image. That makes animated graphics the only instance where you really want to use GIF.

Why to avoid scaling images in HTML

HTML allows you to give smaller dimensions to an image on the page than the image's actual size. For example:

```
<img src="physically200by200.png" width="100" height="100" />
```

This makes sense if you have a second img tag on the page that shows the image's full size. In that case, both the img tags get the same image from cache. If that is not the case, the browser has to load an image that is bigger than needed. This means that more bytes go over the wire, and then the browser has to scale down the received image. As a result, the visitor has to wait longer for the image, which then potentially loses quality in the scaling process, and you pay more for bandwidth. In that case, it is better to resize the physical image so that it has the exact size as required on the page.

Tools

There are many free command-line tools that allow you to convert batches of images to another format, reduce their file sizes, and manipulate them in many different ways. To get you started, here is a short, and by no means complete, selection:

PNGOUT

`http://advsys.net/ken/utils.htm`

This tool converts images from GIF to PNG. This almost always gives smaller files. For example:

`pngout input.gif output.png`

To convert all GIF images in a directory, use:

`for %i in (*.gif) do pngout "%i"`

pngout can also reduce the file sizes of existing PNG images by removing unused "chunks" of image information:

`pngout input.png output.png`

Pngcrush

`http://pmt.sourceforge.net/pngcrush/`

pngcrush reduces PNG image file sizes. It is faster than pngout, but not as effective. For example:

`pngcrush.exe -rem alla -reduce -brute input.png output.png`

Jpegtran

`http://jpegclub.org/`

jpegtran tool strips all metadata from JPEG images, such as copyright information. It reduces file size without affecting image quality. For example:

`jpegtran -copy none -optimize input.jpg output.jpg`

NConvert

`http://www.softpedia.com/get/Multimedia/Graphic/Image-Convertors/Nconvert.shtml`

It is an image conversion program with hundreds of features, supporting over 500 image formats. It is free for non-commercial use, and is good for compressing JPEG files. You will lose some image quality, so inspect the resulting images to see if the reduction in file size is worth it. For example, to compress a file to 75 percent of its original quality, use:

`nconvert.exe -q 75 -o output.jpg input.jpg`

To do this for all images in a directory and write the compressed versions to a subdirectory `compressed`, use:

```
for %i in (*.jpg) do nconvert.exe -q 75 -o compressed\%i %i
```

ImageMagick

`http://www.imagemagick.org/script/index.php`

It is a package of several programs letting you convert images and inspect their properties. It has of hundreds of features. For example, to convert an image to a thumbnail no wider than 100 pixels and no higher than 200 pixels while keeping the original aspect ratio, use:

```
convert -resize 100x200 input.jpg output.jpg
```

Image formats that can be resized this way include JPEG, GIF and PNG.

Combining images

Web pages often contain many small images, which all have to be requested by the browser individually and then are served up by the server. This creates a lot of request overhead. It takes far less time and bandwidth to receive one slightly bigger image than to receive lots of small ones. Fortunately, there is a way to combine images into a single image, while still showing the original images individually on the page, using a technique called **CSS Sprites**.

Take this bit of HTML (in the file `IndividualImages.aspx` in the folder `CombinedImage` in downloaded code bundle):

```
<img src="geography.png" width="38" height="48" />
<p>some html ...</p>
<img src="chemistry.png" width="28" height="46" />
<p>some html ...</p>
<img src="maths.png" width="46" height="45" />
```

This HTML causes the browser to send three requests to the server, one for each image. Let's cut this down to just one request.

First, combine the three images into a single image, as shown in the following figure (file combined.png in folder CombinedImage in downloaded code bundle):

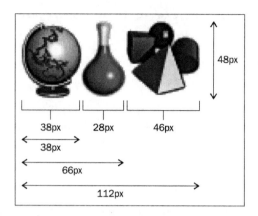

This combined image is created simply by putting the three individual images next to each other. It is 48 pixels high (the height of the highest individual image) and 112 pixels wide (the sum of the widths of the individual images). Note that the chemistry image is 38 pixels from the left edge, while the math symbol is 66 pixels (38 pixels + 28 pixels) from the left edge.

Because of the way png images are natively compressed, you will get a smaller combined image by sticking individual images together horizontally rather than vertically, provided they use the same background color.

So how do you show this one combined image as three separate images on the page? Here is the HTML (file CombinedImage.aspx in the folder CombinedImage in downloaded code bundle):

```
<div style="width:38px; height:48px; background: url(combined.png)
   0px 0px">
</div>
<p>some html ...</p>
<div style="width:28px; height:46px; background: url(combined.png)
   -38px 0px">
</div>
<p>some html ...</p>
<div style="width:46px; height:45px; background: url(combined.png)
   -66px 0px">
</div>
```

Instead of using `img` tags, this HTML uses `div` tags with `combined.png` as the background image. The CSS background property lets you specify an offset into the background image from where you want to show the background image as background. Here, the geography image sits right at the left edge horizontally and right at the top vertically, so it gets offset 0 pixels, 0 pixels. The chemistry image sits 38 pixels away from the left edge, and right at the top vertically, so it gets -38 pixels, 0 pixels. And finally, the math image is 66 pixels away from the left edge and right at the top vertically, so it gets -66 pixels, 0 pixels.

Note that the `div` tags have a width and height equal to the width and height of the original individual images. That way, you only see the portions of `combined.png` that correspond with the individual images.

In addition to fewer requests, combining images also means fewer bytes going over the wire, because one image carries less overhead than three images. In this specific example, you're looking at the following file sizes:

`chemistry.png`	1.5 KB	`combined.png`	3.4 KB
`geography.png`	2.1 KB		
`maths.png`	1.7 KB		
Total	5.3 KB		3.4 KB

On the other hand, if your Waterfall chart shows that all individual images are loaded in parallel without holding up other images, combining them will give you little or no benefit in terms of page load time. *Chapter 1, High Level Diagnosis* showed how to create a Waterfall chart.

Online tools are available that will create the combined image and work out the CSS for you, including:

- CSS Sprites: Online CSS Sprite Builder/Generator
  `http://css-sprit.es/`
- CSS Sprite Generator
  `http://spritegen.website-performance.org/`
- CSS Sprites generator
  `http://csssprites.com/`

Microsoft has released the ImageSprite custom control that combines images and generates the required CSS on the fly, so that you don't have to do this each time you change an image. It comes with good documentation and ASP.NET WebForm and MVC sample sites. At the time of writing, it was still in beta version though, and required .NET 4.

Download the entire package at:

- Sprite and Image Optimization Framework Preview 1
  http://aspnet.codeplex.com/releases/view/50140

A good overview is available at:

- Generate CSS Sprites in ASP.NET
  http://weblogs.asp.net/mikaelsoderstrom/archive/2010/08/10/
  generate-css-sprites-in-asp-net.aspx

Ways to avoid images

Sometimes, you can replace images with HTML and CSS. This section shows two examples of this—rounded corners and utility symbols.

Rounded corners in CSS

Consider the box in the following figure. You could implement the rounded corners with one or more images. However, this means that the browser has to request those images. And if you change the color of the page or the box, you may need to redo the images.

Rounded corners

Many browsers already support rounded corners natively. Firefox has the CSS property **moz-border-radius** (https://developer.mozilla.org/en/css/-moz-border-radius), while Google Chrome supports **border-radius**, a property introduced in CSS3 (http://www.w3.org/TR/2005/WD-css3-background-20050216/#the-border-radius). border-radius is also supported by IE9, but not IE8 or before. This means that unless all your visitors use Firefox, Chrome, or IE9, you'll have to implement rounded corners yourself. Here is how to do this without images.

If you were to zoom in to the top-left corner of the box shown above, it would look as in the following image:

Essentially, the rounding is produced by adding boxes on top of the box with the text. One box is two pixels high and indented one pixel, on top of that are two boxes one pixel high and indented two and three pixels respectively, and on top of that is one box one pixel high and indented five pixels. It translates to the following HTML (folder RoundedCorners in the downloaded code bundle):

```
<div>
  <div class="r15"></div>
  <div class="r13"></div>
  <div class="r12"></div>
  <div class="r21"></div>

  <div class="content">
    Rounded corners without anti-aliasing
  </div>

  <div class="r21"></div>
  <div class="r12"></div>
  <div class="r13"></div>
  <div class="r15"></div>
</div>
```

And translates to the folowing CSS:

```
.r15, .r13, .r12, .r21
{ overflow:hidden; background-color: #c0c0c0; }

.r15 { height: 1px; margin: 0 5px; }
.r13 { height: 1px;  margin: 0 3px; }
.r12 { height: 1px; margin: 0 2px; }
.r21 { height: 2px; margin: 0 1px; }
```

This uses margin to produce the indent. #c0c0c0 is the background color of the box. Set overflow to hidden; otherwise, IE6 will show boxes higher than specified here.

If you look closely at the corners produced by this code, you may find that they are a bit blocky. The greater the contrast between the box and its background, the more this will be apparent.

The solution is to anti-alias the corners by adding pixels whose color is in between that of the box's background and that of the box itself:

You can add the additional pixels by adding a left and right border to the boxes on the top of the main box (in the folder `RoundedCorners` in the downloaded code bundle):

```
.r15, .r13, .r12, .r21
{
  overflow:hidden; background-color: #c0c0c0;
  border-color: #e0e0e0; border-style: solid;
}


.r15 { height: 1px; border-width: 0 2px; margin: 0 3px; }
.r13 { height: 1px; border-width: 0 1px; margin: 0 2px; }
.r12 { height: 1px; border-width: 0 1px; margin: 0 1px; }
.r21 { height: 2px; border-width: 0 1px; margin: 0 0; }
```

The border color `#e0e0e0` is between the color of the background `#ffffff` and the color of the box `#c0c0c0`.

Just in case you prefer not to work out the HTML yourself, a nice online tool that does it for you is **Spiffy Corners** (`http://www.spiffycorners.com/`).

Make sure that your markup works with older browsers, such as IE6 and IE7. An excellent application that lets you test your HTML on IE6 and IE7 engines is **IETester** (`http://www.my-debugbar.com/wiki/IETester/HomePage`).

This entire additional HTML is highly compressible and so, won't add much to the page weight while the page is going over the wire as long as your server has compression enabled (refer to *Chapter 10, Compression*). Still, it doesn't make your markup any cleaner.

To keep the additional HTML out of your markup, add a class to each box that is to have rounded corners, and then have some JavaScript code find those boxes and add the additional lines in the DOM. Visitors with JavaScript switched off will get squared corners, but seeing that this is a presentation issue, you may be able to live with this.

Fortunately, there is no need to write the JavaScript yourself. Firstly, there are many plugins for the popular jQuery library that will give you rounded corners. Search for "rounded corners" at `http://plugins.jquery.com/`. jQuery is discussed in *Chapter 11, Optimizing Forms* in the *Client-side validation* section. If you do not use jQuery, here are some other alternatives:

- CurvyCorners—excellent, free JavaScript library
  `http://www.curvycorners.net/`

- Nifty Corners: rounded corners without images
  http://www.html.it/articoli/nifty/index.html
- Building Rounded Corners With CSS and JavaScript
  http://www.devarticles.com/c/a/JavaScript/Building-Rounded-
  Corners-With-CSS-and-JavaScript/5/
- Ajax Control Toolkit RoundedCorners
  http://www.asp.net/ajaxlibrary/act_RoundedCorners.ashx

Utility symbols

Web pages often contain small utility symbols, such as the phone and the arrows in the following figure:

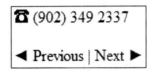

Instead of automatically using images for these symbols, first check whether you can use one of the hundreds of Unicode symbols that most browsers (including IE6) recognize these days. For example, the phone above is a character, with HTML entity &#9742. The graphics and text above can be expressed in HTML as follows (page example.aspx in folder Unicode in downloaded code bundle):

```
&#9742 (902) 349 2337
</p><p>
&#9668 Previous | Next &#9658
```

You're looking at normal characters here. So, you can use CSS to change their color, size, and so on.

Not all Unicode symbols are supported by all browsers. Before you use a Unicode symbol, check whether the browsers used by your visitors support that symbol, for example with the IETester tool mentioned in the *Rounded corners in CSS* section.

Unicode covers the most important languages in the world, which translates to a lot of characters. When you start digging for useful utility symbols, start at the following pages:

- Unicode groups of characters
  http://www.fileformat.info/info/unicode/block/index.htm
- Unicode Characters in the Miscellaneous Symbols Block
  http://www.fileformat.info/info/unicode/block/miscellaneous_
  symbols/images.htm

- Unicode Characters in the Geometric Shapes Block
  `http://www.fileformat.info/info/unicode/block/geometric_shapes/`
  `images.htm`

Alternatively, page `Default.aspx` in the folder `Unicode` in the downloaded code bundle shows the most interesting Unicode symbol characters and their HTML entities.

Shortcut icon

The shortcut icon, or favicon, is the icon shown by the browser next to a website's address. The browser always tries to use a favicon, even if you didn't specify one. As a result, if that icon is not in browser cache, the browser will request it each time it opens a page on your site. This means that even if you don't care about the shortcut icon itself, it still makes sense to provide one simply to stop the browser from requesting it over and over again.

The shortcut icon is a little image in `ICO` format. There are many programs and websites that let you convert a `png` image to `ICO` format such as `http://www.convertico.com`.

One way to give the icon to the browser is to name it `favicon.ico` and put it in the root folder of your site. However, if you decide to change the icon, then all the visitors whose browsers still have `favicon.ico` in their browser cache will continue to see the old icon.

A better way is to explicitly link to the shortcut icon in the head of each web page. That way, you can provide your own icon name and location. For example:

```
<head runat="server">
    <link rel="icon" href="shortcut_v1.ico" />
</head>
```

If you use a cookieless subdomain:

```
<head runat="server">
    <link rel="icon" href="http://img1.mydomain.com/shortcut_v1.ico"
/>
</head>
```

Then, when you decide to change the shortcut icon, you can give it a new name such as `shortcut_v2.ico`, causing the browser to request the new version. This is analogous to putting a timestamp in the image URL, which you saw in the *Caching* section.

Content Delivery Network

All other things being equal, the closer your web server is to the visitor, the faster it responds to requests. You can exploit this by deploying your static content on a **Content Delivery Network (CDN)**. This is a worldwide network of servers that automatically routes requests to the server closest to the visitor. If a US-based visitor requests an image, the request goes to a US-based server, while a request coming from a European visitor goes to a Europe-based server, and so on. In addition to serving images and other static files, CDNs can also be used for streaming content.

In addition to providing better response times, CDNs also reduce the load on your servers, potentially lowering your hardware investment and your bandwidth costs.

If you search for "Content Delivery Network" on Google, you will find many companies that offer to host your content on their CDN. Alternatively, you'll find a long list of providers with descriptions at:

- Content Delivery Networks (CDN) — a comprehensive list of providers
  `http://www.mytestbox.com/miscellaneous/content-delivery-networks-cdn-list/`

If your budget is limited, here are some low cost providers:

- Amazon CloudFront
  `http://aws.amazon.com/cloudfront/`
- CacheFly
  `http://www.cachefly.com/`
- Value CDN
  `http://www.valuecdn.com/`

Find out more

Here are some more online resources:

- Optimizing Page Load Time
  `http://www.die.net/musings/page_load_time/`
- Browser Shots - browser compatibility testing
  `http://browsershots.org/`
- Caching Tutorial for Web Authors and Webmasters
  `http://www.mnot.net/cache_docs/`
- Performance Research, Part 4: Maximizing Parallel Downloads in the Carpool Lane
  `http://yuiblog.com/blog/2007/04/11/performance-research-part-4/`

- Control Adapters
  `http://msdn.microsoft.com/en-us/magazine/cc163543.aspx`

- Using the URL Rewrite Module
  `http://learn.iis.net/page.aspx/460/using-the-url-rewrite-module/`

- CSS Sprites: Image Slicing's Kiss of Death
  `http://www.alistapart.com/articles/sprites/`

- Rounded Corners in Internet Explorer
  `http://msdn.microsoft.com/en-us/library/Bb250413`

- Anti-Aliasing
  `http://www.pantherproducts.co.uk/Articles/Graphics/anti_aliasing.shtml`

- Unicode and Multilingual Support in HTML, Fonts, Web Browsers, and Other Applications
  `http://www.alanwood.net/unicode/`

Summary

In this chapter, we first saw how to store images in the browser cache in the best way. It then looked at preventing cookie overhead in image requests and parallel loading of images, and introduced an image control adapter that addresses these issues.

This was followed by discussions on reducing image sizes, combining images into a single larger image, and replacing images by HTML and CSS.

Finally, we saw how to optimize usage of the shortcut icon, and the use of content delivery networks.

In the next chapter, we'll see how to improve the way JavaScript files are loaded, to speed up rendering of the page.

13

Improving JavaScript Loading

One approach to improving page performance is to shift functionality from the server to the browser. Instead of calculating a result or validating a form in C# on the server, you use JavaScript code on the browser. As a result, fewer user actions require the browser to send a request to the server and wait for the response, greatly improving responsiveness. You also reduce the load on the server. *Chapter 11, Optimizing Forms* goes into more detail.

A drawback of this approach is that it involves physically moving code from the server to the browser. Because JavaScript is not compiled, it can be quite bulky. This can affect page load times, especially if you use large JavaScript libraries. You're effectively trading off increased page load times against faster response times after the page has loaded. This is an issue if a large proportion of your visitors will give up on your page if it takes too long to load.

In this chapter, you'll see how to reduce the impact on page load times by the need to load JavaScript files. It shows:

- How JavaScript files can block rendering of the page while they are being loaded and executed
- How to load JavaScript in parallel with other resources
- How to load JavaScript more quickly
- How to load JavaScript only when needed
- How to load JavaScript without blocking page rendering
- How to load advertisements provided by advertisement networks, such as DoubleClick without allowing them to slow down page loading
- How to improve the loading of CSS stylesheets

Let's start with a major issue with JavaScript files—how they can block rendering of the page while they are being loaded and executed.

Problem: JavaScript loading blocks page rendering

JavaScript files are static files, just as images and CSS files. However, unlike images, when a JavaScript file is loaded or executed using a `<script>` tag, rendering of the page is suspended.

This makes sense, because the page may contain script blocks after the `<script>` tag that are dependent on the JavaScript file. If loading of a JavaScript file didn't block page rendering, the other blocks could be executed before the file had loaded, leading to JavaScript errors.

Confirming with a test site

You can confirm that loading a JavaScript file blocks rendering of the page by running the website in the folder `JavaScriptBlocksRendering` in the downloaded code bundle. This site consists of a single page that loads a single script, `script1.js`. It also has a single image, `chemistry.png`, and a stylesheet `style1.css`. It uses an HTTP module that suspends the working thread for five seconds when a JavaScript file is loaded. Images and CSS files are delayed by about two seconds. When you load the page, you'll see that the page content appears after only about five seconds. Then after two seconds, the image appears, unless you use Firefox, which often loads images in parallel with the JavaScript.

If you make a Waterfall chart, you can see how the image and stylesheet are loaded after the JavaScript file, instead of in parallel (*Chapter 1, High Level Diagnosis* shows how to make Waterfall charts):

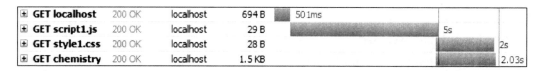

To get the delays, run the test site on IIS 7 in integrated pipeline mode. Do not use the Cassini web server built into Visual Studio. The *Setting up IIS on local Vista or Windows 7 machine* section in *Chapter 14, Load Testing* describes how to set up IIS 7 on your local machine and ensure that Visual Studio uses it while running a site.

If you find that there is no delay, clear the browser cache. If that doesn't work either, the files may be in kernel cache on the server — remove them by restarting IIS using Internet Information Services (IIS) Manager. To open IIS manager, click on **Start | Control Panel**, type "admin" in the search box, click on **Administrative Tools**, and then double-click on **Internet Information Services (IIS) Manager**. For more information about the kernel cache and how to use it to speed up your site, refer to *Chapter 5, Caching*.

Integrated/Classic Pipeline Mode

As in IIS 6, every website runs as part of an application pool in IIS 7. Each IIS 7 application pool can be switched between Integrated Pipeline Mode (the default) and Classic Pipeline Mode. In Integrated Pipeline Mode, the ASP.NET runtime is integrated with the core web server, so that the server can be managed for example, via web.config elements. In Classic Pipeline Mode, IIS 7 functions more like IIS 6, where ASP.NET runs within an ISAPI extension.

Approaches to reduce the impact on load times

Although it makes sense to suspend rendering the page while a `<script>` tag loads or executes JavaScript, it would still be good to minimize the time visitors have to wait for the page to appear, especially if there is a lot of JavaScript to load. Here are a few ways to do that:

- Start loading JavaScript after other components have started loading, such as images and CSS files. That way, the other components load in parallel with the JavaScript instead of after the JavaScript, and so are available sooner when page rendering resumes.

- Load JavaScript more quickly. Page rendering is still blocked, but for less time.

- Load JavaScript on demand. Only load the JavaScript upfront that you need to render the page. Load the JavaScript that handles button clicks, and so on, when you need it.

- Use specific techniques to prevent JavaScript loading from blocking rendering. This includes loading the JavaScript after the page has rendered, or in parallel with page rendering.

These approaches can be combined or used on their own for the best tradeoff between development time and performance. Let's go through each approach.

Approach 1: Start loading after other components

This approach aims to render the page sooner by loading CSS stylesheets and images in parallel with the JavaScript rather than after the JavaScript. That way, when the JavaScript has finished loading, the CSS and images will have finished loading too and will be ready to use; or at least it will take less time for them to finish loading after the JavaScript has loaded.

To load the CSS stylesheets and images in parallel with the JavaScript, you would start loading them before you start loading the JavaScript. In the case of CSS stylesheets that is easy — simply place their `<link>` tags before the `<script>` tags:

```
<link rel="Stylesheet" type="text/css" href="css/style1.css" />
<script type="text/javascript" src="js/script1.js"></script>
```

Starting the loading of images is slightly trickier because images are normally loaded when the page body is evaluated, not as a part of the page head.

In the test page you just saw with the image `chemistry.png`, you can use a bit of simple JavaScript to get the browser to start loading the image before it starts loading the JavaScript file. This is referred to as "image preloading" (page `PreLoadWithJavaScript.aspx` in the folder `PreLoadImages` in the downloaded code bundle):

```
<script type="text/javascript">
  var img1 = new Image(); img1.src = "images/chemistry.png";
</script>
<link rel="Stylesheet" type="text/css" href="css/style1.css" />
<script type="text/javascript" src="js/script1.js"></script>
```

Run the page now and you'll get the following Waterfall chart:

⊞ **GET localhost**	200 OK	localhost	816 B	▬ 503ms	
⊞ **GET chemistry**	200 OK	localhost	1.5 KB	2.01s	
⊞ **GET style1.css**	200 OK	localhost	28 B	2s	
⊞ **GET script1.js**	200 OK	localhost	29 B		5.46s

When the page is rendered after the JavaScript has loaded, the image and CSS files have already been loaded; so the image shows up right away.

A second option is to use invisible image tags at the start of the page body that preload the images. You can make the image tags invisible by using the style `display:none`. You would have to move the `<script>` tags from the page head to the page body after the invisible image tags, as shown (page `PreLoadWithCss.aspx` in folder `PreLoadImages` in the downloaded code bundle):

```
<body>
  <div style="display:none">
    <img src="images/chemistry.png" />
  </div>
  <script type="text/javascript" src="js/script1.js"></script>
```

Although the examples we've seen so far preload only one image, `chemistry.png`, you could easily preload multiple images. When you do, it makes sense to preload the most important images first, so that they are most likely to appear right away when the page renders. The browser loads components, such as images, in the order in which they appear in the HTML, so you'd wind up with something similar to the following code:

```
<script type="text/javascript">
  var img1 = new Image(); img1.src = "images/important.png";
  var img1 = new Image(); img2.src = "images/notsoimportant.png";
  var img1 = new Image(); img3.src = "images/unimportant.png";
</script>
```

Approach 2: Loading JavaScript more quickly

The second approach is to simply spend less time loading the same JavaScript, so that visitors spend less time waiting for the page to render. There are a number of ways to achieve just that:

- Techniques used with images, such as caching and parallel download
- Free Content Delivery Networks
- GZIP compression
- Minification
- Combining or breaking up JavaScript files
- Removing unused code

Techniques used with images

JavaScript files are static files, just like images and CSS files. This means that many techniques that apply to images apply to JavaScript files as well, including the use of cookie-free domains, caching, and boosting parallel loading. You'll find out more about these techniques in *Chapter 12, Reducing Image Load Times*.

Free Content Delivery Networks

As shown in chapter 12, serving static files from a Content Delivery Network (CDN) can greatly reduce download times, by serving the files from a server that is close to the visitor. A CDN also saves you bandwidth because the files are no longer served from your own server.

A number of companies now serve popular JavaScript libraries from their CDNs for free. Here are their details:

- Google AJAX Libraries API

  `http://code.google.com/apis/ajaxlibs/`

  Serves a wide range of libraries including jQuery, jQuery UI, Prototype, Dojo, and Yahoo! User Interface Library (YUI)

- Microsoft Ajax Content Delivery Network

  `http://www.asp.net/ajaxlibrary/cdn.ashx`

  Serves libraries used by the ASP.NET and ASP.NET MVC frameworks including the jQuery library and the jQuery Validation plugin

- jQuery CDN

  `http://docs.jquery.com/Downloading_jQuery`

  Serves the jQuery library

In ASP.NET 4.0 and later, you can get the `ScriptManager` control to load the ASP. NET AJAX script files from the Microsoft AJAX CDN instead of your web server, by setting the `EnableCdn` property to `true`:

```
<asp:ScriptManager ID="ScriptManager1"
  EnableCdn="true" runat="server" />
```

One issue with loading libraries from a CDN is that it creates another point of failure—if the CDN goes down, your site is crippled. *Chapter 11, Optimizing Forms* shows how to overcome this by checking whether the library has loaded and by loading from a fallback location, if it hasn't.

GZIP compression

IIS has the ability to compress content sent to the browser, including JavaScript and CSS files. *Chapter 10, Compression* shows how to enable compression in IIS 6 and IIS 7.

Compression can make a dramatic difference to a JavaScript file as it goes over the wire from the server to the browser. Take for example the production version of the jQuery library:

	Uncompressed	Compressed
jQuery library	78 KB	26 KB

Compression for static files is enabled by default in IIS 7. This immediately benefits CSS files. It should also immediately benefit JavaScript files, but it doesn't because of a quirk in the default configuration of IIS 7.

Not all static files benefit from compression; for example JPEG, PNG, and GIF files are already inherently compressed because of their format. To cater to this, the IIS 7 configuration file `applicationHost.config` contains a list of mime types that get compressed when static compression is enabled:

```
<staticTypes>
  <add mimeType="text/*" enabled="true" />
  <add mimeType="message/*" enabled="true" />
  <add mimeType="application/javascript" enabled="true" />
  <add mimeType="*/*" enabled="false" />
</staticTypes>
```

To allow IIS to figure out what mime type a particular file has, `applicationHost.config` also contains default mappings from file extensions to mime types, including this one:

```
<staticContent lockAttributes="isDocFooterFileName">

  . . .
  <mimeMap fileExtension=".js"
    mimeType="application/x-javascript" />
  . . .
</staticContent>
```

If you look closely, you'll see that the `.js` extension is mapped by default to a mime type that isn't in the list of mime types to be compressed when static file compression is enabled.

The easiest way to solve this is to modify your site's `web.config`, so that it maps the extension `.js` to mime type `text/javascript`. This matches `text/*` in the list of mime types to be compressed. So, IIS 7 will now compress JavaScript files with the extension `.js` (folder `Minify` in the downloaded code bundle):

```
<system.webServer>
  <staticContent>
    <remove fileExtension=".js" />
    <mimeMap fileExtension=".js" mimeType="text/javascript" />
  </staticContent>
</system.webServer>
```

> Keep in mind that IIS 7 only applies static compression to files that are "frequently" requested, as discussed in *Chapter 10, Compression* in the *Setting the request frequency threshold for static compression* section. This means that the first time you request a file, it won't be compressed! Refresh the page a couple of times and compression will kick in.

Minifying a JavaScript file

JavaScript files tend to contain comments and white space that make the file more readable for humans, but these are superfluous as far as the browser is concerned. Minifying a JavaScript file gets rid of those comments and white space, thereby reducing its size and download time. It also encourages developers to write more comments, because they know they won't add to the size of the file as it goes over the wire.

Some minification tools also shorten variable names. This is useful if your server does not use GZIP compression. If compression is enabled, shortening variable names will have little effect, because the compression algorithm itself is very good at shortening repeating strings, such as variable names.

Tools

Here are a number of tools that will minify a JavaScript file for you:

- Microsoft Ajax Minifier

  http://www.asp.net/ajaxlibrary/AjaxMinDocumentation.ashx

  It minifies your JavaScript and CSS files.

- Google Closure Compiler

  `http://code.google.com/closure/compiler/`

  It parses your JavaScript, analyzes it, removes dead code and rewrites, and minimizes what's left. It also checks syntax, variable references and types, and warns about common JavaScript pitfalls.

- ShrinkSafe

  `http://www.dojotoolkit.org/reference-guide/shrinksafe/index.html`

  It is a standalone Java-based JavaScript compressor. It renames local references to short names prefixed with an underscore, and removes white space and comments.

- YUI Compressor

  `http://developer.yahoo.com/yui/compressor/`

  This is another standalone Java-based JavaScript compressor that renames local references and removes white space and comments. It can also be used to minify CSS stylesheets.

- Yahoo! UI Library: YUI Compressor for .Net

  `http://yuicompressor.codeplex.com/`

  It is an excellent .NET port of the YUI Compressor Java project. It includes a DLL that allows you to minify JavaScript in your C# code, as shown:

  ```
  using Yahoo.Yui.Compressor;
  ...
  string compressedJavaScript =
  JavaScriptCompressor.Compress(uncompressedJavaScript);
  ```

- JSMin

  `http://www.crockford.com/javascript/jsmin.html`

  It is a simple minifier program and comes with source code and a description of how the minification process works.

- CompressorRater

  `http://compressorrater.thruhere.net/`

  It is an online tool that allows you to test various minification programs with your JavaScript code, to see which one is the most effective.

Impact of minification

How much effect does minification have compared with GZIP compression? Here are the results of applying GZIP compression and minification (using YUI Compressor) on the uncompressed debug version of the jQuery library:

		Minified		Reduction through minification
		No	Yes	
GZIP Compressed	No	22 KB	78 KB	65 percent
	Yes	48 KB	26 KB	46 percent

This shows that minification has the most dramatic impact if GZIP compression has been disabled on the server (which is not recommended). Still, even with compression enabled, minification makes sense, as the drop from 48 KB to 26 KB is significant.

Implementing minification

A common way to implement minification is to run a minifier program during a release build that minifies the JavaScript files. However, this means that you can't simply copy updated JavaScript files to the production server without going through the minification step.

An alternative is to place JavaScript files unminified in production, and have the website minify the files on the fly before serving them to the browser. To save CPU cycles, you would cache the minified file. To ensure that the site immediately picks up a new version of the file, the cached file would have a file dependency on the physical (uncompressed) file on disk. For more information about caching and file dependencies, refer to *Chapter 5, Caching*.

HTTP handler

You can implement this approach with an HTTP Handler. This is simply a class derived from IHttpHandler, which you put in the App_Code folder, or in a separate class library. To do the actual minification, you can use the YUI Compressor for .NET library, which you saw earlier. The result is code as shown (folder Minify in downloaded code bundle):

```
using System.IO;
using System.Web.UI.WebControls;
using System.Web.Caching;
```

Import the YUI Compressor namespace. To make this work, download the DLL at `http://yuicompressor.codeplex.com/` and add a reference to that DLL:

```
using Yahoo.Yui.Compressor;
using System.Web.UI;

namespace MinifyingHttpHandler
{
  public class JavaScriptHttpHandler : IHttpHandler
  {
    public bool IsReusable
    {
      get { return true; }
    }

    public void ProcessRequest(HttpContext context)
    {
      const string cacheKeyPrefix = "js__";
      string compressedText = null;
      string uncompressedText = null;
      try
      {
```

Get the URL of the JavaScript file that this handler needs to produce. The `PathAndQuery` component will be used as the cache key:

```
Uri url = context.Request.Url;
string path = url.PathAndQuery;
```

Try to retrieve the minified JavaScript from cache:

```
string cacheKey = cacheKeyPrefix + path;
compressedText = (string)context.Cache[cacheKey];

if (compressedText == null)
{
```

If the minified JavaScript could not be found, first read the contents of the file from disk:

```
string filePath = context.Server.MapPath(path);
uncompressedText = File.ReadAllText(filePath);
```

Then, minify the contents:

```
compressedText = JavaScriptCompressor.Compress(uncompressedText);
```

Finally, cache the minified content. Use a file dependency, so that the cache manager automatically removes the content from cache if the file on disk changes:

```
        CacheDependency cd = new CacheDependency(filePath);
        context.Cache.Insert(cacheKey, compressedText, cd);
    }
}
catch
{
}
```

Add a `Cache-Control` header to ask the browser to cache the JavaScript file for 31,536,000 seconds (365 days). You may want to reduce this if it is critical that browsers quickly pick up changes in your JavaScript. For more details about `Cache-Control`, refer to chapter 12.

```
context.Response.AddHeader("Cache-Control",
    "public,max-age=31536000");
```

Specify the correct content type:

```
context.Response.AddHeader("Content-Type", "text/javascript");
```

Send the actual minified content to the browser. If `compressedText` is null, which could happen if an exception occurred, send `compressedText` instead. And if that is null too, send the empty string:

```
        context.Response.Write(compressedText ??
            (uncompressedText ?? ""));
    }
    }
}
```

Configuring the handler in web.config

After you've created the HTTP handler, configure it in `web.config`, so that ASP.NET uses it to handle requests for JavaScript files.

If you use IIS 7 in integrated pipeline mode, simply add your new handler to the `handlers` section of `system.webServer`:

```
<configuration>
  <system.webServer>
    <handlers>
      <add name="Minifying" verb="*" path="*.js"
        type="MinifyingHttpHandler.JavaScriptHttpHandler,
        MinifyingHttpHandler" resourceType="File"/>
    </handlers>
  </system.webServer>
</configuration>
```

If you use IIS 6 or IIS 7 in classic mode, add your handler to `httpHandlers` instead. In that case, don't forget to update your IIS configuration, so that requests for `.js` files are handled by ASP.NET:

```
<configuration>
  <system.web>
    <httpHandlers>
      <add verb="*" path="*.js"
        type="MinifyingHttpHandler.JavaScriptHttpHandler,
        MinifyingHttpHandler" />
    </httpHandlers>
  </system.web>
</configuration>
```

Enabling GZIP compression for dynamic files

Now that you're using ASP.NET to produce the JavaScript, you need to enable compression for dynamic files to have your JavaScript compressed by the server. *Chapter 10, Compression* shows how to do this.

Combining or breaking up

A popular approach to reducing JavaScript load times is to combine several JavaScript files into a single big file, so only that one big file is loaded. An alternative is to do the reverse and break up a big JavaScript file into several smaller files that are loaded in parallel. Here is when each of these approaches makes sense.

When and why to combine

Take for example, a page loading four scripts:

```
<head>
  <script type="text/javascript" src="script1.js"></script>
  <script type="text/javascript" src="script2.js"></script>
  <script type="text/javascript" src="script3.js"></script>
  <script type="text/javascript" src="script4.js"></script>
</head>
```

Older browsers such as Internet Explorer 6 load the scripts one after the other. That way, the browser can be sure that if a script executes code that relies on a previous script, there will be no JavaScript errors. For example, loading the test page in IE 6 resulted in this Waterfall chart:

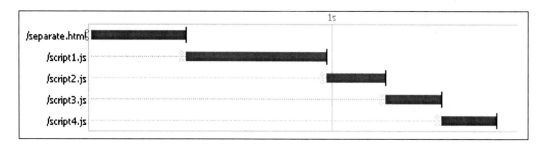

In this scenario, it is attractive to combine files. This is because loading involves a lot more than just loading the bytes in the file. It also involves overhead, such as sending the request from the browser to the server. A site that requests four files one after the other spends four times as much time on the overhead as a site that places a single request for a single large file.

When and why to break up

Loading JavaScript files one after the other may be very safe, but is also wasteful. The browser could load files in parallel, but hold off executing them until the previous files have loaded. Newer browsers, such as Internet Explorer 7 and 8, Firefox, and Google Chrome do exactly the same thing. For example, loading the test page in IE 7 resulted in the following Waterfall chart:

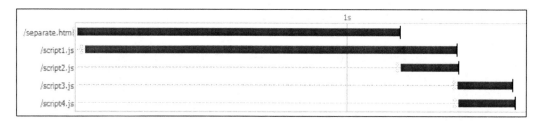

This makes it attractive to consider splitting large JavaScript files into a number of smaller ones, and loading them in parallel. The request overhead would then be incurred in parallel, rather than sequentially. Loading two half-sized files in parallel may take slightly over half the time taken by the single original file, depending on the time taken by the request overhead.

If you load many JavaScript, CSS, and image files in parallel, keep in mind that modern browsers have a download limit of six files per domain (see *Chapter 12, Reducing Image Load Times*).

Measuring each scenario

To investigate this a bit further, I ran tests with two simple test pages — a page `separate.html` that loads four JavaScript files and a page `combined.html` that loads a single big JavaScript file, in which the four separate files are combined. A bit of JavaScript in the HTML files measured the total download time. See folder `ScriptLoadTest` in the downloaded code bundle.

Because the sizes of the JavaScript files might affect the results, I ran a "big" scenario with one 220-KB JavaScript file and three 37-KB files, and a "small" scenario with four 10-KB files. The test pages sat on my hosting account. Your numbers are bound to vary, but you'll get a general idea.

The results for the big scenario were:

Total download times (seconds)	combined.html	separate.html
IE 6	1.3	1.5
IE 7	1.4	0.9
IE 8	1.3	0.7
Firefox 3	1.4	1.2
Google Chrome 5	1.5	1.0

The results for the small scenario were:

Total download times (seconds)	combined.html	separate.html
IE 6	0.2	0.8
IE 7	0.4	0.4
IE 8	0.4	0.4
Firefox 3	0.6	0.2
Google Chrome 5	0.2	0.2

The moral of this story is to find out which browsers are most used by your target groups, and then experiment with different scenarios using those browsers.

Preventing 304 messages

When running your own tests, keep in mind that the browser will store the JavaScript files in its cache. As a result, if you press *Ctrl + F5* to reload the page, some browsers, including Internet Explorer, will send If-Modified-Since and If-None-Match headers to the server, as described in chapter 12. If you haven't changed the files, the server will then respond with a short 304 message indicating that the browser cache is still up to date, instead of a longer 200 message that contains the entire file. This will skew your results.

You can prevent this by running the Fiddler developers proxy (http://www.fiddler2.com/fiddler2), which was described in chapter 1. Its filter feature allows you to neutralize the If-Modified-Since and If-None-Match headers, as shown in the following screenshot:

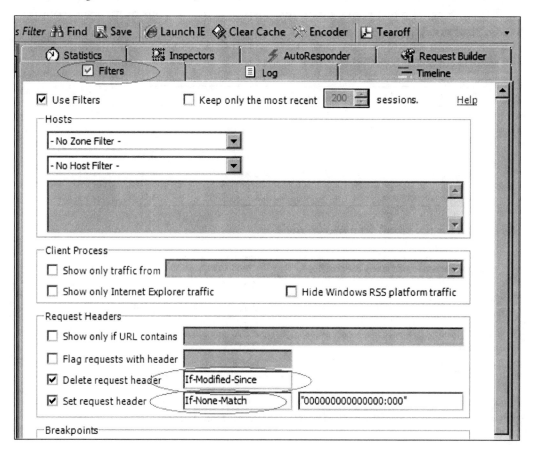

Implementing automatic file combining

If you decide to combine your files, you could do so manually using a simple text editor. However, that would create a maintenance headache. You could also combine the files as part of the build process, but then you would have to modify your `script` tags as well.

The best solution would be to have the site combine the files at runtime. It can then also take care of replacing the individual `script` tags with their counterparts for the combined files.

Here are a number of packages you can add to your site to make this happen:

- ASP.NET `ScriptManager` Control
- Compression (deflate) and HTML, CSS, JS Minification in ASP.NET
- Combres 2.0
- FileCombine

Because CSS files can also benefit from being combined, these packages also support combining CSS files, except for the ASP.NET `ScriptManager` Control.

ASP.NET ScriptManager Control

You include the ASP.NET `ScriptManager` control on your pages to use ASP.NET AJAX controls, such as `UpdatePanel`. It automatically generates the `script` tags for the JavaScript files needed for those controls. It can also create `script` tags for other JavaScript files you nominate.

As of ASP.NET 3.5, you can tell the `ScriptManager` control to combine JavaScript files. It then generates the `script` tag for the combined file and combines the files on the fly. It also compresses the combined files using GZIP if the browser is not Internet Explorer 6. For example:

```
<asp:ScriptManager runat="server">
  <CompositeScript>
    <Scripts>
      <asp:ScriptReference Path="js/script1.js" />
      <asp:ScriptReference Path="js/script2.js" />
    </Scripts>
  </CompositeScript>
</asp:ScriptManager>
```

If you want to use the `ScriptManager` to combine your files without loading the ASP.NET Ajax libraries, use the `ScriptManager` derivative shown in:

- Using `ScriptManager` with other frameworks

  `http://weblogs.asp.net/bleroy/archive/2008/07/07/using-scriptmanager-with-other-frameworks.aspx`

This is probably the simplest way to combine script files automatically. However, a drawback of `ScriptManager` is that it doesn't work with CSS files. Also, it doesn't minify your JavaScript files, and you have to modify your `.aspx` files to make it work. Finally, the URLs of the combined files contain query strings, which means that you miss out on kernel caching and caching in most proxies.

Compression (deflate) and HTML, CSS, JS Minification in ASP.NET

Description and download is available at:

`http://candrews.integralblue.com/2009/05/compression-deflate-and-html-css-js-minification-in-asp-net/`

This package combines JavaScript files and CSS files. It also minifies JavaScript and CSS, and the HTML on the page as well. It compresses your files using the deflate algorithm. And because it uses a custom filter to intercept your HTML to find the script and link tags, there is no need to modify your `.aspx` files.

On the other hand, it uses script and CSS file URLs that contain query strings, which is not good for caching. And those query strings contain the names of the individual files that make up the combined file, which means that they can get very long. The biggest drawback is that it will break your CSS code if your CSS files are in a separate folder and you use relative image URLs, as in the following code:

```
background-image: url(../images/chemistry.png);
```

This is because the combined CSS file is not guaranteed to be served from the same folder, and so the relative URLs no longer refer to the same location.

Combres 2.0

Description and download is available at:

`http://combres.codeplex.com/`

This highly configurable, open source package allows you to organize JavaScript and CSS files into separate resource sets. It automatically detects changes to the files and includes a version number in the combined file URLs, so a browser will never use an outdated file from its cache. It lets you combine, minify, and compress files using either GZIP or deflate. It generates `Cache-Control` and `ETAG` headers. It also supports debugging mode, where files are not minified or cached.

The only drawback to this impressive package is that you can't simply drop it into your website. You have to set up a configuration file to make it work, and you have to maintain that file as your site changes.

FileCombine

You'll find the project `FileCombine` in the folder `FileCombine` in the downloaded code bundle.

This package combines many of the features of Combres with the ability to simply drop it in your site without having to do configuration:

- Combines and minifies both CSS and JavaScript files. To reduce CPU usage, the minified and combined files are kept in server cache. To make sure that you don't serve outdated files from the server cache, a cache entry is removed the moment one of the constituent individual files is updated.

- Limits URL length of combined files by using an MD5 hash over the individual URLs as the combined file URL. The alternative of making up the combined file URL by stringing together the URLs of the constituent files can result in an extremely long URL.

- The hashing algorithm always produces the same hash for the same constituent file URLs, as long as they are in the same order. That way, if you use the same script and CSS link tags in different pages, the browser needs to load the combined file only once, and can then retrieve it from cache for subsequent pages.

- The URL of the combined file includes a shortened version of the last modified time of the youngest constituent file. This stops the browser from using an outdated version from its cache.

- To improve proxy caching, no query strings are used in the URLs of combined files.

- It assigns far-future `Cache-Control` headers, so that if the combined files remain unchanged, they stay as long as possible in browser and proxy cache.

- It replaces relative `url()` properties in CSS files with their absolute counterparts, so that they do not break when used in a combined CSS file.

- It also detects if the site is in debug mode. If in debug mode, it doesn't minify or combine files, and uses `Cache-Control` headers that specify immediate expiry from the browser cache.

Limitations of this package:

- It considers only `script` tags and CSS `link` tags in the head of the page.
- It doesn't minify inline script or CSS.
- It relies on the server to do GZIP compression. To have your JavaScript and CSS files GZIP-compressed (highly recommended), enable dynamic file compression on the server, as shown in chapter 10.

For updates about `FileCombine`, search Google for "FileCombine".

The installation instructions are in the `FileCombine` folder in the downloaded code bundle.

Removing unused code

Because JavaScript code is separate from the HTML user interface elements it supports, it is easy to forget to remove code when it is no longer needed. As a result, your JavaScript files may become bloated with unused code.

Here are a number of tools that help identify unused code. Be careful with this— JavaScript is a very dynamic language, making it difficult for a tool to make sure that a piece of code really is unused.

- JSLint

  http://www.jslint.com/lint.html

  It statically analyzes your JavaScript and reports bad programming practices. It also reports unreachable code and unused variables.

- Jsure

  http://aurochs.fr/jsure.html

  This is another program that statically analyzes your JavaScript. It reports unused functions, variables, and function arguments.

- JSCoverage

  http://siliconforks.com/jscoverage/

  JSCoverage shows which lines of a program get executed, and which ones are missed. It works by instrumenting the JavaScript code used in web pages. Code coverage statistics are collected while the instrumented JavaScript code is executed in a web browser.

Approach 3: Loading JavaScript on demand

The JavaScript code for a page falls into two groups—code required to render the page, and code required to handle user interface events, such as button clicks. The code to render the page is used to make the page look better , and to attach event handlers to for example, buttons.

Although the rendering code needs to be loaded and executed in conjunction with the page itself, the user interface code can be loaded later, in response to a user interface event, such as a button click. That reduces the amount of code to be loaded, and therefore the time rendering of the page is blocked. It also reduces your bandwidth costs, because the user interface code is loaded only when it's actually needed.

On the other hand, it does require separating the user interface code from the rendering code. You then need to invoke code that potentially hasn't loaded yet, tell the visitor that the code is loading, and finally invoke the code after it has loaded.

Let's see how to make this all happen.

Separating user interface code from render code

Depending on how your JavaScript code is structured, this could be your biggest challenge in implementing on-demand loading. Make sure the time you're likely to spend on this and the subsequent testing and debugging is worth the performance improvement you're likely to gain.

A very handy tool that identifies which code is used while loading the page is Page Speed, an add-on for Firefox. Besides identifying code that doesn't need to be loaded upfront, it reports many speed-related issues on your web page.

Information on Page Speed is available at
`http://code.google.com/speed/page-speed/`.

OnDemandLoader library

Assuming your user interface code is separated from your render code, it is time to look at implementing actual on-demand loading. To keep it simple, we'll use `OnDemandLoader`, a simple low-footprint object. You'll find it in the downloaded code bundle in the folder `OnDemandLoad` in the file `OnDemandLoader.js`.

OnDemandLoader has the following features:

- It allows you to specify the script, in which it is defined, for each event-handler function.

- It allows you to specify that a particular script depends on some other script; for example Button1Code.js depends on library code in UILibrary1.js. A script file can depend on multiple other script files, and those script files can in turn be dependent on yet other script files.

- It exposes function runf, which takes the name of a function, arguments to call it with, and the this pointer to use while it's being executed. If the function is already defined, runf calls it right away. Otherwise, it loads all the necessary script files and then calls the function.

- It exposes the function loadScript, which loads a given script file and all the script files it depends on. Function runf uses this function to load script files.

- While script files are being loaded in response to a user interface event, a "Loading..." box appears on top of the affected control. That way, the visitor knows that the page is working to execute their action.

- If a script file has already been loaded or if it is already loading, it won't be loaded again.

- If the visitor does the same action repeatedly while the associated code is loading, such as clicking the same button, that event is handled only once.

- If the visitor clicks a second button or takes some other action while the code for the first button is still loading, both events are handled.

A drawback of OnDemandLoader is that it always loads all the required scripts in parallel. If one script automatically executes a function that is defined in another script , there will be a JavaScript error if the other script hasn't loaded yet. However, if your library script files only define functions and other objects, OnDemandLoader will work well.

Initializing OnDemandLoader

OnDemandLoading.aspx in folder OnDemandLoad in the downloaded code bundle is a worked-out example of a page using on-demand loading. It delays the loading of JavaScript files by five seconds, to simulate slowly loading files. Only OnDemandLoader.js loads at normal speed. As you saw with the test page in the *Problem: JavaScript loading blocks page rendering* section, the delay works only when you run the page in IIS 7.

If you open `OnDemandLoading.aspx`, you'll find that it defines two arrays—the script map array and the script dependencies array. These are needed to construct the loader object that will take care of the on-demand loading.

The script map array shows the script file, in which it is defined, for each function:

```
var scriptMap = [
  { fname: 'btn1a_click', src: 'js/Button1Code.js' },
  { fname: 'btn1b_click', src: 'js/Button1Code.js' },
  { fname: 'btn2_click', src: 'js/Button2Code.js' }
];
```

Here, functions `btn1a_click` and `btn1b_click` live in script file `js/Button1Code.js`, while function `btn2_click` lives in script file `js/Button2Code.js`.

The second array defines which other script files it needs to run for each script file:

```
var scriptDependencies = [
    {
        src: '/js/Button1Code.js',
        testSymbol: 'btn1a_click',
        dependentOn: ['/js/UILibrary1.js', '/js/UILibrary2.js']
    },
    {
        src: '/js/Button2Code.js',
        testSymbol: 'btn2_click',
        dependentOn: ['/js/UILibrary2.js']
    },
    {
        src: '/js/UILibrary2.js',
        testSymbol: 'uifunction2',
        dependentOn: []
    },
    {
        src: '/js/UILibrary1.js',
        testSymbol: 'uifunction1',
        dependentOn: ['/js/UILibrary2.js']
    }
];
```

This says that `Button1Code.js` depends on `UILibrary1.js` and `UILibrary2.js`. Further, `Button2Code.js` depends on `UILibrary2.js`. Further, `UILibrary1.js` relies on `UILibrary2.js`, and `UILibrary2.js` doesn't require any other script files.

The `testSymbol` field holds the name of a function defined in the script. Any function will do, as long as it is defined in the script. This way, the on-demand loader can determine whether a script has been loaded by testing whether that name has been defined.

With these two pieces of information, we can construct the loader object:

```
<script type="text/javascript" src="js/OnDemandLoader.js">
</script>
var loader = new OnDemandLoader(scriptMap, scriptDependencies);
```

Now that the loader object has been created, let's see how to invoke user interface handler functions before their code has been loaded.

Invoking not-yet-loaded functions

The point of on-demand loading is that the visitor is allowed to take an action for which the code hasn't been loaded yet. How do you invoke a function that hasn't been defined yet? Here, you'll see two approaches:

- Call a `loader` function and pass it the name of the function to load and execute

- Create a `stub` function with the same name as the function you want to execute, and have the stub load and execute the actual function

Let's focus on the first approach first.

The `OnDemandLoader` object exposes a loader function `runf` that takes the name of a function to call, the arguments to call it with, and the current `this` pointer:

```
function runf(fname, thisObj) {
   // implementation
}
```

Wait a minute! This signature shows a function name parameter and the `this` pointer, but what about the arguments to call the function with? One of the amazing features of JavaScript is that can you pass as few or as many parameters as you want to a function, irrespective of the signature. Within each function, you can access all the parameters via the built-in arguments array. The signature is simply a convenience that allows you to name some of the arguments.

This means that you can call `runf` as shown:

```
loader.runf('myfunction', this, 'argument1', 'argument2');
```

If for example, your original HTML has a button as shown:

```
<input id="btn1a" type="button" value="Button 1a"
    onclick="btn1a_click(this.value, 'more info')" />
```

To have `btn1a_click` loaded on demand, rewrite this to the following (file `OnDemandLoading.aspx`):

```
<input id="btn1a" type="button" value="Button 1a"
  onclick="loader.runf('btn1a_click', this, this.value,
  'more info')" />
```

If, in the original HTML, the click handler function was assigned to a button programmatically as shown:

```
<input id="btn1b" type="button" value="Button 1b" />
<script type="text/javascript">
  window.onload = function() {
    document.getElementById('btn1b').onclick = btn1b_click;
  }
</script>
```

Then, use an anonymous function that calls `loader.runf` with the function to execute:

```
<input id="btn1b" type="button" value="Button 1b" />
<script type="text/javascript">
  window.onload = function() {
    document.getElementById('btn1b').onclick = function() {
      loader.runf('btn1b_click', this);
    }
  }
</script>
```

This is where you can use the second approach—the `stub` function. Instead of changing the HTML of your controls, you can load a `stub` function upfront before the page renders (file `OnDemandLoading.aspx`):

```
function btn1b_click() {
  loader.runf('btn1b_click', this);
}
```

When the visitor clicks the button, the `stub` function is executed. It then calls `loader.runf` to load and execute its namesake that does the actual work, overwriting the `stub` function in the process.

This leaves behind one problem. The on-demand loader checks whether a function with the given name is already defined before initiating a script load. And a function with that same name already exists — the stub function itself.

The solution is based on the fact that functions in JavaScript are objects. And all JavaScript objects can have properties. You can tell the on-demand loader that a function is a stub by attaching the property "stub":

```
btn1b_click.stub = true;
```

To see all this functionality in action, run the OnDemandLoading.aspx page in folder OnDemandLoad in the downloaded code bundle. Click on one of the buttons on the page, and you'll see how the required code is loaded on demand. It's best to do this in Firefox with Firebug installed, so that you can see the script files getting loaded in a Waterfall chart. Creating Waterfall charts was described in *Chapter 1, High Level Diagnosis*.

Preloading

Now that you have on-demand loading working, there is one more issue to consider: trading off bandwidth against visitor wait time.

Currently, when a visitor clicks a button and the code required to process the click hadn't been loaded, loading starts in response to the click. This can be a problem if loading the code takes too much time.

An alternative is to initiate loading the user interface code after the page has been loaded, instead of when a user interface event happens. That way, the code may have already loaded by the time the visitor clicks the button; or at least it will already be partly loaded, so that the code finishes loading sooner. On the other hand, this means expending bandwidth on loading code that may never be used by the visitor.

You can implement preloading with the loadScript function exposed by the OnDemandLoader object. As you saw earlier, this function loads a JavaScript file plus any files it depends on, without blocking rendering. Simply add calls to loadScript in the onload handler of the page, as shown (page PreLoad.aspx in folder OnDemandLoad in the downloaded code bundle):

```
<script type="text/javascript">
  window.onload = function() {
    document.getElementById('btn1b').onclick = btn1b_click;

    loader.loadScript('js/Button1Code.js');
    loader.loadScript('js/Button2Code.js');
  }
</script>
```

You could preload all your user interface code, or just the code you think is likely to be needed.

Now that you've looked at the load on demand approach, it's time to consider the last approach—loading your code without blocking page rendering and without getting into `stub` functions or other complications inherent in on-demand loading.

Approach 4: Loading Javascript without blocking

The idea behind this approach is to load all (or almost all) script files without blocking rendering of the page. That puts the rendered page sooner in front of the visitor.

There are a couple of ways to achieve this, each trading off more work for a better visitor experience:

- Moving all `<script>` tags to the end of the page
- Separating user interface code and render code
- Introducing page loading indicator
- Loading code in parallel with the page

Let's go through each of them.

Moving all <script> tags to the end of the page

On a basic level, loading JavaScript code without blocking page rendering is really easy to accomplish—simply take your `script` tags out of the head of the page, and move them to the end of the body. That way, the page will have rendered before the `script` tags have a chance to block anything.

Page `ScriptAtEnd.aspx` in folder `LoadJavaScriptWithoutBlocking` in the downloaded code bundle has an example for this. Similar to the test site you used in the previous section, to simulate a slowly loading JavaScript file, this site delays JavaScript files by five seconds; just make sure you run it in IIS 7.

The example page has both render code and user interface code
(`ScriptAtEnd.aspx`):

```
<script type="text/javascript" src="js/Code.js"></script>
<script type="text/javascript">
  // Execute render code
  beautify();
  // Attach event handlers for user interface
  attachEventHandlers();
</script>
```

In this example, the render code simply makes the background of the page yellow,
and turns the caption of the middle button yellow as well. That may be very
simplistic, but that makes it perfectly clear whether the render code is executed.

When you load `ScriptAtEnd.aspx`, you'll see the "raw" version of the page until the
code finishes loading and changes the page's appearance. That's not necessarily what
you want.

This brings us to the next iteration.

Separating user interface code and render code

The code (if there is any) required to render the page tends to be much smaller than
that required to handle user interface events. So, to prevent showing the raw page to
visitors, it can make sense to separate out the render code, and load that upfront. It
will block rendering of the page while it is loading, but in this case, this is precisely
what we want.

Use the **Page Speed** add-on for Firefox to figure out which JavaScript functions are
not needed to render the page.

After you've separated the code, you'll wind up with something similar to the
following (page `SeparateScripts.aspx`):

```
<head runat="server">
  <script type="text/javascript" src="js/Beautify.js"></script>
</head>
<body>
  ... page contents
  <script type="text/javascript">
    beautify(); // run code that helps render the page
  </script>
  <script type="text/javascript" src="js/UICode.js"></script>
```

```
<script type="text/javascript">
  attachEventHandlers();
</script>
</body>
```

The render code is now loaded in the head of the page, so that it blocks rendering the rest of the page. It is executed at the end of the page by calling function `beautify`; otherwise, there is no page content to work with. Only then the user interface code is loaded, so that it doesn't block the call to `beautify`.

If you run `SeparateScripts.aspx`, you should no longer see the raw version of the page. However, if you click any of the buttons while the user interface code is being loaded, nothing happens. This may cause your visitors to think that your site is broken, and move on to some other site, such as your competitor's.

If you look closely, you'll see that the browser shows that the page is busy while the user interface code is loading. However, you can't rely on your visitors to see this. So, let's add a better "page loading" indicator.

Introducing page loading indicator

Introducing a page loading indicator consists of creating the indicator itself, and introducing code to make it go away once all the code has completed loading.

The page loading indicator itself can be any `<div>` tag with a "Loading ..." text. The code below fixes the indicator just below the browser window, so that it stays there even if the visitor scrolls the page (`PageLoadingIndicator.aspx`):

```
<div id="pageloading" style="position:fixed; top: 10px;
  left: 50%;" >Loading ...</div>
```

After all the code is loaded and you've attached the event handlers, make the loading indicator disappear by setting its display style to `none`:

```
<script type="text/javascript">
  attachEventHandlers();
  document.getElementById('pageloading').style.display = 'none';
</script>
```

Alternatively, or in addition, you could disable all input elements after the page is rendered. This dims the captions of all buttons and prevents them from being "depressed" when clicked (PageLoadingIndicator.aspx):

```
<script type="text/javascript">
  beautify();

  function disableButtons(disable) {
    var inputTags = document.getElementsByTagName('input');
    var inputTagsLen = inputTags.length;
    for (var i = 0; i < inputTagsLen; i++) {
      inputTags[i].disabled = disable;
    }
  }
  disableButtons(true); // Disable all input elements
</script>
```

Then after the code is loaded, re-enable them again (PageLoadingIndicator.aspx):

```
<script type="text/javascript">
  attachEventHandlers();
  document.getElementById('pageloading').style.display = 'none';

  disableButtons(false); // Re-enable all input elements
</script>
```

If you run JavaScript code that changes the color of button captions while they are disabled, Firefox, Google Chrome, and Safari will apply the color right away, thereby removing the "disabled" look. Internet Explorer, however, changes only the caption color after the buttons have been re-enabled.

Loading code in parallel with page

In the solutions you've seen so far, loading of the user interface code is initiated after the page has loaded and rendered.

However, if the HTML of your page takes a long time to load, you will want to start loading at the beginning of the page, so that the code loads in parallel with the HTML.

You can achieve this with the OnDemandLoader object that you saw in the previous section. You can get it to load one or more sets of script files while the page itself is loading, and to call a function when each set is done. Finally, it exposes an onallscriptsloaded event that fires when all script files have loaded, which can be used to remove the page loading indicator.

This solution is in page `ParallelLoading.aspx`, folder `LoadJavaScriptWithoutBlocking` in the downloaded code bundle. It breaks into the following parts:

- Initialize the loader object
- Start loading the code
- Ensure that the code runs after the page is rendered

Let's go through each part.

Initializing the loader object

The first step is prepare two pieces of information: the script map array, showing for each function the script file in which it is defined. And the script dependencies array, showing for each script file which other script files it depends on.

Here, the script map contains the two functions you've already seen: `attachEventHandlers` to attach the event handlers after the user interface code has loaded, and `beautify` to execute the render code:

```
var scriptMap = [
    { fname: 'attachEventHandlers', src: 'js/UICode.js' },
    { fname: 'beautify', src: 'js/Beautify.js' }
];
```

Also, list both script files in the array with dependencies:

```
var scriptDependencies = [
  {
    src: 'js/UICode.js',
    testSymbol: 'attachEventHandlers',
    dependentOn: []
  },
  {
    src: 'js/Beautify.js',
    testSymbol: 'beautify',
    dependentOn: []
  }
];
```

If you need to load additional script files, list them in the `dependentOn` array, along the following lines:

```
{
  src: 'js/UICode.js',
  testSymbol: 'attachEventHandlers',
  dependentOn: ['js/UILibrary1.js', 'js/UILibrary2.js',
    'js/UILibrary3.js']
}
```

Finally, create the loader object:

```
<script type="text/javascript" src="js/OnDemandLoader.js">
</script>
var loader = new OnDemandLoader(scriptMap, scriptDependencies);
```

With the loader object established, it is now time to start loading the JavaScript code.

Loading the code while the page is loading

You want the code to load while the page is loading, which means that the JavaScript that initiates the loading needs to sit towards the top of the page. Here is what it looks like (`ParallelLoading.aspx`):

```
<body>
  <div id="pageloading" ...>Loading ...</div>
  <script type="text/javascript">
    loader.onallscriptsloaded = function() {
      document.getElementById('pageloading').style.display =
        'none';
      disableButtons(false);
    }

    loader.runf('beautify', null);
    loader.runf('attachEventHandlers', null);
  </script>
```

If the `onallscriptsloaded` property on the `OnDemandLoader` object is set to a function, the object runs that function when it finds that all script files in the dependencies list have been loaded. That feature is used here to hide the "Loading" box and re-enable the buttons after all the script files have been loaded.

You came across `loader.runf` in the *Approach 3: Load on demand* section. It tells the loader to make sure that all code required to run the `beautify` and `attachEventHandlers` functions has been loaded, and to call those functions once the code has been loaded.

Ensuring that code runs after the page is rendered

There is one last problem to solve: the script files may finish loading before the page itself finishes rendering. This can happen when the script files are in browser cache, left there by another page. The problem is that if the code runs before the page is rendered, it may fail to properly update the appearance of the page, or to attach event handlers to all user interface elements because the page isn't fully there yet.

The way to solve this is to call the `beautify` and `attachEventHandlers` functions not only after they have been loaded, but also after the page has finished rendering. That way, you're sure that these functions will be executed properly, even if the script files were quick to load. You do need a `try-catch` when you call the functions after the page has finished rendering, in case their code hasn't been loaded yet:

```
try { attachEventHandlers(); } catch (err) { }
try { beautify(); } catch (err) { }
```

This means that these functions are called twice — once when the code finishes loading, and once after the page has finished rendering. You don't know in which order this happens. It also means that you need to make sure that the functions do not cause an error message if they run while the page isn't rendered yet.

How do we find out when the page is completely rendered? Here are the usual options:

- Create a handler for the page's `onload` event. This is the most natural solution, but here it has a big problem. When the `OnDemandLoader` object starts loading a script file, it does so by inserting a `<script>` tag into the DOM, as shown in the following code:

  ```
  var se = document.createElement('script');
  se.src = src;
  document.getElementsByTagName('head')[0].appendChild(se);
  ```

  This method loads a script file without blocking rendering of the page, except that in Firefox, it blocks the onload event. This means that if the render code loads quickly and the user interface code takes a long time, execution of the render code will still be delayed until the user interface code finishes loading, which is not good.

- Place a `<script>` tag at the end of the page containing calls to `attachEventHandlers` and `beautify`. Unfortunately, Firefox not only blocks `onload`, but also all `script` tags until all the code is loaded.

- Place an invisible element at the very end of the page, and periodically check whether that element is rendered. If it is, the whole page will have rendered. This slightly pollutes the HTML and couples the invisible element and the polling code because they have to refer to the same ID.

You could make the first two options work by loading the JavaScript code asynchronously using XMLHttpRequest instead of inserting a <script> tag in the DOM. However, that would stop you from loading script files from any host but the one used by your site. For example, you then couldn't load the jQuery library from the Google CDN.

So in this example, we'll use the third method, based on polling for the end of page rendering.

To implement the polling solution, first place an invisible element at the very end of the page:

```
<div id="lastelement" style="display: none;"></div>
</body>
```

Then run the polling code at the beginning of the page, in the same script block where you started loading the JavaScript code:

```
function pollpage() {
  var lastelement = document.getElementById('lastelement');
  if (lastelement == null) {
    setTimeout("pollpage();", 100);
    return;
  }

  try { attachEventHandlers(); } catch (err) { }
  try { beautify(); } catch (err) { }

  if (document.getElementById('pageloading').
    style.display != 'none') {
    disableButtons(true);
  }
}
pollpage();
```

The function pollpage first checks whether the element with ID lastelement exists. If not, the page hasn't finished rendering yet, and so it calls setTimeout to have itself called again 100 milliseconds from now.

Otherwise, the page has rendered, and the function calls attachEventHandlers and beautify. Now that all the buttons will have rendered, this is also a good time to disable all the buttons. However, if the JavaScript code has already loaded, you obviously don't want to do that. So it checks whether the "Loading" box has already been made invisible by the OnDemandLoader object.

Finally, the code calls the pollpage function to start polling.

All this is expressed in the following flowchart:

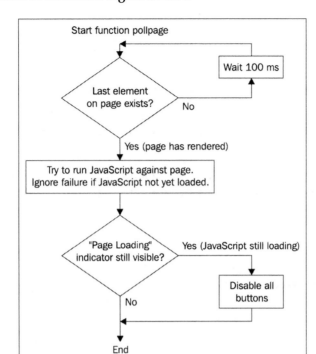

That concludes the four approaches to improving JavaScript loading. We'll now look at two related topics: improving ad loading and improving loading of CSS files.

Improving ad loading

If you use an ad network such as DoubleClick or Google AdWords, they will have given you code to place on your pages along the following lines:

```
<script src="http://adserver.js?....."></script>
```

This loads some JavaScript from the ad server, which then places the actual ad on your site. Easy.

Normally, this works fine. However, the ad server is slow at times. The problem is that while the browser is waiting for the ad server, it holds off rendering the page below the ad. If there is a long delay, this will not look good.

You could prevent this by loading the ads in iframes. However, this will prevent your ad slots from showing variable-sized ads. It also creates a big empty space on your page if the ad fails to load.

A neat way to solve this problem is to load the ads after the entire page is rendered, and then move the ads to their ad slots.

In this approach, you place an empty `<div>` tag at the spot where you want an ad to appear. You can give it the size of the eventual ad (if it has fixed size and you don't mind the empty space on your page) and a progress image to make it look nice (page AdDoesNotDelayPage.aspx, folder AdLoad in the downloaded code bundle):

```
<div id="ad" style="width: 486px; height: 60px; background:
  #ffffff url('/images/throbber.gif') no-repeat center;">
</div>
```

Then at the end of the page, you place the ad loading script within its own `<div>` tag. Make that tag invisible (`display` value is `none`) so that your visitors don't see it while the ad is loading:

```
<script type="text/javascript">
  var scriptloaded = false;
  var divloaded = false;
  function adloaded() {

    . . .
  }
</script>

<div id="tempad" style="display:none">
  <script type="text/javascript" src="http://adserver.js?....."
    onload="scriptloaded=true; adloaded()"
    onreadystatechange="if (this.readyState=='complete') {
      scriptloaded=true; adloaded(); }">
  </script>
</div>
<script type="text/javascript">
  divloaded = true;
  adloaded();
</script>
```

The function `adloaded()` will move the `<div>` to the actual ad slot. But before that can be done, not only the script, but also the `<div>` needs to have loaded. Otherwise, there will be a JavaScript error when `adloaded` tries to move it.

Finding out whether the script is loaded means adding an `onreadystatechange` handler, used by Internet Explorer, and an onload handler, used by all other browsers. Finding out whether the `<div>` is loaded, means simply add a JavaScript block after the `<div>`. If both the variables `scriptloaded` and `divloaded` are `true`, the `<div>` is ready to be moved.

Finally, implement the `adloaded` function:

```
function adloaded() {
    if ((!scriptloaded) || (!divloaded)) { return; }

    var et = document.getElementById("tempad");
    et.parentNode.removeChild(et);
    var d = document.getElementById("ad");
    d.appendChild(et);
    et.style.display = "block";
}
```

This finds the `<div>` holding the script (with the ID `tempad`) and detaches it from its parent, so that it won't show up at the bottom of the page. It then finds the `<div>` marking the ad slot where you want to actually show the ad (with the ID `ad`). Finally, it appends the `<div>` with your ad as a child to the empty ad slot and changes its display property to `block` to make it visible. Done!

Improving CSS Loading

Just as JavaScript files, CSS files also block rendering of the page. This way, the visitor isn't confronted by the page in its unstyled form.

You can see this behavior by running the website in folder `CssBlocksRendering` in the downloaded code bundle. This test has a single page that loads a single CSS file. Generation of the CSS file on the server is delayed by five seconds, using the HTTP Module `DelayModule` in its `App_Code` folder. When you open the page, you'll find that the window stays blank for five seconds.

CSS files also block the execution of JavaScript files. This is because the JavaScript may refer to definitions in the CSS files.

One way to reduce this issue is to load your CSS files as quickly as possible. You can achieve that in the following ways:

- Using techniques used with images such as caching, parallel downloads, and using a CDN. Refer to *Chapter 12, Reducing Image Load Times*.
- Using GZIP compression—refer to *Chapter 10, Compression*.
- Combining or breaking up CSS files.
- Minifying the CSS.
- Removing unused CSS lines.

A sixth option is to load your CSS without blocking rendering.

The first three options were discussed in the *Approach 2: Loading JavaScript more quickly* section.

Let's look at the last three options in more detail.

Minifying CSS

Minifying CSS is very similar to minifying JavaScript. It involves removing unnecessary white space and comments. It also includes replacing long property values by equivalent shorter ones. For example, the color #ff0000 can be replaced by the shorter red.

The impact of minification on CSS files tends to be fairly modest if compression is enabled on the server (as discussed in chapter 10). Here are the results for a typical 4-KB CSS file (style1.css in folder Minify in the downloaded code bundle):

		Minified		Reduction through minification
		No	Yes	
GZIP	No	4.0 KB	2.6 KB	35 percent
Compressed	Yes	1.3 KB	1.2 KB	8 percent

There are many tools that will minify a CSS file for you, including the following:

- Microsoft Ajax Minifier

  http://www.asp.net/ajaxlibrary/AjaxMinDocumentation.ashx

  This tool minifies JavaScript and CSS files.

- YUI Compressor

  http://developer.yahoo.com/yui/compressor/

  It is a standalone Java-based JavaScript and CSS minifier.

- Yahoo! UI Library: YUI Compressor for .NET

  http://yuicompressor.codeplex.com/

  In addition to minifying JavaScript, this .NET port of the YUI Compressor Java project also allows you to minify CSS, like so:

  ```
  using Yahoo.Yui.Compressor;
  ...
  string compressedCSS =
  CssCompressor.Compress (uncompressedCSS);
  ```

You can use this to create an HTTP Handler for CSS files, in the same way as you saw earlier for JavaScript files. See folder `Minify` in the downloaded code bundle for an example.

- CSSTidy

  `http://csstidy.sourceforge.net/`

  This tool is an open source CSS parser and optimizer. Its source code available in PHP and C++.

Removing unused CSS selectors

Because CSS styles are separate from the pages where they are used, when bits of HTML are removed, the styles used with that HTML often remain in the CSS. After a while, you may wind up with a lot of unused styles, causing confusion and file bloat.

A good tool that helps you identify unused CSS selectors is the Firefox add-on Dust-Me Selectors. Download it at `https://addons.mozilla.org/en-US/firefox/addon/5392/`.

After you've installed the add-on, open your site in Firefox. Then, click on **Tools | Dust-Me Selectors | Find unused selectors**, or press *Ctrl + Alt + F*. This reads all CSS files used by the page and finds the unused selectors. You could also right-click on the pink broom at the bottom of the Firefox window.

Now, click on **Tools | Dust-Me Selectors | View saved data** to see the used and unused selectors for each CSS file. There, you also find a button to export the used and unused selectors to CSV files.

CSS files are often shared among multiple pages, and so they may have selectors that are only used on some but not all pages. To make sure you catch all used selectors, navigate through the pages on your site. Dust-Me Selectors will go through each page, and move all the used selectors to the used list. That will greatly weed down your unused list. After you've visited all your pages, consider each selector in the unused list for removal from your CSS files.

If your site has lots of pages, visiting each page would take too much time. However, Dust-Me Selectors can read a site map – click **Tools | Dust-Me Selectors | Automation | Spider Sitemap**. Site maps tell Google and other search engines where to find your pages, so they are good for SEO. Visit `http://www.sitemaps.org` for more information.

Loading CSS without blocking rendering

Getting the browser to load your CSS without blocking rendering is not hard. Consider the following line of code:

```
<link rel="Stylesheet" type="text/css" href="css/style1.css" />
```

Replace it with JavaScript that creates the link element and inserts it into the DOM (folder LoadCssWithoutBlocking in downloaded code bundle):

```
<script type="text/javascript">
 var scriptElem = document.createElement('link');
 scriptElem.type = "text/css";
 scriptElem.rel = "Stylesheet";
 scriptElem.href = "css/style1.css";
 document.getElementsByTagName('head')[0].appendChild(scriptElem);
</script>
```

When you run this page, you'll see that the page becomes visible to the visitor before the CSS is loaded, and then changes appearance when the CSS finishes loading. This may not be the sort of behavior you want, even if it means a page that renders sooner.

Find out more

Here are some more online resources:

- What ASP.NET Developers Should Know About JavaScript

  http://odetocode.com/Articles/473.aspx

- Function.apply and Function.call in JavaScript

  http://odetocode.com/Blogs/scott/archive/2007/07/05/function-apply-and-function-call-in-javascript.aspx

- JavaScript and HTML DOM Reference

  http://www.w3schools.com/jsref/default.asp

- Ecmascript reference

  http://www.devguru.com/Technologies/ecmascript/quickref/javascript_index.html

- JavaScript Kit - JavaScript Tutorials

  http://www.javascriptkit.com/javatutors/

- Object Oriented Programming in JavaScript

  http://mckoss.com/jscript/object.htm

- QuirksMode - JavaScript

  `http://www.quirksmode.org/js/contents.html`

- HowToCreate - JavaScript Tutorial

  `http://www.howtocreate.co.uk/tutorials/javascript/`

- Microsoft CDN for JQuery or Google CDN?

  `http://stackoverflow.com/questions/1447184/microsoft-cdn-for-jquery-or-google-cdn`

- Speeding up website load times: Using a public CDN for Javascript libraries such as jQuery

  `http://gem-session.com/2010/06/speeding-up-website-load-times-using-a-public-cdn-for-javascript-libraries-such-as-jquery`

- CompressorRater

  `http://compressorrater.thruhere.net/`

- On-Demand Javascript

  `http://ajaxpatterns.org/On-Demand_Javascript`

Summary

In this chapter, we first saw how page rendering is blocked by JavaScript `<script>` tags. This was followed by ways to load other components such as CSS stylesheets and images in parallel with the JavaScript to reduce the overall time taken to load the page fully.

We then saw how to load JavaScript files more quickly, including minification, free CDNs, removing unused code, and combining or breaking up JavaScript files.

This was followed by discussions on loading JavaScript code on demand, and techniques specifically aimed at loading JavaScript without blocking page rendering.

Finally, we saw how to load ads from ad networks without allowing them to slow down rendering of your page, and improving the way your page loads CSS stylesheets, including minification and removing unused selectors.

In the next chapter, we'll see how to load test your site.

14
Load Testing

Once you have diagnosed performance issues in your website and made changes to resolve them, you will need to make sure that the improvements you made really improve performance. If those changes were on the web server or the database server, you will need to load test your changes, for which you need a load testing environment.

Additionally, it is a good practice to load test your website as part of acceptance testing of a new release, just to make sure it can still handle the expected loads. And if your marketing department is planning a campaign that will increase the load on your site, you'll want to make sure it can handle the expected load. This is not purely a performance issue; some bugs become apparent only under load, such as bugs triggered by low memory conditions.

A load testing environment simply consists of one or more machines hosting the site under test, plus one or more machines that generate a load by simulating visits by many virtual clients.

In this chapter, we'll see the following:

- How best to do load testing
- Options for hosting your development site so that you can load test it
- How to generate load

Let's begin by looking at how best to approach load testing.

Using a load test environment

Load testing is most often done right at the end of the development cycle as part of acceptance testing. The idea is to subject the new website with the same load it can expect in production. While this is better than nothing, it is not the most efficient way of ensuring that your website will perform well:

- Leaving load testing to the end makes it more likely that the test will unearth problems, making it less likely that you'll meet your release deadline
- It is hard to find the cause of any problems, because you're effectively testing all components of the site in one go

This section shows a more efficient way of ensuring that your website will perform well.

Load testing individual components during development

Just as you do component testing during development to make sure each component is bug-free, it makes sense to load test individual components. For example, you would load test your data access layer, using test stubs for the other layers.

Focusing on one layer at a time makes it easier to find the cause of any problems. And it catches problems in an earlier stage—the same reason why you do component testing in general. The more often you test, the fewer the surprises you face at the end.

Testing page-by-page

To make it easier to find the cause of any problems, it makes sense to do load testing page-by-page. First, load test the hardware and operating system by using trivial "Hello World" pages that use no resources. When that works well, add the home page and test again. If you're happy, add another page, and then continue doing so.

This way, if a test fails, you know right away where to look for the cause of the problem.

Testing performance improvements

Web servers, database servers, and browsers—they are all amazingly complicated pieces of software. No matter what performance improvements you make, be sure to load test them thoroughly before taking them into production.

Acceptance testing

Because your finding problems during acceptance testing is better than users finding them after your new site has gone live, it is a good idea to include load testing as part of your acceptance tests. For this final test, you will want to get as close to the real production environment as you can get:

- Try to get your test site on servers that are similar or the same as the production servers.

- Establish key scenarios of client interaction — visit a product page, place an order, and so on. You may also talk to marketing, look at server logs, Google Analytics, and so on.

- For each scenario, establish traffic patterns such as number of visits per minute, think times, variability during the day (for example, the proportion of order placing to browsing may be higher during the evening), and so on.

- Take burstiness into account — can your site handle a sudden surge of visits?

- Set performance goals for each scenario, such as latency at the browser and throughput.

- If the test site is on an in-house server, generate the load from outside the firewall to include as much hardware and software in the test as possible.

Additional best practices

Finally, for best results of your load tests, follow these best practices:

- Do a cost/benefit analysis. Conducting additional load tests and making your tests mimic the expected load more closely should result in better reliability and performance of your site. However, it also requires an additional investment of time and money. While dreaming up additional load tests, make sure the likely benefits outweigh the costs.

- Use dedicated machines for your load testing. If a web server runs out of memory, you want to know if it is because of the website under load, and not because of the demands of some unrelated application. Likewise, use a dedicated network that doesn't carry unrelated traffic.

- Make sure the load generating machines aren't hitting bottlenecks, whether CPU, disc, memory, or network-related. If they do, add more load generating machines, so that any bottlenecks you hit will be in the web server or database server under load, and not in the load generators.

- Make sure that the operating system and your website work as expected before load testing; there is no point in load testing buggy software.

- Use sufficient warm-up periods, in which load is applied, but no measurements are taken. The warm-up period should be long enough for the servers to populate all caches. You want to get to a stage where there is no real cache-related increase in throughput during the actual test phase. If the load generating software supports it, use a cool-down period as well, where measurement taking is ended some time before the load is taken away. When the load is taken away, the web server is able to process the last requests more quickly—you don't want to pollute your stats with this.

- Ensure that the load tests run long enough. That allows you to see whether performance changes over time.

- Make sure that there are no unexpected errors during the load test.

- Do each load test a number of times in a row. The number of requests per second for each test should be within a few percent of each other. If they are not, use a longer warm-up period and/or a longer test run.

Building a load test environment

As you've seen, a load test environment simply consists of one or more servers hosting the website being tested, and one or more load generating servers. You could use the same servers for both load generation and site hosting to save on hardware, but that would make it more difficult to determine whether any bottleneck on the machine is caused by the site or by the load generator.

If you have a spare server lying around with the same specs as your production servers, that would be great. You'd use that server for the site, and your development machine(s) to generate load.

However, I'll assume that you just have your development machine, and maybe one or more additional machines such as laptops, all running Vista or Windows 7.

In the following sections, some options are listed for hosting your test site. After that, we'll go through some load generation options.

Hosting the website under load

Generally, you have these options when it comes to hosting the test site:

- Use a second hosting account. If your production site is hosted externally by a hosting company, than you could pay for a second hosting account, or for the use of additional servers with the same specs as the production servers. That way, there is no restriction on testing and you would have a testing environment that approximates your production environment.

- Use spare servers. Likewise, if you host the production site on your own servers and you have spare servers with the same specs, then you could use the spare servers. If you use an external load-generating service, make sure that the extra traffic doesn't overload your Internet connection.

- Use the production server. This would be the most realistic test and it wouldn't require additional hardware. On the other hand, you would have to restrict testing to quiet periods, such as the middle of the night, to minimize the impact on your visitors. The production site will also be taking resources away from the test site, thereby skewing your test results. If your site has a global audience, there may be no quiet periods at all.

  If you're going down this route, be sure to switch off any nightly batch processing. You'll also want to keep your test code and data separate from the production code and data, for example using a separate subdomain for the test site.

- Use a development machine running Vista/Win 7. This is easy. However, IIS on Vista or Windows 7 has a built-in limit on the number of clients processed concurrently.

- Use a development machine running Windows Server 2008. This also gets rid of the limit on the number of concurrently-processed clients. You can get a free trial version of Windows Server 2008 that you can use for 240 days. After that, simply buy Windows Server 2008 Web Edition. It doesn't cost much, and unlike Windows Server 2003 Web Edition, you can use it to run SQL Server (except for SQL Server Enterprise).

- Use a development machine running Windows Server 2003. This gets rid of the limit on the number of concurrently-processed clients. This option makes sense if you use Windows Server 2003 on your production servers. Maybe you have a spare legal copy to install on a development machine, or you could buy a legal copy on places such as eBay.

The first three options do not present much of a technical challenge, so I won't discuss them further.

We'll now examine the last three options more closely, and see how to implement them. After that, we'll see how to create a simple site to test our new hosting environment.

Installing IIS on Vista or Windows 7

Version 7 of IIS (Internet Information Server), Microsoft's web server software, is built-in in both Vista and Windows 7. This opens the door to using a development computer as a test server, rather than having to use a real server.

Limitations

However, IIS is not enabled on the Starter and Home editions of Vista and Windows 7, and in the other edition, it has been crippled to stop it from being used in a production environment. Refer to the following chart:

Windows Edition	Available Features	Simultaneous request execution limit
Starter	IIS Disabled	N/A
Home	IIS Disabled	N/A
Home Premium	Some features disabled, including FTP server, advanced Web authentication and authorization, and remote administration	3
Business, Enterprise, Ultimate	All, except remote administration	10

What about simultaneous request execution limit? As the name indicates, this limits the number of requests that IIS can process simultaneously. When an additional request comes in, it is simply queued and processed when it gets to the front of the queue. It isn't rejected, as was the case with IIS on Windows XP.

Is this a serious limit? If it takes 100 ms to process a request, you'll be able to process 10 requests per 100 ms, equaling 100 requests per second on a Vista Ultimate machine. This solution may work for you if your site is fast, or you receive not too much traffic.

Installation

Installing IIS on Vista or Windows 7 is easy:

1. Click on **Start**, and then click on **Control Panel**.
2. Click on **Programs**, and then click on **Turn windows features on or off**.
3. Check **Internet Information Services**.
4. Expand the **Internet Information Services** node, then the **World Wide Web Services** node, and then the **Application Development Features** node.
5. Make sure that **ASP.NET** is checked.
6. Also, make sure that **Web Management Tools** is checked.
7. Click on **OK**.

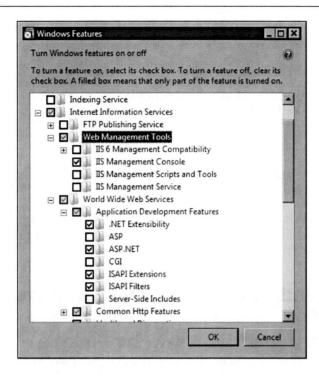

Opening the Firewall

If you will have the load generator on a different machine (highly recommended), then you will need to open port 80 on the firewall, so that it passes through the traffic from the load generator:

1. Click on **Start | Control Panel**. In the search box, enter "firewall". Click on **Allow a program through Windows Firewall**.

2. On the **Exceptions** tab, select **World Wide Web Services (HTTP)**.

3. Click on **OK**.

Installing Windows Server 2008

If you have a copy of Windows Server 2008 that you can legally install on your machine, then you could put it on your Vista or Windows 7 based machine and run both operating systems side-by-side. This allows you to use Windows Server 2008 to host a test website, and use Vista or Windows 7 for everything else you use the machine for.

If you do not have a legal copy of Windows Server 2008, get an evaluation copy of the Enterprise edition at:

- Windows Server 2008 Enterprise

  ```
  http://www.microsoft.com/downloads/details.
  aspx?FamilyId=13C7300E-935C-415A-A79C-
  538E933D5424&displaylang=en
  ```

You can use this for 240 days.

Alternatively, buy Windows Server 2008 Web Edition. This is quite cheap, and would be powerful enough to host the test site.

If you want to run Windows Server 2008 in Virtual PC 2007 as suggested below, be sure to download the 32-bit version. The 64-bit version doesn't run in Virtual PC 2007.

Running Windows Server 2008 alongside Vista or Windows 7

You should be able to install Windows Server 2008 next to Vista or Windows 7 in a dual-boot configuration. However, this requires that you have Windows Server 2008 drivers for your computer, which is not necessarily the case.

The alternative is to create a virtual machine using the free Virtual PC 2007 program, and then install Windows Server 2008 in that virtual machine. This will work only though with the 32-bit version of Windows Server 2008.

Installing Virtual PC 2007

Installing the virtual machine is not difficult:

1. Download and install Virtual PC 2007 from:
   - Virtual PC 2007

     ```
     http://www.microsoft.com/downloads/details.
     aspx?FamilyId=04D26402-3199-48A3-AFA2-
     2DC0B40A73B6&displaylang=en
     ```
2. Start Virtual PC 2007.
3. On the Virtual PC console, click on the **New** button to start the **New Virtual Machine Wizard**.
4. Dismiss the welcome page. On the next page, choose to create a virtual machine.

5. On the next page, choose a meaningful name such as "Windows Server 2008". If you are short on space on the c: drive, click on **Browse** to install your virtual machine on another drive.

6. On the next page, you'll find that Windows Server 2008 is not in the list of operating systems. Simply select Windows Server 2003 instead.

7. On the next page, adjust the RAM to at least 1000 MB. Note that while the virtual machine is running, this RAM is not available to other applications on your physical machine.

8. On the next page, ask for a new virtual hard disc.

9. The next page will want to know where to put the virtual hard disc. Unless you are running out of space on the c: drive, accept the default.

10. Click on **Finish** to end the wizard. You now are the proud owner of a new virtual machine!

Installing Windows Server 2008

Now that you've got your virtual machine, it's time to install Windows Server 2008:

1. Run the Virtual PC program. On the Virtual PC console, click on the **Start** button to start the virtual machine. A new window opens for the virtual machine. It will take a while to boot. After it's done, it will ask for an installation disc.

2. You now need to insert the first Windows Server 2008 installation DVD into the virtual DVD drive of the virtual machine.

    ○   If you have a physical DVD, put it in your physical DVD drive. Then open the **CD** menu on the virtual machine window and choose **Use Physical Drive X:**, where **X:** is replaced by your DVD drive. Hit the *Enter* key to get the virtual machine to start reading.

    ○   If you have an .iso image file, open the **CD** menu on the virtual machine window and choose **Capture ISO Image**. Hit the *Enter* key to get the virtual machine to start reading.

You will now go through the standard process of installing Windows Server 2008. Remember that it all takes place on your virtual machine; your physical machine is not affected.

If you are installing the evaluation version and it asks for a product key you don't have, simply choose to not enter the product key. It will then continue installing. When it asks what version you are installing, go for a full installation version, rather than the Server Core version.

After the installation has finished, you will see the **Initial Configuration Tasks** window. Click on **Provide computer name and domain** and click on the **Change** button to enter a meaningful computer name.

 Important
Do record the administrator password and computer name you entered during the installation. You will need those later.

Getting more out of Virtual PC

While you are waiting for the virtual machine to install Windows Server 2008, now would be a good time to spend a bit more time with Virtual PC.

Keystrokes

Have a look at a few special key strokes for Virtual PC 2007:

Keystroke	Effect
AltGr	Allows you to move the mouse pointer out of the virtual machine.
AltGr + Del	Sends the *Ctrl + Alt + Del* keystroke to the virtual machine. Use this when logging into Windows Server.
AltGr + Enter	Makes the virtual machine full screen. Press *AltGr + Enter* again to go back to a normal window.

The *AltGr* key is the *Alt* key to the right of the space bar on your keyboard.

Screen size

Once Windows Server has switched to a graphical interface, you'll probably find that the screen provided by the virtual machine is very small. Right-click on the virtual desktop and choose **Personalize | Display Settings** to get a bigger screen.

Installing Virtual Machine Additions

Virtual Machine Additions is a package that adds good things to your virtual machine, such as clipboard sharing and better performance.

To install Virtual Machine Additions:

1. Make sure you are logged in to Windows Server as an administrator.
2. Open the **Action** menu on the virtual machine, and choose **Install or Update Virtual Machine Additions**. A wizard will start that installs the Virtual Machine Additions. When it finishes, it restarts the virtual machine—not your physical machine!

Creating a shared folder

When you publish your site on the physical machine, it is easier if you don't then have to move it across to the virtual machine. To solve this, create a folder that is shared between your physical machine and your virtual machine.

Using a network drive or UNC as the home directory of a website is a bit complicated, because IIS needs proper access to the network drive. It's easier to put the actual directory on the virtual machine and share it, so that it is visible on the physical machine.

To make this happen:

1. On the virtual machine, find or create a directory where you want to put the files making up the website. IIS already points at `C:\Inetpub\wwwroot` and it only contains a simple test site that you don't really need, so that folder would be a logical choice.

2. Right-click on the `wwwroot` folder and choose **Share**.

3. Click on the **Share** button.

4. The **File Sharing** window opens. However, it probably obscures a second window, **Network discovery** and **File sharing**. Move the **File Sharing** window to see if that is the case.

5. If there is a **Network discovery** and **File sharing** window, choose to turn on sharing for private networks.

6. When the File Sharing window finishes, it will show how to reach the directory from the physical machine. It will be of the form `\\MACHINE\folder`. Click on **Done**.

Right now, when you want to access the shared folder from the physical machine, you have to provide a username and password. To switch this off:

1. On the virtual machine, click on **Start** | **Control Panel** | **Network and Sharing Centre**.

2. Turn off password-protected sharing.

Now, make sure that the shared folder is visible and writable on your physical machine:

1. Use Windows Explorer on the physical machine to open the shared folder.

2. Make sure the shared folder is writable, by creating a new file in it. Right-click on the folder, choose **New**, and then choose a file type. If all is well, a new file will appear in the folder.

Installing .NET 4 or .NET 3.5 Service Pack 1

If your site uses .NET 3.5 or later, install the version of the framework used by your site on the virtual machine.

1. At the time of writing, .NET 4 was the latest .NET version. Seeing that .NET 4 is included with Visual Studio 2010, its installation file is probably already on your computer. Look for `dotNetFx40_Full_x86_x64.exe`. If you can't find it, download it from:

   Microsoft .NET Framework 4 (Web Installer)

   ```
   http://www.microsoft.com/downloads/details.
   aspx?FamilyID=9cfb2d51-5ff4-4491-b0e5-
   b386f32c0992&displaylang=en
   ```

   If your site uses .NET 3.5, look for `dotNetFx35setup.exe` instead. If it isn't on your computer, download it from:

   Microsoft .NET Framework 3.5 Service Pack 1

   ```
   http://www.microsoft.com/downloads/details.
   aspx?familyid=AB99342F-5D1A-413D-8319-
   81DA479AB0D7&displaylang=en
   ```

2. Copy `dotNetFx40_Full_x86_x64.exe` or `dotNetFx35setup.exe` to the shared folder you just created, so that you can pick it up in the virtual machine.

3. On the virtual machine, open the shared folder and double-click on `dotNetFx40_Full_x86_x64.exe` or `dotNetFx35setup.exe` to start the installation.

Installing and configuring IIS 7 on Windows Server 2008

Install IIS 7 on the virtual machine:

1. Make sure you are logged in as the administrator.

2. Start the server manager. Click on **Start | All Programs | Administrative Tools | Server Manager**.

3. Scroll down to **Roles Summary**, and then click on **Add Roles**. This starts the **Add Roles** wizard.

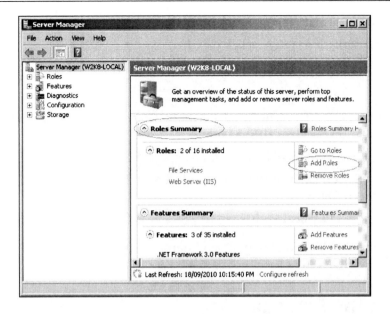

4. On the second page of the wizard, check **Web Server (IIS)**. Click on **Next**.

5. The next page has links to more information. Click on **Next** to move on.

6. The next page allows you to set the role services for IIS:

   ° Under **Application Development**, check **ASP.NET**

   ° Under **Performance**, check **Dynamic Content Compression**

   ° Under **Management Tools**, check **IIS 6 Management Compatibility**

   ° Click on **Next**

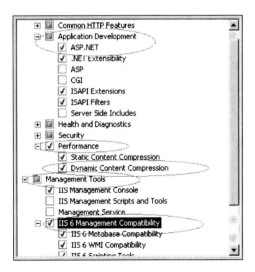

7. On the confirmation page, click on **Install**.

8. Once installation is done, click on **Close**.

If you decided to use a folder other than `C:\Inetpub\wwwroot` for your website files, update IIS:

1. Click on **Start | Control Panel | Administrative Tools | Internet Information Services (IIS) Manager**.

2. Expand the local machine, and then expand **Sites**.

3. Right-click on **Default Web Site**, and click on **Manage Web Site | Advanced Settings**.

4. Change the **Physical Path**.

Now make sure that IIS is working. Open Internet Explorer (click on **Start | Internet Explorer**) and visit `http://localhost/`.

Opening the Firewall

If you have the load generator on a different machine (recommended), then you will need to open port 80 in the firewall, so that it passes through the traffic from the load generator. This applies even if the load generator is on the same physical machine, but not on the virtual machine:

1. On the virtual machine, click on **Start | Control Panel**. In the search box, enter "firewall". Double-click on **Windows Firewall**, and then click on **Allow a program through Windows Firewall**.

2. On the **Exceptions** tab, select **World Wide Web Services (HTTP)**.

3. Click **OK**.

Installing Windows Server 2003

If you have a copy of Windows Server 2003 that you can legally install on your machine, then you could put it on your Vista or Windows 7 based machine and run both operating systems side-by-side. This allows you to use Windows Server 2003 to host a test website, and use Vista or Windows 7 for everything else you use the machine for.

Windows Server 2003 comes with IIS 6, rather than the latest version, IIS 7. If your production environment still runs IIS 6, this would not be a bad solution.

Running Windows Server 2003 alongside Vista or Windows 7

Unfortunately, you can't create a dual-boot system with Vista/Windows 7 and Windows Server 2003 if you already have Vista or Windows 7 on your machine. This is because Vista and Windows 7 use a new boot mechanism based on the new Boot Configuration Database. If you install Windows Server 2003 on a machine with Vista or Windows 7, this will stop the machine from booting properly. Installing Vista/Windows 7 on a Windows Server 2003 will work fine, because the newer operating systems know how to deal with the older boot mechanism.

You'll find more information about this issue at http://support.microsoft.com/kb/919529.

The solution is to create a virtual machine on your computer using the free Virtual PC 2007 program, and then install Windows Server 2003 on that virtual machine. To see how to do that, refer to the *Installing Virtual PC 2007* subsection in the *Installing Windows Server 2008* section.

Installing Windows Server 2003

Now that you've got your virtual machine, it's time to install Windows Server 2003:

1. Run the Virtual PC program. On the Virtual PC console, click on the **Start** button to start the virtual machine. A new window opens for the virtual machine. It will take a while to boot. After it's done, it will ask for an installation disc.

2. You now need to insert the first Windows Server 2003 installation CD into the virtual CD drive of the virtual machine.

    ° If you have a physical CD, put it in your physical CD/DVD drive. Then open the **CD** menu on the virtual machine window and choose **Use Physical Drive X:**, where x: is replaced by your CD/DVD drive.

    ° If you have an .iso image file of the first installation disc, open the **CD** menu on the virtual machine window, and choose **Capture ISO Image**. Press the *Enter* key to get the virtual machine to start reading.

You will now go through the standard process of installing Windows Server 2003, but all on the virtual machine.

 Important

At some stage, the installation will ask you what machine name to use and the administrator password. Do record these items; you will need them later.

While you are waiting for the virtual machine to install Windows Server 2003, now would be a good time to learn how to get more out of Virtual PC 2007. See the *Getting more out of Virtual PC* subsection in the *Installing Windows Server 2008* section.

Creating a shared folder

When you publish your site on the physical machine, it is easier if you then don't have to move it across to the virtual machine. To solve this, create a folder that is shared between your physical machine and your virtual machine.

IIS doesn't want to use a network drive or UNC as the home directory of a website. So we'll put the actual folder on the virtual machine and share it, so that it is visible on the physical machine.

To make this happen:

1. On the virtual machine, find or create a folder where you want to put the files making up the website. IIS probably will already point to `C:\Inetpub\wwwroot`, but Windows Server 2003 will already have put its own site in there. If you want to keep that site, create another folder such as `C:\TestSite`.

2. Right-click on the folder and choose **Sharing and Security**.

3. Select **Share this folder**.

4. Write down the **Share name** of the folder. This will be the same as the folder name, unless you change it.

5. Click on the **Permissions** button.

6. Allow the **Everyone** user group **Full Control**.

7. Click twice on **OK**.

Now make sure the shared folder is visible and writable on your physical machine:

1. Figure out the name of the shared folder. It will be of the form `\\MACHINE\folder`. For example, my virtual machine is called `W2K3SBS` and I used the share name `TestSite`. So, the name of the folder on my physical machine is `\\W2K3SBS\TestSite`. It may be different on your machine.

2. Use Windows Explorer on the physical machine to open the shared folder.

3. Make sure the shared folder is writable, by creating a new file in it. Right-click in the folder, choose **New**, and choose a file type. If all is well, a new file will appear in the folder.

Installing .NET 4 or .NET 3.5 Service Pack 1

Windows Server 2003 was released before .NET 2.0. Refer to the *Installing .NET 4 or .NET 3.5 Service Pack 1* subsection in the *Installing Windows Server 2008* section to see how to install a recent version of .NET on the virtual machine.

Installing and configuring IIS 6 on Windows Server 2003

Now that you have Windows Server 2003 going, let's install IIS 6:

1. On the virtual machine, click on **Start | Control Panel,** and then click on **Add or Remove Programs**.

2. On the left-hand side, click on **Add/Remove Windows Components**. A wizard starts.

3. In the wizard, check **Application Server**. Then, go through the rest of the wizard.

Now configure IIS, so that it will work with your site:

1. On the virtual machine, click on **Start | Administrative Tools**, and then click on **Internet Information Services (IIS) Manager**.

2. In the manager window, expand the local machine node.

3. Click **Web Service Extensions**.

4. If **ASP.NET** is not allowed, click on it and use the **Allow** button. If you just installed .NET 3.5, you will see that only .NET 2.0 is listed. That's ok; .NET 3.5 still uses the .NET 2.0 CLR, and added a number of additional libraries.

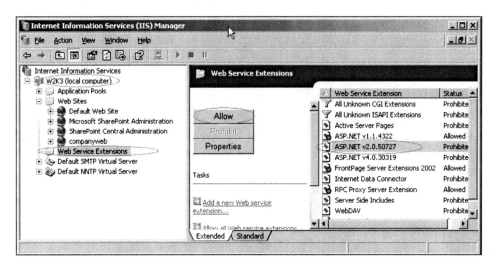

5. Expand the **Web Sites** node under the local machine node.

6. Right-click on **Default Web Site** and choose **Properties**.

7. On the **Documents** tab, make sure your home page is in the list of default documents.

8. If you installed .NET 3.5, then on the **ASP.NET** tab, make sure that **ASP.NET version** is set to 2.0. If you installed .NET 4, make sure it uses that version.

9. On the **Home Directory** tab, enter the location where IIS can find the files that make up your site. This should be the directory that you shared earlier.

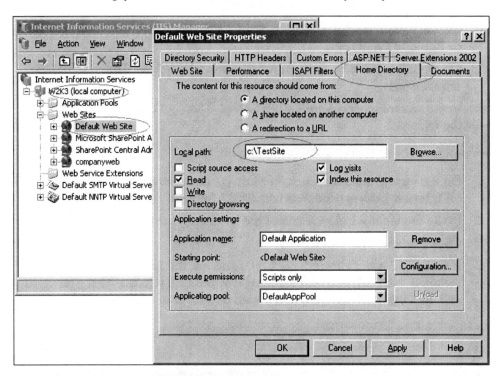

Opening the Firewall

If you have the load generator on a different machine (recommended), then you will need to open port 80 on the firewall, so that it passes through the traffic from the load generator. This goes even if the load generator is on the same physical machine, but not on the virtual machine:

1. On the virtual machine, click on **Start | Control Panel | Windows Firewall**. In the search box, enter "firewall". Click on **Allow a program through Windows Firewall**.

2. On the **Exceptions** tab, click on the **Add Port** button.

3. In the **Name** field, enter "HTTP", and in the **Port number** field enter "80". Leave the **Protocol** as **TCP**.

4. For a bit of additional security, if you know the IP address of the load-generating machine, click on the **Change scope** button and specify for which machines the port should be opened. Click on **OK**.

5. Click on **OK** to close the **Add a Port** dialog. Click on **OK** again to close the Windows Firewall dialog.

ASP.NET test site

Now that you have set up IIS, it would be good to make sure it actually works with an ASP.NET site.

If you don't have a site you want to use for testing, you'll find a very simple site you can use in folder `TestPage` in the downloaded code bundle. It sends messages to the trace log to show that it works well—visit the `trace.axd` pseudo page to see the trace output. More information about tracing is available at:

- ASP.NET Tracing Overview

  `http://msdn.microsoft.com/en-us/library/bb386420(v=VS.90).aspx`

Installing a database

If your website uses a database, and you are hosting the test site on one of your development machines, you will need to install a database server.

Downloading

If you do not have a copy of SQL Server you can legally install on a new machine, there are two free options:

- Use the free SQL Server Express. This edition limits databases to 4 GB, and uses only 1 CPU and 1 GB of memory. You will want to install the Advanced Services edition of SQL Server Express, because it has some very useful additional features, such as Full Text search.

  To download SQL Server 2008 with advanced services, open `http://www.microsoft.com/express/Database/default.aspx`, and then click on the **Installation Options** tab. There, you will find the download link.

- Use SQL Server Developer edition. This includes all of the functionality of Enterprise Edition, but is licensed only for development, test, and demonstration uses. It is also quite cheap to buy. Download a free 180-day trial version at `http://www.microsoft.com/sqlserver/2008/en/us/trial-software.aspx`.

More details about SQL Server 2008 editions are available at `http://www.microsoft.com/sqlserver/2008/en/us/editions.aspx`.

Installation

In an operational environment, the database server and web server should sit on different machines. If you have a number of machines available for load testing, consider putting the database server on a different machine too, so that you get a closer approximation of your operational environment.

1. Start the installation. The **SQL Server Installation Center** page appears.

2. On the left-hand side of the page, click on **Installation**.

3. Choose the **New SQL Server stand alone installation** option. A page appears checking setup rules. If all is ok, click on **Next**.

4. Select free edition or enter the product key, and click on **Next**.

5. Accept the license terms and click on **Next**.

6. Agree to install the required components and click on **Next**.

7. More setup rules are checked. You will probably get a warning regarding the firewall. To manage SQL Server, a port needs to be opened in the firewall, as you will see in a moment. Click on **Next**.

8. You are now on the **Feature Selection** page. Under **Instance Features**, select **Full-Text Search**. Under **Shared Features**, select **Business Intelligence Development Studio, Management Tools – Complete**, and **SQL Server Books Online**. Feel free to install any other features you want. Click on **Next**.

9. On the **Instance Configuration** page, use the default instance unless you have multiple SQL Server instances on the same machine. This way, you don't have to include the instance name in your connection string. Click on **Next**.

10. On the **Disk Space Requirements** page, make sure you have enough disk space. Click on **Next**.

11. On the **Server Configuration** page, select a user account and choose a password for each service. The user accounts you enter need to exist beforehand on the machine. Click on **Next**.

12. The **Database Engine Configuration** page will open in the **Account Provisioning** tab.

13. Select **Mixed Mode**. Enter a strong password for the built-in administrator account. Make sure it is at least eight characters long, and has letters, numbers, and symbols (such as exclamation mark). This way, you will be able to login to the database server with user name "sa" and the new password. More requirements for strong passwords are available at `http://msdn.microsoft.com/en-us/library/ms161962.aspx`.

14. Click on the **Add Current User** button to specify a user account that will act as SQL Server administrator, or add some other user account.

15. On the **Data Directories** tab, make sure you are happy with the location of the files that make up the database. Make sure that there is enough disk space. Also, if you have multiple drives in the machine, consider putting the log files on a dedicated drive that is not used by the database or other programs. This will minimize the number of head seeks on the drive with the log files, thereby increasing overall performance.

16. On the **FILESTREAM** tab, enable **FILESTREAM** access if you need it. This is useful if you store large unstructured objects in the database. More information about FILESTREAMS is available at `http://msdn.microsoft.com/en-us/library/bb933993.aspx`.

17. Click on **Next**.

18. On the **Error and Usage Reporting page**, choose whether to send data to Microsoft. Click on **Next**.

19. The setup rules are checked again. If all is well, click on **Next**.

20. On the **Ready to Install** page, verify the features to be installed. Click on **Install**.

21. The installation starts; this will take a while. Once it is complete, click on **Next**.

22. Read the notes on the last page and click on **Close**.

Opening port in Firewall

To manage SQL Server, you will want to use SQL Server Management Studio — click on **Start | All Programs | Microsoft SQL Server 2008 | SQL Server Management Studio**.

However, SQL Server Management Studio uses a TCP connection to talk to the database server, normally via port 1433. You may need to open port 1433 in your firewall to allow this to happen:

1. On the computer where you installed SQL Server 2008, click on **Start | Control Panel**.

2. In the search box, enter "firewall". Click on **Allow a program through Windows Firewall**.

3. On the **Exceptions** tab, click on the **Add port** button.

4. In the **Name** field, enter "SQL Server Management Studio", and in the **Port number** field, enter "1433". Leave the **Protocol** as **TCP**.

5. Click on the **Change scope** button and specify for which machines the port should be opened. That would be the machine on which you run SQL Server Management Studio.

   To find the IP address of a machine, click on **Start | All Programs | Accessories | Command Prompt**, and then enter the ipconfig command.

6. Done! Close the dialog boxes.

If you use SQL Server Express, there is one complication — by default, it uses a dynamic port. You want to fix that port to 1433, so you only have to open that one port in the firewall.

1. On the machine running SQL Server, click on **Start | All Programs | Microsoft SQL Server 2008 | Configuration Tools | SQL Server Configuration Manager**.

2. On the left-hand side, expand **SQL Server Network Configuration**, click on **Protocols for <instance name>**, right-click on **TCP/IP** on the right-hand side, and then choose **Properties**.

3. Click on the **IP Addresses** tab. You will see a list of IP addresses.

4. For each IP address you want to change, clear out the **TCP Dynamic Ports** field; in the **TCP Port** field, enter "1433". Click on **OK** to close the dialog.

5. On the left-hand side, click on **SQL Server Services**. Right-click on **SQL Server (<instance name>)** and choose **Restart** to stop and restart SQL Server.

Enabling remote administration

If you run SQL Server Management Studio from a different machine than the one running SQL Server, you need to take a few more steps to make this possible.

First, make sure that the SQL Server Browser service is running. This makes it easier to identify instances of SQL Server from a remote computer.

1. On the machine running SQL Server Express, click on **Start** | **All Programs** | **Microsoft SQL Server 2008** | **Configuration Tools** | **SQL Server Configuration Manager**.

2. On the left-hand side, click on **SQL Server Services**. Right-click on **SQL Server Browser** and choose **Properties**.

3. Click on the **Service** tab. Set **Start Mode** to **Automatic**. Click on **OK**.

4. Right-click on **SQL Server Browser** again, and then choose **Start** to start the service.

Now enable TCP/IP, so that SQL Server Management Studio and SQL Server can communicate over the network:

1. Still in SQL Server Configuration Manager, on the left-hand side, expand **SQL Server Network Configuration**, and click on **Protocols for <instance name>**. If TCP/IP is disabled on the right-hand side, right-click on TCP/IP, choose **Properties**, and then set **Enabled** to **Yes**. Click on **OK** to close the dialog.

2. On the left-hand side, click on **SQL Server Services**. Right-click on **SQL Server (<instance name>)** and choose **Restart**. This way, the service picks up the change you just made.

Test page

You will want to test the database, especially if it sits on a different machine than the web server. To do that, you'll find a simple test site in the downloaded code bundle, plus two .sql files to set up the simple database used by the site:

- tuneup.database.sql has the script to set up the TuneUp database. It also creates a login tuneup with password fast3rweb! and adds a user with that login to the TuneUp database.

- tuneup.table.sql creates the Trace table in the TuneUp database.

- `TestPageDb` contains a simple website with a one-page site. That page shows the most recent 100 records in the `Trace` table. It has a single button that inserts a new record in the `Trace` table.

- Before you use `TestPageDb`, change the connection string in its `web.config` file, to set its data source to your database server.

Setting up a load generator

Now that you've hosted the test site, it is time to generate some load. Here are the basic options:

1. Use a load-generation service. In simple terms, you sign up at a website, define which pages to hit with how many simultaneous users, and start the load test. Most services have many more features than this. There are services that are very affordable, or even free.

   This would be the easiest way to generate load. However, you may find that these services are lacking in features, and you may have to spend some money. In a moment, you will see a number of free and low-cost load generation services.

2. Run a load-generation software package on one or more machines. There are lots of packages available, ranging from free, open source software to very expensive enterprise-class software.

   Further down you will find instructions on how to use two widely used load generator packages – Microsoft's free WCAT, and the load tests provided by Visual Studio 2008 Team Edition and Visual Studio 2010 Ultimate.

Load generation services

There are many online load-generation services that you can use to generate traffic to your site. You get them to run a test with a given number of virtual browsers accessing pages you specify. After the test run, they provide statistics with response times, and so on. Some are cheap and provide a simple website to operate their service; others are aimed at large corporations.

The advantages of these services are:

- Very easy to use. No need to install and configure software.
- Ability to send traffic from locations around the world.

The disadvantages are:

- Limited freedom in devising traffic patterns
- The virtual browsers sending traffic during a test do not always support all features of real browsers, such as browser caching (discussed in *Chapter 5, Caching*)

The following table is a comparison of the features of three low-cost, easy-to-use services, as of the time of writing:

Available features	LoadStorm	Load Impact	Dotcom-monitor
	loadstorm.com	loadimpact.com	dotcom-monitor.com
Free plan	Yes	Yes	No
Server location	Virginia, California, Ireland, Singapore	Sweden, United States (several)*	United States (several), Europe (several), Canada, Israel
Visitor think time	Yes**	Yes	Yes
Ramp up load in steps	Yes	Yes	No
Send POST	Yes	Yes	No
Session Recorder	Yes	Yes*	Yes
Scheduled Tests (so that you can run a test at night)	Yes	Yes*	No
Automatically increase load until web server times out	No	Yes*	No
Virtual browsers simulate caching	Yes	No	No
Maximum number of virtual browsers	50,000	5,000***	3,000
Page requests can be grouped in scenarios with relative frequencies#	Yes	No	No
Images and JavaScript files are optionally loaded along with the page	Yes	No	No

Available features	LoadStorm	Load Impact	Dotcom-monitor
	loadstorm.com	loadimpact.com	dotcom-monitor.com
Use random visitor details from a list	Yes	No	No
Series of different tests can be run in one go	No	No	Yes

*Paid plan only

**Can be randomized.

***No limit for custom load tests.

\# For example, frequent browse scenarios and infrequent buy scenarios

Now that we have seen three load generation services, let's have a look at a load generation software package, WCAT.

WCAT

WCAT (Web Capacity Analysis Tool) is a free and a very fast load-generation tool by Microsoft. It uses simple configuration files that can be created by any text editor. Alternatively, you can use third-party software to record a browser session into a WCAT script.

WCAT lets you generate load from multiple machines, and control them from a central controller machine. Each machine can simulate multiple clients (WCAT's term for browsers). It is extensible via DLLs written in C. It supports SSL requests and NTLM authentication requests. Also, it produces a basic numbers-only report after each test run. You'll find more features in the user's guide, which is part of the installation.

This is a nice, lightweight, but a fairly basic package.

Installing WCAT

1. Download WCAT at:

   WCat 6.3 (x86)

   http://www.iis.net/community/default.aspx?tabid=34&i=1466&g=6

2. Install WCAT on the machine that will generate the load.

3. Open the command prompt. Click on **Start | All Programs | Accessories | Command Prompt**.

4. In the command window, go to the folder where WCAT was installed. The default installation folder is `C:\Program Files\wcat`.

5. In the command window, issue the following commands:

```
cscript //H:Cscript
wcat.wsf -update
```

This will cause the machine to reboot!

To reduce typing, the last three steps are in file `installwcat.bat` in the downloaded code bundle.

Creating a simple test

A full discussion of WCAT would be outside the scope of this book. Full documentation is in the user's guide, which you'll find in the `doc` folder under the installation folder. Here, we'll go through the basic features to quickly get you started using this tool.

Settings and scenario file

To get started with WCAT, let's set up a simple test, which load tests a single web page.

Each test involves two files telling WCAT how to carry out the test:

- A settings file, showing which web server to test, how many virtual clients to use, and so on

- A scenario file, showing which pages on the web server to test, POST data, and so on

Here is a simple settings file (`settings.ubr` in the downloaded code bundle):

```
settings
{
  server = "10.1.1.4";
  clients = 1;
  virtualclients = 2;
}
```

This says that the web server is at IP address `10.1.1.4`, that there is one machine doing the load testing, and that each load-testing machine runs two virtual clients. Instead of an IP address, you can specify a machine name or a domain.

Here is a simple scenario file (test1_scenario.ubr in the download section):

```
scenario
{
  name = "test1";
  warmup = 5;
  duration = 100;
  cooldown = 5;

  default
  {
    setheader
    {
      name = "Connection";
      value = "keep-alive";
    }

    setheader
    {
      name = "Accept-Encoding";
      value = "gzip, deflate";
    }

    setheader
    {
      name = "Host";
      value = server();
    }

    version = HTTP11;
    statuscode  = 200;
    close = ka;
  }

  transaction
  {
    id = "test1_transaction1";
    weight = 1000;
    request
    {
      url = "/default.aspx";
    }
  }
}
```

Let's go through this file bit-by-bit.

Scenario attributes

The scenario file first sets a few attributes for the scenario itself:

- `name`: Identifies the scenario.

- `warmup`: Length of the warm up period in seconds, during which the virtual clients are started one-by-one. Make this long enough so that your site can populate caches, and so on.

- `duration`: Length of the test run in seconds. During this time, the virtual clients are all sending requests to the server and receiving responses, and the results are recorded by WCAT.

- `cooldown`: Length of the cool down period in seconds. During this time, the server is still under load, but the results are no longer recorded by WCAT. This is useful, because when the load is taken away, the server will be able to respond to the last requests without having to deal with new requests coming in. You don't want the results of these atypical requests recorded by WCAT.

Default element

After the attributes, you'll see the default element, which sets default attributes that apply to every request sent to the server. That way, you don't have to repeat those attributes over and over again.

Within the default element, you first see the headers that will be sent as part of each request. Notice that the `Host` header is set to the output of the `server()` function. The `server()` function returns the name of the server you specified in the settings file. WCAT has lots of similar handy functions.

It then sets a few more attributes for each request:

- `version`: Version of HTTP to use. The default is 1.0.

- `statuscode`: Status code for WCAT to expect from the server. If the server sends a different status code, that will be recorded as an error.

- `close`: Specifies what to do with the connection after the request has completed. Use `ka` to keep the connection alive, `graceful` to attempt to let all pending sends and receives complete and then close the connection, and `reset` to forcefully close the connection.

Transaction

Finally, every scenario file contains one or more transactions. Each transaction in turn has one or more requests to be sent to the server.

During a test run, WCAT picks transactions at random and assigns them to the virtual clients. A virtual client sends out the requests and receives the responses from the server in the order given in the transaction. When it's done, WCAT picks a new transaction at random and gives it to the virtual client.

In this very simple example, the transaction has just two attributes:

- `id`: Identifies the transaction in the log file that WCAT produces at the end of the run
- `weight`: Determines how likely the transaction is to be picked. If there are two transactions, one with weight 1000 and the other with weight 2000, the second transaction is twice as likely to be picked as the first transaction

This transaction has only one request element, with just one attribute: the URL of the page to be visited by the virtual client. By default, the virtual client will send a GET request. WCAT can also send POST requests, use SSL, and handle authentication and more.

This is only a short selection of WCAT attributes. You'll find the full story in the user's manual in the doc folder under the installation folder.

Running a simple test

Time to take the settings and scenario files you've just seen and use them in a load test.

1. Modify the server field in the settings file, so it points at a real website. If you followed the earlier sections about setting up IIS, you will have set up a test site that would be good to use here. Use the trace.axd pseudo page of that test site to see the progress of the test.

2. Copy the settings and scenario files into the folder where WCAT was installed.

3. Open a command prompt. Click **Start | All Programs | Accessories | Command Prompt**.

4. In the command window, go to the same WCAT installation folder:

   ```
   cd "C:\Program Files\wcat"
   ```

5. In the command window, to start the load test, issue the command

   ```
   wcat.wsf -run -t test1_scenario.ubr -f settings.ubr
   ```

After the test has finished, you'll find a report with test results in the file `log.xml` in the WCAT installation directory. Double-click on that file to open it in a browser.

Recording scenario files using fiddler

Hand coding a scenario file for a single request isn't all that difficult, but it quickly gets laborious and time consuming once you start to create complicated scenarios. Fortunately, a combination of two free tools allows you to record this type of interaction in a scenario file, simply by going through the steps yourself in a browser.

First download and install Fiddler and the Fiddler plugin WCAT Scenario Creator:

1. Download and install the free tool Fiddler from `http://www.fiddler2.com/fiddler2/`.

    Fiddler is a proxy which logs all HTTP and HTTPS traffic between your browser and the network, including loopback traffic to the same machine.

2. Download the WCAT Scenario Creator. This plugin for Fiddler allows Fiddler to take a recorded session and convert it into a WCAT scenario file. That includes all the pages you visited and the events coming from the pages such as button clicks because those events are sent in POST data, which is captured by Fiddler.

    The WCAT Scenario Creator is available at `http://fiddler2wcat.codeplex.com/`.

    After the page has opened, click on the **Download** tab. On the right-hand side of the page, you'll see the latest release. Download that release.

3. WCAT Scenario Creator comes in the form of a DLL. Copy that DLL to the scripts folder under the `Fiddler2` installation folder. The default folder is `C:\Program Files\Fiddler2\Scripts`.

Now record a session:

1. If you have any web pages open, close them now. Some sites refresh periodically, which would spoil the recording of your session.

2. Start Fiddler.

3. Open your test site in a browser. Navigate around, click a few buttons, or create other events that will be processed on the server.

4. In Fiddler, press *F12* to stop capturing any more traffic.

5. On the left-hand side of the Fiddler window, you will see a recording of all your actions. Click on the actions you want to include in your scenario file. Hold down the *Ctrl* key while clicking on multiple actions. To include all actions, click on **Edit | Select All**.

6. On the bottom-left of the Fiddler window, you will find a black input line. It works the same way as Windows Command Prompt window, except that it shows only one line.

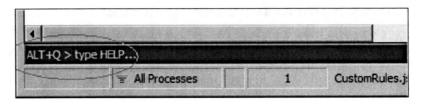

In that line, issue the following commands. After each command, press the *Enter* key:

wcat reset

wcat addtrans

wcat save "C:\Program Files\wcat\test2_scenario.ubr"

This saves the session in the form of a scenario file in C:\Program Files\ wcat\test2_scenario.ubr.

7. Open the scenario file C:\Program Files\wcat\test2_scenario.ubr you just saved. You'll see that it contains a single transaction, with a request for each page you visited. Each button-click or other event that resulted in a postback will have been recorded as a request, with the proper POST data, so your ASP.NET application will interpret the correct event.

You may want to change the warm up, duration, and cool-down periods at the top of the file.

Adding thinking time

In the real world, visitors spend time thinking in between actions. To simulate this, add sleep elements to the scenario file, as in the following:

```
scenario {
  transaction {
  request {
    ...
  }

  sleep
    {
      id    = "sleep1";
      delay = 2000;
    }
```

```
request {
  ...
}

sleep
  {
    id   = "sleep2";
    delay = 1000;
  }
  }
}
```

As you see here, sleep elements are part of a transaction, sitting on the same level as request elements. In this scenario, after the first request has been executed the virtual client waits for 2000 milliseconds. It then executes the next request and finally waits for 1000 milliseconds.

Other free load generation tools

WCAT is by no means the only free load-generation tool. Other popular options include:

- JMeter

  http://jakarta.apache.org/jmeter/

- WebLOAD

  http://www.webload.org/

After having seen a free and fairly basic load generation package, let's have a look at a more sophisticated and far from free option—Visual Studio Team System 2008 Test Edition and Visual Studio 2010 Ultimate.

Visual Studio Team System 2008 Test Edition/ Visual Studio 2010 Ultimate

Visual Studio Team System 2008 Test Edition and Visual Studio 2010 Ultimate are top-of-the-line editions of Visual Studio 2008 and Visual Studio 2010. They include an excellent load-testing feature, which is a lot more sophisticated than WCAT. It includes features such as simulating different browser mixes and network mixes, and the ability to run reports comparing the results of two different tests, making it easy to pick up any performance improvements.

If you do not have Visual Studio 2010 Ultimate, you can try it for free for 90 days. Download the trial version at:

- Visual Studio 2010 Downloads

    `http://www.microsoft.com/visualstudio/en-us/download`

As is the case with WCAT, you can generate load from multiple machines, using a central controller machine. To keep it simple for now, here we'll use just one machine for load generation. To use multiple machines:

- If you use Visual Studio Team System 2008 Test Edition, you will need to install and run Visual Studio Team System 2008 Test Load Agent, at:

    Visual Studio Team System 2008 Test Load Agent (90-day Trial)

    `http://www.microsoft.com/downloads/details.`
    `aspx?FamilyID=572e1e71-ae6b-4f92-960d-`
    `544cabe62162&DisplayLang=en`

- If you use Visual Studio 2010 Ultimate, visit:

    Distributing Load Tests Across Multiple Test Machines Using Test Controllers and Test Agents

    `http://msdn.microsoft.com/en-us/library/dd728093(v=VS.100).aspx`

Rather than taking you through every single load testing feature, this section shows how to create a basic load test. For more information, read the online documentation at:

- Working with Web Tests (for Visual Studio Team System 2008 Test Edition)

    `http://msdn.microsoft.com/en-us/library/ms182536.aspx`

- Working with Load Tests (for Visual Studio Team System 2008 Test Edition)

    `http://msdn.microsoft.com/en-us/library/ms182561.aspx`

- Testing Application Performance and Stress (for Visual Studio 2010 Ultimate)

    `http://msdn.microsoft.com/en-us/library/dd293540(VS.100).aspx`

Setting up a demo site

To get you going quickly, the download section of this book contains a website to load test, in folder `CustomerManagement` and file `TuneUpCustomers.database.sql`. Later on, you will also need file `newcustomers.csv`, so download that as well.

The difference with other demo sites you've seen in this chapter is that this one has a few additional pages and some database access. We'll need to explore some of the features provided by Visual Studio.

To install the demo site:

1. Run `TuneUpCustomers.database.sql` in SQL Server Management Studio to create the simple `TuneUpCustomers` database.

2. Copy the `CustomerManagement` folder to your system, and open it with Visual Studio.

3. Modify the connection string in the `web.config` file so it uses your database server.

4. Publish the website to an IIS web server. Earlier in this chapter you saw how to do this.

If you take the demo site for a spin, you'll see that the home page simply shows a list of customers which is initially empty. There is a link to a page where you can enter new customers. And once you've added customers, you'll see that each customer in the list has a select link taking you to a details page, where you can modify the customer.

Creating a simple web test

A web test, or web performance test in Visual Studio 2010 Ultimate, lets you test the functionality of a website. You first record a visit to your site into the web test, and then run the test again later to see if the site still works well. A load test is essentially one or more web tests executed by a large number of virtual clients.

It makes sense to define a number of web tests, matching different types of visits. One type of visit would be inserting a new customer; another would be updating an existing customer, and so on. Some types of visits will be less common than others. When you combine the web tests into a load test, you can set how often each web test is executed in relation to the other web tests.

To create the first web test:

1. In Visual Studio, open the website in the `CustomerManagement` folder of the downloaded code bundle.

2. Add a new Test project. In Visual Studio, click on **File** | **Add** | **New Project**. Expand the **Visual C#** tree and click on **Test**. Make sure you are happy with the name and location of the test project, and then click on **OK** to create the test project.

3. Now, add a web test to your newly created test project. Right-click on your new test project, choose **Add**, and add a **Web Test** (**Web Performance Test** in Visual Studio 2010 Ultimate). A new browser window will open, where you'll record the steps making up the web test.

4. In this new browser window, navigate to the **New Customer** page of the demo site. If the demo site is on your local machine, make sure that you do not use localhost because the load test does not like this. Instead, use your machine's IP address, as in `http://<ip address>/New.aspx`.

   Note that 10.1.1.3 is the IP address of my machine. Use the `ipconfig` command line utility to find out the IP address of your machine.

   You'll see your action being recorded on the left-hand side of the window.

5. On the right-hand side, enter some dummy values in the three input fields such as "title", "company", and "name". We'll replace those values in a moment. Then click on the **Insert** link to insert the new customer.

6. On the left-hand side, click on the **Stop** button to finish recording. Visual Studio will now spend some time detecting dynamic parameters. This relates to query string parameters and form values that change for every page load, which is outside the scope of this discussion.

7. You now have a valid web test, but it will always use the same details. That's a bit boring. Let's get those details from the input file `newcustomers.csv` instead.

   On the left-hand side, click on the data source icon:

8. Double-click on the CSV file icon. Then, enter the location of the `newcustomers.csv` file on your hard drive; you got this from the code bundle. Close the wizard.

9. You now have the `.csv` file as a data source in your test. Before using it, we need to set its access mode to random. Expand the data source and the **Tables** node. Click on **newcustomers#csv**.

This will show the properties of the data source on the right-hand side.

10. Open the **Access Method** drop-down. You will see there are three (four in Visual Studio 2010 Ultimate) access methods:

   ° **Do Not Move Cursor Automatically**: The web test always uses the first row.

   ° **Random**: The web test picks a random row.

   ° **Sequential**: The web test picks each row in order. If there are four rows, then the web test is executed four times—once for each row. In a load test where the web test is executed over and over, the web test will go back to the first row after it has done all rows.

   ° **Unique**: Same as **Sequential**, but without going back to the first row. Do not use **Unique** in a web test that will be part of a load test.

   Set the **Access Method** to **Random**. This way, when we run the load test, each time the web test is run by a virtual client, we get a random row from the newcustomers.csv file. This approximates the real world a bit more closely than always, using the same input.

11. Now that you have a data source, change the script you just recorded, so that it inserts values from the data source instead of the fixed values you entered during the recording.

   Expand the second **http://10.1.1.3/New.aspx** entry. Expand **Form Post Parameters**. You'll now see all the POST parameters sent by the browser when you recorded the script, including the values you entered into the form:

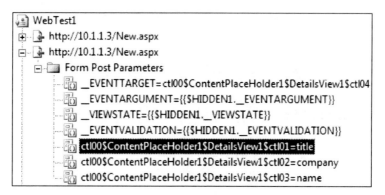

12. Click on one of the POST parameters you entered. On the right-hand side, a property window opens. Open the drop-down of the **Value** field, and expand the data source. You'll see a list of columns in the `newcustomers.csv` file. Click on the one you need for this POST parameter:

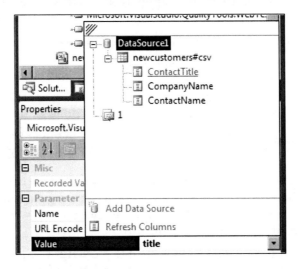

13. Going back to the left-hand side, you'll see how the POST parameter has now been bound to the column in the data source you just picked.

14. Do the same with the other two POST parameters.

15. Don't forget to save the web test:

16. Run the web test a few times, to make sure it works correctly:

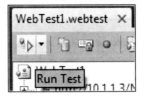

Creating a second web test

We'll do a second web test, so that we can have a mix of web tests when we set up the load test. This is also a good opportunity to show another data source—a database table:

1. Right-click on the test project, choose **Add**, and add a **Web Test (Web Performance Test** in Visual Studio 2010 Ultimate). A new browser window will open, where you'll record the steps making up the web test.

2. In the new browser window, open `http://10.1.1.3/Details.aspx?id=1`.

   Note that 10.1.1.3 is the IP address of my machine. Use the `ipconfig` command-line utility to find out the IP address of your machine.

   This should open the details page for the first company that was added when you ran the previous web test.

   You'll see your action being recorded in the left-hand side of the window.

3. On the **Details** page, enter new values in the three input fields. Then, click on the Update link. This will update the database.

4. On the left-hand side, click on the **Stop** button to finish recording.

5. You now have a valid web test, but it will always open the **Details** page of the same customer. Let's make it so that the **Details** pages of all customers will be opened. To do that, we need to get the `CustomerIDs` of all customers in the `Customers` table in the `TuneUpCustomers` database, so that we can then pass them on to the ID query string parameter of the details page.

   On the left-hand side, click on the data source icon.

6. This time, instead of double-clicking on the csv file icon, double-click on the database icon. Provide connection details to your database server and specify the `TuneUpCustomers` database. Then, select the `Customer` table and finish the wizard.

7. You now have the `Customer` database table as a data source in your test. Before using it, make sure it is set to `Sequential`; that way we'll get the **Details** pages of all customers in the database.

   Expand the data source and the **Tables** node. Click on **Customers**. Its **Access Method** should already be set to **Sequential**.

8. Now that you have a data source, change the script you just recorded, so that it takes the ID query string parameter from the data source.

Expand the first **http://<ip address>/Details.aspx** entry. Expand **QueryString Parameters**. You'll see that the ID query string parameter is set to **1**.

9. Click on the query string parameter. On the right-hand side, a property window opens. Open the drop-down of the **Value** field and expand the data source. You'll see a list of columns in the **Customer** file. Click on the **CustomerID** field to bind it to the query parameter:

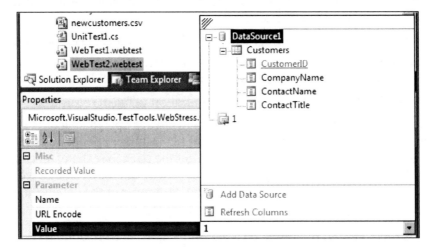

Going back to the left-hand side, you'll see how the query string parameter has now been bound to the **CustomerID** column in the data source.

10. Now do the same with the second ....**Details.aspx** entry.

11. At the moment, each customer whose **Details** page is opened with this web test will have their details updated to the values you entered in step 2. If you run a load test with this web test, a lot of customer records will wind up with those same details.

    If you want each customer to keep their details, simply expand the **Form Post Parameters** of the second ....**Details.aspx** entry and replace the values you entered with values taken from the data source. This way, both the **CustomerID** for the query string parameter and the values being POSTed come from the same database record.

Alternatively, if you want to update the details with a different value, add a second data source to the test, and bind the form post parameters to that second data source.

12. Don't forget to save the web test.

13. Run the web test a few times, to make sure it works correctly.

Coded web tests

In most cases, recording a session and tweaking it so that it takes values from a data source is enough. But if your requirements are a bit less conventional, a coded web test will give you ultimate flexibility.

A coded web test is a web test written in C# or another .NET language. Essentially, it is a class derived from the class `WebTest`. You can use it in a load test like any other web test.

In this example, we'll create a web test that does the same as the web test you just created, but instead of updating each customer with fixed values or values from a second data source, we're going to make sure that absolutely every customer is updated with new and unique values, even if there are thousands of customers in the database.

To reduce the amount of code to write, we'll base the new coded web test on the code underlying the web test you just created:

1. Double-click on the web test to open it.

2. Click on the **Generate Code** button to generate the underlying code of this web test:

3. A dialog will appear asking how to name your new coded web test. Let's call it `WebTest2Coded` for now. Click on **OK**.

4. A window with the actual code will open, ready to be edited. Near the bottom of the window, you'll find the following lines of code:

```
request2Body.FormPostParameters.Add
   ("ctl00$ContentPlaceHolder1$DetailsView1$ctl01", ...);
request2Body.FormPostParameters.Add
   ("ctl00$ContentPlaceHolder1$DetailsView1$ctl02", ...);
request2Body.FormPostParameters.Add
   ("ctl00$ContentPlaceHolder1$DetailsView1$ctl03", ...);
```

5. Replace those lines with:

```
long ticks = DateTime.Now.Ticks;
request2Body.FormPostParameters.Add
  ("ctl00$ContentPlaceHolder1$DetailsView1$ctl01",
  ticks.ToString());
request2Body.FormPostParameters.Add
  ("ctl00$ContentPlaceHolder1$DetailsView1$ctl02",
  (ticks + 1).ToString());
request2Body.FormPostParameters.Add
  ("ctl00$ContentPlaceHolder1$DetailsView1$ctl03",
  (ticks + 2).ToString());
```

This first puts the ticks of the system clock in the `ticks` variable. It then uses ticks as the value for the first POST parameter, `ticks+1` for the second POST parameter and `ticks+2` for the third POST parameter. This way, all values are unique. Adding 1 or 2 to `ticks` will not lead to duplicate values when the next customer is updated because of the time lapse in between customer updates.

6. If you bind to a CSV-based data source in a coded web test, you'll get a runtime error. If you added a CSV file as a second data source in the web test, find all lines with `DataSource2` and remove those lines. It's okay to bind to a database table-based data source.

7. Save your new coded web test.

8. Rebuild the solution.

9. Make sure that the new coded web test works. In the Visual Studio menu bar, click on **Test**, then **Windows**, and then **Test View**. The **Test View** window will open. Right-click on **WebTest2Coded** and choose **Run Selection**.

   This will run the coded web test once, against the first customer record in the table. But if you use the coded web test in a load test, it will sequentially go through all its customers, just as the web test on which it is based.

Combining web tests into a load test

Now that you have a few web tests, it is easy to combine them into a load test. In this simple example, one machine will generate the load:

1. Right-click on the test project and click on **Add | Load Test**. The **New Load Test Wizard** will start. Click on **Next** to dismiss the welcome page.

2. The **Scenario** page allows you to enter a descriptive name for the test. It also lets you set think times. The options here are:

   ° **Use recorded think times**: When running a web test, uses your own think time when you recorded the web test.

◦ **Use normal distribution**: Smoothes out the think times by using a standard distribution based on your think times.

◦ **Do not use think times**: Turn off think times completely. You would only use this when stress testing the server, rather than simulating real-world users.

Finally, if you know how much time there normally is in between test iterations, enter that in the **Think time between test iterations** field. For example, you may have found that each user thinks about 10 seconds in between entering a new customer or updating a customer. Click on **Next** to continue to the next page.

3. The **Load Pattern** page lets you define the number of virtual clients executing web tests at any time. The **Constant Load** option will keep the number of virtual clients the same during the test, while the **Step Load** option increases the number of virtual clients in steps. The latter is useful if you want to study the system at differing load levels, to find its breaking points. Click on **Next** to continue to the next page.

4. On the **Test Mix Model** page you get to indicate how you want to structure the mix of your web tests:

◦ **Based on total number of tests**: Lets you specify that for example, 25 percent of all the tests carried out use one web test, while 75 percent of the tests use another web test. If you have more than two web tests in your load test, you would divide up the tests among however many web tests you have.

◦ **Based on the number of virtual users**: Lets you specify that for example 25 percent of all the virtual users run one web test, while the other 75 percent run another web test. The difference with the previous option is that if one web test executes faster, it will be executed more often if you base the mix on number of tests.

◦ **Based on user pace**: Lets you specify how often a particular test should be run over the course of an hour.

◦ **Based on sequential test order**: (Visual Studio 2010 Ultimate only) Each virtual user cycles through all the web tests continuously.

Click on **Next** to continue to the next page.

5. The **Test Mix** page asks which web tests to include in the load test, and their distribution. Here is where you set the percentages that will be applied by the text mix model that you set in the previous step. Click on **Next** to continue to the next page.

6. The **Browser Mix** page lets you indicate the mix of browsers used by the virtual users. The type of browser used influences page load times; for example, IE6 uses only two connections per domain to load images, while newer browsers use six or more.

   If you use Visual Studio 2010 Ultimate, you'll find that it has the **Network Mix** ahead of the **Browser Mix** page.

   Click on **Next** to continue to the next page.

7. The **Network Mix** page lets you indicate the mix of simulated networks used by the virtual users. For example, if you know that 30 percent of your users are still on dial-up modems, you would enter that here. Remember that a user on a slow connection takes longer to load a page. Click on **Next** to continue to the next page.

8. The **Counter Sets** page lets you pick counter sets to monitor. If your test is run on multiple machines, you would specify those machines here. Click on **Next** to continue to the next page.

9. Finally, on the **Run Settings** page, you specify how long the test will run, either by setting a runtime, or by setting the number of test iterations. When you set a run time, you can specify the warm-up time, during which the web tests are run, but no data is collected. Make this long enough to ensure that all caches are populated by the time the warm up period ends. Click on **Finish** to finish the wizard.

Running the load test

To run a load test, double-click on it to open it and click the **Run** button.

While the test is running, you will see a series of graphs tracking the most important counters. Note the drop-downs on top of each graph, allowing you to select a different graph in that window.

More stats about the counters being tracked are below the graphs such as minimum, maximum, and average. Select a counter to highlight its line in its graph:

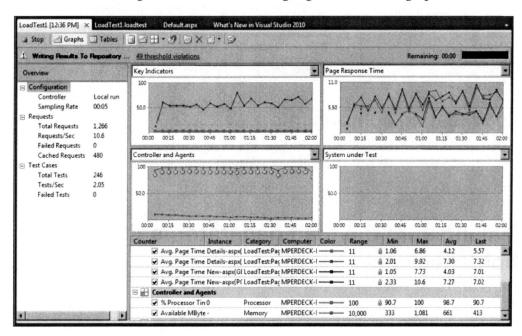

To stop the test midstream, hit the **Stop** button.

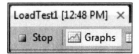

After the test has finished, the graphs are replaced by a load test summary. To get the graphs back, click on the **Graphs** button near the top of the window:

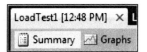

Click the little Excel button in the button bar to export the stats to a spreadsheet. This includes graphs as well as the numbers. In addition to a report on just this test, you can get a numerical and graphical comparison between different load tests. This way, you can see whether things have improved, and by how much.

Finally, the results of each test are stored in the load test. To see the results again after you closed the results window, double-click the load test to open it, and then click on the **Open and Manage Results** button near the top of the window:

Load testing components

Web tests are not the only tests you can use as part of a load test. You can add unit tests too, in the same way as you add web tests.

This makes it very easy to load test components, such as the data access layer.

Making sure the load generator isn't bottlenecking

You need to make sure that the load generating software doesn't put too much stress on the CPU of the machines it runs on, or their network interfaces, disk drives, or memory. Otherwise, they can't reliably generate the load that you expect them to generate.

To make sure that a load generating machine isn't stressed, use the Reliability and Performance Monitor:

To open the monitor, run `perfmon` (`resmon` on Windows 7) from the command prompt (**Start | All Programs | Accessories | Command Prompt**). This opens the monitor window.

The monitor window shows how busy each of the four main hardware subsystems is, and how to detect bottlenecks:

Section	Description
CPU	The first column shows the percentage of time that the processor is busy. You will want this to be below 80 percent most of the time.
	The **Maximum Frequency** column will show 100 percent if the CPU is going at full speed, or a lower number if it has been slowed down by Vista or Windows 7 to save power.

Section	Description
Disk	The first column is the amount of disk I/O.
	The **Highest Active Time** column shows the percentage of time that the physical drive(s) were busy. You do not want this to be consistently over 85 percent.
	The **Highest Active Time** percentage can be high even if there is little disk I/O. This would indicate lots of disk head seeks, which could be caused by a highly fragmented disk, or by accessing lots of small files.
Network	The first column is the amount of network I/O.
	The **Network Utilization** column shows the percentage of network bandwidth in use on the network segment that the network card is connected to. If the card is on an Ethernet network using a shared hub or router, you will want to keep this below 30 percent most of the time.
Memory	The first column, **Hard Faults/sec**, shows how often the machine swaps memory pages to the page file on disk due to a shortage of physical memory. Obviously, swapping to disk takes much longer than reading or writing to memory. And it takes CPU cycles and Disk accesses. You do not want this number to be consistently high. If it is, add more memory. This will reduce load on the CPU and Disk as well.
	The **Used Physical Memory** column shows the percentage of physical memory that is being used.

Find out more

Here are some more online resources:

- Real-World Load Testing Tips to Avoid Bottlenecks When Your Web App Goes Live

  http://msdn.microsoft.com/en-us/magazine/cc188783.aspx

- Beyond performance testing

  http://www.ibm.com/developerworks/rational/library/4169.html

- Rapid Bottleneck Identification - A Better Way to do Load Testing

  http://www.bitpipe.com/data/document.do?res_id=1255388747_681

- A Load Testing Strategy

  http://www.borland.com/resources/en/pdf/white_papers/load_test_whitepaper.pdf

- Modeling the Real World for Load Testing Web Sites

  http://www.methodsandtools.com/archive/archive.php?id=38

- Overview of IIS 7.0 differences Across Windows Vista Editions and Windows Server 2008 Editions

  `http://learn.iis.net/page.aspx/479/iis-70-features-and-vista-editions/`

- Troubleshooting WCAT(Web Capacity Analysis Tool) Problems

  `http://blogs.iis.net/mukhtard/archive/2009/03/16/troubleshooting-wcat-web-capacity-analysis-tool-problems.aspx`

- Windows Vista Performance and Reliability Monitoring Step-by-Step Guide

  `http://technet.microsoft.com/en-us/library/cc722173(WS.10).aspx`

Summary

This chapter discussed how to do load testing, and how to build a load-testing environment. We first saw how it makes sense to run load tests not only during acceptance testing, but also during development. This was followed by various options to host the development site being load tested, which included installing Windows Server 2003 or Windows Server 2008 on a test server.

We then saw how to generate the required load, using free or low-cost web-based services, the free load generator program WCAT, or load test projects, a feature of Visual Studio Team System 2008 Test Edition and Visual Studio 2010 Ultimate. The chapter concluded by showing how to make sure the load generator isn't bottlenecking.

This was the last chapter. In this book, you saw how to diagnose performance problems, beginning with Waterfall charts and then drilling down further, using mainly performance counters. After you pinpointed the main bottlenecks, you saw how to remove these. This journey took us from the web server and the database server, to client-side issues such as image and JavaScript loading, to finally load testing in this chapter. Improving website performance isn't a black art and doesn't need to be time consuming, as long as you go about it in a structured manner.

Index

website, publishing 33-35
Site-Perf.com 23
Slimtune tool 67
Spiffy Corners tool 328
SqlCommand property 123
stopWatch class 66
StringBuilder class
  about 77, 78
  capacity 56
  strings, concatenating 55
  use, avoiding 56
  using 55
sys.dm_exec_cached plans 176, 177

T

tempdb file 214
test site, hosting
  ASP.NET site 393
  IIS, installing on Vista 379
  IIS, installing on Windows 7 379
  options 379
  production server, using 379
  second hosting account, using 378
  spare servers, using 379
  Windows Server 2003, installing 388
threading
  counters, in perfmon 77
  overhead, reducing 77
thread locking
  .NET CLR LocksAndThreads category 156
  about 156
  delay reducing, ways 156
  lock duration, minimizing 156
thread starvation 30
thread usage, bottlenecks
  about 30
  counters, adding 31
  default available threads 30
  Requests Current 31
  Requests Executing 32
  thread starvation 30
TimeoutAsync method 121, 127
timeouts
  setting 140, 141
time to last byte 217
toJson function 297

tools
  ANTS Performance Profiler 67
  Slimtune 67
  Visual Studio Performance Profiling 66
Trace class 143

U

Universal Disk Formats. *See* **UDFs**
unmanaged resources
  about 57
  counters 59
  IDisposable interface 58
unnecessary processing
  avoiding, ways 82
  HTTP pipeline, trimming 82
unwanted request
  about 40
  CAPTCHA 41
  hot linking 41
  scrapers 42-45
  search engine bots 40
  usability testing 45
UtcNow
  using 79

V

Validate JavaScript library, client-side
    validation
  about 282
  built-in methods 283
  CDN 286
  error messages, formatting 285
  homepage 282
  initialization 283
  overhead 287
  validation methods, adding 284, 285
ValidationGroup attribute 281
ViewState
  about 219
  compressed ViewState, measuring 220
  compressions 230
  controls, identifying 223, 224
  controlstate 219
  database cache, reloading from 224, 225
  disabling 221, 223
  issue area, tracking 220

Thank you for buying
ASP.NET Site Performance Secrets

About Packt Publishing

Packt, pronounced 'packed', published its first book "*Mastering phpMyAdmin for Effective MySQL Management*" in April 2004 and subsequently continued to specialize in publishing highly focused books on specific technologies and solutions.

Our books and publications share the experiences of your fellow IT professionals in adapting and customizing today's systems, applications, and frameworks. Our solution based books give you the knowledge and power to customize the software and technologies you're using to get the job done. Packt books are more specific and less general than the IT books you have seen in the past. Our unique business model allows us to bring you more focused information, giving you more of what you need to know, and less of what you don't.

Packt is a modern, yet unique publishing company, which focuses on producing quality, cutting-edge books for communities of developers, administrators, and newbies alike. For more information, please visit our website: www.packtpub.com.

Writing for Packt

We welcome all inquiries from people who are interested in authoring. Book proposals should be sent to author@packtpub.com. If your book idea is still at an early stage and you would like to discuss it first before writing a formal book proposal, contact us; one of our commissioning editors will get in touch with you.

We're not just looking for published authors; if you have strong technical skills but no writing experience, our experienced editors can help you develop a writing career, or simply get some additional reward for your expertise.

ASP.NET 3.5 CMS Development

ISBN: 978-1-847193-61-2   Paperback: 284 pages

Build, Manage, and Extend your own Content Management System

1. Create your own Content Management System with the understanding needed to expand it and add new functionality as your needs grow

2. Learn to build a fully functional application with very little code and set up users and groups within your application

3. Manage the layout of your site using Master Pages, Content Placeholders, Themes, Regions, and Zones

4. A step-by-step guide with plenty of code snippets and screen images

ASP.NET 3.5 Social Networking

ISBN: 978-1-847194-78-7   Paperback: 580 pages

An expert guide to building enterprise-ready social networking and community applications with ASP. NET 3.5

1. Create a full-featured, enterprise-grade social network using ASP.NET 3.5

2. Learn key new ASP.NET topics in a practical, hands-on way: LINQ, AJAX, C# 3.0, n-tier architectures, and MVC

3. Build friends lists, messaging systems, user profiles, blogs, message boards, groups, and more

4. Rich with example code, clear explanations, interesting examples, and practical advice â€" a truly hands-on book for ASP.NET developers

Please check **www.PacktPub.com** for information on our titles

Lightning Source UK Ltd.
Milton Keynes UK
UKOW020727280513

211353UK00001B/8/P